A Coach's Life

Les Hipple as he appeared during the glory years.

A Coach's Life

Les Hipple and the Marion Indians

Dan Kellams

iUniverse, Inc.
New York Bloomington

A Coach's Life
Les Hipple and the Marion Indians

iUniverse books may be ordered through booksellers or by contacting:
iUniverse
1663 Liberty Drive
Bloomington, IN 47403
www.iuniverse.com
1-800-Authors (1-800-288-4677)

ISBN: 978-1-4502-2147-4 (pbk)
ISBN: 978-1-4502-2146-7 (ebk)
ISBN: 978-1-4502-2145-0 (hbk)

Library of Congress Control Number: 2010905397

Printed in the United States of America
iUniverse rev. date: 6/21/10

For all the boys

And for Elaine

It's not the size of the dog in the fight that counts.
It's the size of the fight in the dog.

—Motto on Les Hipple's wall

Not many of you should be teachers, my brothers and sisters,
for you know that we who teach will be judged with greater strictness.

—James 3:1

Contents

Author's Note

When this project began, I made three promises: to do as little as possible to open old wounds, to refuse to use reporter's tricks and threats to wheedle information from people who didn't want to talk to me, and to respect the memories of those who did. I've tried hard to keep those promises.

I also believed that the story of Les Hipple and his teams had to be put into the context of the times, when Marion was a much smaller town, and many things were different. Thus, the book offers a few excursions into those vanished times, and I occasionally appear as a minor character, recalling events I witnessed or experienced. I hope these passages will trigger similar recollections among older readers and enlighten or amuse younger ones.

Dan Kellams
South Kent, Connecticut
January 2010

Chapter 1
First Encounter

The window is open and the room is frigid when the boy awakens with a start.

"Danny, it's almost six o'clock." His father is calling through the door. His parents are up, believing they will have to prod him into action.

But the boy is wide awake and shivering with excitement. Wednesday morning in November. As dark as night. Marion, Iowa, 1947. Around town, at least twenty other sixth-grade boys are also stirring.

"Wake up, Danny. You'll be late."

He is out of bed and pulling on his clothes. His gym bag was packed the night before. It contains basketball shoes and socks, shorts, a T-shirt, a towel. And a jock strap. He never had one of those before.

He dresses quickly, bounds downstairs, and heads for the back door.

"You have to have breakfast."

"I'm not hungry."

"You have to have breakfast."

His mother and father sit with him in the kitchen. They smoke their cigarettes, drink their black coffee, and watch him eat some oatmeal and toast and drink two glasses of milk. His little brother is asleep in his room upstairs.

"I have to go now."

"Good luck, Danny."

The sky is beginning to lighten as he bolts out the back door, leaps down the steps, and turns up the driveway, starting the half-mile run to the high school gym.

Basketball practice begins today for sixth graders. He is going to play basketball for Coach Hipple. He is going to become a Marion Indian.

—

Some of the youngsters who gathered in the gym that morning were seeing their coach up close for the first time. Les Hipple was thirty-four years old, trim and straight-backed at just under five feet seven and weighing 150 pounds. He wore a gray T-shirt and blue satiny sweatpants with a white stripe down the legs. A whistle hung from his neck, and he carried a clipboard. The coach walked with a slight limp, and some boys sensed that each step caused him pain. His expression gave no indication that it did. His light-brown hair was thinning. His nose, in profile, was sharp and slightly hooked. His skin was pale. His eyelids drooped slightly. His mouth was small, set in a straight line.

Hipple did not smile at these awkward young players. He tousled no one's hair. He told no jokes. He conferred no nicknames. He did nothing to charm the boys or set them at ease or suggest that practice would be fun. Instead, he put them to work.

For some of the sixth graders, much of the excitement that morning came from playing basketball on a real court. The high school gym was essentially the only one in town, and some of the boys had never set foot on it. They had learned the rudiments of the game outdoors on concrete or dirt, and now they were eager to scrimmage on hardwood, to hear the squeak of their shoes as they bolted across the floor. They were impatient that morning to shoot at a regulation basket with its orange rim, white metal backboard, and roped net—to finally taste the game for real. They were to be disappointed.

Hipple did not let them shoot that day, nor for many practices to come. Instead, they drilled. Hipple taught them the proper way to catch a ball: on the fingertips, the index fingers at the center of the ball on each side—so that upon catching the ball they were immediately able to pass it.

He taught them how to dribble using a slight wrist action and moving their fingertips in a small, squeezing motion, the ball never touching the palms of their hands. Dribbling was necessary, but passing was important. It was the key to successful basketball, Hipple believed.

He taught them the two-handed chest pass, arranging the boys in circles, showing them how to get into position, feet shoulder-width apart, their weight slightly forward. He taught them to get the feel of the ball on their fingertips, how to hold it away from the palm, stepping forward with the left foot, pointing the fingers downward, then bringing the ball near the chest, moving the fingers upward to snap the wrists, releasing the ball off the index fingers of both hands, extending the arms in the critically important follow-through, following through all the way, so that arms, hands, and fingers point exactly to where the ball should go, teaching them to hit their man in the chest or the waist so he did not have to reach for the ball, so he could catch it and quickly pass it on.

He drilled them on the one-handed bounce pass, the two-handed bounce pass, the overhead pass. After they knew how to pass, he taught them to run and pass, pass and cut. They passed and ran all winter until it became a habit. Then he taught them how to pivot, how to set a screen, how to take a defensive position with the hands up and the arms outstretched, how to move when guarding the man with the ball, how to get in position for a rebound.

At last he taught them how to shoot. The one-handed push shot, the jump shot, the lay-up all required the same wrist and hand motion: the ball always on the fingertips, released softly off the first two fingers, the wrist snapping and the hand dropping as the ball is released, then coming back up to point toward the target. Everyone must shoot exactly that way. He stressed free-throw shooting, insisting on the two-handed underhand shot, the ball sliding off the fingertips with a minimum of wrist action.

The boys practiced and practiced all that winter and never got into a scrimmage.

First you grind, Hipple told a reporter many years later, and then you polish.

—

When those hopeful sixth graders gathered at the Marion High School gym that early morning in November 1947, Les Hipple was in his third year at Marion, in charge of the boys' and girls' physical education programs and head coach of all of Marion's varsity teams: football, cross-country, basketball, and track. All were boys' teams. There were no varsity sports for girls.

In his brief time at Marion, Hipple had turned around a floundering sports program. His teams had begun to stir the imagination of the townspeople with their spirited play, their victories, and their prospects for even greater achievements. The sixth graders knew that, or sensed it, and they wanted to be part of it. In fact, years of athletic glory, beyond the wildest dreams of the townspeople and the sixth graders, lay just ahead and would continue for more than a decade. Hipple's teams would dominate their conference and rank among the best in their class, creating a palpable sense of pride among the players, the students, and the townspeople.

Hipple himself would become a legend, one of the few high school coaches whose name was known throughout the state. He would become one of the few men in Iowa to be inducted into both the Basketball and the Football Coaches Halls of Fame. In time, the expression *Hippleman* would become famous as well. It described not only a Marion player but also a boy forged by the coach's austere disciplines and strict rules—requirements that not only closely governed athletic technique, conditioning, and on-field behavior but also regulated a boy's private life and intruded upon his relationship with his family. Hipple's rules were considered the strictest in the state and the most zealously enforced. Playing for Hipple meant a life of rigor, clean living, modest behavior, and self-denial. Being a Hippleman was more than being an athlete. Like being a Marine, it marked a boy forever.

Even as Hipple's teams were winning thousands of fans, his rules and tactics were making enemies and sparking controversy among a few parents and citizens. Eventually, as the times and the town and the school changed, Hipple would come under fire.

But the coach's triumphs and troubles all lay in the future that Wednesday morning in 1947 when the sixth graders gathered in the gym. Hipple was far ahead of his time in starting players young. Most school systems offered no organized sports before high school. On Tuesday nights, Hipple's varsity team usually had a game, yet there he was the next day at dawn in a cold and dusty gym to work with sixth graders. On other mornings, the junior high principal coached the seventh and eighth graders. But Hipple worked with sixth graders because he wanted to see what talent was coming down the pike. He wanted them to learn basketball the right way from day one. His way.

Chapter 2
Iowa

A friend used to say, "I always thought Iowa was one of those square states," lumping it with Kansas, Colorado, Nebraska, and other states on the Great Plains. My friend is from Michigan, a state anything but square, and not so far from Iowa that she might have known better. But she is to be forgiven: Many people think of Iowa, if they think of it at all, as a state somewhere out West, and far away from wherever they are.

On a map of the United States, Iowa is more or less in the middle of the nation, actually tending toward the East, and admittedly square-like in shape. It would be even more so without the Missouri and Mississippi rivers, which make its western and eastern borders so curly. On a map of Iowa itself, if the towns, roads, and rivers were removed and nothing left but the lines that mark the borders of each county, there would be ninety-nine more or less square counties laid across the state in rows from top to bottom, as if a child had covered the map with playing cards, not worrying too much about precision.

In each of these ninety-nine counties, more or less at its center, is a small town that serves as the county seat. In the center of many of these towns is a small, square park, and in that park is an essentially square building, the county courthouse. Business establishments line the streets around the park. Iowa formed ninety-nine counties to assure that every farmer could make the trip to town in a horse-drawn buggy, conduct his business, and return home before nightfall.

From the air, squares and rectangles also define the Iowa landscape. The roads, many of them gravel, mark off the farmland in right angles. Travelers flying into Cedar Rapids on a commuter jet can sometimes see a farmer's truck kicking up dust as it scoots along a gravel road, headed to town on an errand. Iowa has hundreds of small towns, more, it has been said, than any other state, scattered along rivers, railroads, and crossroads to serve the area farmers. The farmlands, too, as seen from the air, are laid out in hard-edged geometries, softened here and there by a wooded stream or a curving swath of green land planted in grass or cover crop to prevent erosion.

When the first settlers arrived, Iowa was covered in prairie grass so tall in places that a man on horseback could tie it across his saddle horn. The land was virtually treeless because prairie fires regularly incinerated every growing thing for miles around, and the grass recovered more quickly than the trees.

Originally, 75 percent or more of the state was covered in grassland. Today, all that land is under cultivation. There is almost no prairie grass left in the state, except where it is cultivated as a tribute to the past. There are no great forests here, no mountains or deserts, but a landscape thoroughly tamed, with farms following upon farms until, before long, a town appears.

From the air, Iowa looks flat. But out in the farmland in the eastern part of the state, where this story is set, the land is not flat at all. In November, when the earth is bare and the cows are eating the corn stubbles, travelers can see clearly how the ground undulates, swelling and heaving around them. This fertile land is all soft curves, belly and thigh, round, full, and fat. This is Grant Wood country. There are places in eastern Iowa where motorists looking out their car windows realize that the artist exaggerated only a little in his famous paintings of the rolling earth.

Glaciers shaped the land in Iowa and left it rich with topsoil. But some people see in the undulating land a reflection of the ocean waves that covered it millions of years before the glaciers arrived. Iowa Poet Laureate Robert Dana described it this way in his poem, "A Short History of the Middle West": "Under this corn, / these beans, / these acres of tamed grasses, / the prairie still rolls, / heave and trough, / breaker and green curl, / an ocean of dirt tilting and tipping. / Its towns / toss up on the distance, your distance, / like the wink / of islands."

One of the towns winking in the distance is Tipton.

Chapter 3

The Early Years, 1913–1932

Lester Charles Hipple was born April 1, 1913, in a farmhouse his family rented north of Tipton, Iowa. No physician attended his birth, and there probably wasn't a midwife, either. Money was scarce. The baby's family worked in farming. Everyone knew the work of bringing a new life into the world. Lester's sister Bess, who was five and would witness the birth of three more Hipple children, said she was almost certain that her father, Charles, assisted in the delivery. "Pop was right there whenever a baby was born," she remembered. Also on hand were a group of aunts, uncles, and cousins. All worked as hired hands for Iowa farmers, living together and sharing the costs.

Lester was the third of six children born to Karolina and Charles Hipple, their first boy. His older sisters, Bess and Florence (called Floss), were born in 1908 and 1910 respectively. After Lester came Helen in 1916, Don in 1919, and Shirley in 1924.

Charles Hipple was born in Silver City, Iowa, on June 15, 1885. He became a blacksmith and set up shop in Tipton. The Hipple name is said to be German, but it's not known how long the family lived in the United States. Lester's great-grandfather, Reuben Jackson Hipple, came to Iowa from Indiana in a covered wagon and, in 1855, married Leah McClain. They had eight children, one of whom was Lester's grandfather, John Hipple.

Lester's mother, Karolina (called Lena) Olsson, was born in Sweden on April 15, 1886, the second daughter of Lars Olsson and Anna Jonsdotter. Lena was four years old when she came to the United States with her mother, a sister, and a brother, following her father, who had moved to the new country earlier. The Olssons had been farmers in Sweden, but were drawn to new opportunities in America, saving their money for at least two years to help pay their passage.

When Lena and Charles married, in 1907, Charles was twenty-two, and had a secure job in his father's smithy. Lena, twenty-one, grew up on a farm, and it was a life she loved. She soon persuaded Charles to give up working with iron and fire and take a position as a hired hand on area farms.

Life was tough. The men rose early to milk the cows and feed the animals before they had their own breakfasts. Horses were still used for plowing. Much of the harvesting was done by hand. Bess, the oldest child, remembered long, tedious days of husking corn in a wagon box pulled by horses. She and the other hands worked late into the night and so far into the fall that the weather turned wintry and her hands became chapped and raw.

While the men labored in the fields and barns, the women cared for the children, prepared the meals, did the housework, fed and raised the chickens and geese, and tended large vegetable gardens. All the children had chores around the house, and they were occasionally assigned a goose or duck to raise. Lester learned at an early age the value and necessity of hard work. But an education was important, too. The children's principal jobs were to do their schoolwork. Farms had no electricity, so the children studied by the light of kerosene lamps on the dining room table. On Saturdays, the family often went to town to shop or see a movie. This was a special treat for the children, but Bess remembered that the family always had to return home in time to milk the cows.

Life as a hired hand was nomadic. The growing Hipple family moved often to new rented houses when work ran out or disagreements arose with employers, or when bad feelings erupted among members of the extended family. In addition, there was a constant tug of war between Charles and Lena. He wanted to go back to town; she didn't want to leave the farm.

Getting the kids to school was a major task. Thousands of one- and two-room schoolhouses dotted the Iowa landscape in those days. If a family could spare a horse from farm work, a child could get to school fairly easily. But many had to walk. Bess recalled leading her little troop to school across the frozen midwinter countryside. She and Floss were wrapped in heavy coats. Lester, in the first grade, was bundled in an old fur coat of his mother's that she had cut down for him. Bess, with Floss tagging along, pulled him across the snow-covered fields on a sled. "That year we had two miles to go to school," Bess said. "So I would pull him and we would stop along the way at Mr. and Mrs. Nolan's house to warm up. Then we went across a field and stopped sometimes at a log cabin owned by Mr. and Mrs. Butler. Then we cut across another field to the school."

One winter day, with Bess home sick, Floss, perhaps in third grade, took Lester to school. The snow was so high it blocked the roads. The two children made their way cross-country on the sled. During recess, Floss watched as Lester took the sled and walked out of sight down a hillside. A few minutes later, she saw him walking back into view, pulling the sled, his face covered in blood.

Lester had belly-flopped down a hillside and run full tilt into a barbed wire fence buried in the snow. The barbs cut a deep gash in his right cheek and left smaller cuts in his forehead and near his eye. "His face was full of blood," Floss said. "I took him in to the teacher and she tried to stop the bleeding with a handkerchief, but it didn't work. I asked the teacher if I should take him home and she said yes, so a boy and I put him on the sled and got him there. When we got home, we put out a general ring and found out there was a doctor in the neighborhood." (To send a general ring, which signaled an emergency, callers cranked the bell handle on the party-line telephone ten times. Everyone on the line then ran to the phone to see which neighbor needed help.)

"When the doctor came, Mom and Bess were so upset that I was the one who had to hold Lester down while the doctor put in stitches. But he never cried or resisted at all. Maybe he was in shock." The cuts left permanent scars on Lester's face that turned red in cold weather, making him look angry.

The next year, the Hipple family rented a house closer to Tipton so the children could go to school in town. Sometimes they rode to school in a large wagon drawn by a team of horses driven by older boys.

When Lester entered school in Tipton, the teachers found he had not learned much at the country schoolhouse, and they made him repeat first grade. Seven-year-old Lester was angry and ashamed. "He said he would never let that happen again, and his grades were always good from that time on," Bess said.

Lester was strong-willed and quick to anger as a child, Bess said, but he calmed down as he got older. Lester fought often with Floss, who was three years older. "I could beat him up, but I didn't dare," she recalled. "If I tried to hurt him, I'd get punished. You know, I was the second girl but he was the first boy, so my parents sided with him." Once, for no good reason, Lester kicked Floss in the eye. "Mom said, 'Charlie, you've got to do something about this boy.'" Lester got a good spanking for that, Floss said, still relishing the justice of it all, more than eighty years later.

His sisters remembered a cheerful child who loved a good joke. He could also be silent and private, "like he was thinking all the time," said Floss. Bess added, "He was quiet and didn't complain, but he was a laugher. His baby pictures from the day he was born show him laughing." He liked to tell a joke subtly, starting out as if discussing a serious matter then revealing the punch line with a twinkle in his eye.

As a young boy, Lester had blond hair to go with his pale brown eyes. Later, his hair turned brown, but, "He was a Swede all the way through," said Shirley. He had very fair skin, which would turn red and peel when exposed to the sun. Shirley remembered a time as a very small girl when her brother, eleven years older, sat patiently as she pulled pieces of sunburned skin from his back. Together, they held a white patch up to the sun and peered through it, seeing the dark spots where the pores were. "He burned easy," Shirley said.

—

The tug of war between Charles and Lena was resolved in 1926, when Lester was thirteen. After years of saving, the Hipples bought a house on the edge of Tipton for no more than $2,500. Now Charles could return to being a blacksmith. They also acquired an adjacent vacant lot for about $500. This became Lena's farm.

The house was at 108 Spruce Street, in what Shirley called "the industrial section," about a block from the railroad and not far from a brickyard, a corn canning factory, and a plant that made cheese. A former side porch had been walled in to create a single long, narrow room that served as a kitchen and dining room. There was a trap door in the kitchen that opened to stone steps leading down to a small cellar with a dirt floor where the family stored potatoes, apples, and other fruits and vegetables. The rest of the house consisted of a living room and four small bedrooms.

The new Hipple home had electricity, a luxury the family never enjoyed before. However, there was no indoor plumbing. Fourteen years would pass before this amenity was added, when Shirley was a sophomore in high school and Lester was launched on his coaching and teaching career. It was common to live without indoor plumbing in those days, remembered Bess. "All our friends had outdoor toilets."

The Hipples pumped water from a well in the side yard or gathered it from a cistern that captured rainwater just outside the kitchen door. They carried the water inside in a bucket to fill a reservoir in a giant cast-iron stove, which heated the water for cooking or washing. When it was time to take a bath, a tub was filled with hot water from the stove. When baths were in order for more than one person, the cleanest went first, the grimiest last. Shirley, by far the smallest, usually enjoyed the first dip, while Pop, the blacksmith, was always the last to take a bath in water that was lukewarm at best.

The kitchen stove, which burned wood or coal, was the primary source of heat for the house, augmented by a pot-bellied stove in the living room. Lester and his little brother, Don, were responsible for chopping wood and bringing it inside, which they did every day without complaint. The boys shared the front bedroom, assigned to them because it was the coldest.

The neighborhood swarmed with children. "I think there were fifty-nine kids in our part of town," said Bess. "We all played ball," added Shirley. "Bess was the best player in school. She played baseball and football with the boys. She learned to drop kick a football."

"We didn't have any money, but we didn't care," said Bess. "We had a lot of fun and we played ball."

Lester loved sports. As a kid he was always in the pickup games that sprouted as if by magic in schoolyards and vacant lots. He learned to swim at the Cedar Valley quarry outside of town. The Hipple children wore out two Montgomery Ward croquet sets in endless matches under the shade of a huge maple tree in their side yard. Lester flew all over town on his bicycle. Among all the Hipple children, only he and Shirley owned bikes. Hers cost $10, and it was such a treasure that she kept it at the foot of her bed.

—

Tipton, the county seat of Cedar County, had a population of about twenty-five hundred during the 1920s, but somehow earned the title "city," which was officially bestowed only on municipalities with a population of three thousand or more. Nevertheless, it was the biggest town in the county, and it had a new, $250,000 school, constructed in 1925. The "consolidated" school took students who previously had attended nineteen different rural schools in the surrounding countryside. It served students from kindergarten through high school and was the largest consolidated school district in the state. There was even a two-year junior college in the building. The structure was "in the vanguard of everything which was up-to-date in education," said a city history, including "electric clocks and ventilating systems, which were quite new to this section of the country."

All the Hipple children graduated from Tipton High School, to the immense pride of their parents; neither of them had gone beyond eighth grade. Both Lester and Don graduated from Tipton Junior College on their way to undergraduate degrees.

"Tipton was a typical small town," wrote Shirley many years later. Like many midwestern county seats, the business district surrounded a square that held a park and the county courthouse. Local merchants occupied the streets facing the square, with commercial buildings on the side streets as well. "The streets downtown were paved, but the rest [in town] were just tar over dirt," Shirley remembered. "That stuff would be shiny black and smelly for days until it soaked in. It was nasty on shoes and tires." The array of downtown merchants was sufficient to meet almost all the needs of the local residents and the farmers who came to town on Saturdays.

After working briefly for two other businesses, Charles opened his own blacksmith shop just off Main Street. The shop's sign read, "C.C. Hipple Blacksmith." At the turn of the century, every town had at least one blacksmith and many had several. Making horseshoes and shoeing horses was a core part of the business, but blacksmiths also sharpened tools, repaired wagons and wagon wheels, fashioned gates and hinges, and forged tools. "They worked in both wood and metal, over hot forges and around skittish horses," wrote Michael W. Vogt in *Iowa Heritage* magazine. Photographs of shops in the magazine show dim interiors with racks and piles of heavy tools for bending metal and shaping wood. The environment calls up images of smashed fingers, bruised shins, and burnt flesh, a place where a forgetful misstep could lead to serious injury.

—

Hard times came to Iowa during the 1920s, well before the Depression gripped the nation in 1929. In the mid-1920s, the government removed subsidies for farmers that had been instituted during World War I. Farm prices were cut almost in half. Small-town banks and businesses felt the effects almost immediately. Jobs became scarce. Iowa entered a twenty-year period of economic strain that did not end until after World War II. When the Depression officially arrived, things got worse. Farm prices dropped to as little as one third what they had been during World War I.

Some farm families burned their corn for heat because they couldn't sell it at a decent price and it was cheaper than coal. Parents made clothing for their children from flour and seed sacks. Many farmers who had expanded their land holdings during the war were now stuck with mortgages they could barely pay. They could eat what grew, but cash was scarce. Sometimes they couldn't afford the twenty-five cents Charles charged to sharpen their plows. He extended credit and kept meticulous records in a large ledger that he stored in an old school desk in his shop. Bartering was common, and farmers often paid him with produce or animals.

One farmer gave Charles a baby pig, a runt, and Charles brought it home and nursed it. It was kept for a time behind the stove where it would squeal for milk. One day the family heard strange noises from behind the stove. "Sounds like a pig eating coal," someone said, and from then on the phrase became the standard way of describing any strange sound. Eventually the pig, named Gloria, was moved to the garage and an open pen behind the house, where the children helped feed her and refill her water hole in the summer. In time Gloria grew into a large, healthy hog—and was butchered. Lena canned the pork that wasn't consumed right away, and the family feasted on Gloria for months.

With income from the blacksmith shop unpredictable during the Depression, Lena's gardens became a major source of support for the family. She transformed the vacant lot into a miniature farm. She built a coop and kept chickens. Using the garage for a barn, she raised, at one time or another, cows, sheep, pigs, and white rabbits. For a time, she kept a cow in the back of the blacksmith shop in town.

In summers, Lena's gardens were a virtual Eden of vegetables, fruits, and flowers. "She had every kind of bush in creation," said Shirley. "She raised sweet corn and potatoes and all kinds of vegetables. She raised strawberries, raspberries, gooseberries, boysenberries, peaches, pears, and grapes. I remember the kitchen table full of boxes of berries. People drove by and would stop and buy strawberries. Some people phoned in their orders." People also bought her cut flowers: tulips, asters, roses, foxgloves, daisies, and mums.

"Mom was in the garden so much her fingernails were black," said Shirley. "Whenever she went to town she wore white gloves so people wouldn't see her hands."

Everyone worked. The girls were assigned most of the housework to give their mother more time to tend her gardens and animals. She made all the children pull a row of weeds before they went to school. Shirley and Don dug potatoes together and hauled them to the cellar. In the fall, some of Pop's clients invited him to their orchards to gather windfall apples. He took the kids along and they brought home basketsful for Lena to can. "All she ever worried about was those kids having enough to eat," said Shirley. "We had nothing. Nobody did. But we ate."

The Hipples had a charge account at Montgomery Grocery in town. Sometimes the bill got uncomfortably large, and to help pay it down, Lena would sell her cow's milk to the store. Shirley and her older brother, Don, had the job of delivering the milk to the store. "I carried one quart bottle and Hooter [Don's nickname] carried two quarts," Shirley said. "One day I dropped a quart of milk, and the bottle broke." She was horrified, but there was no punishment when she ran home and confessed what she had done.

In time, Pop was able to pay off the grocery bill. "Mom took Hooter and me down to the store and told us we could have anything we wanted because we had worked so hard to pay the bill. Boy, was that a big deal. I got a pack of gum and a candy bar."

The children came home every day from school for lunch, and Charles walked the five or six blocks from his shop to join them. He was always tired, Shirley said. After the meal, he often leaned back in his chair, balancing it on two legs, bracing its back against the kitchen wall. Then he put his head back against the wall, closed his eyes, and rested for a few minutes, perhaps even dozed. After a little while, he brought the chair back down on four legs, stood up, and went back to work. In time, Shirley remembered, a dark spot formed on the wall where Pop's head had touched it so many times as he leaned back for that moment's rest.

—

Pop was short, about five feet five, but broad and muscular. Mom was only about five feet tall and very gentle. Mom never cursed, and Pop did so only when provoked. He had thick hands with heavy fingers and could crack nuts in his bare hands. He was quiet, but commanded respect. He liked to give his kids nicknames: Shirley was "Tootsie," Don was "Hooter," and Helen was "Toody." No one remembers exactly what inspired these names, but they stuck forever. Lester remained Lester, the name the family always used.

In photographs Charles and Lena stare grimly into the camera. They seem severe and humorless, but the pictures are misleading, their children said. Lena and Charles were neither demonstrative nor talkative, but the Hipple children never doubted that they were deeply loving and devoted to one another and to the children. "During the Depression, if your parents fed you, you were loved," said Shirley. "We had great parents," said Bess. "They took great care of us all. Their first concerns were always for us. They never had a real vacation." For Lena and Pop, a day at the Cedar County Fair or attending a family reunion was a vacation.

Lester got his quiet, commanding manner from his father and his industriousness and organizational ability from his mother, his sisters said. Lena was the driving force in the family, while Charles tended to be content with things as they were. "We would never have gotten that house if it weren't for Mom," said Floss.

Lena was an excellent seamstress. For years she made all the girls' clothes. Every year she sewed three new dresses for each of them to wear to school. "I never had a ready-made dress until I was thirteen," said Bess. "Mom was too sick to sew that year, so Pop took me downtown, and we bought a dress." Lena taught all the children to sew, and Lester became adept at it. He learned by shortening the sleeves of his shirts and jackets, which were often too long for him. He would use the skill all his life.

Lester wanted no part of blacksmithing or gardening. When he was about twelve, he began working at a grocery store owned by Doan Winslow, the father of one of his best friends, Ralph. No one knows how Lester was able to secure a paying job in such hard times. Grown men hunted without success for jobs and, unable to find them, were forced to go on relief or leave home for jobs on government projects. Money was tight, and Doan Winslow was not known for his generosity. Perhaps Lester was just around the store a lot, because that's where his friend was, and began to make himself useful.

In the end, Winslow may have had no choice but to pay a small wage to this young, tireless worker. Barely a teenager, Lester began a decade-long career in the grocery business that would not only put a few dollars in this pocket but also put him through college.

Young Lester did not squander the money he worked so hard to earn. He kept a jar of coins in the kitchen cupboard, where the other children eyed it enviously. "We called him 'the miser' because he had money and we didn't," said Floss. When Lena served one of her delicious pies, precisely cutting equal slices for each child, Lester offered to buy Don's or Shirley's slice for a penny or a nickel. Shirley hated to part with her pie, but it was the only way to make money. The whole family loved sweets. Sometimes Lester brought home containers that had held bulk chocolate. The children picked pieces of chocolate from the sides of the bucket and devoured them ecstatically. The cleaned bucket became a wastebasket.

Ralph Winslow had a younger sister named Wilma. She was in Lester's class, and the two became friends when they were very young. Wilma said she knew Lester liked her from about the fifth grade on, because that was when he threw a rotten apple at her, which burst in a splat all over her brand-new coat.

Wilma had thick, coal-black hair and wide-set hazel eyes. She was a quiet girl, well behaved, with a sharp sense of humor. Wilma and Lester were always good friends, but it appears they didn't date often during high school, and they certainly didn't go steady. His ability to take girls on dates was sharply hampered because Pop refused to allow Lester or any of his other children to drive the family car, a rule that frustrated and angered the young man. Even so, Lester had little time for dating. He was busy with school, sports, and work. After working for several grocers, he landed a job at the local A&P store. He showed an interest in only one other girl in high school, and perhaps dated her a few times, but Wilma was clearly his favorite.

Ralph and Wilma's father, Doan Winslow, was a stern and dour man. His first wife died, and his second was given to long, unexplained disappearances. Early in her high school years, Wilma began complaining of stomachaches. Some days the pain was so bad she couldn't go to school. Her father, unwilling to spend money on a doctor, hoped the problem would go away. He told Wilma to ignore the pain, bind her abdomen with tight clothing, and carry on. Soon her appendix burst, spilling poison into her body and nearly killing

Wilma. It took her so long to regain her health that she fell behind in her schoolwork and did not have enough credits to get a diploma when her class graduated.

—

Lester was an outstanding student. He was regularly on the honor roll, and during his senior year was elected to Tipton High School's first National Honor Society. Lester was a serious student who had little interest in movies or novels and confined his reading largely to textbooks.

In sports, Lester earned three varsity letters in basketball, two in football, and went out for track all four years. He was small, about five feet seven, and weighed less than 150 pounds, but he was very strong and quick, with powerful thighs. Basketball was his best sport.

As a senior, he was captain of the basketball team and its only senior starter. The team had to get by with two freshman guards, which undoubtedly contributed to its record of 6–12. The season came to an end with a 32–27 loss to West Liberty in the first game of the sectional tournament. "Lester Hipple might be mentioned among the best forwards in Class A, for he made four baskets in the last half of the game," wrote the local newspaper.

Summarizing the season, the paper reported that Hipple was the team's top scorer by far, notching 101 points, more than twice as many as any teammate. If the paper can be believed, Lester's shooting accuracy was shockingly poor by modern standards. He attempted 213 field goals that season and made only 34 of them, for a woeful average of 14 percent. He was 33 of 69 in free throws, for 48 percent accuracy, also poor by later measures. It was a different game. None of Tipton's shooters came close to matching today's scoring percentages. The most accurate shooter on the team had a field goal average of only 28 percent, and another key player made only 6 of 66 attempts.

Lester was quarterback on his football team as a senior, a triple-threat man who ran, passed, and drop-kicked extra points. He also played in the defensive backfield, intercepted at least one pass, and returned punts. In one game, he had to tackle a teammate. The Tipton player, in possession of the ball, became confused and began running toward his own goal line. Lester gave chase and hauled the boy to earth before he could get there. Lester led Tipton to a 6–1–2 record, with the team's only loss a 28–0 pounding by

Marion. It may have been in football that he sustained an injury to his left hip that was to plague him for almost all his life.

Although Lester went out for track all four years, there is no record of his receiving a letter, and his name doesn't show up in reports of meets that appeared in the local paper.

He loved sports so much he wanted to become a coach. To do that, he would have to earn a college degree. That cost money, which was one thing his family didn't have.

Chapter 4
College Man, 1932–1937

Pop Hipple was proud that Lester had graduated from high school, but he didn't want him to go to college. Pop believed his son should continue working for the A&P, with the goal of becoming a store manager. The A&P offered stability, security, and food—Pop thought that was an unbeatable combination. Lester's ambition to be a teacher and coach seemed unattainable. "Lester didn't argue with Pop, he just went on with his plans," remembered his sister Floss. "He had his head set on what he was going to do, and that was that."

So in September 1932, at the age of 19, Lester Hipple became the first member of his family to go to college. He entered Tipton Junior College, which had an enrollment of 40 students and was housed in the same building as the high school.

The Depression still held Iowa in its grip. Unemployment was widespread as businesses of all sizes went under. In 1932, two banks in Tipton closed their doors several months apart, setting off a panic among the citizens. They made a run on the only bank remaining in town. Its officers hurried to banks in nearby towns for cash. The bank honored $40,000 in withdrawals on the first day of the run and withstood the panic. Then bank officials assembled $100,000 in currency and "stacked it up like cordwood where everyone could see it," the local paper reported. The bank also increased its insurance against robbery and hired extra guards to protect the stack of money. Thus calmed, local business owners continued making deposits, and within three days the panic was over.

Tuition at Tipton Junior College couldn't have been very high, but it was likely that Lester had to bear most of the cost himself. Although Lena's garden was feeding the family and her sewing was clothing them, cash was scarce. Lester continued to live at home and work at the A&P. The financial pressure of raising six children had eased somewhat for Lena and Charles. Their oldest daughter, Bess, had graduated from high school four years earlier and moved about forty miles away to Cedar Rapids. She counted herself lucky to land a job as clerk in Kresge's Five and Dime at $11 a week. A few years later, Floss also moved to Cedar Rapids to work

Wilma Winslow, meanwhile, worked for about a year in a Tipton restaurant and then moved to Monroe, Wisconsin, her birthplace, to enter a school of nursing. She and Lester often wrote letters to each other.

Despite his work and studies, Lester had time for sports. Tipton Junior College was too small to field a football team, but it did offer basketball. Lester lettered both years in junior college and was captain of the team his second year, when the team finished 8–5. Hipple was the team's third-highest scorer with eighty-nine points and was named to the all-conference second team in the Northeast Iowa Junior College Conference. The Tipton paper praised his play several times, notably in a hard-fought 25–21 victory over Roosevelt Military Academy of Aledo, Illinois. "Captain Hipple sank three goals in the first two minutes of the last quarter to give his team the lead which they maintained throughout the remaining minutes of play. Hipple showed more of his old time fighting spirit than he has at any time this season, demonstrating his ability to come through in tight places when points were most needed."

Early in Lester's second year at the junior college, a fellow student drowned in the Cedar Valley quarry. The quarry, just outside Tipton, served as the swimming pool for the area and was a favorite gathering place. The tragedy happened during a school outing. It was night and somehow the young man lost his footing and fell backward into deep water. The victim couldn't swim, and as he thrashed and screamed, Lester pulled off his watch and shoes and plunged into the water. In a few minutes at least one other rescuer joined him. They swam around in the darkness, yelling for their friend, until they were exhausted. The boy's body was not found until much later. Lester never talked about this event as an adult. Occasionally his wife brought it up, pointing out that Lester was the first one into the water because he didn't remove any clothing before diving in. Others, more prudent, or less confident of their swimming ability, stripped away their clothes before entering the dark waters.

Lester Hipple received his associate's degree from Tipton Junior College in 1934, one of only fourteen graduates. By this time, he was firm in his determination to become a coach, he told the *Cedar Rapids Gazette* many years later. How he was going to accomplish his goal remained a big question. He had no money for tuition, room, and board at a four-year college. So he stayed in Tipton, working full time for the local A&P.

After a year of this, he parlayed his grocery experience into a job with an A&P in Iowa City, about twenty-five miles from Tipton. With that as his base, he went to classes at the University of Iowa in the morning and worked from noon to 6:00 PM at the store. With Saturday work, he put in forty hours a week. His pay was twenty-five cents an hour.

Part of the Hipple legend, recounted by several who knew him, is that he injured his left hip while playing football at the university. One version is that the injury occurred when he was trying out for the Iowa team. While it is almost certain that his work schedule would have prohibited his playing intercollegiate sports, the injury could have occurred during an intramural or pickup game. In one version of the story, there was a huge pile-up of bodies, with Hipple at the bottom. He crawled out with a damaged hip that would torment him for fifty years.

Lester's university transcript suggests that combining full-time work and study was a difficult challenge. Hipple was essentially a C student, with a few D's (in math courses) and B's (in physical education). His only A during the full two years came in basketball theory. Good grades weren't the objective here; getting a degree was.

Les Hipple graduated on time, in 1937 at the age of twenty-four, with a BA in education and without failing a course. The next challenge would be to land a teaching job. Such positions were in short supply during the Depression. If he could find one, his days as a grocery clerk would be over for good.

Chapter 5
Callender, 1937–1940

Lester C. Hipple, twenty-four, Bachelor of Arts, found his first professional position in the crossroads village of Callender in western Iowa, just south of Fort Dodge. It was two hundred miles from his home in Tipton, a grueling trip by car over rough roads. He had never been so far away from home, and he never would be again.

Somehow, in the depths of the Depression, the Callender school district had built a new high school and a new gymnasium. Now it needed a coach to establish an athletic program and a principal to handle administration for the school. Hipple, with no prior experience in either position, was hired to do both, in addition to teaching mathematics classes. He surely received supportive recommendations from his university. No doubt he made a good impression in his interviews. Then again, his salary requirements may have helped. He was paid $900 a year to start (about $12,000 in 2007 dollars).

The new Callender High School had about sixty students and a nine-person faculty. There were only eleven students in the 1938 graduating class. Either the school was growing, since the senior class represented less than its share of the total enrollment, or students drifted away as they got older, taking up work on the farm or landing a job that helped the family survive.

Hipple worked at Callender for three school years, from the fall of 1937 through the spring of 1940. He coached the boys' and girls' basketball teams and a boys' baseball team that played in the fall and the spring. A sparse record of those years was preserved in a scrapbook kept in the Callender public library. The scrapbook contains faded newspaper clippings and roughly typed programs for school events such as graduation exercises, student plays, and declamatory competitions. It also has photos of the basketball teams Hipple coached; the pages appear to be part of a yearbook.

One photo shows Mr. Hipple with his boys' basketball squad, seventeen members strong, and the first of thirty teams he would lead. In the photo, the coach stands to the far right, looking no older than his players. He wears a slightly rumpled double-breasted suit. His blond hair is neatly trimmed, short and parted just off the center of his head to his left. His arms are folded behind his back, and his body looks fit and strong. His gaze is steady, his expression serious. The boys standing beside him in his row are only slightly taller than his five feet seven. The taller boys are seated in the second row; the reserves sit cross-legged on the floor. The names of the players and coach are printed by hand beneath the photo in a careful, formal alphabet. Did Hipple himself print those names: *"B. Kruse, D. Wing, J. Vesey,"* and so on? It seems possible, for the handwriting style did not change in three years.

Hipple was so young, and had such serious work to do, handling myriad administrative chores, leading the faculty and staff, teaching, coaching, and disciplining these boys and girls nearly his own age, that it must have been at Callender that he developed his disciplinary style, learning the role of a stern taskmaster and honing all the methods that made him so intimidating in later years. Surely he faced repeated challenges from the tough farm boys he was hired to control and inspire. As coach, he could not threaten them with a trip to the principal's office. He was both coach and principal; the matter had to be settled on the spot. He had to learn how to see trouble coming and beat it to the punch—to establish his dominance in any situation. He was not one to back down. Perhaps the double duties of coach and principal made him doubly tough.

The Callender scrapbook has nothing about the record of Hipple's first boys' basketball team, but it does show those of the two teams that followed. Judging by the later results, that first year must have been sheer misery. In Hipple's second year, 1938–1939, the team went 3–14, suffering some brutal losses by such scores as 40–13, 33–8, and, against Webster County power Gowrie, a Class A school, 67–20. The following year brought dramatic improvement as the team finished 8–12 and the scores were lower and closer. Clearly, the coach was stressing defense: Scoring for both teams was lower, and mighty Gowrie was held to a 35–18 victory.

Hipple did not coach the girls' team in 1937–1938 but took over the following year. Apparently he inherited a talented group. These teams went 9–5 and 10–6 in the two seasons under Hipple, but they too were no match for Gowrie. Although Hipple coached the girls' team, he did so under the watchful eye of fellow faculty member Miss Prestegard, whose title was "chaperone."

Girls' rules in those days severely limited running and dribbling. There were six players on each team, three on defense and three on offense, with no crossing of the centerline. A player could dribble only twice before passing the ball. (These rules were essentially preserved in Iowa until 1993, when the last six-player tournament was held. Beginning in 1985, tournaments were held for both the six-player and the five-player versions.)

The boys' game, too, was much slower and more conservative than it would become in the 1940s. The rule dictating a jump ball after each basket had been eliminated in 1936, the year before Hipple became a coach, and that opened the game up somewhat. The photos of the Callender players suggest that they favored the two-handed set shot. Don King, long-time Iowa coach and basketball historian, wrote:

> Coaches were resistant to change. Everything with the ball except dribbling was a two-handed game. Coaches then were horrified by such ideas as cross-court passes, passing off the dribble, passing after jumping. Players were not as skilled. The pace of the game was much slower. Playground basketball had not happened yet. There was not the abundance of driveway courts with goals on the garage that we see now, so that shooting and other skills were not as readily developed pre-40s as they were later. The ball itself was not as good in the old days (they had laces at one time). So it was a combination of factors [that made the game slow and conservative and kept scores low].

In the years just ahead, basketball would undergo many changes, most of which Hipple embraced and helped popularize. But for his time at Callender, he was caught in the current mode of cautious play. There are two clues in the scrapbook that show Hipple's influence at work. One is that by his final year at Callender, he had established junior high basketball teams for both boys and girls. These tiny athletes of the future are pictured holding a ball twice the size of their heads. And there is this comment in an unidentified newspaper article: "The basketball boys have received new sweat shirts, all members have been practicing good."

The scrapbook contains very little about the baseball team. There are a few news clippings and scorecards, which do not suggest much success. The one team photo shows only nine players.

At Callender, Hipple husbanded his savings and purchased his first new car, a 1939 Chevrolet. When he drove it back to Tipton, his 15-year-old sister Shirley asked him to give her a driving lesson. He reluctantly agreed. They sat in the car, Shirley at the wheel. Hipple said nothing. Shirley sensed that he wanted her to try driving, so she turned the key and started the car. Observation had taught her the rudiments of shifting, so she put it in low and tried to work the clutch and accelerator. The car bucked and died.

Lester looked his sister in the eye and said, "Now I'm going to tell you once, and I'm not going to tell you again, how to drive a car." And that's what he did. Shirley said she was able to learn the basics from that single lesson. "It just proves that if you paid attention to his instructions, you could accomplish the nearly impossible," she wrote.

Throughout these years, Hipple continued to take summer school courses at Iowa University in special areas of physical education, mathematics, and school administration. He got all B's and C's, a marked improvement over his undergraduate grades. He did enough course work to earn his master's degree, but never completed his thesis. After three years at Callender, Hipple's salary had risen 15 percent to $1,035 and he was ready for a bigger challenge.

Chapter 6
Walker, 1940–1942

Lester Hipple and his childhood friend, Wilma Winslow, were married on June 5, 1940. He was twenty-seven, she was twenty-six. The two had gone their separate ways after high school. She had stayed in Monroe, Wisconsin, to work after graduating from nursing school. Lester and Wilma exchanged letters and saw each other from time to time on visits back to Tipton, but the romance, if there ever had been one, had cooled.

"Wilma got interested in someone else, some Norwegian. I think his name was Marvel Rundhaug," said Lester's sister Bess. When Lester heard the news, he was upset. The development was no secret in the Hipple family. "Mom told him, 'If you want her, you better go get her and you better do it right away,'" said Shirley. Lester did not hesitate. "He wrote to Wilma immediately and then he went right up and got her," Bess said.

They were married in a civil ceremony at Davenport, Iowa, where Wilma's sister, Zelma, lived with her husband, Frank. Zelma and Frank were to be witnesses to the wedding; there were no other guests. But Zelma fell ill at the last minute, so a church custodian was recruited to join Frank as a witness. It was not unusual that none of Lester's family attended the wedding. Matrimony was often a cut-and-dried affair in those hard times when money was short. Honeymoons were often foregone as the new husband and wife returned immediately to work, and that is probably what Lester and Wilma did.

That September, Hipple took the reins at Walker High School, serving as principal, math teacher, and coach of boys' basketball and baseball. Walker, a small town in northern Linn County, was only marginally larger than

Callender, with a ten-person high school faculty, but Hipple was back in eastern Iowa, much closer to home, and his salary had risen to $1,125 a year (worth about $16,000 in 2007).

The Walker girls' basketball team was a county power under Coach Rita Houlahan. In 1940–1941, the girls posted a 23–3 record, winning the county and sectional championships and finishing second in the district tournament. The boys, by comparison, were so prone to losing that fans streamed out after the girls' games, leaving the boys to perform before nearly empty bleachers.

Hipple's task, as at Callender, was to turn the situation around. In his first year, the team went 5–9, "which seems like a very poor record," wrote a student correspondent for the *Walker News*. "However, it is much better than last year's, and if the team keeps improving under Coach Hipple I'm sure it will have a much better record next year." Although the team reportedly got better, its record didn't. In February 1942, the *News* reported that the boys were 4–11. The girls were 17–2–2. That year, however, marked Hipple's first victory in state tournament play. His team defeated Palo in the opening round of the sectional tournament, 26–14. This was followed by a loss to Center Point, 33–17.

Efforts to research Hipple's Walker years turned up scant information. No yearbooks came to light. What can be learned comes from the *Walker News*, a six-column paper devoted to notes on the activities of the area's citizens. The paper's front page featured a weekly column, "School Notes," submitted by student reporters, but sports, and all other matters, were covered haphazardly. Here are some items contributed by Fulton Ross in 1940–1941 and Luella Bare in 1941–1942.

- Coach Houlahan has a fine, winning team. Coach Hipple is drilling the boys in many detailed ways and is teaching the team many fundamentals which were missed prior to this time.
- The basketball girls will certainly look beautiful now as they have secured a mirror in which they may see all of themselves. It's just what they've been wanting for quite some time. They raised the money by selling candy one evening at the show. They hope to raise enough money to buy a shower curtain.
- Coach Hipple is certainly giving the boys' basketball team some long needed drilling. We are really improving.

- Mr. Hipple's baseball boys are hard at work (when the weather permits, today the diamond was almost completely under water). The team this year is made up of boys who are quite small but Mr. Hipple says they are making up for height with their zip and willingness to work.
- 19 boys have reported for basketball practice … The boys are to hold practice every day! Boy! That really is some going. We hope Miss Houlahan doesn't get the same idea for the girls.
- Coach Hipple has improved our basketball backboards by painting them black, to resemble the new smaller backboards. The forwards appreciate this because it improves their eye for the basket.
- The boys were defeated by Troy by the score of 28–26. The game was very exciting. The boys led during a good share of the game and at one time had a lead of 10 points. The boys' brand of basketball has certainly improved this season.

There is almost no hint in "School Notes" that during this time Europe was under Hitler's domination, that the Japanese had attacked Pearl Harbor, and that America had been at war since December 1941.

Had World War II not yet scarred the people of Walker, it would do so soon enough.

Chapter 7
West Branch, 1942–1945

Superintendent Leonard A. Maley at West Branch High School was losing a good man. His athletic coach, Grant Peterson, had decided to join the Navy. This war, less than a year old for the United States, was not going well. His country needed him.

Peterson would be difficult to replace. He was a good coach who had built a winning program in football and basketball. Finding young male teachers and coaches was difficult. Teachers were leaving the field not only to join the military, but also to take jobs left vacant by others who went to war. The war was stirring the economy, creating opportunities that paid more than teaching.

Maley did not have to look far to find Les Hipple. West Branch, in Cedar County and not far from Iowa City, was sixty miles from Walker and only about twenty miles from Hipple's boyhood home of Tipton. Maley may well have met Hipple or known of his reputation for hard work, discipline, and integrity. But if the supply of candidates had been as plentiful as in the past, he might never have picked Hipple.

West Branch was considerably larger than Walker, with slightly more than one hundred students in high school and another fifty or so in junior high. Hipple's dedication as a coach was clear, yet his ability to produce winning teams was open to question. Another negative was that he had never coached football. Maley, a former athlete who taught manual training at West Branch, believed strongly in the value of sports and was proud of his school's winning teams. Football mattered. In 1941, the West Branch Bears went 7–0–1 in the tough Eastern Iowa Conference that also included University High of Iowa City, Tipton, West Liberty, Monticello, and Mount Vernon.

For his part, Les Hipple, twenty-nine and married, with a child on the way, had five years' experience as principal and coach, had completed most of the course work for his master's degree, and was ineligible for military service because of his damaged hip. He also had been an excellent high school quarterback. Maley hired him as high school principal and coach. His starting salary was $1,495 (about $20,000 in 2007). Hipple, wrote an area newspaper, "really picked himself a spot to start teaching grid maneuvers," since he had no prior experience coaching the sport.

That fall, Lester and Wilma welcomed their daughter, Patty Jo, into the world. She would be their only child, born September 5 in an Iowa City hospital. Hipple always insisted he was the first to see her, although Wilma disputed the claim. Since fathers did not participate in hospital births in those days, the likely explanation is that Wilma was still unconscious when nurses brought the newborn out to show the father.

At the practice field, Hipple was overseeing a squad of thirty players. Eight were returning lettermen, but only three had been starters. Peterson, it appeared, had been more generous in awarding letters than Hipple would be. Even more foreboding was the loss through graduation of the Bears' gifted running back, Floyd Christensen, who made third-string All State as a senior.

Thus it was something of a surprise when West Branch opened the season by trouncing Brooklyn, 27–0, in a torrential downpour that caused the field lights to fail several times. The following week, the Bears beat Wapello by the identical score of 27–0. When the team followed that by whipping Mount Vernon 19–0 in their first conference game, West Branch fans happily observed that their team had out-pointed its opponents by the cumulative score of 73–0. Maybe, some dared to think, this team and its new coach could be as good as last year. But West Branch was pounded by conference powers Tipton (28–0) and University High (20–7), lost to archrival West Liberty (13–8), and tied Monticello (7–7). All in all, the newspaper coverage indicates that the town was satisfied with the season's 5–3–1 record.

Although Hipple had to make do without All-State Christensen, he inherited an arsenal of multitalented weapons in the Rummells boys. There was Don, the oldest, a junior that year and a returning letterman. Right behind him were the sophomore twins, Warren and Wayne. All three played in the backfield that year and, when basketball season rolled around, often comprised 60 percent of the starting lineup. The Rummells boys were not big (Warren was five feet ten and 150 pounds as a senior), but they were wiry, fast, and tough—willing workers who were passionate about sports. They were the kind of kids Hipple would have so much success coaching in the years to come—the kind of kid Hipple himself had been.

The *West Branch Times* and its student-edited insert, *The Purple and the White Weekly*, were assiduous in covering football, but tended to pay less attention to basketball. The paper reported that the basketball team won 69 percent of its games that first year under Hipple, giving him his first winning season as coach of a boys' team. The team finished in a three-way tie for first place in its conference and won both the county tournament and the sectional championship, the first level of play in the state tournament.

Hipple started a spring baseball program, spending "no less than two hundred and fifty dollars" on new uniforms and equipment, the paper reported, and the team went 6–3 in the regular season. West Branch also fielded a track team, which operated concurrently with the baseball team, apparently with Hipple as coach. Several boys won letters in all four sports—football, basketball, baseball, and track.

In football, the Bears were on a roll. In 1943, with Don Rummells at quarterback and the twins in the backfield, the football team went 7–2, tying for second place in the conference. That winter, the basketball team went 16–7, good for a first-place tie in the conference, and again won the county title and sectional championship.

Things were even better the following year. Don Rummells had graduated, but Warren replaced him as captain and quarterback, while Wayne stayed at halfback. West Branch had a veteran team, its heaviest in five years, averaging 160 pounds per man. Even before the season opened, the town knew it had a powerhouse. The Bears swept to an undefeated 9–0 season, outscoring their opponents 268–51, beating University High for the first time in years, and capping the season with a satisfying 32–6 drubbing of West Liberty. Warren Rummells was named to the All-State third team, and Wayne received honorable mention along with two other teammates.

In basketball, with Wayne at forward and Warren at guard, West Branch finished second in the conference to powerful University High. However, the

Bears again won county and sectional titles, losing, as in the past, in the first round of the district tournament.

After five years of frustration at Callender and Walker, Hipple proved he could produce winners. Yes, he built on a strong foundation, but who could argue with a three-year football coaching record of 21–5–1 and, in basketball, a .700 winning record, shares of two conference championships, and six out of a possible six county and sectional championships? This man had the right stuff.

—

Research of Hipple's West Branch years reveals a stern disciplinarian with a list of rules and an almost supernatural power to turn unruly teenaged boys into obedient, disciplined athletes.

Reached some sixty years after his high school playing days, Warren Rummells remembered that Hipple had strong support from Superintendent Maley and that "people couldn't believe how hard he made us work and how tough he was." Rummells himself, for all his skill as an athlete, felt intimidated, but not frightened, by the man. "Without a doubt," Rummells said, "Hipple made me a better athlete and a better person."

A promising freshman athlete, Winton Gable, took an algebra class taught by Hipple. One day, as the students worked quietly on a series of problems, a fly began to taunt the boy. It landed on his desk, rubbing its legs and flexing its wings, and then took off, buzzing his face before landing again. It would not go away. Winton ignored the creature as long as he could. Then, as the fly sat preening on the edge of his workbooks, the boy made a sudden swipe with his hand to catch it. At that moment, he looked at his teacher. Hipple's glare across the room penetrated Winton's very heart. The boy was frozen in mortification. Hipple at West Branch had mastered his full ability to paralyze a boy with his eyes.

On another day, Winton was walking down a school hallway, munching a piece of cake that had been given to him by a girl who had baked it in home economics class. At this moment of gluttony, Hipple spotted him. The two stopped, facing one another. As Hipple watched, Gable choked down the rest of the cake.

"Was that good?" Hipple asked.

"Yes. But I only took it because I didn't want to hurt my friend's feelings."

"Well, good, because it's going to cost you ten laps on the track tonight before practice. And I'll be there to time you."

At West Branch, Hipple's rules banned between-meal sweets. The following was found among the coach's papers:

Football Training Rules

1. No improper language is to be used on or off the field, on trips, and around the building as it reflects directly on your school. Be a gentleman all the time.
2. You are to be in bed at 10:00 PM every night except Friday and Saturday. (This does not mean starting from downtown, but it means in bed by 10:00.) On Friday and Saturday night you are to be in bed by 12:00.
3. If you are caught smoking or drinking you are through as far as athletics are concerned.
4. Your diet is important, do not eat between meals. Sweets may be eaten at meal time after your regular meal, but do not make a habit of this practice as sweets are hard on the wind.
5. If it is reported to the coach that you are breaking training, you will be asked in front of the squad in regard to your situation. It's a tough spot to be in; don't let it happen to you.
6. If you own a car or drive the family auto, use it only when absolutely necessary; besides, walking is better for you.
7. You may have dates if you desire; however, don't let them interfere with your football training; if you fall in love, you'll have to make your choice, as a boy in love does not make a good athlete.
8. You must attend every practice or report to your coach before practice if you expect to be excused; otherwise a cut practice.

9. All football shoes are to be put on and taken off at the back doors, not in the dressing room or under the shade tree on the lawn.
10. You will be on the team if:
11. 1. You are considered good enough.
    2. You are training.
    3. You hustle, have the will to succeed, show perseverance, enthusiasm, pluck, spirit and courage.

Hipple continued to enforce these rules throughout his career. In time they became more specific and demanding, although the reference to eating sweets was dropped.

Hipple's philosophy of sacrifice and dedication was spelled out in a 1944 issue of the school paper. The article has no byline, but its author is unmistakable.

> Every boy, at all times, must put aside all thoughts of personal gains and give all he has for the good of the team. He must be big enough to refuse to let any personal differences come between himself and his teammates. In other words, every boy must take enough responsibility on himself so he will be in there 100% all the time … Our boys know that a team that won't be defeated can't be defeated.

—

World War II was raging overseas. Former students who were now soldiers came back to address pep rallies. Servicemen's letters to the school were printed in the paper. Readers could track the progress of former coach Peterson as he went through naval training school, attained the rank of ensign, and was put in charge of a gun crew on a troop ship. Instead of writing a traditional recap of football games, the *Times* printed play-by-play accounts intended especially for those in the service. The author set the stage with a description of the weather, field conditions, and pre-game activities. Then he, with the help of several assistants, reported each play and its result. Servicemen overseas loved this approach. As they read the accounts, they could see the game unfold in their minds.

In November of 1942, America had been in the war for less than a year. The school conducted a somber commemoration of Armistice Day, which had marked the end of World War I—the first such day celebrated with the nation again at war. Following a minute of silence, the Rev. James Gable of the Methodist Church, father of Winton and his younger brother Barrie, gave the invocation and, after some songs and other speeches, presented a "very stirring Armistice Day address."

Less than two years later, in the summer of 1944, the Rev. Gable, his wife, and his two young sons moved to Marion, where he took the pulpit of the Methodist church. It probably couldn't be called an act of divine intervention, but the move led to the best thing that could have happened for the future of sports at Marion High School.

Chapter 8
Marion at War, 1942–1945

The world was at war, and the sons of Iowa were in it. They began joining the service when war broke out in December 1941. They were uprooted from farms and small towns, spun off to places they had never heard of, and thrown into chaos and horror.

At home, families gathered around the radio every evening to hear the news from Gabriel Heatter, H.V. Kaltenborn, and Lowell Thomas. They studied the progress of the war in their newspapers and pinned maps to their kitchen walls to track the locations of their sons and daughters overseas. They learned about islands, cities, and countries they had never cared about.

The first boy from Marion reported to have died in the war was Lt. Donovan Goodyear of the Army Air Force, who perished in the sinking of the U.S.S. Langley off the coast of Java. Others also may have "made the supreme sacrifice," said the *Marion Sentinel*, but their deaths could have gone unreported because of distance and censorship.

The boys continued to enlist as they came of age and war raged on, and by 1943 almost every weekly issue of the *Marion Sentinel* contained reports that ripped at the hearts of families living in Marion and nearby villages in Linn County.

Peace reigned inside the paper, where long gray columns chronicled the modest social activities of the people of Marion, Springville, Walker, Peralta, Buffalo, Center Point, and Toddville. Each week, there were dozens of brief paragraphs telling of relatives visiting a local family, children's birthday parties, neighbors entertaining guests on a Sunday afternoon, children spending the night at their grandparents' home, a boy coming home from college for a visit. There were marriages, births, and deaths, too, but most of the news described uneventful, peaceful gatherings.

The front page was different. It contained the official news of the area, and a lot of it was bad. Photos of young men in uniform were accompanied by headlines telling how their parents had received "the dread news" of their deaths. Readers learned of boys killed in action, or missing and presumed dead, or lost when their ships sank or their planes crashed. One soldier was cut down by malaria, another killed under a falling tree as it toppled from cannon fire. A county boy on a prison ship died when the ship was sunk, apparently by Allied forces. A father received his son's last letter after being informed of his death.

The bodies of the dead came home to Marion in caskets carried in a Milwaukee Railroad baggage car. The caskets had been loaded and unloaded from a series of trains to make the shuttling journey from the East or West coasts. The train men knew the contents of the caskets, and word reached Marion ahead of the train when a boy's body was coming home. Neighbors and friends gathered at the depot to pay their respects and to follow along as the casket was taken off the train and transferred to the Yocum Funeral Home a block away.

When a son was killed or wounded, taken prisoner or missing in action, the news was delivered to his family in a small envelope carried by a boy on a bicycle. He wore a billed cap with the word "Telegraph" on the front. He was dispatched from the train depot, where the news had been sent by wire from Washington, D.C.

One morning, teenager Joyce Fosdick Parks was outside her house enjoying the day with two neighbor women, one with a boy in Europe, the other with a son in the Pacific, both officers. There was a motion or a sound down the street, and they looked up to see the telegraph boy pedaling in their direction. The two women froze in place and turned pale. Joyce could not breathe as the cyclist approached. He rode toward them and then past them and the women sighed and then shook their heads. They knew where he was going, just a few doors away, where another mother learned that her son had been taken prisoner.

Many families with a boy in the service hung a cloth banner with a blue star in a front window of their house. Some windows had two blue stars. If a boy was killed, a gold star was sewn over the blue one.

Reports on funerals and memorial services for the dead boys were a regular feature of the *Sentinel.* Their brief obituaries recounted their accomplishments in high school. This boy had been on several sports teams; this one played in the band. There were stories, too, of prisoners still alive, of miraculous rescues at sea, of wounded men sent home to grateful families, of transfers, promotions, and medals.

Servicemen home on leave gave interviews to the *Sentinel.* Others spoke to church gatherings or service clubs. Marion's former coach, Lieutenant (jg) Don P. Wolfe, visited home after "several months in Guadalcanal and New Guinea," the paper reported. He couldn't talk about his specific role, but warned, in the *Sentinel's* paraphrase, "that the Japs fight hard and at times make their blows count." A Marion sailor told of eighteen grueling and ultimately boring months "spent entirely in the rocky, storm-tossed, fog-ridden Aleutians."

Some of the servicemen on leave, and others, badly wounded and out of it for good, sat on benches in the town square after supper and told their stories to the men and boys who gathered around them. They did not talk about fighting and killing as much as about the physical misery of war—the freezing filth of fox holes, relentless attacks by insects in sweltering jungles, going weeks without changing clothes, or contracting diseases that could cripple or kill. As the soldiers talked and the sun set, high school girls walked by, giggling among themselves and shooting shy glances at the men. Ed Failor, a high school boy who listened to the veterans, remembered that no matter what story was being told, its basic theme was always the same. "Always, the talk was of us winning the war," he wrote, of ending it so normal life could resume. The day after he received his high school diploma in 1945, Failor was on his way to training camp for the Army Air Corps.

Like Failor, high school boys were not deterred by the veterans' horror stories or by the deaths of boys they had known in school. Many enlisted as soon as they graduated. Others left school even earlier, at sixteen, and lied about their ages. Some of these dropouts continued their studies while in the service. The lucky ones came back to school after the war to receive their diplomas. Many did not return. By the end of the war, the honor roll of the dead at the Methodist church, the largest in town, bore as many as fifteen names. Jon Edward Smith, who graduated from high school in 1943, wrote that every boy in his class entered the military service. "Some of the best were killed in action. We still cry for them every day."

—

The greatest homecoming was held in September 1942 for the town's most prominent hero, Major William N. "Bill" Reed, a pilot in China with Claire Chennault's legendary American Volunteer Group, the Flying Tigers. Reed, who had been an outstanding student and athlete at Marion High School and Loras College in Dubuque, was credited with shooting down at least eleven Japanese planes. He was one of about ninety pilots who were granted leave from the regular air forces to go to Burma to help defend China against Japan a few months before the United States officially entered the war. The unit was later incorporated into the Army Air Corps. In 1942, Reed was chosen by the Defense Department to join a troupe of celebrities and soldiers that toured the country to promote savings bonds. One of his first appearances was in Marion.

When Bill Reed came home, more than ten thousand people (twice the population of Marion) are said to have turned out to hear him speak from the bandstand in the park. The *Sentinel* did not report his words, so they must have been brief and modest, aimed at spurring the sale of war bonds. More than $21,000 worth was sold in Marion that day, with Reed himself making a large purchase. Congratulatory advertisements were placed in the *Marion Sentinel* by sixty-three businesses. Three major newsreel companies covered the event, and the report from Fox Movietone News was shown a few days later at the Marion Theater. Iowa Governor George A. Wilson gave a stirring address that included these words:

> This is Iowa. This is very near the very heart of the greatest republic ever organized. This is the victory garden of America. Here are the people one hundred percent American. There are no notes of discord as the tones of the Liberty Bell roll over these lands that were never marred by slavery nor stained by treason.

Reed stayed in the area a few days, making appearances and spending time with his mother, Mayme, and his nephew William "Dick" Reed, who was also a fighter pilot. The *Sentinel* reported that Bill Reed's term of enlistment would end on July 4, 1943, and speculated that he might leave the Air Corps to accept a job flying commercial transport.

Instead, in August 1943, after eleven months of stateside touring with such companions as movie stars James Cagney, Pat O'Brien, Walter Abel, and Jinx Falkenberg, Reed returned to China and the Flying Tigers. At about that time, his nephew Dick was shot down in a dogfight over Sicily. He was rescued by sailors, captured by the enemy, and later freed by American troops. He returned to his unit and continued to fight.

In August 1944 Bill Reed was promoted to Lieutenant Colonel in China. He continued flying. Four months later, on December 19, 1944, as he returned from a mission, his plane was diverted from landing because the airstrip was under fire. His plane crashed into a mountainside, and Reed was killed.

"We shall never know whether the crash was due to bad weather, enemy-inflicted damage to his airplane or lack of gasoline," General Chennault wrote to Reed's mother, "for mercifully he died instantly and without pain." Reed had flown seventy-five missions and had received the Silver Star, the Distinguished Flying Cross with oak leaf clusters, and honors from Britain and China. "Bill had successfully coped with danger for so long that he was regarded as well-nigh indestructible," Chennault wrote.

—

Even as its young men were at war, so was the town, in its own way. Gasoline, sugar, butter, meat, shoes, clothing, and many other commodities were rationed and in short supply. Often, these goods were unavailable even when families had ration stamps enough to buy them. Nylon was used in parachutes, so women's stockings were hard to obtain. Women who wanted to appear stylish drew a line along the back of their legs with an eyebrow pencil to simulate the seam of a stocking. Men's trousers were made without cuffs to save cloth.

Shortages of fabrics and clothing encouraged some mothers to continue the Depression-era practice of making clothes for their children from flour and grain sacks. A shortage of lumber and building supplies brought home construction and remodeling in town to a standstill; only farmers were allowed to build. Newspaper delivery boys sold savings stamps for ten cents; when enough stamps were purchased, they could be turned in for a $25 savings bond. Little boys wore beanies with patriotic slogans, such as "Remember Pearl Harbor."

Because gasoline and rubber tires were hard to come by, people walked a lot. Automobile production all but ceased as factories produced war machinery day and night. When the reverse gear went out on Bill Lundquist's Plymouth, he couldn't get it fixed because parts weren't available. So he had to be careful where he parked. If the car had to be backed up, only gravity could provide the power.

Recycling was rampant. Every scrap was needed for the war effort: cooking fat (for explosives), old newspapers, metal. Boy Scouts and other groups conducted paper and metal drives. Families cut the bottoms and tops out of vegetable cans, removed the labels and stomped the cans flat before taking them uptown to a depository in the park. Because sugar was rationed, candy and gum were hard to come by. When children acquired some with a foil wrapper, they carefully removed the wrapper from the rest of the packaging, added it to the ball of foil the family was saving, and eventually took it to the park depository.

There was a major drive for scrap metal in 1942, and the town contributed two World War I pieces of field artillery that had graced the park. A one-day drive netted 600,000 pounds of scrap metal, equal to 125 pounds per capita, but "more, much more, is needed," said the *Sentinel*. Elementary school children collected old keys, and a single boy at Irving came up with 1,000 of them, equal to one-third the school's total.

Troop trains often came through town and stopped so their steam locomotives could take on water. These were big occasions for people who lived nearby. Townspeople weren't supposed to know when a troop train came through, but the trains were so long, came through so often, and were so easy to spot that word got around quickly. Some people came to the town park just to watch, munching popcorn purchased at Charlie's stand. Sharron Ozburn Grundy and her mother had a stash of homemade cookies, and they hurried to the train and ran alongside it, offering treats to the soldiers. John Ballard and some other pre-teen boys had less charitable intentions. They gathered comic books, newspapers, and magazines and handed them to the servicemen, fully expecting, and often receiving, a handful of coins for their industriousness.

As the war ground on, some of the trains carried wounded soldiers on their way home or to hospitals. Sometimes, when the train stopped, the soldiers who could walk got out and bought ice cream at a nearby store. More than once, the storeowner came out at night, after the store had closed, to open it for the soldiers.

—

During the day, boys and girls halted their play when they heard the sound of aircraft. Comic books and playing cards sometimes printed silhouettes of both U.S. and enemy warplanes, so children looked up anxiously to see whether the noise was coming from friend or foe.

No enemy plane or rocket could reach Marion. Yet the citizens obeyed federal law and rehearsed for that possibility by staging blackouts, which required that all lights be out or windows blocked with an opaque covering. Townsmen served as air-raid wardens, one man responsible for each block. The wardens patrolled their blocks to assure that no light seeped from the houses. Sirens wailed all over town announcing a blackout; children in their beds heard the sound and feared that, this time, the attack would be real.

The war was central to the lives of young boys. Not the real war but the one they learned about at the movies. By a certain age, say eight or nine, a boy could go to the movies by himself or with an older brother or friends. Kids could walk to the Marion Theater from almost anywhere in town. There they watched a steady stream of war movies, absorbing all the lessons Hollywood could teach about friendship among men, courage, sacrifice, and the importance of defeating the enemy.

A dime on Saturday entitled kids to a double feature, with Westerns often paired with war movies. Most boys had accumulated a small arsenal of toy guns, and they sneaked their pistols into the theater and fired back at the action on the screen.

When the movies ended, and the boys gathered near their homes, one of their favorite games was "guns." "Let's play guns," they would say. "Do you want to play Cowboys and Indians or War?" Either choice was good, for Hollywood had taught them how to fire their weapons, and how to die dramatically, clutching the wound and staggering backward, spinning several times before falling to earth. But they rose quickly to take up arms again. "I'm a new guy," they would say.

The games of War and Cowboys and Indians were similar, except for one thing. When the boys played War, almost no one wanted to be a German or Japanese. So they had to hunt down imaginary enemies in the bushes and alleys. But when they played Cowboys and Indians, there were always boys who wanted to be Indians, for they knew from the movies that Indians moved like the wind and were fierce and honorable in their savagery and martyrdom.

Chapter 9
Vernon at the Helm, 1943–1945

When World War II reached its midpoint in 1943, C. B. Vernon had been Marion's superintendent of schools for seventeen years. He was fifty-one years old and would remain in charge for another thirteen years. That he held such a controversial position so long is testimony to Vernon's wisdom, propriety, and sense of duty. Many years after he passed away, acquaintances still referred to him reverentially as "Dr. Vernon."

From his office in the high school two blocks south of Main Street, Vernon oversaw three other schools as well. Next door was the Lincoln Building, formerly the high school, housing kindergarten through eighth grade. Over on the north side of town were two small grade schools, Emerson and Irving.

Chester B. Vernon was born January 24, 1892, in Kansas, the son of a Methodist minister. He attended high school and college in Kansas, and then made his way to New York City, where he received a master's degree in education from Columbia University in 1917. He then returned to the Midwest and, in a few years, was named superintendent of schools in Vinton, Iowa. He came to Marion for the 1926–1927 school year.

Vernon ran a tight ship. In a photograph that often appeared in the *Marion Sentinel*, he presented a dour image in his rimless glasses. A seven-year-old boy, studying that picture, might shiver at the prospect of running afoul of such an implacable presence. In fact, students discovered that if they attended to their studies and stayed out of trouble, they were unlikely to so much as exchange a word with him.

He was a disciplinarian who equated study with work. One day, Vernon's son John, a high school student, got into trouble in music class. That night, Vernon told his son, "I have my job to do here and you have yours. Your job is to be a good student and stay out of trouble." If John didn't like that job, his father said, he was free to get another one—the meat-packing plant in Cedar Rapids was always looking for workers.

A teacher's job was to teach, and a student's job was to learn. This could only occur, Vernon felt, in an environment where teachers maintained discipline and students were at their desks, working. Vernon delegated authority. If teachers did their jobs of instilling knowledge and maintaining order, they had his support should challenges arise from unruly students, parents, or even the board of education.

Teachers were expected to set a stellar example for students and to live apparently blameless lives. Female teachers were absolutely forbidden to smoke, and male teachers were forbidden to smoke in public or on school grounds. Sometimes a male teacher or staff member sneaked to the basement boiler room to smoke. There was trouble if they were caught.

Vernon was a careful man with a dollar, a trait the community prized. During the Depression, he received phone calls at home at night alerting him that a light had been left on over at Emerson or Lincoln schools. In 1945, the *Sentinel* reported that the annual cost per pupil in the Marion school system was $72.06, the lowest of any of the 113 Iowa school districts measured, and significantly below the $121.50 spent in the nearby big city of Cedar Rapids. The paper praised Vernon for the "magnificent piece of work in providing excellent schools with the small amount of money available." The school population is large and the tax base small, the paper said, and Marion's citizens "tax themselves to the limit to provide as well as possible for the children's education."

—

Vernon was not happy with the high school athletic program—which consisted of football, basketball, and track for boys only. Apart from its character-building aspects, Vernon saw sports participation as an important way to channel male energies away from mischief-making or more destructive activities. Further, high school athletes who lived disciplined lives set an example for the whole school. In the largest sense, Vernon believed, a well-run sports program contributed immensely to the success of the whole school district and the spirit of the entire town.

In the fall of 1944, Vernon hired a new athletic coach, Everett Scherich. It may not have been a good decision. Scherich's specialty was track, and he seemed to know little about football and basketball. More importantly, he was lax as a disciplinarian.

Marion was having disciplinary problem with some of its youngsters. Bob Brooks, a legendary sportscaster who was later to broadcast many Marion games, had learned that a pattern of fighting had developed between Marion boys and those from the closest Cedar Rapids school, Franklin. Clearly the town fathers were worried about something. "At the request of numerous citizens," reported the *Sentinel* in October 1943, the city council considered passing a curfew law, but decided instead "to give the young people a chance first to cooperate." If they didn't stay off the streets after hours and out of places they didn't belong, the council warned, "Marion will soon have a good stiff curfew law that will crimp the style of the young roisterers."

The sports program was on Vernon's mind for another reason as well. In 1943, the WaMaC athletic conference was formed, consisting of eight schools in a section of eastern Iowa drained by three muddy rivers. The names of the rivers, combined, gave the WaMaC Conference its name: the Wapsipinicon, the Maquoketa, and the Cedar. Marion had a long history of playing some of these schools in other conference formats, but the new WaMaC was likely to focus even more attention on high school sports, and Vernon knew that the townspeople would expect a decent showing—within reason.

The beginning had been auspicious. Marion finished second at the first WaMaC event, the conference track meet held in the spring of 1943. The football and basketball seasons the following school year, 1944–1945, Scherich's first at the helm, were far less successful.

The football team's record was 2–5, which included a loss to conference foe Independence made memorable when the opposing team tried an audacious deception. The Independence players took the field wearing all-white uniforms and all-white helmets—and used a game ball painted white to make it almost invisible against the team's uniforms. A vigorous protest forced Independence to use an unpainted ball, but it couldn't prevent a 25–0 Marion loss.

The basketball season was even worse. Marion won only two or three games (the record is unclear), and the coach pronounced the team jinxed because it had lost so many close contests. Partial redemption came in track season, when Marion won the conference championship.

In the summer of 1944, the Rev. James Gable, a Methodist minister, was transferred to Marion from West Branch. One of the possessions the family brought to Marion was a basketball hoop forged by a blacksmith in West Branch. It was promptly mounted on the garage of their new home so the Gable boys, Winton and Barrie, could improve their game. The Gables and Vernons lived on the same block, on opposite sides of the street. Winton Gable and John Vernon, classmates and, by nature of their parenting, model students, soon formed a close friendship. Their fathers, prominent, community-minded men, got to know each other well.

Winton, who had seen some action as a freshman on West Branch's undefeated football team under Les Hipple, reported for the sport at Marion. He was shocked to discover that some members of the team drank, smoked, and skipped practice, yet were allowed to continue playing. Winton remembered that the coach cursed at his young players, tried to humiliate them, and even kicked and shoved them at times. Equipment was in short supply and shoddily maintained. Because he was a sophomore, Winton was issued neither a helmet nor shoulder pads, so his father ordered them from Montgomery Ward at $2 each. Later, as he began to see action, he was issued shoulder pads but had to borrow whatever helmet was available when he went into games.

Despite all this, Marion's football team won the WaMaC championship in 1944, going 6–2–1 overall. Ed Failor was the senior quarterback. He remembered a group of dedicated athletes who, while unqualified for sainthood, were largely self-taught, independent, and feisty. Some took a drink when they could and some smoked, but they were disciplined in other ways. From an early age, they determined they would become champions.

The summer before the 1944 season, many of the players met regularly at the football field to practice and work out, and thus entered the season in good condition. During the season, Failor met with Coach Scherich every day to look over plays that were diagramed in a coaching magazine. As a result, the team was constantly learning not only new plays, but also new formations. "We ran the single wing, the double wing, the T, and short punt offenses," Failor wrote. "We were disciplined in football and we had speed to burn. We were fortunate to have some very good athletes."

One of them was Bob (Dutch) Coon, who played in the backfield with Failor. In the huddle during one game, Failor outlined a pass play. Coon would be the passer and Failor would go deep to draw the defense away as an end crossed over the center of the field. Coon was to throw the ball to the end. As Failor sprinted down the field, he looked back to see how the play was unfolding and spotted the ball coming right at him. "I caught it and took it in for six!" Failor wrote. The play went ninety-six yards, still a Marion record for longest touchdown pass. "I had a very good arm, but Dutch could throw it farther than I could." Coon was one of Marion's great athletes. He was drafted by the Cleveland Indians and appeared to be an excellent major league prospect, Failor recalled. But he injured his arm and never made it to the majors.

In the football season opener that year, Marion humiliated Lisbon, 53–7, in a game played on an eighty-yard field. Coach Scherich seemed to be running up the score unmercifully, John Vernon recalled, prompting an uncharacteristic intercession from Superintendent Vernon, who left the stands and ordered the coach to send in substitutes. The *Sentinel* later reported that the coach substituted freely, to the extent of playing an all-freshman team.

The games were much closer after that. Following a 15–0 loss to University High, the team went 5–1–1 in the conference, losing to Vinton and tying Tipton in the last game of the season. Neither Vinton (3–1) nor Tipton (2–0–1) played enough conference games to qualify for the title, so it was Marion's alone.

The basketball season was a repetition of the prior year: disastrous. The team won only two games. After the final contest of the season, the discouraged *Sentinel* reporter sought to find something positive or hopeful to say, then gave up: "It is over, and we were licked, so why dwell on the details."

"Our coach just threw the ball out in practice and told us to scrimmage," recalled Failor. The balls themselves were in sad shape. The team had one good ball for games and a motley collection of practice balls, many with bulges that made shooting difficult and dribbling all but impossible.

John Vernon was a sophomore that year and played on the freshman–sophomore basketball team. In those days, coaches drove the players to away games in their own cars; there was no school bus available. Because their games were curtain raisers, the freshman–sophomore basketball team left town earlier than the varsity. On one game day, the coach driving the car made a short detour and stopped at Marion's pool hall. He told one of the boys to go inside and tell the varsity players there had been a change in the schedule, and their driver would pick them up at a different time or place. Stopping at the pool hall was the surest way to get this message to the varsity players. The coach, Vernon realized, didn't want to go into the pool hall himself because he was afraid he would catch the players smoking—and then have to face the dilemma of looking the other way or disciplining them for breaking the rules.

The track team, hurt by the illness of one star and the failure of another to show up, finished fifth in the conference meet that year.

C. B. Vernon discussed his concerns about the athletic program with the Rev. Gable. The minister told his neighbor that there was a man named Les Hipple at West Branch who could turn the Marion athletic program around and make the boys toe the line—if Marion could only land him. Superintendent Vernon decided to look into it. He drove to West Branch and watched the young coach lead his charges in a basketball game. He liked what he saw.

The WaMaC Conference
As formed in 1943

Anamosa Raiders
Independence Mustangs (also Maroons)
Manchester Manhawks
Marion Indians
Maquoketa Cardinals
Monticello Black Panthers
Tipton Tigers
Vinton Blue Jays

WaMaC – Named for three rivers: Wapsipinicon, Maquoketa, and Cedar.

Chapter 10
Hipple Is Hired, 1945

As the 1944–1945 school year came to a close, Les Hipple was ready for his next career move. In his three years at West Branch, his teams had achieved impressive success. He was known throughout the eastern part of the state. So well known, in fact, that he could list as one of his references Pops Harrison, the successful head basketball coach at the University of Iowa. Hipple was more than a coach. At the age of thirty-two, he also had eight years of experience as high school principal and thirty-six hours of graduate study under his belt. Bigger schools were courting him.

The superintendent at West Branch, L. A. Maley, didn't want to lose Hipple and, in fact, offered him more than twice the salary Hipple had received when he started there three years before—$3,000 a year if he would stay. (Worth about $33,000 in 2007).

When Marion Superintendent C. B. Vernon and the Rev. James Gable met with Hipple to discuss the Marion job, the coach gave them no indication that he was being heavily recruited by other schools. Typically tight-lipped, Hipple was absolutely sphinx-like during their first meeting, saying almost nothing for an hour. This was particularly puzzling to Gable, who had been Hipple's neighbor for two years at West Branch, where the two families sometimes visited in each other's homes. As the two men left, Hipple finally spoke, thanking his visitors for their interest and saying he would consider the Marion position.

The most likely reasons for Hipple's silence were that his plans for the future were falling apart and he had no idea what to tell his visitors. At about the time of his meeting with the Marion representatives, Hipple was attempting to juggle offers from other schools—and through no fault of his own, they kept slipping through his grasp.

Hipple's quandary, C. B. Vernon later discovered, was that he had decided to leave West Branch and had accepted a position at Mount Pleasant. Superintendent Maley, though disappointed, gave his blessing and turned his efforts to finding a replacement. Shortly after that, University High of Iowa City offered Hipple a job that included coaching the basketball team.

As home for a university, Iowa City had one of the best school systems in the state. A coach there would receive strong support and statewide exposure. He would interact with the athletic department at the University, and this offered almost unlimited potential. Hipple already was on good terms with Pops Harrison, the Hawkeye's head basketball coach. Finally, SUI was Hipple's alma mater. This was a plum job, one of the top coaching positions in the state, one he simply had to try for. So he asked Mount Pleasant to release him from his agreement. The school refused, leaving Hipple no honorable choice but to decline the Iowa City offer.

Shortly after that, officials at Mount Pleasant had second thoughts. Apparently insulted by Hipple's request and fearful that even if he did join the staff he wouldn't stay long, they withdrew their offer. Hipple was now free to accept the coveted Iowa City job. But when he got back in touch with officials there, he learned that they had already filled the position. In a matter of weeks, his offers from West Branch, Mount Pleasant, and Iowa City had all dissolved. Hipple had no live prospects whatsoever—except for Marion.

When Vernon and Gable visited a second time, Hipple was more cordial and forthcoming, and he accepted the job.

In his application for employment by Marion, Hipple stated in response to written questions that he had no physical defects, was married and living with his wife, belonged to no organizations, had engaged in no extracurricular activities during college, that he refrained completely from the use of tobacco and alcoholic beverages, and that he was willing to commit to three years at Marion. He was asked to select one of two educational viewpoints that most nearly reflected his own.

> Our schools should prepare boys and girls for adult responsibilities through systematic training (in various subjects), requiring mastery of such subjects and, when necessary, stressing discipline and obedience …

Or

> Our schools should make central the informal learning of experience and activity work, placing much less stress on formal, systematic assignments, discipline and obedience … with teachers, while in control, serving primarily as guides.

It takes no guessing to identify the viewpoint Hipple favored.

—

Hipple's personnel file does not reveal his starting salary at Marion. It seems likely that Vernon, parsimonious though he was, would have wanted to at least match the $3,000 that West Branch had offered. Hipple no longer would fill the role of principal, which would tend to drag his salary down. On the other hand, Marion's high school, at nearly three hundred students, was almost triple the size of West Branch's, which made the role of athletic coach more demanding and time consuming. Vernon's solution was to structure a pay package based on the multiple tasks that Hipple would perform. There was a base salary for his jobs as athletic coach, director of physical education, and math teacher. On top of that, he received much smaller amounts for repairing equipment, maintaining the football field and track, and for administering and coaching a summer baseball program. The result was that Hipple had duties that would fully occupy him more than eight hours a day fifty-two weeks a year. He had done essentially the same thing at West Branch, and he apparently relished the work.

On May 31, 1945, the *Marion Sentinel* revealed the news:

> Lester C. Hipple, who has returned his signed contract with the Marion independent school board to become director of athletics at Marion High School the coming years, comes with a record of splendid ability to develop athletic talent in the youth under his direction. He is a graduate of Iowa University and has taught three years in the schools of Callender, two years at Walker, and three years at West Branch. His athletes at West Branch made a splendid record. He is 32 years-of-age, married, and has a three-year-old daughter. He hopes to move here as soon as a home can be secured.

The touch of dignified pride in the announcement suggests that C. B. Vernon himself may have penned it.

Hipple hit the ground running, according to a letter from Winton Gable, the minister's older son, who wrote:

> When Les arrived at Marion during the summer of 1945, he immediately did four things. First, he went to work to improve the condition of the track and football field. Second, he began to repair and upgrade all equipment. Third, he ordered the best available football and basketball uniforms. And fourth, he typed up a set of stringent training rules for discussion with all interested athletes.

The boys at Marion High School, accustomed to relaxed athletic standards, were in for the shock of their lives.

Chapter 11
Hipple's Way, 1945–1946

On a blazing August afternoon in 1945, the Marion High School football team gathered for one of its first practice sessions under the new coach. The mood was buoyant. Doug Hutchins, a senior center and one of only four lettermen from last year's championship team, was kidding around with his buddy, Bob Whittemore.

"We were joking around, just like we always did," Hutchins recalled. "Whittemore said he was going to take my position away from me. I was a holler guy, a baseball guy, and I yelled, 'Oh, shut up!'"

At that moment Hipple, dressed in canvas football pants, a gray T-shirt, and blue baseball cap, walked up to Hutchins. "I don't know your name," he said, "but you don't need to talk like that. You're through for the day. Go on up to the school."

"Just like that, he threw me out of practice," Hutchins remembered. The boy was stunned, but he did as he was told.

After practice that day, Hutchins sat in the locker room, still in his uniform, totally confused, wondering whether he had been thrown off the team. A teammate said to him, "Mr. Hipple wants to see you." Hutchins went to the coach's office, angry and defensive, prepared to turn in his equipment.

"We can't have everyone talking in practice," the coach told him calmly. "If something needs to be said, I'll do the talking. Go take your shower. I expect to see you at practice tomorrow."

"I was totally befuddled," Hutchins said. Hipple never mentioned the incident again. "You know," said Hutchins years later, "Sports are supposed to be full of banter and shouting and emotion, but Hipple wouldn't allow that kind of behavior. He ran practice like a classroom. He was a man in canvas pants teaching a bigger game than football. Oh, I loved that man. Not then, but later."

—

Hipple's job that fall was to reshape a muddled athletic program, establish his authority, and instill in his players a level of discipline beyond anything they imagined.

From the very first day the forty-eight players reported for practice in 1945, they could see that things were different. For starters, there was more equipment to choose from. That summer, Hipple had pounced on an offer for "our entire stock of football equipment," from Lisbon High School, which was giving up the game. Equipment for sale included sixteen helmets, "some good as new," fourteen hip pads, twenty-one shoulder pads, twelve white practice jerseys, footballs, football shoes, pants, and other items. The typed sales list from Lisbon is covered in penciled notes in Hipple's handwriting. It appears he bought the lot for $288.

When the players showed up to get their equipment, it was laid out neatly. Coaches were on hand to help fit the players. There was enough gear for everyone. A year earlier, the boys had scrambled through a jumble of equipment on their own, and some players had shared helmets.

The year before, the team had used plays torn from coaching magazines—or made them up on the spot. They had freelanced their way to a championship on sheer ability and determination. Now, Hipple diagrammed a handful of plays and drilled the players on every aspect of every play, making them repeat the plays again and again in practice.

"Coach Hipple has had some of [his team] out limbering up this week," said the *Marion Sentinel* that August, "and already has made them understand that he expects to have a squad that is well-trained." The paper added that with few returning veterans, "Marion's new mentor will have to start from scratch."

Hipple told his charges that practice would be tough, much tougher than any game, and that their labors on the practice field would give them the endurance they needed to outlast their opponents in games. He made them run and do calisthenics until their bodies ached. He drilled them in the fundamentals of blocking and tackling. The school had no blocking dummies or sleds, so he sent the boys against one another at full speed. "Put your heart and mind into the tackle and your body will follow," he told them, quoting one of his favorite slogans.

At thirty-two, Hipple still mixed it up with some of the players. John Vernon remembers him going against lineman Merle O'Neil. Merle didn't want to hit the coach with everything he had, but Hipple taunted him, "Come on, Merle, is that the hardest you can hit?" Merle increased his effort, but still held back, and Hipple scolded him again. Merle, angry now, charged Hipple hard, knocking him on his butt. Hipple got up, saying, "Yes, Merle, that's more like it. Keep it up." He never challenged Merle again.

Players who blew assignments or goofed off or talked too much were sent running laps. All during practice bulky figures in their leather helmets circled the field to pay for their misdemeanors. Running laps taught lessons and sharpened the memory, as well as improved conditioning. It could be embarrassing for a boy to have to run laps. It was something like being the cartoon dunce, having to sit in a corner with a cone-shaped hat on his head. The humiliation was even greater because running laps meant that in some way a player had let his teammates down. On the other hand, sooner or later, nearly everyone ran laps.

Hipple often did not speak to a boy when he sentenced him to run laps. That is, he did not say, "(Boy's name here), you have screwed up by (insert screw-up here), so start running." He just looked at the culprit, raised his right hand next to his ear, pointed to the sky with his index finger, and made small circles with his hand. It meant: Start running. Players did not need to ask him why they had to run. They knew the reason, and he knew they knew it. They ran. If by some chance it seemed to them that Hipple had made a mistake in judgment, they did not question it. That would have been extremely unwise, and they already had been foolish enough. They ran. Nor did they ask him how many laps they would have to run. They simply began running, watching him as they lumbered around the field, and at some point he would raise his hand beside his ear, point his index finger up, then hook it down with a few tap-like movements. It was their signal to stop running and rejoin their unit.

That sequence—Hipple signaling a boy to start running, then signaling him to stop, and never exchanging a word about it—is often recalled with laughter by his former players, who, as grown men, see the sequence as wistfully funny. It was the essence of playing for Hipple—being completely under his control—and in retrospect it made them laugh.

—

The Marion Indians of 1945 discovered that Hipple did not yell much. He never cursed at his players or punched or kicked them as his predecessor had. He sometimes growled. He fumed when his players did not live up to his expectations, but the emotion was transmitted not in a scream but in a grimace, a head shake, or a cold stare. Some said his lips trembled when he was really angry. He governed his players not so much with words as with gestures, postures, and facial expressions. His glare was so icy it could freeze a boy in his tracks.

Hipple had, as other players have said about their coaches, "God-like tendencies"—superhuman powers of observation, the ability to see what was in their hearts, and judgment that was as immediate and ruthless as it was fair. Some players over the years feared him. A few saw a twinkle in his eye or sensed subterranean warmth under his severity, but they were a minority. Most of his players regarded him with fear-tinged awe. He held their fate in his hands. He was deadly serious about what he was doing. This day's effort, he let his players know by his every action, was important in every aspect. Whatever was going on here, it wasn't just a game.

And though Hipple was relentless in his concentration on fundamentals and conditioning, a meticulous student of the games he taught, a masterful strategist, a keen judge of character and talent, and a genius at motivation who could turn gangling boys into disciplined athletes and good athletes into great ones, he was not unique among coaches in these matters. In his dedication to his craft and his success in terms of victories, he ranked with the very best, but other coaches had winning percentages as good or better. Hipple outdistanced most great coaches in one respect, however: he repeatedly turned out championship teams in four different sports—football, basketball, track, and cross-country. He was elected to the state halls of fame for basketball and for football, an honor he shares with only a few other men. When Hipple started coaching, multi-sport head coaches in high schools, especially small ones, were common. When he stopped, some thirty years later, they were rare. His commitment, his love of coaching, his versatility, and his sheer stamina set him apart from all but a very few coaches.

His rules made him unique. Over the years, they became the most significant aspect of his coaching reputation. Eventually, he was known all over the state as much for his rules as for his victories, and since his rules were often a matter of rumor instead of fact, his reputation for fearsomeness grew far beyond reality.

With the onset of the 1945 football season at Marion, he introduced his rules to players and parents who had been accustomed to a casual approach to sports. "Hipple told all the players to bring their parents to the school for a meeting," recalled John Vernon, a junior that year. "He handed out the rules and read them aloud, and all of us, parents and players alike, had to agree to abide by them. It was kind of like joining the military. You take a step forward, make a pledge, and you're in, for better or worse." Both the parents and the players had to sign a statement agreeing to the rules.

No copy of the 1945 football rules has been found. To see how they were presented a few years later, refer to the Appendixes. Here are the rules in summary. They are similar to those Hipple used at West Branch, but at Marion they became more specific and more stringent.

1. No smoking or drinking.
2. In bed by 10:00 PM every night except Friday and Saturday, "when we may stay out until 12:00, although this will not be done often."
3. Dates with girls must be kept at a minimum. No going steady. "If we must see a particular girl friend between classes or at noon, we will drop athletics."
4. We will not miss practice. If for any reason you must miss practice, you must receive permission ahead of time.
5. We may not drive cars except on Sundays during specified hours and even then we will not "just drive around town."
6. We will use only proper language at all times.
7. We will take the best possible care of our equipment.
8. We will keep our dressing rooms clean, at home or away.
9. We will take off and put on our football shoes outside when it is muddy, in the lower exit when not muddy.

"You, as a Marion Indian, cannot do some of the things other students do," Hipple wrote in 1952. "If you think more of smoking, drinking, dating or going steady, staying out late at night, or riding around in automobiles, then you are not willing to 'pay the price' and it is best for you not to take out a uniform ... To be on a championship team you have to be a champion yourself."

These were only the written rules. As Hipple's players were to learn over the years, there were unwritten rules as well—a host of them. The most famous was his requirement that anyone wishing to play football had to go out for track the spring before. And if a boy wanted to go out for basketball, he had to go out for track the year before and either football or cross-country in the fall. Therefore, a basketball aspirant, regardless of his or his parents' wishes, had to become a three-sport man. That way Hipple kept his players in condition and under his control, obeying the football rules for all or most of the school year. As a result, Marion had large track squads even though at least half the boys hated the sport. Hipple was not a great fan of track himself, but he understood its value and made all his players run the quarter mile, which he considered the most effective distance for developing both speed and endurance.

Hipple believed that his rules were central to the development of championship teams. Just as important, Hipple wrote to parents, the rules contributed to physical well being, moral strength, mental alertness, and helped instill "the confidence and courage for which all men are respected."

That first year, the new Marion coach gathered the eighth-grade boys in the gym for a pep talk. He had no football equipment for them, but he would begin drilling them without pads. "Do you want to be a champion?" he asked them. "Yeah! Yeah!" the boys hollered back. Then he held up a sheet of paper. "These are the rules you will have to follow to be a champion," he told them. The boys cheered again. "We just had this feeling that something special was going to happen and we were going to be part of it," remembered George Murdoch, one of the eighth graders who wanted to be a champion.

From the first, there were complaints from a few parents about the rules, said John Vernon. The one that seemed to bother them the most was the ban on driving. Those parents who disliked it saw it as usurping their authority—they couldn't send their boys on errands in the car. Hipple's rules affected parents, too; the coach had assumed an inconvenient presence in their lives.

In 1945, gas rationing limited driving and some families didn't even own cars. After the post-war prosperity kicked in and cars became more widely owned, objections increased.

"Complaints about the no-driving rule mystified my dad," said John Vernon. The way C. B. Vernon saw it, parents did not want to buy their boy a car or let him tool around in theirs, so here was the opportunity to shift the blame to Hipple. "Why don't they just support Hipple and tell the boy they would be glad to lend him the car but for the coach's rules?" the superintendent wondered. That was Vernon's approach: He supported Hipple completely, and when a parent came to him with a complaint of any kind, he told them, "Hipple's the coach. Go see him."

Some parents were bothered by the three-sport requirement. They may not have wanted their son to go out for football, where he could easily lose some teeth in the era before facemasks, or perhaps break a limb. They may have wanted their son to have time for other activities, such as music, or to hold a job and contribute to the family income. Farm parents needed their sons at home, especially in the spring and fall.

Parents did not object to the ban on excessive dating. They saw its danger: an unwanted pregnancy. This would mean ostracism for both the boy and the girl and pain for both families. The two children would have to leave school and, in all probability, get married. A whole range of future options would be cut off, and two teenagers would be chained together in a union they may not have wanted and neither was ready for. For Hipple, the rule involved a simpler proposition: girls, and especially girls and cars, meant distraction from the important formative work at hand. That work was, first, being a student and, second, being an athlete. Both roles were crucial to their lives as adults. "Falling in love is much worse for a boy than driving a car," Hipple told fellow coaches. There would be all the time in the world later for girls and cars.

Hipple's rules were enforced with a hierarchy of punishments that only he understood. Most punishments involved running laps, but others included being sent home from practice, being demoted, being benched for all or part of a game, or, very rarely, being thrown off the team. Hipple's rules were not lightly made, lightly enforced, or lightly broken. Even though most punishments required no more than running laps, the boys who accepted the rules were afraid to break them and even more afraid to be caught breaking them. "He put the fear of God into us," said Chuck Kent.

"Hipple's training rules were the most extreme and unequivocal of any I've ever heard of," said Don King, a high school and college coach who knew Hipple well. "He went farther in his rules and enforcing them of any coach I've heard of. As a result, his teams were always in top condition and extremely disciplined mentally."

Hipple's sister Shirley saw the rules from the family's point of view and found them neither very onerous nor surprising. "What rules?" she scoffed. "That was the way we grew up."

—

Hipple's first Marion football team that year had a dismal season, finishing 1–6–1. The Indians were shut out in four games, scoring a total of only thirty-one points while allowing opponents 102 points. Several of the games were close and all were hard fought. The *Sentinel* reported, "The boys are training faithfully … playing the fourth quarter as strong as the first. Some of these days they will be mowing down the championship aspirants, if they keep fighting."

The high school yearbook, *The Quill*, summarized the season this way: "By following Coach Hipple's instructions and example, (the team) respected sports instead of abusing them … They learned that anyone working for individual glory will fall far below the level of first string material." The second sentence sounds as if Hipple wrote it.

—

That fall, Hipple found time to round up some runners to enter an annual race at Iowa City called the state team mile run, which was scored like a cross-country meet, according to the finishing places of team members. Marion finished second. A few weeks later, the runners went to Ames for the state cross-country meet, and came home as champions. This was the first of what would be eight consecutive state championship cross-country teams coached by Hipple, from 1945 through 1953 (the meet in 1947 was rained out). Marion won a ninth state championship in 1958 under John Schippers. As late as 2005, the nine state cross-country titles were more than had been won by any other school.

Jerry Walker, who twice won the state cross-country individual title for Marion in the 1950s, said that the race in Ames traversed a golf course and was only about 1.8 miles long. Only a handful of teams in Marion's class entered the race, perhaps as few as six, Walker said, and because of the low turnout, he felt that the championships did not count as great accomplishments. Over the years, the *Sentinel* devoted little space to these events, sometimes not even reporting the outcome. But no other team won them year after year, only Marion. Measured in state championship trophies alone, Hipple stands as the most successful high school cross-country coach the state has ever seen.

He achieved this, at least in part, by spotting talented runners from his large track squads. They may have been out for track only because they wanted to play football or basketball, but because they tended to be whippet-thin and small, they had a difficult time in those sports. Hipple then channeled them into cross-country, where they experienced victories at a level they never achieved in the other sports.

Because he coached football, Hipple had little time to watch the cross-country team train. He depended on the team captain, each day handing him a paper outlining the run for the day. Most often, the boys were assigned a route south of town, a run of three or four miles, circling what Walker remembered as a "castle-like" house. On the way they invariably aroused a few dogs that chased the little clutch of sweat-suited runners until they were discouraged by a volley of rocks the boys had gathered ahead of time for just that purpose.

Three miles was a fairly long run in those days, when a cross-country race covered less than two miles. (The standard in Iowa is about three miles today.) "Maybe that's why we won every year," Walker suggested. "We ran three miles in training. Maybe no one else ran that far."

—

The basketball team in 1945–1946 had a rough year, going 5–13 as the boys and the coach continued to adjust to one another. The team was "pitifully inadequate offensively" in an early game, reported the *Sentinel*, and performed with "something less than brilliance" a few weeks later. The *Sentinel* was accustomed to writing about poor basketball teams, but the coverage turned more positive as the year progressed. Marion lost its first six games, but went 5–7 for the rest of the regular season before losing to Wilson of Cedar Rapids by four points in the first game of the state tournament. It was the last losing basketball season Marion would have for fourteen years.

Winton Gable, a junior who had played quarterback in football, became a leader in basketball, too. He was perhaps Marion's last practitioner of the two-handed set shot. In each game, he would launch several ceiling-scraping shots from well beyond the top of the key. The crowd held its breath as the ball plummeted toward the basket, then exploded in joy if it pierced the net or groaned in anguish if it trampolined high off the rim. Gable also had a driving, "one-handed angle shot now famous among Marion opponents," the *Sentinel* said. Both of the shots were copied from Dick Ives, a high-scoring guard on Iowa University's championship basketball team. Winton's father took his sons to Iowa games, and the boys came back and practiced on their driveway what they had seen at the Hawkeye field house.

Winton was Marion's first sports star in the Hipple era. Short, stocky, powerfully built, Winton was a handsome boy involved in many high school activities. Pictured in the *Sentinel* in his double-breasted pin-stripe suit and his slicked-down black hair, he looked like a 1940s movie star—either the villain or the hero. Of his junior high years at West Branch, Winton wrote, "I had become a real problem at school: hyperactive, belligerent, and rebellious. Hipple straightened me out faster than any counselor might have [and] became an indelible influence in my life."

Basketball was changing as players' speed and skills improved. Perhaps the most visible evidence of this was the demise of the two-handed set shot. In January 1946, reporter Ray McHugh of the *Cedar Rapids Gazette*, back home after three years in military service, noticed the change immediately. One-handed shooting was not new, he wrote, but before 1941 one-handed shots tended to be hook shots or driving shots. "From stationary positions beyond the foul circle, the two-handed set shot was considered practically mandatory." McHugh polled a few coaches and found that they all supported the one-handed shot as being harder to diagnose and harder to stop. In a follow-up article the next month, other coaches weighed in on both sides of the question, some insisting that beginners should be taught a two-handed shot. When it came to free-throw shooting, however, there was unanimity: the two-handed shot was best, either underhanded or overhanded.

Hipple did not stop Winton Gable from using the two-handed set shot, but he didn't encourage it with youngsters. He was adamant about free throws, however. He made every player use two hands underhanded. He would hold that belief all his life, and it would cost him.

—

When track season rolled around, Hipple's rules insured a good turnout, and his large team finished second in the WaMaC championship meet. The Indians lost by only three points to Vinton, 58 ½ to 55 ½, with the outcome undecided until the last event, the half-mile relay. The second-place finish was a favorable omen for future track teams and the sports program in general.

—

That summer, after an absence of several years, Marion reinstated a baseball program for boys. Hipple was paid by the school to coach the team, which operated under the auspices of the American Legion and was sponsored, at least for some seasons, by Stuber Motors. About twenty boys signed up. The team practiced several evenings every week and played about ten games over the summer. The turnout was small because rural kids could not leave the farm to play baseball, and most town kids had jobs. This was a program for sports nuts and baseball fanatics, boys who would race from their summer jobs to get to the practice field at 5:30 or so.

Compared to his approach in other sports, Hipple was a casual baseball coach. He did not devote a great deal of time to the finer points of technique as he did in football and basketball. He told pitchers, "Don't walk him; make him hit it." Hitting instruction was little more than urging his players to choke up on the bat and try to make contact. He taught players to go down on one knee when fielding ground balls, so when they missed the ball it would bounce off their bodies instead of scooting between their legs. Tom Domer was a good fielder but had a lousy arm. Hipple put him at third base and told him to scoop up the grounders and then throw the ball to the pitcher rather than heave it all the way across the diamond with the almost certain result that the first baseman would have to chase it down in the weeds as the runner took an extra base. Better to grant the batter a single and hope for a miraculous double play.

Most days, Hipple organized his players for practice sessions that resembled game situations and let everyone play a lot of positions. Boys could play baseball whether they went out for any other sport or not. Many of Hipple's off-the-field rules did not apply in the summer (although he never said so), but he was unrelenting in requiring proper language, gentlemanly behavior, and serious effort.

Bob Page, who played four sports under Hipple in the 1940s, never forgot the time he was third baseman when a batter hit a high pop fly in foul territory. Page circled under the twisting ball, calling out, "I got it, I got it, I got it." He missed it. When the ball landed an embarrassing distance from his glove, Page began laughing at his own ineptitude. "Oh, Hipple bawled me out after that. He really gave it to me," Page said. The scolding came not because Page missed the ball, but because he laughed after missing it. Hipple probably said no more than, "What's so funny, Page?" The man did not harangue his players. A few words and a scowl at the right moment could last a lifetime.

The baseball team that year lost most of its games, establishing a pattern that persisted for the next twenty years. Only a smattering of parents showed up for these games. Hipple never seemed to care whether the team won or lost, and for some of those who played all four sports, baseball was the most fun.

—

In May 1945, the Allies achieved victory in Europe. While New Yorkers celebrated with a massive street party in Times Square, the people of Marion attended a solemn service at the Methodist church, thankful that the end was in sight, but prayerful about the fighting in Asia.

Then, in August, the *Marion Sentinel* heralded the surrender of Japan with a huge headline: PEACE! The subhead read: "It's Over—Pearl Harbor Has Been Avenged." The announcement came in the evening, and that night the Marion citizens went uptown to celebrate. A double line of cars drove up and down Main Street and the air was filled with "the din of automobile horns, sirens, bells, and yells," wrote the *Sentinel.* Most stores were already closed. "Stores dispensing food stuffs of any kind did a big business," the paper said. The state liquor store closed promptly. Some taverns closed, others stayed open. Boys tied strings of tin cans to their bicycles and rode clanking through the streets.

At last, people could get back to their real lives. Shortages and rationing would persist for a time. Boys would continue to come home from overseas, some whole and hardy, others wounded or broken from years in prison camps. The *Sentinel* continued to report on deaths that only then could be confirmed. There were still a few short, sad trips from the train station to the funeral home. But the effects of the war were diminishing. Gas rationing had curtailed many sports programs during the war. Coe and Grinnell Colleges resumed football programs that had been shut down for the duration. Small-town amateur baseball teams and leagues—"cow pasture leagues" they were sometimes called—started up again. Gradually, stories of men at war faded from the front pages of the *Sentinel* and were replaced by stories of boys at play.

In March of that year, the *Sentinel* was sold by its owner of eighteen years, L.L. Papes & Son, to Ralph P. Young. Under Young's editorship, the paper would devote a lot of space to the fortunes of the Marion Indians.

Chapter 12
Landmarks, 1947

When Hipple came to Marion, the town had between four thousand and five thousand citizens who lived in neat homes gathered closely together on a total area of about two square miles. Marion was a good-sized town; more than a village, less than a city. It was ringed on three sides by farmland and on the fourth by a narrow strip of largely undeveloped land that separated Marion from Cedar Rapids, which had a population of about sixty thousand. The two communities were so close together it was difficult to tell where the town ended and the city began.

The people of Marion were happy they didn't live in Cedar Rapids. They could take advantage of the city for shopping or entertainment, but then retreat to the small-town life they preferred. In 1943, with the war at its midpoint and turning in favor of the Allies, the *Sentinel* wrote:

> People do like to live in Marion, where they can enjoy its companionable people, its good schools and churches, its inexpensive living, its good spring water, its excellent utility services, and at the same time enjoy its nearness to the larger town while escaping some of its taxes. Yes sir, when people can again build homes, there will be a lot more people living in Marion.

By 1947, with rationing ending, Marion's business district was beginning to prosper. For a town of its size, the district was small, stretching for parts of three short blocks along Main Street, with more businesses trailing off the side streets. It was small because Cedar Rapids, a fifteen-minute bus ride away, had more and larger stores. Marion had enough merchants to offer the basics for citizens and area farmers who didn't want the hassle of going to the larger city.

The Marion business district was called "uptown," perhaps because people had to go uphill from three directions to reach it—and many walked there. Main Street ran along a ridge that rose from the south, west, and north, and then extended east into the countryside. (Cedar Rapids was "downtown.") Marion's skyline was typical: Buildings uptown ranged from one to three stories, with the water tower rising above them near the center of town. After the water tower, the tallest structures were the spires of the two largest churches, the Presbyterian and the Methodist, which faced each other on opposite corners a block from Main Street. Four other churches were not far away: the Baptist, Catholic, Christian, and Congregational.

There were more churches than taverns in Marion. Three taverns were on side streets. Chesley's Club Royale sat on Main Street and dispensed gallons of Hamm's and Pabst beers, but nothing with greater alcoholic content. Serving liquor or wine by the drink was illegal. In the summer, the Club Royale's front door was often left open, and the narrow room exhaled the smell of stale beer and wet sawdust.

It may have been an act seen through the open door of the Club Royale that prompted a crackdown by the Marion City Council in 1947. A councilman looked into a tavern one night and saw a woman dancing while holding a small child. The outraged councilman said he wanted "to go on record that if women were dancing in taverns while carrying children, he was against it," the *Sentinel* reported. Other councilmen were concerned. One "doubted that the sale of beer and dancing should be allowed in the same place." Others demanded that taverns be cleaner and have better lighting. That spring, the council passed an ordinance prohibiting minors from entering taverns.

The Club Royale, on 12th Street, was the eastern anchor of a block that led to the town park and to the side street opposite the park that ran down to the train station. To reach either destination, pedestrians walked past Storm's, a Ben Franklin Five and Ten Cents Store, and the K-V Café, the town's best restaurant, where businessmen gathered for coffee and the Lions Club met in the back room. Sometimes high school students danced to music from a jukebox in that room.

The Iowa State Liquor Store sat across the alley from the K-V Café. It was the only place citizens could purchase wine or liquor, which were treated like controlled substances. Customers entering the store scanned a board listing the brands and types available. Then they filled out a form with their choices and handed it to the clerk behind his small window. He went back among tiers of metal shelves to pick the order and bring it to the front. The customer then produced his small blue liquor book and offered it, along with cash, to the clerk, who wrote into the book some numbers describing the purchase. The book's purpose was to limit the number of gallons an individual could obtain in any given month. It was a hard way to purchase liquor in a prudish state, but the Illinois border was one hundred miles away, and a thirsty man without underworld connections had little choice. Other citizens often noted a customer's visit. Irwin Renfer, who owned the shoe store next door, once saw a customer who owed him money making his way down the street with a paper sack full of newly purchased bottles. Renfer felt well within his rights to ask the man why he could spend money on liquor when he owed money for shoes. The man replied that he was simply carrying out an errand for a friend and that Renfer would be paid soon, which he was.

The Snack Shop occupied a narrow niche just beyond Renfer's shoe store. Tucked into the building housing the Farmer's State Bank and a dentist's office, the Snack Shop had room only for a griddle, a counter, and a few stools. It featured hamburgers and homemade pies, and did a heavy trade with high school students.

Thus, after a stroll of only a few hundred feet, a pedestrian reached 11th Street, and could walk down to the train station, which everyone called "the depot." This was Marion's toughest and most exotic block, a series of small storefronts hung with a jumble of signs. Some high school girls would not walk down this block, not so much because they were afraid, but because they were worried what people might think of them.

The block began with Kepros's Shoe Repair, where pulleys, belts, and grinding machines howled in a dark window. The smell of leather, shoe polish, oil, and rubber seeped out the door.

The next store was a dark, narrow beer tavern. Beyond that was the pool hall, an important gathering place for the sporting crowd. A glass case displaying cigarettes, candy, and gum sat just inside the door on the right. (Condoms, though not on display, were available for those who had reasons not to ask the druggist for a supply.) Beyond the counter was a cooler for soft drinks and above that a large blackboard where major league baseball scores were chalked up as they came in over the radio. A cigar humidor and two pinball machines lined the left wall.

The real name of the business was Phillips Cigar Store, but no one called it that. The narrow room contained a series of pool tables set one behind the other in a row parallel to the front window. Farmers in overalls, merchants in white shirts, and boys in jeans hunched over the tables. Players waiting their turn sat on wooden benches along the right wall, sharing the space with other men and boys who were there to watch. Hooded lamps hung over each table, their lights cutting through the haze of tobacco smoke.

Strings of beads looped above the tables for keeping score. Ceiling fans turned slowly in the murky air. Beyond the pool tables was a back room, where men played cards for money and sipped hard liquor in violation of the law. The room had a doorway leading out into the alley. The back door was handy for customers, and especially high school athletes, who wanted to be discreet about their visits. Patrons could try their luck at a mildly illegal form of gambling called a punchboard. They paid a small sum, a quarter perhaps, and used a wooden peg to punch out a little square or circle among the many on the face of a rectangular cardboard box the thickness of a small book. At each punch, a tiny scroll came out of the bottom. It told the player whether he had won a watch or other item that the manufacturer packaged with the board, or some amount of money, or, of course, nothing at all.

Kenneth "Shine" Domer managed the pool hall for several years on the promise from Harold Phillips that he could one day buy it. Shine, who had been a smooth Marion basketball player in his time, was superlative at pool, a master of strategy, force, angle, and spin. Shine could spot a hustler the minute his shadow fell across the pool hall's dust-specked window. Many times he out-hustled the intruder at his own game, pretending to be drunk and lucky as the bets mounted up, and then turning cold-eyed and deadly when all the money was at stake.

Tom, Shine's son, worked in the pool hall some nights, racking balls for the players and dusting off the tables until his father said, "You've sucked up enough smoke for the night, go on home." Shine never taught Tom how to play pool, and Tom made no serious effort to learn. In fact, on the few occasions he tried to get into a game, the others wouldn't let him play, figuring he would be too good for them.

One day, Harold Phillips walked into the pool hall with a stranger and introduced him to Shine Domer as the new owner. Shine quit in a cold fury and went to work at the liquor store.

The next business was another beer tavern. Two taverns flanking a pool hall was reason enough for girls to avoid the block.

The next business was the White Way Café, which opened early for railroad workers and closed late for revelers from the beer taverns. The White Way was the kind of place where, if customers absent-mindedly allowed their fingers to explore the underside of their tables, they were certain to recoil at the touch of gum stuck there by a previous diner. Investigating the gum phenomenon at the Hallwood Café, a slightly more upscale restaurant diagonally across the park, *Marion Sentinel* reporter Fred E. Dice once counted 636 "gobs" of gum stuck to the bottom of a single table. He calculated that this meant that Hallwood's tables accommodated a total of 8,904 gobs, a sum that didn't include whatever was pasted under the counter. Considering the White Way's position in the hierarchy of Marion diners, its gob population was probably denser than Hallwood's.

The last store on the block, in a solid brick building, was the creamery, which specialized in dairy products: milk, cream, butter, rich ice cream. The air inside was cool and damp from refrigeration, and heavy with the smell of fresh milk. A slight odor of wet hair hung in the air, as if a cow was being kept in the back room.

The Marion depot sat alone on the railroad tracks, separated from the other buildings by a parking lot. The depot was one of the town's most important buildings. Marion was a stop on the Milwaukee Railroad, which employed about a thousand Marion residents—engineers, conductors, firemen, freight agents, telegraph officers, mail handlers, and section workers. The railroad conferred economic stability that farming alone could not provide.

Built in 1888, the depot was two stories high, covered by a slanting, high-peaked green roof that made it seem even taller. There was a ticket booth out front, a telegraph office inside, and a dusty, paneled waiting room. A curving stairway, a graceful architectural touch, led past stained-glass windows to the railroad offices on the second floor. The depot extended eastward as a rectangular structure devoted to freight handling and storage. Huge handcarts were lined up outside the depot to haul luggage or cargo. Freight trains came through often, and two fast passenger trains, the Hiawatha and the Arrow, each stopped in Marion twice a day on their routes between Chicago and Omaha. Their great, deep whistles reminded everyone how big the world was.

Marion's town park was directly across the street, occupying a full block square. It contained a statue honoring Civil War soldiers, a Civil War cannon pointed toward Cedar Rapids, a bandstand, and a drinking fountain reputed to deliver pure spring water; people came there from Cedar Rapids to fill up jugs. The park's most important feature for many youngsters was a small, white building that sat on the northeast edge of the park. The structure, about ten feet wide and five feet deep, was Charlie's popcorn stand.

Charlie was a former railroad man who lost both legs in a train accident. He sat inside his tiny stand wearing a green eyeshade and making the best popcorn in the world—small, sweet, white kernels popped in fragrant oil. Charlie's popcorn came in two sizes, each served in a white paper sack. The regular size cost a nickel; a large sack was a dime. Charlie put the butter on, but customers could add salt from a tin shaker on his counter. For a special treat at double the price, customers could have their popcorn mixed with warm redskin peanuts.

On summer evenings, Charlie's popcorn perfumed the air of all uptown. Breezes carried it to surrounding neighborhoods. As citizens headed uptown for a band concert, the scent of Charlie's popcorn came to them before they heard the horns tuning up or saw the lights of the business district. It was the smell of home.

—

Southwest of town, along the road to Cedar Rapids, lay Marion's Thomas Park, an eighteen and a half-acre meadow named after a pioneer settler, Richard Thomas, who once owned the land.

In the 1940s and 1950s, the park contained a few pavilions for picnics and, at its southern edge, one of Marion's greatest treasures, the American Legion Memorial Swimming Pool. A dirt road and parking area ran next to the southern edge of the pool. Across that road was the field where the football players practiced twice a day in the late summer. As sweat poured from them in the August heat, they could hear the screams of children frolicking in the pool.

The swimming pool was Marion's second-largest body of water after Indian Creek. The creek bordered the town to the north then flowed south through Thomas Park and along the edge of the pool. Indians once camped along the creek, inspiring the name for both the creek and Marion High School's sports teams. Indian Creek was just deep enough in a few places to provide swimming holes for Marion youngsters seeking a cheaper, more natural, and private experience than the pool offered. Every few years, the creek rose in a flood and dumped its muddy waters into the swimming pool, shutting it down until the flood receded and the pool could be cleaned.

In an era without air conditioning, the swimming pool was Marion's Riviera, the most important summer gathering spot for young people. Preteen-age kids biked there from all over town and exhausted themselves in wild play. Their shrieks formed a canopy over the pool. Young mothers took their toddlers there for relief from the confinement of their homes. Teenagers swam and dove—and looked. And looked and looked, for nowhere else could they see so many members of the opposite sex in so little clothing. Boys leaped off the diving boards in trunks no bigger than boxer shorts. Girls lay out in the sun wearing one-piece suits of heavy latex that rose from below the hips to above the breast line. Desire smelled like chlorine, sweat, and coconut oil.

Marion's pool probably was the largest in the county in both water surface and gallons. It had an unusual, amoeba-like shape, with only one ninety-degree corner, the result of a decision when it was built in 1929 to fit it among five large trees. The pool had three sections: a small baby pool with less than a foot of water at its shallowest point, a vast four-foot-deep area for playing and swimming, and a diving area ten feet deep. There were four diving boards, two about three feet high, one six feet high, and one ten feet high.

Admission was twenty cents for children, thirty-five cents for adults. On hot days early in the season, as many of five hundred people lined up to get in, said Ed Reed, who worked there many years. Customers walked through a gate, paid their entry fee to someone in a small booth, got a ticket, walked about ten feet to the basket room, handed the ticket to the attendant, and received a basket and a rubberized wrist band with a metal number hanging from it that served as the receipt for the basket.

The changing rooms were so dark and wet they could have been underground. A dank corridor with a cement floor ran the length of the building, with small changing stalls and showers on either side, shielded by mildewed canvas curtains.

After their shower, customers took their baskets down the corridor, waded through a small puddle of icy water containing a chemical that killed athlete's foot, turned in their baskets and, if the mood struck them, broke into the sun by running through the baby pool, diving over the rope that marked its edge, and stroking for the far side.

Staff members regularly patrolled the area, enforcing the requirement to shower. The staff was always on the lookout for kids with open sores, which could set off ringworm or impetigo, two highly contagious diseases. "If a kid with sores got past the ticket seller, it was rare he got past the people in the basket room," Ed Reed wrote. They shouted, "Hey, kid, you can't come in here. You got sores on you." They gave the kid his money back and sent him home, often in tears. "Come back when you're cured," they yelled at his retreating back.

Others were also denied admittance. The swimming pool discriminated against people of color. As an enterprise owned by a private organization, the American Legion, the pool apparently had that right. Many young people were only dimly aware of this policy, if they knew it at all. Ed Reed saw it invoked only once, when a black couple with two children tried to get in. An assistant manager turned them away with these words: "We have the right to refuse admission to anyone." Marion High School in those days had only one person of color. He was Hispanic. The boy played on the football and basketball teams, was an honor student, and was voted one of the leaders of his class. He wasn't much browner than a lifeguard, but he couldn't go to the pool.

Chapter 13

"We Can't Have Dishonesty," 1946–1947

In August 1946, the *Marion Sentinel* ran on its front page an article that was repeated almost every year for the next two decades, with only slight changes in language. It was Hipple's preseason message to football players.

Get your football shoes, now, he advised, and begin wearing them a little each day. That way, they will be broken in when football season begins, and players will avoid getting blisters. Near the end of many of these annual notices, readers were told that anyone who had shoes that no longer fit should bring them to the coach. And anyone who needed shoes should go see the coach. The message was clear: Even if a boy's family couldn't afford football shoes, he could still go out for the team.

Football was no longer a game just for "toughies," Hipple told parents in his annual letter. That time ended, he said, when "fine red-blooded men and boys found what a thrilling game football really was." Nor did size matter, he said. "To any boy who wants to play football but feels he is too small, I want to emphasize that it's not the size of the body that counts, it's the size of your heart. We don't weigh players to find out how good they are." Football, like all sports, was good for every boy.

All over Marion, boys acquired their ankle-high black football shoes with screw-on black rubber cleats and began punching holes in their parents' lawns as they worked the heavy leather into shape.

As practice began that year with a turnout of forty-eight players, Hipple was typically closed-mouthed about the team's prospects, but the *Sentinel* reported that the Indians' "excellent morale pleases the coach a good deal." In fact, the team was shaping up well, with a veteran backfield of Winton Gable, Bob Page, John Schlotterback, and Dallis Carsner. Gable, the captain, would play quarterback, halfback, and fullback before the season was over, and Page would play both quarterback and halfback. The line was bolstered by a group of tough underclassmen, including two freshmen who both went on to earn four varsity letters—Corky Abernathy and Dave Rathje.

The Indians "displayed mid-season form" in their first game, the *Sentinel* said, defeating Belle Plaine, 20–0. But the win was followed by a virtual collapse against University High. The Indians lost 20–0, due in large part to a severe case of "buck fever," Hipple huffed afterward, but they also played without Gable, who was dealing with an injury known as "water on the knee."

As conference play opened, Marion squeaked by Monticello, 13–12, still without Gable, and then pounded Independence, 19–2, as Gable, apparently fully recovered, returned a punt forty yards for a touchdown. Then the Indians beat Vinton, 20–0.

Thus Marion found itself in a race for the WaMaC title, with some difficult teams yet to face. Maquoketa, in something of an upset, beat the Indians in a defensive brawl with the only score coming on a safety, 2–0. The Indians rebounded the following week, celebrating homecoming with a victory over Manchester, 19–6. The game was marked by a sensational run by Bob Page, playing at quarterback. Marion was ahead in the fourth quarter but was pushed back to its own fifteen-yard line by a series of penalties. With Manchester bunched up to stop the run, Page called a quarterback sneak, but sent a man in motion. As the Manchester line shifted to adjust for the flanker, Page burst through the line, shook off a tackler, and raced eighty-five yards for a touchdown. It was a heady victory and Marion was back in the title race. (Page's gallop is tied for eighth among the longest touchdown runs from scrimmage in Marion history.)

The Monday after the homecoming game, Hipple gathered his team in the end zone at the north end of the field. He told them to sit on the ground. He had something to say, and no one was going to like it.

"I know that some of you are breaking training rules by smoking," he told the team. "I'm going to ask each one of you if that's the case. I expect an honest answer."

He began with the team captain.

"Gable, have you been smoking?"

"No," Gable said.

Then he asked Vernon, the son of the superintendent. Again the answer was no.

The coach went on asking each player, seniors first, one at a time, staring at each intently as the other team members watched anxiously. Most said no. Then one said, yes, sir, he had smoked cigarettes during training. Then another said yes, and then another.

Kenny Otting, a sophomore, was trembling in fear as he waited for his turn. "I was completely innocent," Otting recalled, "but I was so scared I was shaking." Otting managed to squeak out his denial.

Hipple had now questioned every player. But he wasn't finished. "Some of you are lying," he said. "Be a man. We can't have dishonesty." He turned to a junior player, riveted him with his eyes, and asked him again if he had broken the rule against smoking.

Oh, my God, Otting thought, *he knows.*

When Hipple had finished, about ten players had admitted smoking. Hipple dismissed them from the team on the spot. If they followed the training rules, he said, they could come out for basketball.

The night after the mass dismissal, the phone rang constantly at the Vernon house. "People were really pissed off," John recalled. "My dad had the same answer for each one: 'Hipple's the football coach; you need to take your complaints to him. I'm not going to interfere.'" A few people tried to take their objections to the board of education, but the board wouldn't hear them. The boys knew the rules, the board said informally, and so did the parents.

There was no mention of Hipple's Monday massacre in either the *Sentinel* or the *Cedar Rapids Gazette*. In its advance story on the next game, the Gazette said that Hipple planned a number of lineup changes, and then listed several players who were out because of injuries. Hipple had to juggle the lineup so much that Otting, who had never played halfback, started at that position. "I wasn't too great," he recalled. Anamosa defeated the Indians, 7–0, on a muddy field.

Some of the injured players came back to play in the last game of the season, so it's impossible to determine who was thrown off the team. Marion lost its last game, to Tipton, 32–2, finishing the season with a 5–4 record overall and fourth place in the WaMaC.

Otting always believed that Hipple's action created the foundation for a winning tradition. "I think it established Mr. Hipple's position for many years," he wrote. "We knew the rules, we knew the consequences of disobedience, and we gained great respect for his principled behavior."

—

The word "Hippleman" appeared in the *Cedar Rapids Gazette* on October 5, 1946, apparently for the first time in print, in a story by Larry Tanner. Tanner later became news editor for the *Marion Sentinel*. While working for those two papers, he covered Hipple's career from beginning to end.

—

That winter, the sprinkling of fans who followed Marion basketball were pleasantly surprised by the team's first winning season in at least four years. The Indians finished third in the conference with an 11–6 record and won their first game in the sectional tournament. "Marion teams have shown steady progress and improvement under the tutoring of Coach Hipple, and we hope and believe this progress will continue until WaMaC and state tournament trophies are added to the collection in our trophy case," said the high school yearbook. "We are proud of our season's record, but we are equally proud that our relationship with our neighboring schools is fully as friendly, if not more so, than it has ever been. In defeat as well as in victory we have tried to be good sports."

If warmer feelings truly had been fostered between Marion and other schools, they weren't going to last.

—

Sorg Drug, a relatively new business in town, became a supporter of Marion athletics. During the 1946–1947 basketball season it sponsored a guessing game, announced in a one-column ad in the *Sentinel*. Contestants were required to pick the winner of an upcoming contest and predict the combined scores of the two teams.

When I won the contest, my parents were delighted, but I received the news calmly because, after all, that was the reason I had entered in the first place. I was ten years old. I was not a close follower of Marion basketball, but I was very interested in a dollar's worth of trade at Sorg's. When I went to Sorg's with the authorized postcard, my first stop was the rack for magazines and comic books, tucked into a V-shaped nook at the front of the store. I studied the comic book offerings: *Superman, Batman, Wonder Woman* (no), *Green Hornet, Plastic Man, Captain Midnight, Archie* (no) *Shana, Queen of the Jungle* (hmm), *Joe Palooka, Captain Marvel,* and so on.

In a process that may have taken as long as thirty minutes, I soberly selected five comic books. That gave me fifty cents to go. I headed for the candy counter in the back of the store near the cash register. I handed the card to the clerk without saying a word and studied the assortment arrayed before me. Mars bars cost a dime, but they were delicious, so I took one. Then a Milky Way, an Almond Joy, perhaps a Baby Ruth, a package of Walnettos, a box of Milk Duds. Bit-O-Honey was a taffy-like bar divided into six sections. It did not taste great, but it was a good value, since it took several minutes of sucking and gnawing to reduce each rubbery block to a size that could be safely swallowed.

Finally I handed my dollar's worth of treasure to the clerk: five comic books and eight candy bars. She put them into a paper sack and handed it to me. I took the sack silently, turned, and walked out the door.

—

The *Marion Sentinel*'s news editor in 1947 was Fred E. Dice, who had been a reporter for the *Gazette*. Like many townspeople, Dice became very fond of the Marion Indians. He was also an exuberant and funny writer. Here is an excerpt from his account of Marion's 39–28 loss to Manchester in a basketball game marked by sixty-four fouls, or two for every minute of play: "Any worries that the coach would have to put the water boy into the game when he ran out of players were dispelled when the final gun ended the game along toward morning."

Dice discovered that Hipple had seventh and eighth graders practicing basketball before school started. The news warranted several paragraphs in one of the reporter's columns. "This is part of Coach Hipple's plan to stimulate basketball, and it is apparent that some of the fighting now is for positions on the cage teams three and four years ahead." It would also assure Marion many years of dominance in the WaMaC Conference.

—

The track team that year had seventy-two members, fourteen more than had gone out for football in the previous fall. The huge turnout delivered Hipple his first WaMaC championship as Marion scored 81 ½ points and finished 17 ½ points ahead of second-place Tipton.

In other news, the postwar building boom predicted by the *Sentinel* was underway. On a single day in August 1946 the town granted building permits for five new houses, ranging in price from $1,000 to $9,000. Growth would be continuous and at times rampant for the next sixty years.

Chapter 14
Coach Lyle

In mid-twentieth century Marion, playing sports came to boys out of the culture of childhood, as naturally as marbles or tag. They learned from each other, or from older boys who let them into their games. A few fathers helped them develop their skills, but the boys were mostly self-taught. They shared tips picked up from magazines or instruction books that fell into their hands, and passed on techniques they learned from watching adult players in the town's softball leagues or on the minor league Cedar Rapids Raiders. Hipple's high school athletes were role models in basketball and football.

By the fourth or fifth grade, many boys abandoned gunplay for sports. They played touch or tackle football on vacant lots and backyards, and urged their fathers to hang baskets from their garages. The backboards were always made of wood. Rims and nets were purchased, but commercial backboards were either nonexistent or too expensive.

Marion had few playing fields. The two best softball diamonds were on opposite sides of town. In the south, the town's clay field had benches, a pitcher's rubber, a home plate, and a backstop. In the north, the sneakered feet of generations of boys had pounded base paths into the pebble-strewn earth of Emerson schoolyard. The diamond was otherwise unequipped. Players put down cardboard or sticks for home plate and the bases. They scratched a line in the dirt for the pitcher's mound. Boys with the oldest, most battered bicycles lined them up behind the batter's box so the spokes stopped balls that got past the catcher, relieving him of chasing them out into the street.

Fathers never coached softball games and rarely attended them. Mothers would not think of being present.

Then, in the late 1940s, Lyle Touro began to pursue his dream of creating a softball league for boys. When I became one of his players, Lyle had been working toward this goal for a few years, but the best he could do on most days was put together the fragments of two teams and set them against each other as he served as manager and coach for both sides.

This is not to diminish Lyle's accomplishment. He was ahead of his time. Little League Baseball was still a local program in Williamsport, Pennsylvania in 1940, and it did not get a foothold in Marion until many years later.

Lyle Touro's quest was complicated by the fact that he was severely handicapped with developmental disabilities. In that time it would not have been considered cruel to describe Lyle as retarded, although the word probably would not have been spoken to his face. Lyle also had a speech impediment. When he talked, his *l* and *r* sounds turned into *w*. He pronounced his name *Wy-owe To-woe*. His diction was imprecise in other ways, too, so it was difficult to understand him until his speech patterns became familiar. He was able to read and write, but with great difficulty, and the boys who spent time with him recognized that his mental skills were not greatly advanced over their own.

He was physically imposing. Born in 1917, he was about thirty when I played for him. There was nothing about Lyle that was not thick: his legs, his body, his neck, his arms, his fingers. His wide torso was usually covered in overalls and a denim shirt. He wore heavy work boots. He was a farmer, the son and grandson of farmers; his lineage went back to Marion's first settlers. His face was red from the sun until it turned white at his forehead, which he exposed when he tore off his cap and hurled it to the dirt in mock anger when misfortune befell his team. His players understood that he was simply re-enacting behavior he had witnessed by some professional manager or coach, and the boys took no offense. They did not feel in any way threatened by him.

Lyle sometimes took a turn at bat. His swing was mechanical and constricted, all arms, and he missed the ball as often as his players did. But when he connected, it went a long way.

Lyle was unable to drive a car. Yet he had to travel three or four miles from his parents' farm to town for a practice or game. Sometimes he rode his old bicycle, sitting down all the way, pumping steadily with his heavy legs, making good time over the gravel roads. But he discovered that he could get to town quicker by walking. He would set off down the road, striding briskly, swinging his right arm in an exaggerated arc, like a soldier on parade. Before long, someone in a passing car picked him up and drove him the rest of the way.

Ken Touro, Lyle's nephew, worked with Lyle on the farm during summers. He remembered how Lyle suddenly stopped working in the late afternoon when it was time to leave. As his father fumed at the loss of a good hand, Lyle walked to the road and turned toward town. Lyle believed fully in the decency and generosity of others, and the first driver to see him usually confirmed his faith.

Nothing could deter Lyle from his love of sports. Once, he had a falling out with his father, perhaps over this matter, and tried to live on his own. He took a job at a meatpacking plant in Cedar Rapids, but things didn't work out, and Lyle returned home after a few weeks.

Despite his limitations, Lyle knew how to work the phones, and that was how he pulled his teams together. He called several boys and assigned them to call others and to report back to him. Thus he determined the availability of talent and, when enough pieces fell into place, he declared a game. I was one of Lyle's prime organizers, and the constant calling back and forth sometimes caused my mother, normally a stoical, uncomplaining woman, to mutter about the incessant interruptions.

In our home, the phone sat on its own table in a small nook at the end of a short hallway between my grandmother's room and the bathroom. If, when the phone rang, my mother was upstairs, ironing clothes in the bedroom she shared with my father, she had to walk down a short hallway, go down a flight of stairs, make a right hand turn and take a few more steps to reach the phone. It was a long way to go for a barely comprehensible message from Lyle Touro. My mother did not like telephones much. She viewed them as costly devices to be used only in an emergency or to pin down an important fact, such as the time of a bridge club, not for conversation. Lyle's many calls exceeded what she considered a reasonable limit.

The telephone was a heavy, black two-piece object with a circle of plastic on its face instead of a dial. In the center of this non-existent dial, a smaller circle of clear plastic protected a piece of paper on which my mother had written our phone number: 343J.

To call my best friend, I picked up the handset and waited. Perhaps there was a buzz. Then:

"Number, please." A woman's voice.

"Four two four."

"Oh, hello, Danny. Tommy's not home. He's over at Denny Petersen's. I'll ring there."

"Okay."

Tommy's mother was a telephone operator. What she did was against company policy and perhaps illegal. Mothers knew best in Marion.

By game time, despite the phone calls, there was often severe fallout among the boys who said they would show up. So Lyle organized a scrimmage or a game of workup. He took his role seriously, so seriously that when an umpire's call went against him—even though the umpire was one of us—he sometimes threw down his hat, stomped his boots in the dust and shouted, "I pwo-test; I pwo-test this game." We were afraid he would suspend all play at that moment.

"Lyle," we said, "You can't protest the game. You run the league. There's no one to protest to."

"I pwo-test anyway," he insisted, apparently lodging his complaint with heaven as play resumed.

Boys seldom said cruel things to Lyle. When a few tried it, others stepped in to silence them. Lyle was hard to tease, because he tended to go along with the joke, enjoying it even if he wasn't sure what the point was.

—

Lyle's teams often scrimmaged on the town's softball diamond, a cement-like patch of clay near the football field. Here I had one of my most vivid experiences in sports. I was pitching, probably because it was my turn to do so, since I was unable to deliver a flat, accurate pitch, and would not have been assigned the position in a real game. I had to arch the ball to get it over the plate. Shorty Novotny, a year older than I, was on third base, no doubt having stretched a single into a triple, since Shorty Novotny was very fast. He was also very quick, which he immediately demonstrated by stealing home. He got there before the ball. The catcher had no chance to tag him.

"No stea-wing, no stea-wing," yelled Lyle, ordering Shorty Novotny to return to third. Shorty did not really deserve his nickname. He wasn't tall, but there were other kids shorter. He was only slightly on the short side, and must have picked up his handle when he was very young. His real first name was Marvin. Shorty's mouth was naturally set in a sort of quarter-smile, which gave him a look of slightly amused confidence. People who didn't now him might think he was laughing at them in a small, private way, but that was just the way his mouth was set.

As Shorty Novotny, back on third base, stared at me, I detected no mockery in his smile. But I could also see that Shorty Novotny had every intention of stealing home again.

And he did, effortlessly sliding under the flattest, hardest pitch I could deliver.

As Lyle again ordered Novotny back to third base, I had a vision of eternity: *I was a pitcher alone on a sun-blasted softball field, yellow clay as hard as iron, and Shorty Novotny was on third. No matter what I did, no matter how hard I threw the ball, no matter what the rules were, Shorty Novotny would go on stealing home, forever. I would never get out of there.*

Hopelessly, I delivered the next pitch. The batter took matters into his own hands and drove a double into center field even as Shorty Novotny was sliding into home. Shorty Novotny was cleared off third base and home safe, and my torment was over.

—

Somehow, Lyle was able to arrange occasional games against teams in Cedar Rapids. It's hard to imagine how he did it, but he was a persistent man on the telephone, so one day we found ourselves, probably transported by our fathers, on a grassy field in a strange neighborhood. Here I had another of my most memorable moments in sports.

I was playing left field when the batter belted a hard line drive right at me. As the ball rocketed toward me on a straight line I couldn't tell whether it was going to drop at my feet or scream on over my head. The ball came on, straight as a bullet, and I stood rooted by indecision.

Now the ball was upon me, clearly on its way over my head. In total futility, I jumped and thrust my glove into the air. The ball hit it and stuck. I brought the glove down and gazed in amazement at the ball. Then, because it was the third out, I trotted to our bench along the third base line.

Lyle was ecstatic. "I wish I had a Kodak of that," he said. "I wish I had a Kodak of that." He kept saying it, over and over, with a huge smile on his face. It was the most genuine, unrestrained praise I ever received from a coach, and his joy in my accomplishment was thrilling. I was too embarrassed to tell him the catch was sheer, blind luck.

Chapter 15
Falling in Love, 1947–1948

Iowa's hot, muggy weather in August is good for the corn but hard on football players during preseason practice. The heat wave in late August of 1947 was the worst on record, with the mercury topping one hundred degrees for seven straight days then remaining in the high nineties into September. Sixty candidates for the Marion football team labored that summer in cauldron-like temperatures on the practice field just across Indian Creek from the game field.

The practice field was known as the American Legion field, and in the summer Marion's baseball team played there. The vast expanse of the outfield, which had no fences, provided plentiful space for football practice and helped preserve the game field. Hipple tended the game field all summer long, and it was always in superb condition. The practice field was anything but. Grass grew there, but the land had more in common with a pasture than a real outfield, with ruts, gullies, small rocks, and patches of dirt. The baseball infield was a stony plateau with no hint of grass.

The practice field had a water spigot—not a fountain, but a faucet on the end of a pipe rising a few feet out of the ground. Here the players were allowed to bend down for an occasional sip of water. Assistant coaches policed the process to be certain no boy got more than a gulp or two. Too much water, it was believed, could make a player sluggish, while going without it made him tough.

Hipple may have allowed a greater ration of water that year because of the scalding temperatures; there were no reports of heat exhaustion among the players. Some players went to extraordinary lengths to get more than their allotted share of liquid. It became a ritual over the years for boys to sneak down to the field and plant caches of water among the trees that rose on a hillside—called the bluffs—at one end of the practice field. Then, during practice, claiming the need for a bathroom break, the boys stole among the trees and filled up on the hidden water. This story, repeated by former players over the years, sometimes takes on the aura of myth. Several former players insisted that when Hipple discovered milk cans on the hillside filled with water, he had someone get a rifle and shoot holes in the cans.

To augment their sips of water, players were allowed to suck on chunks of cut lemons. They were to eat the fruit, then deposit the peel in a receptacle. Some boys managed to hide extra lemons in their equipment with the aim of enjoying them during a break in practice. One day, a player took a tremendous hit during a drill. The impact was so great that it twisted his helmet sideways and left him dazed on the ground. As coaches and players gathered around the fallen player, they were shocked to see a whitish pulp oozing out of the ear hole of his helmet. They feared brain damage at first, but on closer inspection discovered that the discharge was actually a piece of mangled lemon the player had stowed in his headgear.

—

With eleven returning lettermen in 1947, Hipple had his best Marion football team yet, a true contender. The season opener was not auspicious, however, as the Indians lost four fumbles while staggering to a 6–6 tie with Belle Plaine. This was followed by a 12-0 victory over Mt. Vernon. These two games exposed a weakness that would prove fatal to the Indians later in the season: They sometimes had trouble making extra points.

Marion opened conference play with an impressive 20–0 defeat of Monticello, and then traveled to Independence for what would be one of Marion's most memorable games. The contest was played in a downpour of biblical proportions. The rain began during the bus ride to Independence and continued relentlessly until well after the game. The field had very poor drainage and became a quagmire. By game time, the field was "100 yards of soggy mud," wrote Fred Dice in the *Sentinel*, with much of it "submerged in a measured three inches of water." A few hardy fans hunched together under blankets, reported the *Independence Conservative*. A few more sat in cars ringing the field. Only about one hundred people saw the game.

Out on the field, visibility was limited and mobility almost impossible. As the rain pounded down, the two teams tried to mount their running attacks but went nowhere. Ball handling was treacherous. Players on both sides slipped and stumbled. Runners who fell face down after being tackled would find themselves up to their ears in puddles deep enough to drown them. The first half ended in a 0–0 tie, and it was hard to see how that would change.

But Bob Page, Marion's handsome blond quarterback, had an idea. "Moments after the second half started, Page flipped a wobbly pass to left end Don Whittemore, who plowed forty yards through the mud for a score without being touched," reported Dice. "Whittemore slipped behind the Maroon's defense and took the pass over his shoulder.

"A few minutes later, with Marion on its own 47-yard line, Page drew back and let fling a pass to Ken Otting on the Maroon 40 who rambled down the sideline for a second third-quarter touchdown." And then, as if the moon were out on a cloudless night, Page passed again to Otting for the extra point. Page, one of the few Marion quarterbacks over the years who favored the pass, said he called each of those plays. The game ended in a Marion triumph, 13–0.

After the game, Hipple, who must have been soaked to the skin, ordered his mud-caked players to take their shoes off outside the building and walk directly through the dressing room and straight into the showers without removing their uniforms. Once under the showers, they were told to undress and wash the muck off their equipment and themselves. When everyone was clean, the players used towels to swab down the shower and locker rooms, leaving them spotless. Hipple later received a letter of gratitude from the Independence superintendent, who said he had never before experienced such an extraordinarily thoughtful act by a visiting team. (See Hipple Rule Number 8: We will keep our dressing rooms clean and neat, at home or away.)

In its next games, Marion beat Vinton 20–0, then held off Maquoketa, 27–20, in a contest that was not as close as the score suggested. The Maquoketa victory came at a heavy price, though, as quarterback Bob Page broke his lower right leg early in the game. "I lateraled the ball to [Dick] Jeffery [fullback], and then he lateraled it back to me. When I was tackled, someone fell across the back of my leg and it broke," Page said. He was rushed to a Cedar Rapids hospital in a Marion police car. He was still in his uniform when he was taken to the emergency room. There, nurses started to cut his uniform off him. "I knew how serious Coach was about taking care of our equipment," Page said. "When they started to cut it off, I thought, *Oh-oh, Coach isn't going to like this.*"

Page's replacement, junior Jack Ratliff, performed ably against Maquoketa, throwing two touchdown passes to Ken Otting, and in the next game against Manchester he passed for two more touchdowns and an extra point in a hard-fought 19–0 victory.

At this point, Marion had won five straight conference games by the cumulative score of 99-20. But the next opponent, Anamosa, was also undefeated, and impressively so, for the Raiders had allowed only one touchdown by an opponent all season. The game, to be played at Marion, would be a defensive battle, wrote Dice, and Anamosa was favored by a touchdown. The Indians had captured the hearts of Marion fans with their stylish play and their victories, Dice wrote, and many people were planning to get to the field by 6:00 PM to be certain of a good seat. The WaMaC championship was riding on this game.

Anamosa scored all its points in the first half as quarterback Bob Purcell had touchdown runs of fifty-five yards with a punt return and thirty-five yards with an interception. Marion retaliated in the second half with two scores by fullback Jeffery, one on a forty-seven-yard run and another on a short plunge late in the game. For its first extra point attempt, Marion tried a place kick, and for its second, a pass. Both failed, depriving the Indians of the chance to win or tie. Marion lost a heartbreaker, 13–12.

After the game, Dice of the *Sentinel* blamed a muddy field for stifling Marion's passing attack. He pointed out that Marion outgained Anamosa by 268 yards to 107 and began promoting a post-season rematch. Larry Tanner's report in the *Gazette* focused so much on Marion's comeback that the director of music at Anamosa High School wrote a letter to the editor extolling his players' superiority and calling for more accurate reporting. This brought a response from the Marion Coffee Club, whose members sent a letter pointing out that Marion had dominated the offensive statistics.

Arguments over football superiority were quashed in the final games of the season when Tipton, which played only four conference games and won only one of them, held a dispirited Marion team to a 0–0 tie and Anamosa won its game to post a 7–0 conference record. Marion, at 5–1–1, finished second.

A rivalry had been born, and basketball season was at hand.

—

The 1947–1948 basketball season opened with a game against Mount Vernon. The contest was tied, 40–40, with six seconds left when Mt. Vernon's Don DeCamp was fouled. He had one shot coming—the shot that could win the game. He stepped to the line. Then, in the words of Fred Dice, "DeCamp, reaching an excited pitch that appeared to overcome him, called time out and stretched out on the floor before making the toss."

The next game found the Indians once again in the clutches of the Anamosa Raiders, who won handily on their home court, 50–42, with Big John Beardsley, Anamosa's six-foot-four, 220-pound center, dominating the game with twenty-one points. But just behind him in the scoring column was a tall, skinny Marion forward named Lloyd Olmstead, with seventeen points. "Skinny" may be too generous a word to describe Olmstead in his junior year. The boy, who was about six feet four, had powerful legs, but his upper body was skeletal. Despite his frail appearance, Olmstead moved with fluid grace and shot with deadly accuracy. He had perfected a sort of semi-hook shot that was hard for defenders to stop because, like a hook shot, it came off the shoulder farthest from the defender. Hipple did not permit hook shots, and Olmstead finished the shot with the wrist and finger movement of a standard one-handed shot.

A referee, after watching Olmstead play a few times, told Dice, "He's the best boy I've seen this season. That slow, easy-moving push or twist shot reminds me of the movements of a hillbilly, but his shot is as sharp and beautiful as any you will find in high school."

After losing their first two games, the Indians hit their stride, winning five straight. This set up their second meeting with Anamosa. It was shaping up as a grudge match. As the Indians began winning that year, fan enthusiasm increased and basketball became a hot ticket. Now, in preparation for the Anamosa game, 110 reserved-seat tickets were held at Sorg Drug. They cost eighty cents a seat, a hefty increase over the standard admission price of fifty cents, but well worth it to fans who couldn't get to the gym early.

The game was a sellout. Marion's WaMaC record was 4–1, Anamosa's was 6–0. Marion would have to win to keep its title hopes alive. If winning the title and wreaking revenge on Anamosa wasn't enough, Marion had another motive for winning. Ken Otting, then a junior guard, explained that a few days before the game, "Marion's new home uniforms arrived. They were Marion's first home whites and they were beautiful."

Hipple wanted to get maximum impact when the new uniforms were introduced, Otting wrote. "We still had old warm-ups, and Mr. Hipple had us go out with them closely fastened up for our pre-game warm up." After the warm up, the players returned to the locker room. Then the starting five took off their sweats and led the team back onto the court. As the team burst out of the locker room in its new home whites, "the crowd went wild and so did we," Otting wrote.

The game was an end-to-end thriller. Wrote Fred Dice, "An overflow crowd jammed the Marion high gymnasium Friday night to watch a fighting tribe of Indians knock off the conference-leading Anamosa Raiders 51–49." Marion led most of the way, but Anamosa forged ahead 47–46 on a field goal by guard Jerry Swanson with about two minutes left. Then Olmstead, who had 24 points for the night, scored twice to make it 50–47. A goal by Big John Beardsley cut the lead to 50–49. As Marion stalled, Dick Smith drew a charity toss and made it. Beardsley had a final shot to tie the game, but missed, and the Indians held the ball as the final seconds ticked away.

"The rafters shuddered with the howls and screams of frenzied fans during the final minutes of play," Dice wrote. "When the whistle ended the photo-finish contest, fans poured from the bleachers like a broken dam releasing a fury of water. The Marion cagers were swamped by excited spectators and the fervor dimmed only when the victorious lads left the gym for the showers."

Marion went on to win nine of its next ten regular season games, losing to Independence, which also beat Anamosa. Both Marion and Anamosa lost two games, but Marion was named champion because it played one more conference game. It was Marion's first WaMaC basketball championship, and the fans were thrilled.

They were even more ecstatic when the team won three straight state tournament basketball games. The first two victories made the Indians sectional champions, while the third carried them to the district finals where they lost a thriller to Belle Plaine, 37–36, in what some called an upset.

No Marion team had won a sectional tournament before. One of the sectional victims was Immaculate Conception, a Catholic high school in Cedar Rapids with a strong basketball tradition. Marion won, 27–24, in a brutal defensive contest. Epic battles between Marion and I. C. would continue to highlight tournament play for years to come.

The *Sentinel*'s Dice, looking back on the year, praised Hipple's program.

> That sectional tournament trophy hanging over at the Marion high represents more strategy by Les Hipple than an infantry maneuver behind enemy lines. The Indian coach has built up a winning outfit on the idea of starting them young and then making them toe the mark. Over a period of years the lads have had little rest ... Track, football, basketball—their bodies and minds have been given thorough training ... It requires hard work, conditioning, sacrifice—Coach Hipple has proven to the boys he knows his stuff.

This was evident in boys as young as ten, Dice continued. "These youngsters can see what is required to be a good athlete. They can see what it takes to be a champion, practicing hours before school starts in the morning and on Saturdays and Sundays."

Further proof of the benefits of starting players young came that year from the success of the freshman–sophomore basketball team, which had an undefeated 18–0 season. The team was coached for the first time that year by Frank McLeod, a tall, bald man with a gruff manner, a broad smile, and a kind heart. In addition to coaching the freshman–sophomore basketball team and the junior varsity football team, he served as Hipple's assistant varsity coach for football (line coach), basketball, and track.

Handsome uniforms and good equipment were an important part of Hipple's strategy, too, Ken Otting wrote. "A lot of Hipple's program involved instilling pride. He did this by making us feel we were better conditioned, better coached and, indeed, better looking than our opponents. In the next two years we got new traveling red uniforms, yellow T-shirt uniforms, and new warm-ups. In football we got new red jerseys and gold pants, new gold jerseys with red pants, and new white jerseys. We were by far the best-dressed team in the conference."

Before long, the football team would have new pads and plastic Riddell helmets with suspension straps and rubber lining. The old woven leather helmets, along with pads and practice uniforms, were passed down to the junior high team. "After leaving Marion," Otting continued, "I played football and basketball at Cornell College. The equipment—not just uniforms, but pads, helmets, everything—at Marion was vastly superior to that at Cornell."

In his review of the sports year, Fred Dice praised Bob Page, who had re-injured the leg he broke in football and could not rejoin the basketball team until late in the season. Page had been the basketball team's high scorer the year before, and had he not been hurt, both Marion's football and basketball teams might have had even greater seasons. (Years later, Page said that if it were not for sports, he wouldn't have wanted to go to school. "I guess my parents would have made me go, though," he added. He went on to graduate from Cornell College and become an educator and coach.)

Dice then commented about Marion's teams as a whole.

> It's a pleasure to write about such a worthwhile gang of fellows. … Their love of the game along with their sportsmanlike attitude echoes the loyalty that has long been an outstanding characteristic of Marion High School athletics. … The boys are not alone in this recognition, however … They exhibit the pattern that is drawn from within by Coaches Lester Hipple, Frank McLeod, and Harold Yeoman … The coaches mold their players like an author molds his characters—both in the effort to make the results of the work as successful as possible.

That spring, Marion won its third straight WaMaC Conference track championship without taking a single first place. It was the only team that did not win at least one event. The large squad prevailed as the Indians out-pointed second-place Tipton 54 ½ to 49 ⅓. Thus the Indians won two of three WaMaC titles that year—basketball and track—and narrowly missed one in football. This pattern of dominance would persist for nearly a decade. Hipple's glory years had begun, and the people of Marion were in love with the Indians.

Chapter 16

Racing into the Glory Years, 1948–1949

NO SEATS read the sign taped to the locked door of the school building. Inside, the six hundred-seat gymnasium overflowed with fans who had arrived early to be sure of getting seats. They watched the freshman–sophomore team play in the curtain raiser while scores of fans outside turned away in disappointment. The place could not begin to hold everyone who wanted in. The wisest fans lined up as much as two hours before the doors opened. They stomped their feet in the dark and sent plumes of steam into the frigid air. They chatted with one another as they waited, gladly enduring the discomfort to see their boys play basketball.

"We idolized those boys," said Irwin Renfer, who owned the shoe store in town. He and other business owners closed early on home-game nights to line up at the school. They had reversed the long-standing policy of keeping their stores open late on Friday nights. It would have been disloyal to stay open when Marion played a football or basketball game. The stores would have been empty anyway. (Not every establishment closed. The taverns, the pool hall, and the movie theater stayed open. The pleasures of life, if not all of the necessities, were still available on Friday nights.)

The Marion Indians of 1947–1948, by winning WaMaC titles in basketball and track, and reaching the finals of the district basketball tournament, had inaugurated the glory years of Les Hipple's reign. Hipple once said that he wanted Marion to win only its fair share of conference championships—half for Marion, half for the other teams. During the nine glory years, Marion won more than its fair share: seventeen of the twenty-seven championships contested in football, basketball, and track.

A romance is sweetest and most exhilarating in its earliest days, and the teams that followed over the next two school years, 1948 to 1950, were surely the most beloved of them all. These teams reached heights never before scaled by Marion—and rarely matched in the years that followed. The fans loved the Indians for the way they won fiercely contested games through discipline, crisp play, and courage. And they were charmed as well by the demeanor of the coaches and players, who at all times bore their successes with humility.

In 1948 Bob Brooks had begun broadcasting Marion basketball games for KCRG radio in Cedar Rapids, covering five home games. At least sixty businesses co-sponsored the broadcasts. Each contributed $11 to fund the effort, priced at $660 for the five games. There were too many sponsors for individual advertisements, but each was mentioned during the broadcast as a booster of the "Marion is a better place in which to live and shop" campaign.

Brooks later called football games for several years and was at the mike for basketball games at home and away for about a decade. Fans at opposing schools hated to see him arrive, he said. "We sold the daylights out of those broadcasts," Brooks recalled. "The whole town was involved."

Print coverage of the Indians was extensive, too. There were usually at least two major articles on Marion sports in every issue of the *Marion Sentinel*, plus a column by the news editor. For several years, the paper also carried a syndicated column on sports by Tait Cummins, the former sports editor of the *Cedar Rapids Gazette,* who had become a sports broadcaster for WMT radio. There were also brief reports in the paper on such matters as school letters awarded, games by junior varsity teams, and awards banquets. The *Sentinel* devoted as much space to Marion sports and high school activities as it had to the county's soldiers in World War II. Its coverage of high school sports was far more extensive than in the newspapers in other conference towns, and this contributed a great deal to fan interest.

In 1948, revenues from football attendance soared to $3,373, allowing Hipple to spend $1,948 for twenty helmets, thirty-seven pants, twenty rib pads, and other items. When a few townspeople expressed concern over such expenditures, C. B. Vernon assured them that the sports program was not only self-funding but actually generated excess cash for the school at large.

The football program usually operated at a loss, but revenues from basketball made up the difference and paid for track, with something left over for the general fund.

—

In the fall of 1948, Hipple began his fourth year as athletic coach at Marion. He had delivered two track championships and one basketball title. His football teams had shown steady improvement, but had not won a championship. This could be the year. Marion had eight returning lettermen—four linemen and four backs—pictured in the *Gazette* in their sweat-soaked jerseys and hard leather helmets. The heart of the line would be occupied by center George Murdoch, guards Corky Abernathy and Jerry Jeffrey, and tackles Larry Yauslin and Jerry Kelso. The veteran backfield consisted of halfbacks Dick Krog and Ken Otting, the 200-pound fullback Dave Rathje, and quarterback Jack Ratliff. The entire squad numbered more than seventy hopefuls.

The talk around the conference was that Marion was a cinch to win the title, wrote Fred Dice in the *Sentinel.* Hipple hated that kind of talk. "Coach Hipple is still shaking his head," Dice wrote. "He's not giving out any dope yet. By the end of the season he'll still be shaking his head and not giving out any dope. He never lets optimism carry him away."

The Indians raced through their first five games as if fulfilling the prophecy of the conference pundits, outscoring their opponents by 151–6. This run included a 28–0 pounding of Anamosa in a grudge match that drew spectators from miles around, even from Cedar Rapids. "It was the largest crowd in years," Dice reported. Gate receipts were $905. In this and other games, Otting and Rathje repeatedly thrilled fans with long runs behind outstanding line play. Rathje was so powerful on offense and defense that a fan wondered, "What is he, a man or a tractor?" Otting made eighteen touchdowns. (He is tied for fifth place among Marion's all-time leaders in touchdowns per season.)

In the next three games, Marion slipped by Maquoketa, 19–12, crushed Manchester, 49–0, and subdued Independence, 18–7. The Indians had run up 237 points to the opponents' 25. Now they would face undefeated Tipton in the final game of the season for the championship. But the Indians seemed to be faltering, Dice wrote. They had been sluggish against Independence, winning largely because of lucky breaks. The sense around the conference was that Tipton would win.

An enormous crowd of thirty-five hundred people showed up for the game at Tipton, including six hundred from Marion. There were not enough seats, so fans formed a ring around the field and watched standing up, enduring a driving rainstorm in the early November chill. It was a thrilling game, marked by fumbles, goal-line stands, and daring pass plays, but Tipton prevailed, 13–7. The Tigers overcame a Marion lead of 7–6 in the fourth quarter, and then held off Marion's answering drive by stopping Rathje on a fourth-and-six-inches plunge on the Tipton twenty-seven-yard line.

It was a disappointing finish for one of Hipple's best football teams ever. The 1948 team allowed its opponents a total of only thirty-eight points. (The team remained tied for first place by this measure among all Marion squads through 2008.) At the gridiron banquet that year, Hipple listed three factors that had made the season a success: the cooperation of the team, the cooperation of the student body, and the cooperation of the townspeople.

—

One of the more curious sights of the football season, Dice wrote, was the appearance of Marion's basketball star, Long Lloyd Olmstead, in a football uniform. Hipple had urged Olmstead to come out for football for the first time. At a skinny six feet four, he was not built for the sport. He towered over the other players and, when he got down into his stance, looked unnaturally off balance, as if constructed from mismatched parts.

Olmstead played end and saw action in several games. Teammate George Murdoch remembered that Hipple had wanted Olmstead to play football to toughen him for basketball. Olmstead would be switching from forward to center, and football would make him more aggressive and physical around the backboard. This is not a choice every coach would make. Some might reason that the prudent course would be to have the potential All-State basketball player go out for cross-country. He was not a factor in football, and being on the cross-country team would not only reduce the risk of injury but also give the boy practice time in the gym after his three-mile run. But playing football caused a "complete turnaround" in Olmstead's play, Murdoch insisted. "He was soft as a junior but as a senior he was all elbows, knees, and butts."

As the basketball season opened, great things were expected of Olmstead, but Dice wondered whether other scorers would emerge to take some pressure off the tall center. Dice needn't have worried. Two juniors, Barrie Gable and Jack King, immediately established themselves in the forward positions. Ken Otting was back at guard, joined by junior Dick Krog. The team took off like a rocket and never looked back.

The Indians had only one starter taller than six feet, but they were blazingly fast, sure ball-handlers, and ferocious defenders. Gable, listed at five feet ten, was a preacher's kid. He had the face of a choirboy but the guts of a cat burglar. King, only five feet nine and weighing about 140 pounds, "runs like mad," Dice wrote, showing total disregard for his own safety as he finished fast breaks by crashing high against the padding on the wall under the baskets. Otting, five feet eleven, and Krog, five feet ten, both football halfbacks, also could fly.

They were adept ball-stealers. They confounded opponents by knocking the ball out of their hands, scooping it up, and dashing down-court for easy lay-ups. Olmstead, gathering rebounds, hit the outlet man with quick passes, and the Indians were off to the races again. They could not be slowed by a full-court press. They flawlessly executed the weaving pattern from Hipple's drills and broke free for easy baskets.

The team simply left its foes in the dust. Until the final game of the regular season, the closest game Marion played was a 41–31 victory over McKinley High School of Cedar Rapids. But the last regular season game, at Monticello, was a squeaker. It was also anticlimactic, coming after Marion had sewn up both the conference title and the sectional championship. Marion won, 33–31, in a foul-filled slugfest. Marion's victory came at the free-throw line. The team made seventeen free throws to Monticello's seven, despite the "hysterical" behavior of the Monticello fans, who were chided by Dice for their poor sportsmanship. Whenever a Marion player prepared to shoot a free throw, Monticello fans "set up a noisy demonstration in an effort to rattle the shooter." In the second half, "the crowd got out of hand and had to be checked by an official. Bitterness seemed to hang heavy over the gym," Dice wrote.

The victory over Monticello gave the Indians an undefeated regular season at 19–0. Earlier, in January, with the season half completed, the fans and the press began to talk about the state tournament, and especially about the wealth of top teams in the Class A bracket in the eastern part of the state. (Teams played in one of three classes—AA, A, or B—until they reached the state finals, a sixteen-team tournament that produced a single champion.)

In January that year, undefeated teams included Marion, Immaculate Conception of Cedar Rapids, West Liberty, and Montezuma. Other good teams included St. Patrick's and Wilson of Cedar Rapids. If Marion hoped to reach the state tournament, it would have to claw its way through a thicket of top teams. "What a battle it will be," wrote Gus Schrader in the *Gazette*, if Marion and I. C. met again.

What a howl the fans in Marion and Cedar Rapids set up when the pairings were announced a few weeks later. Marion and I. C. were matched against each other in the opening game of the sectional tournament—to be held at Marion. It was a travesty, fans said, to pit two of the hottest teams in eastern Iowa against each other in the very first game of the tournament. They should have been seeded, at least, to meet in the second game, the sectional finals, or better yet, sent to separate sectionals to delay their clash until the district tournament. Marion was undefeated and I. C. had lost one game by that time. Whatever the result of that first game, it would be an injustice for the loser.

It was a crime, I. C. boosters wailed, for the game to be played at Marion where the Indians had home court advantage. And when the fans realized that Marion's gym would have no room for them, they were ready to riot. C. B. Vernon, faced with the Solomon-like duty of parceling out tickets for the game, calculated that the capacity of the gym was 604 seats, of which 540 would be available after accommodating players, cheerleaders, and tournament officials. Since Marion's enrollment (325) was almost exactly double I. C.'s (163), Marion would receive 360 tickets and I. C. 180. Marion's tickets would be distributed by way of a pecking order that would allow the purchase of three tickets first by members of the basketball team, then the cheerleaders, then the seniors, juniors, sophomores, and freshmen. If any tickets were left, and there was small chance of that, faculty members could buy them. Students could buy tickets for anyone they chose, but scalping would be strictly forbidden.

This meant no seats for the public. The public hated the plan. Vernon was under fire. He wanted to move the game to the Coe field house, but the school's Colonial Ball was scheduled for the night of the game. "We didn't ask for this tournament in the first place," Vernon said, pointing out that venues are assigned by the Iowa State High School Athletic Association.

As the turmoil swirled about them, Vernon and Hipple came up with another plan: Change the date of the game and hold it at Coe. The Coe field house could accommodate two thousand spectators, two hundred of whom would have to stand. The ISHSAA approved the plan, and Vernon announced that Marion's allotment of twelve hundred tickets would go on sale at the high school about a week before the game. There would be a limit of two to a customer.

Long before the doors opened for the ticket sale, fans crowded together on the steps to the high school. The knot of anxious townspeople stretched all the way out to the street, recalled Alice Wallace, school secretary assigned to handle the sale. She had to fight her way through the crowd and up the steps, and the going was so tough that a button was ripped off her new coat. Luckily, there were enough tickets for everyone. Despite the change of venue, Marion's share of the proceeds did not change: It was limited to $200.

In his column, Tait Cummins hailed Vernon and Hipple for "an almost unique act of generosity in the field of sports" in giving up the home court advantage and allowing the game to be moved to Coe. They would have been "well within their rights to keep the tournament game in their home gym," he said.

Although I. C. had taller players, Marion was the slight favorite, according to Dice. A lot of money was bet on the game, Dice said, with the top amount placed in a single bet reaching $700 (the equivalent of $6,000 in 2007). As for a bettor asking for odds, "Don't be silly," wrote Schrader. If a bettor on either side hinted that his team didn't have an even chance of winning, "he'd be read out of the clan. There's no such thing as a favorite in this game. Figure it any way you can, the game is a toss-up."

When the two teams finally met, the Coe gym was "packed to the rafters with a frenzied and howling crowd," Dice wrote. The game was a sell-out; people without tickets tried a variety of ruses to get in. One kid shamelessly claimed that he was the son of Tait Cummins, and since Tait wouldn't be attending the game, he'd asked the boy to go in his place. The ticket taker, throwing the boy out, replied that he had just greeted Tait a few minutes earlier. A man falsely identified himself as a good friend of C. B. Vernon. The police caught someone trying to sneak in through the window to the ladies' room.

The game was a furious defensive battle in which both teams were tighter than bowstrings. Neither played up to its potential. I. C. led at the half, 13–12, with Olmstead scoring only five points. He broke loose in the second half, however, and finished with seventeen. As the fourth quarter opened, Marion led by 24–18, and held onto its lead as I. C. "became too frantic to work the ball in with customary finesse," Schrader wrote. Marion won, 31–25. Field goal averages were abysmal. The Indians made 26 percent of their shots, while the Greyhounds made only 16 percent.

Marion then stormed through the next two games, pounding St. Patrick's, 58–37, and DeWitt, 53–38. In the district finals, Marion met a towering Wilson team. Marion trailed at the half, but scored three baskets in the first twenty-seven seconds of the third quarter to take the lead. With slightly more than three minutes to play, Marion went into a stall, displaying "some of the finest ball-handling, dribbling, and passing" ever seen, Dice wrote. "The ball darted back and forth in front of (Wilson players') eyes … but completely out of their reach." During that entire three minutes, Wilson never touched the ball, and Marion won, 34–28.

With that victory, the Indians entered the substate tournament. Only twenty Class A teams reached that exalted position. Marion had never been in a substate tournament before. They celebrated by crushing West Liberty, 55–25. Now only Montezuma stood between Marion and the Sweet Sixteen. Marion fans were beside themselves with joy and tension. The team captivated even Gus Schrader of the *Gazette*. Taking a page from Grantland Rice, he began his game reports with four lines of doggerel. For example, after the McKinley game, he penned:

Wanna know what it was
That got McKinley treed?
Long-legs Olmstead
And speed, speed, speed.

The last two undefeated Class A teams in the state clashed at the substate final at the university field house in Iowa City. For three quarters it looked as if Marion would triumph over the much taller Montezuma five. The Indians held leads of as much as eight points on six different occasions as they "fast broke, snatched rebounds, stole passes, and delighted the crowd [of 10,501] with their spunk," Schrader reported. But the lead deteriorated to 38–34 at the end of the third quarter as the Indians tired under relentless pressure by Montezuma.

Montezuma pulled even, and then went ahead by one point, 39–38, with about 4:30 left. A free throw by Olmstead tied the game at 39–39, but it was the only point Marion scored in the fourth quarter. With three minutes to go, Bob Van Cleve of Montezuma made a ten-foot shot and, wrote Schrader, "The scoring—but not the fighting—was over." Gable broke free for a shot, but was fouled. When he missed his first free throw, Marion elected to take the ball out of bounds (an option then permitted), but the Indians couldn't convert.

"In the final minute, Marion threw caution to the winds and committed seven fouls, sending Otting and Gable to the sidelines," the *Gazette* reported. "Countless times Gable was able to tie up the Montes, but each time he had the chance at jumping against the towering winners—who controlled the tip and continued to stall." (Tie-ups always resulted in a jump ball; ball possession did not alternate between teams.) The tournament darlings lost, 41–39, and Schrader offered this epitaph:

Marion's speed and guts
Finally bowed to terrific height.
But remember the Indians
And their unrelenting fight.

Olmstead was the team's high scorer for the season with a total of 338 points for an average of 14.1 per game, and was named to the All-State first team as a forward by the Iowa Daily Press Association, which polled coaches and officials. The press lauded his defensive play, rebounding, and passing. Olmstead was the first Marion player to be so honored. When the *Sentinel* interviewed him, he displayed the modesty typical of all Hipplemen. "They picked me because our team was so good," he said. He had learned to shoot so well by practicing every night at a hoop attached to a neighbor's barn. "Coach Hipple would show me how to shoot and I'd go practice it."

The Indians had fallen just three points short of making the Sweet Sixteen, but Marion fans were ecstatic over its team of one tall guy and four short ones "who knocked off many a rugged five who looked down on them in height, but who looked up to them in heart, speed, guts, and brains," Dice wrote.

"We're from Marion, couldn't be prouder," went the cheer, and no Indian fan thought it was corny to feel that way. How could the town be anything but proud of the Indians? They had run through the WaMaC undefeated. They had triumphed over everything Cedar Rapids threw at them, beating Wilson twice and topping McKinley, I. C., and St. Pat's, and no one need ask who had bragging rights for all of Linn County. It would take a drive of more than one hundred miles to find a town with a Class A team as good as Marion. Why, the Indians were as good as—well, damn near as good as—any other team in the whole state. And that meant the town of Marion was just as good, too. Les Hipple had done that.

"These boys have brought to this city a package of glory that will not be duplicated for years and years to come," Dice predicted. If he meant an undefeated regular season, Dice was cannily prophetic. Through 2009–2010, no other Marion basketball team managed an undefeated regular season. But if Dice referred to the Indians' tournament performance, he could not have been more wrong. Over the next six years, five teams would match the Indians' record in tournament play, and two of them would exceed it.

Tait Cummins wrote that he was in awe of the composure shown by the Marion players. Every team they faced was obsessed by the goal of knocking them off. That's the way it would remain for years to come.

Chapter 17
Sweethearts, 1949–1950

As Marion prepared for the 1949–1950 sports seasons, the Chamber of Commerce voted to sponsor radio broadcasts of all Marion games—nine in football and eighteen in basketball. Bob Brooks had continued at the microphone for Marion through the basketball tournament the year before, and the fans wanted more. However, KCRG had already arranged to cover other football games on Friday nights. The station wanted to air Marion basketball, but the Chamber of Commerce saw it as a package deal for both football and basketball, and signed a contract with KWCR, a new Cedar Rapids station.

In other media shifts, Fred Dice left the *Sentinel* and was replaced by Larry Tanner, who had covered Marion and its teams for the *Cedar Rapids Gazette.* Tanner, a graduate of Franklin High School in Cedar Rapids, became devoted to the Indians and their coach. He whipped around town covering Marion general news for both the *Gazette* and the *Sentinel,* but his heart was in sports, and for many years he was a familiar presence at every Indian contest. He even rode along when Hipple drove one or two of his track stars to state meets.

Tanner developed a close relationship with Coach Hipple, and was a frequent guest in his home. Reporters on other papers sought out Tanner's views on the teams, and he functioned almost as a part-time sports information director. The opinions in his weekly column, "Larry's Line," were often synonymous with those of the coach, and were studied diligently by athletes, their parents, and fans.

The football team that year was a powerhouse with ten returning lettermen, including four-year lettermen Dave Rathje (fullback) and Corky Abernathy (guard). Barrie Gable took over the quarterback slot and was joined in the backfield by Dick Krog, a slashing runner, and a bruising junior, Bob Williams. Prominent among the linemen were the tackles, Bob Jeffrey and junior George Palmer, a muscular 225-pounder. The line averaged 180 pounds and significantly outweighed its opponents. "Les Hipple at Marion is a man [opposing coaches] all fear," wrote Tait Cummins.

The Indians opened the season by crushing two non-conference foes, Belle Plaine, 34–0, and Wellman, 46–0. The victory over Wellman was widely hailed because it broke a long winning streak by that school. "There's magic in Hipple's coaching kit," wrote Cummins. "[He] rates the bouquet as high school coach of the week."

Hipple wanted no bouquets. He knew that the Wellman team was not up to par. He told Tanner that Marion wasn't ready for a really tough game. He was right. The over-confident Indians were roughed up in the next game by Monticello. With time running out and facing a fourth-and-eleven, Gable hit Krog on a pass that took the ball to the Monticello four-yard line. Krog punched the ball over with twenty seconds remaining to tie the game at 26–26. Marion would have won had Williams made the extra-point kick.

Over at KWCR, sportscaster Jim Norvell was having his troubles, too. After the Belle Plaine game, he appeared before the Marion Chamber of Commerce to apologize for the incoherence and dead air during his broadcast. He was slow in setting up the equipment, he explained, because he had to climb a telephone pole to plug in his line. To give himself the best possible vantage point, he had arranged for seats on the fifty-yard line on the top row of the bleachers—only to discover when he got to the game that the bleachers were just four rows high, which accounted for his inability to identify players. As for the dead air, well, someone pulled out his electrical power cord.

The Indians, apparently aroused by the Monticello tie, performed much more ably for the rest of the season, overpowering opponents with their ground game. In a 35–7 win over Anamosa, Marion piled up 462 rushing yards to Anamosa's 49. Other games were similarly lopsided. The Indians ran up five conference wins, outscoring their opponents by a combined 115–20.

Now, just as it had the year before, Marion faced unbeaten Tipton in a game to decide the WaMaC title. Marion had not beaten Hipple's alma mater in four previous meetings. "This appears to be Hipple's best and last chance," wrote Tanner. "They better win this year if they expect to own a conference championship—at least for the next few years." (This was probably Hipple talking. Cummins had written earlier that "Marion's reserves, mostly freshmen and sophomores, are terrific.")

The teams clashed in a bruising game on Marion's field before thirty-five hundred shivering fans. Marion, with a line averaging twenty pounds per man more than Tipton's, dominated the statistics, making fourteen first downs to Tipton's nine, and accumulating 246 total yards to Tipton's 111. But Marion turned the ball over twice on fumbles and lost a touchdown when a clipping penalty nullified a sensational, thirty-eight-yard broken field run by Krog. All the scoring came in the first half. The game was not decided until late in the fourth quarter, when the Indians halted a Tipton drive on Marion's fifteen-yard line to preserve a 14–7 victory.

"With the conference title on the line, the boys gave it everything they had," wrote Gene Kovarik in the *Gazette*. "This resulted in several roughing penalties when tempers got a little short. The injured went on and off the field with alarming regularity, but always returned in an attempt to bring victory to their team." Both teams played only fifteen men. The hard-fought victory gave Hipple the first of three undefeated football teams he led at Marion. (Monticello, the team that had tied Marion early in the season, finished in fourth place with a 2-3-2 record.)

Hipple was surely delighted with the championship and the news that his team was ranked twentieth in the state according to a poll of forty-two daily newspapers. But he was just as proud of another accomplishment. Of the eighty-three boys who came out for football, eighty-one were still on the squad at the end of the season. That turnout equaled half of the 165 boys in school.

At the football banquet that year, Iowa football coach Eddie Anderson told his audience of 220 players, parents, and teachers, "Pattern your life after Nile Kinnick. Go to college with the idea of 'What can I give to the school,' not 'What can the school give to me.'" Kinnick was the great Iowa Heisman Trophy winner who was killed in a plane crash during World War II.

—

As the basketball season opened, fans wondered how Marion would fare without Olmstead and Otting, especially after the Indians lost in their third game of the season, to Wilson of Cedar Rapids, 38–32. The Indians were ice cold, and the final score would have been humiliating except for a late rally in which Marion scored seven unanswered points.

Toughened by another year of football, Barrie Gable and Jack King were back at forward, as fiery as ever, furious ball-hawkers and masters of the fast break. As the season progressed, someone, probably Tanner, gave them the nickname, "the DUZ twins," because DUZ, a detergent, was incessantly advertised in a jingle that ended, "D-U-Z does everything."

Late in the season, Gable was averaging thirteen points a game and King ten. Dick Johnson, six foot three, was the center. He had been a valuable reserve the year before. He did not have Olmstead's grace, but he could run, he worked tirelessly on defense and rebounding, and he gave the team balanced scoring with an average of almost ten points a game. Dick Krog, termed "indispensible" by a reporter, returned at guard, joined by junior Bob Williams, a burly six feet two and an emerging star. Sixth man was another junior, Don Christensen, who, at six feet, was a strong rebounder who could play any position.

After the loss to Wilson, Marion found its footing and went undefeated through the rest of its regular season of fifteen games. Unlike the previous year's team, it did not dominate all its foes. The team narrowly escaped Monticello, 37–35, as Marion stalled successfully for five minutes. It slipped by Independence, 37–33, in the Mustangs' cracker-box gym, and beat McKinley of Cedar Rapids, 34–28, at the Coe field house. It took a furious rally in the last 3:30 for the Indians to beat Manchester, 43–41, cinching a tie for the conference title.

The Indians then faced Monticello in the last game of the regular season. Monticello had lost only to Marion that year, so the Indians needed a win to take sole possession of the crown. Marion built a commanding lead in the early going, but Monticello refused to quit and pulled within two points with a minute to play. "Then came the real turning point of the game," Kovarik wrote. "A double foul was called on Marion's Dick Krog and Monti's John Schneiter. After John missed his free one, Dick calmly dropped his to give Marion a three-point edge, which it eventually expanded to seven, mainly on free throws in the last thirty seconds." Marion made seventeen of nineteen free throws, while Monticello connected on only fourteen of thirty-one. The final score was 51–44.

The Indians finished the regular season at 18–1, undefeated in the conference, and delivered Hipple his third straight WaMaC basketball title. But the team was not as dominant as the one that preceded it, and fans' tournament hopes were not as high.

In the state tournament's opening game, Marion throttled Coggon, 64–40. In the next game, the Indians were nearly bounced by Springville on that team's home court. Marion had crushed the Orioles early in the season, but was taken by surprise in what turned out to be a sizzler. Springville led at the half by two points as Marion consistently missed easy lay-ups. But the Indians had gained fame for their third-quarter bursts, and they did it again, outscoring Springville by ten points and taking a 32–24 lead into the fourth quarter. Springville fought back, "and nearly pulled the game out in the final three minutes," Kovarik wrote. Then the Orioles missed four out of five free throws and faded as Marion salvaged a 40–36 victory.

This year, tournament officials wisely seeded Marion and Immaculate Conception in separate sectional tournaments, but the two teams were on a collision course in the first game of the district tournament in the Coe field house. The game sold out more than a week before it was held.

The contest, like each of its predecessors, was a defensive battle with tense players performing before a screaming crowd. The noise was so great that the referees couldn't hear the buzzer at the scorer's table signaling that Marion wanted to send in substitute Jim Bailey. "Two times the timer sounded the buzzer after a ball had gone out of bounds, but each time the noise was so terrific that the officials could not hear it," Kovarik reported. On the third attempt, after a Marion foul, the referee heard the buzzer and waved the kid in.

Holding a slight lead with three minutes to play, Marion went into its famous stall. This time it didn't work. I. C. forced several turnovers, but couldn't convert. In the end, the Greyhounds outshot Marion from the floor, twelve field goals to ten, but faltered at the free-throw line, making twelve of twenty-four chances, compared to Marion's nineteen of twenty-four. "If only we had made more of our free throws," mourned I. C.'s center, Ron Peck. Marion won, just barely, 39–36.

It was Marion's third straight squeaker over the Cedar Rapids team. I. C. had a new coach that year. He was young Bob "Red" Jennings, who had been a fiery floor leader for the Greyhounds only a few years earlier. He had returned to his alma mater after graduating from Iowa. After the game, Jennings walked around the dressing room, staring into space. "I guess it just isn't supposed to be for us to ever beat Marion," he said. In the Marion locker room, the team was giddy with relief.

During the I. C. game, Bob Williams severely injured his back and was later hospitalized. A fractured vertebra was feared. He listened to the broadcast of Marion's next game, against Monticello, from his hospital bed. A few days later he returned to school, his back in a canvas cast. He wanted to suit up but was held out and eventually sidelined for the rest of the season. Junior Don Christensen stepped in "to perform brilliantly both on offense and defense," wrote Jack Ogden in the *Gazette*, as Marion pounded Monticello, 65–35. The Panthers were jittery, making only 20 percent of their field-goal attempts. Fouls hurt them, too. On his way to twenty-one points, Monticello's Schneiter had seven field goals nullified because fouls were called just before he launched the ball.

In his locker room feature after the game, the *Gazette*'s Kovarik offered this note on the eating habits of young athletes: "The Indians claimed a dinner of wieners Monday noon cut down their efficiency in the Marion–Immaculate Conception game … Friday night, after walloping Monticello, the Indians were equally certain that a dinner of beans was the big factor in the win."

The Indians opened substate play against Washington at the University of Iowa field house, and ran away with the game, 70–46. "Fans Gasp at Double-Barreled Marion Blast," said the *Gazette* headline. Marion's seventy points tied the second-highest total in any substate game and could have eclipsed the seventy-eight scored in 1942 by Davenport had Hipple not flooded the game with reserves. King made twenty-three points and Gable twenty-one. The two "gamboled about the huge Iowa floor as unpredictable as spring lambs," said Gus Schrader in the *Gazette*. "They terrorized Washington with their half-pressing defense, ball-hawking, and ever-eager fast break."

Next, in the substate final, Albia, an energetic, fast-breaking team, shocked the Indians with a full-court press and broke out to a 9–0 lead. Marion responded with its own press and fought back to 9–9. The score was

26–24 in Marion's favor at the half. Although the battle raged on, Marion maintained control, extended its lead slightly, and won, 45–41. The press cost Albia dearly as five of its players fouled out trying to keep up with the Indians. Marion could have put the game safely away had its free-throw shooting been better. The Indians made only seventeen of thirty-five tries.

The victory put Marion in the Sweet Sixteen for the first time in history. This hardscrabble team had captured three of its six tournament wins by a total of only eleven points. Each easy win was followed by a nail biter. Here was Marion, one of the shortest teams in the finals with only one starter over six feet. It was almost beyond belief. Congratulatory telegrams and letters poured into Hipple's office from all over eastern Iowa, even from WaMaC foes such as Monticello, and from West Branch fans, including the butchers at Albin and Sons meat market, who remembered Hipple's years there as coach and Barrie Gable's as a promising grade school athlete.

At Marion and other Sweet Sixteen schools, pep rallies were held before every game. Mary Ann Ross, who wrote the "School Daze" column in the *Sentinel*, viewed such goings on wryly:

> The gym at the school was decorated last week with some colorful signs naming the teams Marion had already defeated in tournament play … Friday Mr. McLeod led us in his favorite yell, "INDIANS." The pep band was supposed to play at Friday's assembly, but when the meeting started, there were only three members present. It seems that Sue Cary (trumpet), Lyle Fisher (trombone), and Marge Lala (baritone) were all at a band clinic.

Mary Ann Ross kept her perspective while many about her were losing theirs over the Indians. She wrote:

> I don't know whether this year's team was the first team to enter the state tournament or not. Well, anyway, we reached the same point that last year's team did. I was awfully glad of this myself, because several of last year's seniors made remarks to the effect that we'd have a good team this year, but we just wouldn't have quite enough to put us in the same category as the last. However, they will be forced to admit they were wrong about us.

Mary Ann Ross aside, it was no small matter to reach the final sixteen. There were more than nine hundred Iowa high school basketball teams, classed in three categories according to school size. Nearly seven hundred of the teams were in class B—those with the fewest students. More than two hundred mid-sized schools, including Marion, were in Class A. The forty largest schools were in Class AA. In the sectional, district, and substate tournaments, schools played within their class, but those that reached the Sweet Sixteen were matched against one another according to an alphabetical system to produce a single state champion.

Marion's first opponent in the state finals was Class AA Loras Academy of Dubuque, a boys' school with 539 students. Loras came into the game with a 14–5 record. It had lost twice to I. C., but was said to have vastly improved.

It was "a whale of a ball game," wrote Gus Schrader in the *Gazette*—for most of the first half. Then, "lightning struck" as Marion scored eleven points in the last 1:46 of the first half and went into the locker room ahead, 30–19. Marion pulled relentlessly away and led by as many as twenty points until Hipple began sending in reserves. The final score was 53–39. The team had dazzled the tourney crowd of more than fifteen thousand spectators. "I've never seen such unselfish play," said Bob Schultz, a former Davenport All-Stater who would coach at Iowa and Coe. "They love to pass off and they aren't worried about who gets the points. This King and Gable combination is really smooth."

Marion had reached the rarified heights of the state tournament quarterfinals. Only eight teams remained. Marion fans could focus on nothing else. The Chamber of Commerce arranged a city-wide closing of businesses so anyone who had tickets to Marion's next game, which was to be played in the afternoon, could attend. The chamber handled the distribution of the tickets allotted to Marion, yet some fans were unable to get seats. The Iowa field house had an official capacity of more than fifteen thousand spectators, but more than sixteen thousand people jammed the arena, setting a new attendance record.

If the easy game/hard game pattern persisted, the Indians could expect this one to be really tough. The foe was Ankeny, an undefeated team led by "Cosmic" Ray Fontana, the youngest of three brothers who had powered Ankeny to three straight appearances in the state finals. Fontana was a six-foot-four center with a feathery touch. In the opening round against Melrose, he set a new scoring record of thirty-six points—and he did it in three quarters as Ankeny won, 56–45.

Ankeny, it turned out, was not a one-man team. Marion's swarming defense held Fontana to fifteen points as he made only five of twenty-four shots, but other players broke through to score. Ankeny threw a tough defense against Marion, stationing guard Barney Alleman far down court whenever Marion got the ball. His teammates also rushed back on defense quickly, hobbling Marion's fast break. The game was rough. Gable suffered an ankle injury in the first quarter and King hurt his hip. Gable had his ankle taped at halftime and would not admit how much it hurt, "for fear Coach Hipple would take me out of the game," he said.

Both Gable and King fouled out, as did Krog, who committed his fifth foul as the final buzzer rang. Ankeny had a 31–19 lead after three quarters, and controlled the fourth quarter despite a twenty-one-point surge by the Indians. Ankeny's defense was tough and the Indians were ice cold, making only fifteen of eighty shots for a .188 average. Ankeny wasn't much better, shooting .238. Each team made fifteen field goals. The difference was Ankeny's seventeen points on free throws to Marion's ten. Ankeny won, 47–40. Gable, despite his injury, led Marion scorers with fifteen points.

Trying to generate some firepower, Hipple sent in sophomore Hugh Leffingwell, who did not hesitate to launch the ball. He took five long shots and made four of them, "and was nearly the spark the Indians needed to ignite their attack," wrote Ogden. "Hugh might be a handy man to have around when the present seniors are missing next fall."

The team was gracious in defeat, Ogden wrote. "It was the coldest game we had this year," Hipple said. "It was just one of those games. It was hard to see the boys lose out when you know they can at least play better ball than they were doing." Ankeny, said Hipple, was not the best team the Indians had faced this year. "For clever ability, I think Immaculate Conception of Cedar Rapids was the best." Gable's ankle injury was so bad that he would not have been able to play in the next game had Marion won. Ankeny went on to the finals, where it lost to powerful Davenport, 67–28.

Gable was elected to the IDPA All-State third team. The senior trio of Gable, King, and Krog had enjoyed extraordinary careers. As sophomores, their team was undefeated in eighteen games. As varsity starters, their teams went 48–3. Over those three years, in compiling a record of 66–3, they were undefeated in conference play and lost only one regular season game.

—

Meanwhile, the town of Marion was experiencing the growth and prosperity that the *Sentinel* had predicted during the war years. In 1948, the population rose to 5,725, up from 4,714 in 1940. In a single year, from 1948 to 1949, high school enrollment rose 10 percent, from 314 to 344. A two-bedroom home with no basement could be built for $6,500, and excavation sites pocked many neighborhoods.

Over at the post office, Virgil Mozena surprised his fellow workers by going out and buying a car. He got tired of riding buses, Virgil said. He chose a Studebaker because it was the only model he could get without waiting sixty days. He and his brother drove four thousand miles all over the state as Virgil learned how to operate the machine. He got his license right after that and then went back to work.

Chapter 18
The Gym

The handwritten note read:

12/2/49
Mr. Hipple:

The sixth grade teachers say that their boys are late on Friday mornings getting to their classes because they are in the gym. Will you see that they are out of the gym in time to get to their rooms by 9:00 o'clock?

C. B. V. [C. B. Vernon, superintendent]

On dark December mornings, the vacant gym was cold. It smelled of dust, sweeping compound, and dried sweat. But at 6:00 AM, the lights went on and a trickle of boys ran in, followed by a swarm. Their noise and energy awakened the day. The gym would not be still again until long after dark.

The gym was a basketball court, nothing more, about three-fourths the size of a standard court today. There were four baskets in the gym, two with metal backboards on the main court and two with wooden backboards against the north walls. The bleachers folded up to create a small playing space at the side baskets. A heavy climbing rope hung from the ceiling near one of the side baskets. During the day it was usually drawn up out of the way by a smaller rope on a pulley. When basketball practice started, the players had to climb the big rope twice before touching a basketball.

Jumping ropes were draped on a wooden rack on the east wall of the gym. No sporting goods company issued these ropes. They were common heavy ropes fit for farm work. There were about twenty of them, hacked into different lengths. Tape was wrapped around the ends to make handles. Basketball players had to make three hundred jumps before each practice. Nearby was a wooden rack on wheels that held about twelve basketballs, some of them lopsided. That was the extent of the equipment in the gym: baskets, balls, and ropes; no tumbling mats, no fitness equipment, no golf clubs.

The south side of the gym held another set of bleachers that worked its way up to a platform. Behind the bleachers was the girls' gym, which was another basketball court. A sliding wall separated the boys' gym from the girls' gym, and the wall was almost always in place. The boys' and girls' gyms were separate domains.

The school's teams played their home games in the boys' gym on Tuesday and Friday nights. There were at least sixty high school boys out for basketball and an equal number from junior high and sixth grade. The younger boys practiced at dawn. The freshman–sophomore and varsity teams practiced after school. The junior varsity and freshman squads practiced after supper. No one was cut. If a boy wanted to be on a team, he could be.

After the morning practices, and even earlier when basketball wasn't in season, boys of all ages were given free run of the place until classes started. Custodian Fred Lang opened the gym at 6:00 AM. Hipple often showed up. He gathered groups of fourth or fifth graders and showed them how to hold a ball and how to pass and shoot it. Sometimes he led a little cluster of boys across the playground to the audio-visual room in the Lincoln building. He showed them home movies he had made of high school players, pointing out the smooth motion of their shooting form. The movies showed the stars outside, on rocky ground, shooting at a backboard behind the gym, because the 8mm camera needed daylight to capture images.

On Saturdays the gym was open all day, with specific times set aside for certain age groups. It was thronged. One season, the supervising coaches estimated that an average of 232 boys played there each Saturday. On Sundays, the gym was ostensibly closed, but sometimes Coach Hipple slipped the keys to a trusted high school player or two who wanted to work harder.

On school mornings, after the last kid left the gym and hurried off to class, physical education sessions began for students of all ages, ranging from as low as fourth grade through high school. When lunch hour came, hundreds of students ate what was called "hot lunch" on tables set up on the gym floor. During the 1950s, a student could buy thirty lunches for $6.00. Some students worked for their lunches by setting up and taking down tables or helping to serve the meal of the day.

After lunch, tables were cleared and the basketballs came out again for open play. The afternoon brought more physical education classes, followed by basketball practice for the freshman–sophomore and varsity teams, and followed in turn by practice for the reserve squads.

The next dawn it all began again. Each morning boys waited at the back door. When they were admitted, they descended a flight of gray concrete steps to the basement, turned right, and passed the freshman–sophomore locker room, always dank and reeking from mold and sweat. Then they turned left and sprinted up a half-flight of steps to the gym. The early birds wanted to get the best balls.

Coach Hipple, who often opened the gym in the morning, once told a colleague that no matter how early he got there, there was always at least one boy waiting to get in.

—

During school hours, most athletes went to the gym through a door leading to a small alcove. They chose this route because Hipple posted his messages and plans on a bulletin board just inside the alcove. A flight of steps from the alcove led to Hipple's tiny office, with its small desk covered in a jumble of papers, broken equipment, and coaching books. Beyond Hipple's office was the varsity locker room. Hipple wrote his messages neatly by hand on white paper with blue lines. "The following boys will dress for the Anamosa game. The bus leaves at 5:30 PM." Or, "The following boys will suit up for the Homecoming Game vs. Tipton." Each boy's name was written in blue ink, respectfully, in columns. There was a fresh sheet for each game, all the names written anew. The sheet was always signed, "Coach."

—

It was forbidden, absolutely, to step onto the court wearing street shoes. No one did it. It was unthinkable. This was a Hipple rule. If boys were not wearing sneakers, they had to slip off their street shoes and shoot baskets in stocking feet. If anyone were ignorant or brazen enough to try to break the rule, five other students enforced it. There was no chance a boy could get on that court in street shoes—except during hot lunch, when hundreds of kids did exactly that, lining up to get their food tray and taking their place at tables set up across most of the court. Genny Tanner (Larry's wife), who grew up in Ames and moved to Marion as a young teacher, was stunned by the abuse the gym floor took, especially in light of how successful the teams were and how important basketball was to the school.

Genny Tanner taught fourth grade. Sometimes she brought her class to the gym, where Coach Hipple showed them how to pass a basketball. The kids, especially the boys, wanted to climb the big rope to the ceiling, perhaps thirty feet high. Tanner was reluctant to permit this, fearing they might fall, but Hipple said to let them try. If they can get up it, he said, they can get back down. And so they could. The girls were better climbers than the boys; Barb Tefer made it to the ceiling three times. After each climb, the girls wanted to go again, but no boys did. Hipple also advised Tanner that making fourth graders run laps was not effective discipline. Kids that age like to run, he said. If you want to discipline them, make them sit still and be quiet.

—

The Marion basketball court was for many years the largest in the WaMaC Conference, and was often selected as the site for sectional competition, the first round of the state tournaments. For all the wear and tear it received, the gym floor had no soft spots; the balls bounced true everywhere. Each year during the summer it was covered with a hard-finish sealant and then buffed to a new gloss. At its largest, the gym could hold up to fifteen hundred spectators packed tightly together and crowded into every available spot for standing room. A few fans were allowed to stand behind the out-of-bounds line behind the baskets, but not directly under them.

The backboards were made of metal, painted white. Glass backboards were not in vogue for high schools. There was no need for them; two feet beyond the out-of-bounds lines at both ends of the court was a brick wall. Dirty canvas-covered pads similar to wrestling mats were hung along the wall from hooks. Marion players finishing off a fast break knew they would crash into the pads as they came down from their lay-ups. The secret was to hit the pad with their arms, shoulder, or back, keeping their heads from banging one of the hooks, or, worse, hitting the brick wall just above the mat. Few of them could jump high and far enough to hit the brick, but they had seen others come close.

—

Hipple's physical education classes could be grueling. The man believed in conditioning for everyone. Just as he pushed his athletes to explore their limits, so did he push every boy in his P. E. classes. Hipple had studied graduate level physical education practice and theory at the University of Iowa, so the exercises he imposed may have been sanctioned by experts. But in later times, some came to be considered dangerous.

A class often began with push-ups, an exercise Hipple favored. He stood on the platform overlooking the basketball court and commanded his class to do ten, then ten more, then five, then one more, and still another, and another, until every boy lay face down in a puddle of his own sweat. He knew which boys were faking it, and he walked among the sprawled bodies, challenging the malingerers to rise up again, be a man, and finish their workouts. "You're only cheating yourself," he told them.

He had the boys turn on their backs, lift their legs up and straight out, just six inches from the floor, and hold them there until the pain in their stomachs felt like fire, their legs trembled, and their feet dropped to the floor. Then up again, and hold it, hold it.

The real agony came next. Hipple lined the boys up in groups of four at one end of the gym for relay races. Running was only a warm-up. Next were duck walks. Crouched with their rears nearly dragging on the floor, the boys had to waddle all the way to the other end of the gym and back again. It was great for the thighs, but the exercise would later be criticized for the damage it could do the knees.

Another exercise, the wheelbarrow, involved two people. One boy assumed a position similar to a push-up. A second boy grabbed his ankles and the first boy, the one in the prone position, had to walk on his hands the length of the court while the other boy carried his legs. The boy carrying the legs often went too fast, overrunning the poor slob laboring to stay up on his hands, and the two of them would collapse in a tangled heap. They were not interested in winning the race. They only wanted to finish it.

The worst exercise was the reverse wheelbarrow. Here the boy on the floor was upside down, trying to walk backward on his hands. He did not get far. His shoulders gave way, his stomach muscles collapsed, his feet flew over his head, and again the two boys ended in a pile. Hipple may have invented this form of torment, but he did not impose it in every class. Perhaps he was experimenting.

—

Boys didn't know what happened in the girls' gym. There were no varsity sports for girls, but there were physical education classes and intramural sports such as basketball and volleyball. Most of the girls who played these sports were inept and didn't play seriously. They dissolved in giggles, and the games disintegrated, which disgusted and infuriated the girls who were good athletes and took the contests seriously. These girls, the ones most interested in sports, often became cheerleaders. It was the closest they could get to being athletes, and they loved going to the games. In addition to being attractive and peppy, cheerleaders needed to understand the game, for their jobs included rallying the crowd with cheers for specific situations. In football, for example, there was a cheer called "First and Ten, Do It Again," and, to bolster the defense, "Hold That Line."

Cheerleaders practiced in their gym twice a week. They were taught how to spin properly, keeping their arms down at their sides to hold their skirts closed so their legs were not exposed. The movement ran counter to human physiology. Their arms should have been spread wide, their skirts flaring up, and their legs moving in dazzling patterns.

One Marion girls' physical education teacher told her charges that females should not engage in strenuous sports because doing so could result in a tipped uterus. No one knew what that was, but no one wanted one, either. On warm, sunny days, this teacher liked to lead her charges on a walk. When they got a few blocks from the school, she took off her blouse, exposed her shoulders to the sun, and worked on her tan as she and her students counted off a mile or so.

—

On Friday nights, after home football and basketball games, dances were often held in the gym. For big dances, such as homecoming or Sadie Hawkins Day, the gym was decorated with streamers and special lighting, and students were allowed to dance in their shoes. But most often the dances were held in an unadorned gym with the lights turned low. These dances, sponsored by school clubs or classes as fundraisers, were called "sock hops," because participants had to take off their shoes. A large, wood-encased record player was set up on a table in a corner of the gym. Somebody put on the 78- or 45-rpm disks and the dancing began. As the records played "Tennessee Waltz" and "Blueberry Hill," boys and girls who were going steady fell into a familiar embrace and began moving ever so slowly, taking tiny steps.

Only a few of the boys—the braver, more talented ones—danced with more than one girl. A cluster of shoeless boys occupied one end of the gym. Mostly underclassmen, they had no intention of walking over to the girls standing nearby and asking one of them to dance. The girls hated being wallflowers. Some spent most of the dance in the rest room. Some danced together. When Hipple was chaperone, he broke up the group of sullen boys, ordering them to go ask a girl to dance, thus sowing anxiety between both sexes.

There were a few fast dances—a bunny hop, an experiment with the limbo—but most of the dances were cheek-to-cheek and body-to-body, as intimate as two people can be while remaining upright, in motion, fully clothed, and managing not to kiss. Physical contact was otherwise frowned on. When a girl dared to sit on a boy's lap, chaperones moved immediately to unseat her.

The dancers almost all used the same step, a foxtrot taught to them in seventh grade by Miss Haffa. She lined up the boys on one side of the old gym in the Lincoln building and the girls on the other side, and then had them march around the room as she called out, "One, two, three, four … step-together-step, step-together-step." This elementary routine, drilled into them as preteens, was the only dance step many of the boys ever learned. After the youngsters practiced alone for a while, Miss Haffa ordered the boys and girls to pair up for real dancing. The most aggressive of both sexes darted across the room to snare a favored partner, while the rest mingled about, leaving the matter to fate, and, as often as not, ended up grimacing in the arms of a virtual stranger.

The dances in the gym ended at 11:00 PM with the playing of "Goodnight, Sweetheart" or "Goodnight, Irene." Athletes had to be home by midnight and so did just about everyone else. There might be time for a hamburger and a Coke at Bailey's Milk Bar. Some of the more adventurous might range out to Todd's on First Avenue or all the way to Nick's in Cedar Rapids. Boys and girls going steady often preferred to walk to the girl's home and then stand on the dark porch, kissing until it was time to stop. Then, after seeing the girl inside, the boy, if he were a good Hippleman, would turn, jump off the porch, and begin his run toward home.

Chapter 19
Shooting Star, 1950–1951

Sometimes players on opposing teams shook their heads and laughed as they watched him warm up before a basketball game. "*That's* the great Hugh Leffingwell?" they said. "He doesn't look like much."

At first glance, he didn't. In that time before weight training, good athletes tended to be raw-boned and lean, with hard, wiry muscles, like greyhounds. In contrast, Hugh as a high school player looked more like a St. Bernard, bulky and undefined at six feet three and just under two hundred pounds. He had big feet and hands, and it was immediately apparent that he wasn't fast. He didn't look very smart, either. He wore glasses with clear plastic rims that were often bent out of shape and sat crookedly on his nose. His face often bore a distant expression. His mouth hung slightly open. His light blond hair was shaved on the sides and cut very short on top, so he looked like an Army recruit about halfway through basic training. There was no hint of vanity or pride in his appearance, and if people wanted to be cruel, they might even say he looked a little goofy.

A few of his opponents may have called him that, or worse. They did their best to get on him. "Four eyes," they called him, and riffed up insults based on his name: *Huge*, or *Hugo*, or worse. When the game started, they banged him hard to see if he would flinch or tire out.

It's unlikely that Hugh Leffingwell said much of anything in return. Instead, he just went out and showed them he was probably the smartest, toughest, most gifted basketball player they ever saw.

—

Former teammates and neighbors vividly remembered how hard Hugh Leffingwell worked at his game and how deeply he loved sports. The quotation under his senior photo in the yearbook reads, "Everyone has a constant longing; his is for sports."

The Leffingwells, Hugh and his parents, Wally and Olive (often called Pat), lived in a former elementary school converted into several apartments. Because it had held a school, their lot had space for a playground, and it became a magnet for neighborhood kids. On the lot, Wally built the best home basketball court in town. Most baskets were attached to garages, but this one was freestanding. As Ron Franklin, who lived nearby, recalled, Wally sank a sturdy steel pole in the ground and mounted on it an oversized wooden backboard about four feet high by six feet wide. He treated the area in front of the basket with finely crushed black cinders, which helped keep the ground smooth, hard, and dry, even after a rain. The playing surface was as wide as many gyms, and looked like black concrete. Wally strung up lights so Hugh could continue practicing after nightfall. It was said that Wally had to replace the nets often, because Hugh shredded them with his shooting.

There was room in the yard for games of touch football and kickball, but the dominant feature was the basketball court, worn smooth and broad in all seasons. Hugh Leffingwell practiced day and night, rehearsing the moves and polishing the strokes that gave him what many said was the purest, sweetest touch and shooting form they ever saw. Hugh taught himself to dribble and shoot with either hand, skills that few high school players possessed.

The most familiar sight on Fourth Avenue and Eighth Street was Hughie, out on that court, all alone, practicing ceaselessly. Ray Fuller was a grade-school kid who lived across the street. The last sounds he heard before falling asleep at night were the bang and rattle of Hughie's basketball on the backboard. The same sounds woke him in the morning.

On Saturdays, when the high school gym was open to all the boys in town, the scene was disorderly and noisy, crowded with boys whose skills fell short of Hugh's by several orders of magnitude. Yet he often showed up anyway, drawn by the sheer joy of a gym full of shouting, panting youngsters. Some of them, who never suited up for a varsity game, always remembered what it was like to try to guard Hugh Leffingwell.

On Sundays the gym was officially closed, but Hipple often slipped a key to Leffingwell and his close friend and teammate, Russ Seeks, and the two worked out together, with the pounding of the ball and their own gasps echoing in the nearly empty gym. Sometimes Hipple dropped by, unannounced, to see that everything was as it should be.

—

Hugh was a private person, somewhat shy and withdrawn, Russ Seeks said. The two lived near each other and grew up as friends and teammates through grade school. "We were very close friends," Seeks said, "I can't stress it enough. I don't think he had very many other friends.

"He was sports crazy and I was sports crazy," Seeks said. "But I can't remember him enjoying himself, having fun. He never dated girls, except maybe for big dances like a prom or the Big Ten Ball."

Another childhood friend, Don Roby, a year older than Hugh, had a slightly different take. He said Leffingwell was mischievous in grade school. "He was in trouble all the time. I remember when Miss Harlan called him out in the hall to spank him with a paddle. I could hear him yelling."

By the time he reached high school, Hugh was well mannered and a good student, wrote one of his teachers, Margaret Doty Robson. She taught only one year at Marion, when Hugh was a junior, and did not at the time "realize he was one of Marion's greatest athletes." Leffingwell was an honor roll student in each of his four high school years, yet rarely took books home at night.

Seeks often slept over at Hugh's house, but always felt uncomfortable around his parents. Hugh was an only child. "His parents were tough on him," Seeks said. "His dad pushed him hard to be good in sports. Really pushed him. Told him not to take second place from anyone." Wally was a large man, taller even than his son, standing at least six feet five. He had been a star athlete in high school. (An article in the *Cedar Rapids Gazette* said he had been an All-State basketball player in Illinois.)

"I remember Wally at games, up in the stands, yelling at Hugh to do this or that," Seeks said. "Maybe it was good for Hugh. My dad was interested, but only saw about half our games."

Jim Lang, a year behind Hugh, remembered Wally's involvement before Hugh's senior year in football. Wally had learned that Hugh was slated to play quarterback that year. Lang was in line to play center. The team the previous year "had been plagued by fumbles during the center snap," Lang wrote.

"Wally was not going to put up with that with Hugh involved. I don't know whether he had Les Hipple's blessing or whether he just did it, but Wally had Hugh and me down at the park on most Sunday summer afternoons, practicing the center snap. It did pay off—I don't believe we ever fumbled." It was unusual that Wally knew Hugh would be quarterback. Hugh had played end the year before. Hipple often juggled his players' positions from year to year, but he was normally closemouthed about his intentions.

Don Roby had a different take on Wally, describing him as "more of a supporter" than a driver. "Hughie drove himself," Roby said. "He wanted to be perfect." Hugh would willingly run quarter miles just for conditioning, Roby said. "Big, heavy-footed guy. Just wanted to get stronger and faster. Who do you know would run 440s because they wanted to?"

—

In 1950, Hugh's junior year, he started at end on the football team. Some key players were injured, and Bob Williams, who starred as a halfback the year before, had moved to Anamosa (after, some say, a falling out with Hipple). Early in the season, Marion trounced the Anamosa team led by Williams, 32–7, in what Larry Tanner called "a performance that rivaled anything ever to appear on a Marion gridiron under the tutelage of Hipple."

Marion was in the title hunt all season, but lost its final two games, to Independence, 13–6, and Tipton, 19–0, finishing in fourth place with an overall record of 4–3–1. Meanwhile, Anamosa went undefeated the rest of the way and won the WaMaC crown, so perhaps the rebellious Williams had the last laugh. The Indians' Bill Hintz, a ferocious 200-pound lineman, had injured his knee in the Anamosa game and was out for the season, a loss that Tanner said could have cost the Indians the title.

—

Eleven days after the football loss to Tipton, Marion played its first basketball game. The Indians had only three lettermen, including Leffingwell, who had seen limited duty as a sophomore, returning from what Tanner called "probably the greatest basketball team in the history of Marion High School." The starting lineup included three juniors—Leffingwell and Seeks at forward, Jim Hayes at guard—who joined seniors Don Roby (guard) and Don Christensen (center). Christensen was only six feet tall and was more naturally a guard, but he was agile and a great jumper, so he was assigned to spend the season battling much bigger men.

Tanner had his doubts about this team matching the records of past squads. The early games were rugged affairs, marked by "many fouls that would have meant yardage on the gridiron." But by the Christmas break Marion had won eight straight, and people were beginning to talk about another run to state. "Let's just finish the season first," Tanner wrote.

By the end of January the Indians were still undefeated and 6–0 in the conference, with Tipton on their heels at 5–1. Leffingwell was scoring at a tremendous rate, averaging more than twenty points a game. With even more tournament talk in the air, Tait Cummins wrote in his *Sentinel* column that Marion and Sioux City might be getting all the attention among the A schools, but people shouldn't overlook Grinnell. It was an A school, but played several AA teams, and was winning steadily against the bigger schools.

Meanwhile, WaMaC opponents couldn't shut down Hugh Leffingwell. Leo Cabalka, coach of the strong Monticello team, told the *Cedar Rapids Gazette,* "We used everything on Leffingwell, but nothing stopped him. We used a man-for-man, jammed three men around him in the pivot, tried a zone and man-for-man, a zone combination, and everything else."

With opponents ganging up on Hugh, Hipple told his two seniors, Roby and Christensen, to protect him with hard checks. But Marion's offensive strategy wasn't based on getting the ball to Leffingwell. That wasn't Hipple's way. "I can't remember our ever running plays specifically to get the ball to Hugh," said Seeks. "We just ran our regular plays." Leffingwell could score with opponents hanging on his arms. He had a keen instinct for the path of the ball, and he was a surprisingly quick and powerful rebounder. Many of his points came from putting back shots his teammates missed.

Leffingwell had a full arsenal of shots he could make with either hand, including hook shots, which Hipple did not permit. If a player took a hook shot during a game, Hipple yanked him, so Hugh obeyed the rules. Hugh didn't like it, though. He often walked home from practice with teammate Bob Christensen, who remembered Leffingwell complaining about the restriction. "I can make hook shots as well as any other shot," he would say, "so why won't Coach let me use them?" When he tried it in practice, Hipple stopped the scrimmage and sometimes sent Hugh to the showers. "Go home, Leffingwell," he would say. "Just go home."

In early February, Marion and Tipton met for the first time that season, with the Indians squeaking by, 46–41. Tipton used a full-court press and played ball control in an attempt to slow the Indians' scoring. It didn't work. Leffingwell made thirty-one of his team's forty-six points, including two free throws that clinched the victory. In its next game, Marion barely escaped Vinton, winning 58–55 in overtime. "We had many hard-fought games," Seeks said.

After clinching a tie for the WaMaC title with an easy win over Manchester, Marion faced Monticello on the Black Panthers' home court. A victory would give the Indians sole possession of the championship. For this game, Coach Cabalka listened to fans who urged a drastic defensive plan. They told him to have his boys foul Hugh every time he took a shot. "He won't make many points that way," the fans said.

Cabalka's scheme backfired, setting up one of Leffingwell's greatest feats. Fouled repeatedly, he took seventeen free throws—and made all seventeen. Moreover, he added twelve field goals for a new WaMaC scoring record of forty-one points. The Indians romped, 72–53. Leffingwell had now made eighteen straight free throws, including one from the previous game.

After the Monticello game, Larry Tanner went into the dressing room to see how the Indians were celebrating their conference championship. He expected a fairly riotous scene because the freshman–sophomore team also beat Monticello to clinch a title. Instead, he found "amazing quietness and calmness. Even the sophomores weren't whooping it up," Tanner reported. "They sat around in small groups rehashing the game, or talking about girls, but mainly just taking it easy." The varsity players "were laughing a little, but no whooping or hollering."

In the final regular season game, Tipton came to town, shot better than 50 percent from the field and won, 50–46, depriving Marion of an undefeated season. The loss was the Indians' first to a WaMaC foe in three years and the first at home in four years.

Against Tipton, Leffingwell got four free throws and made them all, extending his streak to twenty-two. The *Gazette* said he now held the "unofficial" state record for consecutive free throws. No official records were kept, but apparently research by the newspaper discovered that the previous best was twenty-one in a row. So, as Marion prepared for what was expected to be a relatively easy state sectional tournament opener against Coggon in the Alburnett gym, all the talk was about Hugh Leffingwell's free throw string and whether he could keep it alive. The suspense ended fairly quickly. Hugh made his first two, and then missed, ending the string at twenty-four. Fans were so focused on his free throws that few of them realized the young scoring wonder was pulling off another amazing feat.

Perhaps some people keeping score realized it. The kid hadn't missed a field goal. He took layups, jump shots, set shots. They all went in.

He was doing this while under constant pressure from a young Coggon player who was dogging Hugh's every step and waving his hands in his face. The Coggon player was Norm Rathje, the younger brother of a former Marion football star, Dave, whose family had moved to Coggon that year.

Rathje was only a freshman and several inches shorter than Leffingwell. But he was chosen for this assignment because he was fearless and tireless. Whatever he lacked in experience and height, he made up for in energy.

Coach Riddle of Coggan had given Rathje these instructions: "Go wherever Hugh goes and keep your hands in his face all the time." And this Rathje was trying to do—match Leffingwell step for step and wave his hands in front of his eyes, whether he had the ball or not. This tactic was known as "face guarding," and it was illegal. Rathje didn't know that, and to this day he doesn't think his coach knew it either. Instead, it was to be the defense that would finally put a clamp on Leffingwell. "We worked religiously in practice that week on face guarding," Rathje wrote. "In practice I could face guard anyone. I thought I was ready to do what no one else had done against Hugh. Shut him down!"

The tactic failed miserably. Not only was Leffingwell scoring at will, Rathje kept drawing technical fouls. He fouled out of the game before the first half ended, and only then did an official tell him what he had done wrong. Leffingwell continued shooting, and when he was taken out of the game the official scorecard showed that he had shot a perfect 1.000 from the field, taking fourteen shots and making every one of them. It had to be a record of some sort, but there was no mention of that in the newspapers. (Later, Leffingwell's short biography in the University of Iowa media guide said that his performance that day set a national record and that his 17-for-17 free-throw shooting against Monticello was a state record.)

After the game Rathje heard his coach tell a visitor, "I knew the kid didn't have a chance, but I thought it would be good experience for him." Wrote Rathje, "Hughie didn't take it easy on me. I always respected him for that."

(Several Marion people said in interviews that in one game or another, Hugh made every field goal *and* every free throw he took. They insist it is so and that they saw it. However, I could find no evidence. It appears that Hugh's feats in two separate games held close together have merged in their memories.)

Marion encountered a far more stringent defense in its next game against tournament archrival Immaculate Conception of Cedar Rapids. They met in the opening round of the district tournament at the university field house in Iowa City. Both teams entered the contest with only one defeat. The defensive play was so fierce that the score at halftime was 14–13, with Marion in the lead.

John "Pete" Kassler, a Marion player, remembered what happened when the two teams assembled at halftime in separate areas of the large university locker room. Hipple talked quietly to his team, but was suddenly interrupted by a noisy outburst from across the room. It was Coach Red Jennings, "screaming and yelling at his players," Kassler wrote. Hipple stopped talking and made a small gesture in the direction of the noise. Marion players had never heard anything like it. "I think we won the game at that point," Kassler said.

In the second half, Marion broke away to an eight-point lead, but later fell behind at 37–36. It was tied at 39-all with 1:30 remaining when Seeks scored. I. C. couldn't answer, and when the Indians got the ball they went into a stall, which led to a basket by Leffingwell with less than a minute remaining. I. C.'s Don Jennings made a thirty-foot shot with ten seconds left, but Marion had the game wrapped up. The final score was 43–41.

I. C.'s Sid Stemmler swarmed all over Leffingwell throughout the contest, holding him to seventeen points on seven-for-seventeen shooting. Marion won the game at the foul line, making eleven of twelve attempts, while I. C. could convert only five of ten. Marion had now beaten I. C. four straight times—by a total of only fourteen points. "What do we have to do to beat

Marion?" asked Coach Jennings. "Last year we got more field goals than they did and they won. Same thing this year. When will our turn come?"

Marion followed the I. C. victory with relatively easy wins over Monticello (64–51) and St. Columbkille of Dubuque (74–51) to advance to the substate finals. The St. Columbkille game started as if it might be close, with a strong defense proving effective against Leffingwell. But Seeks broke through and made six of his first seven shots, forcing the opposing team to adjust. Then Leffingwell went on a rampage, scoring thirty-one points.

One more victory would put the Indians in the Sweet Sixteen again. The opponent was Grinnell, which, like Marion, had lost only one game. The big worry for the Indians was Grinnell's huge junior center, Dick Ritter, who stood six feet five. He proved to be the difference as Marion trailed all the way and lost, 55–47. Ritter scored twenty-seven points to Leffingwell's twenty-five, but more importantly he dominated the backboards. Marion's six-foot Don Christensen and his teammates, for all their agility, couldn't overcome Ritter's height advantage.

Some commentators thought Marion was the victim of bad schedule making by tournament officials. Had Marion been sent to Waterloo for the substate (wrote Tanner) or had Grinnell been sent to Des Moines (wrote Cummins), Marion would have made state. The WaMaC, Cummins had written earlier, was a very good conference. Five of its eight teams won their sectional championships and two of those who didn't were victims of another WaMaC team. Marion had impressed fans and the press with its discipline and heart, and the team deserved to go to state, Cummins wrote.

In the state tournament, Grinnell advanced to the semi-finals then fell to Keokuk, which had another fine, tall junior center, a kid named Bill Logan, who outplayed Ritter in a 51–38 victory. Keokuk then lost to Davenport, setting up the storybook final in which the largest school in the state, Davenport (with nineteen hundred students), played one of the smallest, Roland (with eighty-four). Roland's leader was a five-foot-six sophomore giant-killer named Gary Thompson, who would grow four more inches, lead his team to state for two more years, and go on to star at Iowa State. The game had its thrilling moments, but Davenport won, 50–40.

The Indians finished the season with a record of 23–2. Leffingwell scored 609 points for an average of 24.4 points a game and was named to the IDPA All-State second team.

—

That spring, Marion finished second in the WaMaC track meet, scoring eighty-nine points as a strong Tipton team set a new conference record with 102.5 points. In his six years at Marion, Hipple had delivered eight WaMaC championships—four in basketball, three in track, and one in football.

His reputation was growing. Wrote Tait Cummins, "Coaches … say the best-conditioned cage teams in this section of the state are Marion and Belle Plaine. It may be just happenstance, but both coaches—Hipple at Marion and Deaton at Belle Plaine—have by long odds the toughest set of rules, and they enforce them to the letter."

—

Sports lover that he was, Leffingwell joined the small corps of kids who raced down to the American Legion field several evenings a week after their summer jobs to play baseball under Hipple. Although Marion teams seldom won, Leffingwell excelled as a pitcher. It was not unusual for him to strike out seven or eight opponents in a five-inning game. In one seven-inning game he notched fifteen strikeouts as Marion defeated Central City, 4–3. Marion's fielding was always error-prone and its hitting was feeble. Late that season, Hipple released statistics showing that Leffingwell was leading the team in batting—with an average of .262.

Baseball was fun. Football and basketball were serious, and Leffingwell had a lot of work ahead of him.

Chapter 20
The Peak of Glory, 1951–1952

"We have the most explosive offense of any team in the WaMaC ... Yet after the kids shove over a couple of scores they seem to be content to relax .... We are the best team in the conference in football. Still, we are in second place ... one might believe the boys on the squad don't care whether they win or lose ... If, inside themselves, the lads really possess no feelings toward winning or losing, they should remove themselves from the team, making way for youngsters who wish to compete and win."

This outburst appeared under Larry Tanner's byline in the *Sentinel* late in the 1951 football season. Tanner typed the words, but the sentiments were surely Hipple's. Tanner warned that Hipple might be planning some major changes in the lineup.

The team had just come off two disappointing performances. The first was in a game with Tipton. Marion was leading 12–0 in the third quarter. Tipton then exploded for nineteen straight points before Marion responded with a seventy-nine-yard touchdown run by Russ Seeks, who then scored the extra point, running wide after a fake plunge by fullback Jim Hayes. Behind quarterback Wally Sheets, Tipton drove to Marion's three-yard line, but the defense held, and Tipton had to give up the ball with twenty-four seconds left on the clock. Marion tried a Statue of Liberty play, with Shorty Novotny, a junior rocket, racing the ball back to midfield, where he was tackled as time expired. The game ended in a 19–19 tie.

The following Friday, Marion committed three fumbles and lost to Vinton, 18–14. Anamosa, last year's champion, despite an early season loss to Marion, was again leading the conference. Marion, Tipton, and Vinton were tied for second place a half game behind. It was the tightest WaMaC race on record, Cummins wrote.

Hipple was furious. Losses did not bother him if the players worked hard. Considering the talent on the team, he believed only a failure in commitment could have produced the poor showings.

The Indians responded the following week with a 28–6 win over Independence, but still lost the ball twice on fumbles. They closed out the season with a 35–6 win over Manchester. During these weeks, other contenders clashed, and when the dust had cleared, Marion and Vinton were tied for the championship. It was Hipple's second football title at Marion.

Leffingwell played quarterback that year, and in at least two respects he was an unusual choice. Hipple typically chose quarterbacks who were smart and good ball handlers, which Leffingwell certainly was, but Hipple also chose good runners whose nimble footwork was critical for option plays. Marion quarterbacks rarely passed. Some people felt Hugh was wrong for this offense.

Leffingwell's second drawback was even more serious, but it was one he overcame spectacularly. The boy needed glasses to see well, and in this time before face masks and contact lenses, he had to play without them. His receivers must have been no more than a blur of color, but he threw and completed more passes than almost any Marion quarterback before him. In the final game against Manchester, in subfreezing temperatures, he completed ten of fourteen passes, his highest totals of the season.

Leffingwell demonstrated he had the skills to play quarterback, but the real star of the football team was his friend, Russ Seeks, the team captain, whose 700 yards rushing accounted for about 40 percent of the team's total. Seeks scored ten touchdowns and ten extra points (kicking and running). "Russ can run, pass, block, tackle, is good on pass defense, kicks extra points, and could probably punt if called upon," said Tanner. "He's the best backfield man we've seen this year."

—

Five games into the basketball season, Marion was undefeated but had not been impressive, wrote Tanner. The team "was ragged and baffled" in a narrow 40–37 victory over Anamosa and had only looked good for six minutes in blasting Wilson of Cedar Rapids, 51–37, on the strength of a 25-point last quarter. But Leffingwell was on target again, scoring mightily and rarely missing a free throw. Just before the Christmas break, he made nine straight free throws against Manchester at home to run a new streak to twenty-six, beating his former string of twenty-four and setting a new state record (it had been twenty-five). When play resumed in January, he made two more before missing against Mt. Vernon. With this accomplishment, Leffingwell held two state records for free-throw shooting (his string of twenty-eight straight and his 17-for-17 against Monticello) and one national record in field-goal shooting for his 14-for-14 against Coggon.

The Indians had won ten straight when they traveled to Tipton and suffered a surprising 46–34 loss in which Leffingwell was held to only eight points. The Tigers were led by "Big John" Sissel, a rugged six-foot-three center who pushed the surprised Marion team all over the floor and scored twenty-three points. The next time the two teams met, Hipple started Bill Lundquist, who was a lanky six feet four, at guard to help center Bob Christensen deal with Sissel. It apparently worked, because Marion triumphed 60–44, with Leffingwell scoring thirty-two points to Sissel's twenty-two.

Thus evolved a six-man starting rotation that saw the Indians into the post-season. It had veterans Leffingwell and Seeks at forward, Christensen, a six-foot-three junior and Don's younger brother, at center, and Lundquist alternating with junior Jerry Peck and senior Jim Hayes at guard. Two tough juniors, Harry Oakley and Shorty Novotny, were on the bench to spell the regulars. It was a formidable lineup, and it carried Marion to its fifth straight WaMaC title.

Leffingwell routinely faced double and triple teams, but continued to score at a torrid pace. Games could be very rough. Against Vinton, the two teams committed forty-five fouls as Marion won handily, and Leffingwell scored thirty-two points, ten on free throws. In the regular season finale against Monticello, he scored forty-two points, his all-time high, including eighteen field goals (still a Marion record in 2008).

In their state-tournament run, the Indians simply crushed their first five opponents, winning every game by twenty points or more. This included a 62–37 thrashing of Immaculate Conception in which Marion shot 62 percent in the first half and 45 percent for the whole game. "Not only were the Indians uncanny at shooting, but they controlled the game from all aspects," reported the *Gazette*. "Their sharp, definite passing and strong rebounding could not be denied. This superiority unleashed many fast breaks."

Having reached the substate finals, the point at which they fell the previous year, Marion again faced its WaMaC nemesis, Tipton. Asked what he planned to do to stop John Sissel, Hipple just shrugged and said, "We haven't been able to stop him yet."

It was Marion's first pressure game of the tournament, and it turned out to be a defensive battle that thrilled 5,500 fans at the Iowa field house. The two teams made only ten points combined in the fourth quarter, which featured Marion's famous stall. The game was rough. Seeks was removed after taking an elbow that smashed his glasses against his eyebrow, opening a cut that streamed blood into his eyes. Sissel played most of the second half with four fouls. The final two points came on a basket by Leffingwell with one second left on the clock. Marion squeaked by, 43–38.

The media and fans had concocted a rivalry between Leffingwell and Sissel—suggesting the possibility of animosity—but both players praised one another after the game. In their three meetings, Sissel had outscored Leffingwell sixty-two to fifty-eight, and some Tipton fans thought he was the superior player. Tipton was the best team the Indians faced all year, Hipple said. The Tipton coach said the same about Marion.

For the second time in three years, Marion was in the Sweet Sixteen, and again the town was thrilled. Stores closed early and flocks of residents caravanned to Iowa City. This year, those who didn't go to the games had their choice of two radio stations that broadcast Marion games. Bob Brooks was at the mike for KCRG, but now he was up against a new station called KPIG. The interloper had rounded up enough sponsors to cover games that year and would continue to do so for the next several years.

All over Marion, people listened to the Indians, especially when they played out of town. Kids put their hands on the radio as they tried to send energy and good luck across the wires. At the pool hall, a group of men clustered around their radio as Shine Domer, the manager, used sign language to "wig-wag" the action to some men who were deaf.

In the opening round of the state tournament, Marion returned to form, racing past Ogden, 72–42. The victory was so easy that some people started thinking about a Marion-Davenport final. While Leffingwell was still making a lot of points, other players were scoring, too, often on the end of blistering fast breaks. "I think this club is better balanced than the one we had at state two years ago," Hipple said. "Leffingwell has been a high scorer all season, but the other boys have been shooting more in the tournaments, and that helps."

Everything collapsed when Marion faced Keokuk and its star six-foot-six center, Bill Logan, in the quarterfinals. "Logan played one of his best games of the year as he led his mates to an early lead that they never relinquished," reported the *Gazette*. Marion narrowed Keokuk's lead to 31–27 early in the third quarter, but then Keokuk turned up the gas and won pulling away, 55–39. "Keokuk's Bob Williams … did the best job of the year guarding Marion's shooting sensation, Hugh Leffingwell, as the sharpshooter was held to fourteen points," the paper said. Leffingwell made only five of nineteen shots. Meanwhile, Logan, often triple-teamed, made ten of his twenty-seven attempts, scoring twenty-six points in all. "The boys weren't up to par today," said Hipple after the game.

Keokuk then beat Roland, 55–43, after which Keokuk's coach, Don Shupe, said Marion was better than Roland because of the team's height. As Keokuk prepared to face Davenport in the finals, Shupe experienced a mutiny. Three boys—the sixth, seventh, and eighth men—suddenly quit the team because they weren't getting enough playing time. The boys almost immediately were remorseful and asked to be taken back, but Shupe would not allow it. This rupture in team unity, to say nothing of the loss of key reserves, surely played a role in the championship game against Davenport, which Keokuk narrowly lost, 48–45. Logan was in foul trouble early and fouled out with eight minutes left and Keokuk ahead by a point. A few days later, the three boys appeared before the Keokuk student body to apologize for their "terrible mistake."

In the space of three years, two Marion teams had made it to the quarterfinals at state. Which team was better? Larry Tanner asked in a column, and then provided his answer "without consulting Hipple, who wouldn't give me a concrete answer anyway." He decided that the 1952 team had the edge, with better shooting ability, greater bench strength, and more height than the 1950 team led by Barrie Gable and Jack King. The 1950 players, Tanner said, were better ball handlers and "a shade better on defense." The clincher was the difference in height, which gave the 1952 edition better rebounding. In addition, Tanner thought the competition was tougher in 1952.

—

In track that year, Marion set a new record for total points (104 1/10) behind outstanding performances by Leffingwell and Seeks, who each won three events. Demonstrating both strength and coordination, Leffingwell won the shot put, the discus, and the football throw. Seeks won the 100-yard dash, the 120-yard high hurdles, and the 180-yard low hurdles. Thus the Marion Indians of 1952 accomplished what no other squad could do: win all three WaMaC titles—football, basketball, and track. The glory years had reached their highest point.

Hipple's popularity was at a peak. The Marion community believed in the Indians and the values they represented. Paul Moon, the great Davenport basketball coach, spoke at the sports banquet and praised the citizens for helping to enforce Hipple's rules. Decency and piety were seen as public virtues. The *Sentinel* ran a series of advertisements, supported by twenty-one "patriotic" merchants, urging parents to take their children to church so "they will not willingly commit a crime against society."

—

Marion lost a stalwart assistant coach as the school year came to a close. Frank McLeod resigned to teach and coach at Roosevelt High School in Cedar Rapids. He left behind an extraordinary record. His freshman–sophomore basketball team again went undefeated, giving McLeod a forty-game winning streak over three years. His teams won the conference championship in each of his five years as coach, compiling a record of 83–7. Three of his teams were undefeated. His junior varsity football teams were highly successful as well, but no record seems to exist. "My Marion years were the best in my career," McLeod said many years later.

McLeod's successor was Lynn Brown, who had had won nine letters at Wartburg College in football, basketball, and track, and had been an assistant and then head coach in his two years at Hansell, Iowa. Hipple played no part in the interview process. Brown heard about the opening on a radio broadcast by Tait Cummins and thought it would be a great learning experience to work with Hipple.

After applying for the job, Brown met Superintendent Vernon in Marion and was later interviewed by Wally Leffingwell, a member of the board of education, at a state track meet in Ames. They sat in the stands talking for several hours. "He and Dr. Vernon were very aware of the strictness of the rules and how tough Coach could be on athletes," Brown wrote. "Mr. Leffingwell stressed to me that part of my job would be to pat an athlete on the back and encourage him after Coach had gotten on him." Brown's plan was to spend a few years learning what he could at Marion and then move on to a head coaching job. Instead, he stayed for eight years and was invaluable to Hipple. "We liked Marion so much we didn't want to leave," Brown said.

"What will Lynn Brown find as he joins the Marion coaching staff?" wrote Tanner.

> He will see a group of youngsters who are as eager to compete on the sports field as anyone in Iowa and perhaps in the United States. He won't have to worry about instilling a fighting spirit in most of the lads …
>
> He will work with boys who are used to winning and expect to win. In fact, some of them take winning for granted. The word defeat is never mentioned on an Indian practice field or floor, and could almost be termed a profanity. He will see lads who put team spirit ahead of personal desire … These lads realize, too, that only through the success of their teams do they have the ghost of a chance to gain recognition.
>
> He will work with one of the most respected coaches in the state. A man who is a stern taskmaster, who expects a lot from his players, gets a lot from them, and expects still more in return. Brown will work for a man who feels that if a youngster learns to produce to the utmost of his ability while still in school, he will continue to do so when he reaches maturity.

—

When the All-State basketball teams were announced that spring, Leffingwell was a first-team selection. John Sissel of Tipton made the second team. Three Marion players received honorable mention: Seeks, Lundquist, and Christensen. The 1952 All-State team had three players who went on to be named All-Americans in college: Keokuk's Bill Logan, who starred at Iowa, Gary Thompson of Roland, who played at Iowa State, and Carl Widseth of Davenport, who went to Tennessee. Leffingwell would never get the chance.

Chapter 21
Leffingwell Out

It was time for Hugh Leffingwell to select a college. He was "getting a terrific play by Kansas State," wrote Tait Cummins, "one phone call after another." Kansas State was also interested in Seeks for football, so the two friends drove there in Hugh's family car to check it out. "He was a terrible driver," Seeks remembered. "He had no mechanical knowledge of a car at all. He scared me most of the time we went out and back."

The school greeted them warmly and lined up dates for them, "but we never gave it a thought that we would go to school out of Iowa," Seeks said. Seeks went to Coe, started on the freshman football team, started on the varsity as a sophomore, but then quit college to join the Army.

Hugh went to Iowa, a member of perhaps the greatest group of basketball players ever to enroll in a single freshman class. The freshman squad that year included two first-team All-State players from Iowa, Leffingwell and Keokuk's Logan, and two from Illinois, Bob George from Highland Park, and Carl "Sugar" Cain from Freeport. Also on the squad were Bill Schoof, Homewood, Illinois; Milton "Sharm" Scheuerman, a football and basketball standout from Rock Island, Illinois; Bill Seaberg, a four-sport star from Moline, Illinois; and Dick Ritter, the Grinnell ace.

Cain, Logan, Seaberg, Scheuerman, and Schoof would earn fame as "The Fabulous Five," a team that achieved a three-year run of success "that is unparalleled in school history," according to *Black and Gold Memories*, by George Wine. Over three years, they went 35–7 in the Big Ten, "far and away the best three-year period in the annals of Iowa basketball," Wine wrote. As sophomores, they came within one game of sharing the Big Ten championship.

They won the title as juniors and seniors, going to the NCAA Final Four as juniors and reaching the final game as seniors. In that last game, they lost to the undefeated San Francisco Dons, led by the legendary Bill Russell who, at six feet ten, knocked Iowa's shots off the rim (as pre-goaltending rules then permitted), captured twenty-seven rebounds and scored twenty-six points. The Iowa teams' accomplishment was so great that the numbers of all five starters were retired.

Had he not fallen ill before his sophomore year, Leffingwell would have been part of all that. "They would have had to change the nomenclature," said Bob Schulz, who was the Iowa freshman coach at the time. They would have had to call them the Sensational Six, Schulz said. "Leffingwell ranked among the top five or six guys, maybe within the top five. He was so good. I recruited him out of Marion. When I scouted his games, he was head and shoulders above everyone he played against."

The whole freshman group was extraordinary, Schulz said, with the talent going deeper than any other squad he saw. "I used to go down to the Jefferson Hotel to talk about the freshman team [to booster groups], and I told them the freshmen here were capable of winning a Big Ten championship someday. I don't think Paul Brechler [the athletic director] liked that."

Head coach Bucky O'Connor knew how good those freshmen were. Practice typically ended with a scrimmage between the varsity and the freshmen. "Bucky wouldn't let me send out my best five men," Schulz said. "He told me, 'Send out two good ones and three hamburgers.'"

Big Ten rules were strict. Freshmen could not play on the varsity or in any intercollegiate games. The basketball season did not start until December and was limited to 22 regular-season games. To gain experience, the freshmen played curtain raisers starting at 6:00 PM before home games. The freshmen teams were constantly scrambled ten to a side, with each player getting in for half the game.

Several Marion sources said that Leffingwell was the top scorer among all freshman players that year. "We didn't keep stats like that," said Schulz, "but he was certainly equal to the task. I think Logan or Cain could have scored more." In one game, the *Sentinel* reported, Leffingwell scored thirty-four points. The *Daily Iowan* mentioned games in which he scored fifteen and eight points. Although no official statistics were kept, box scores apparently were available and it's easy to imagine that Wally Leffingwell attended each game and kept a tally of his son's scoring.

Late that winter, Marion's team was at the Iowa field house practicing for a tournament game when Rollie Williams, a former Iowa coach who was then an official in the athletic department, stopped to chat with Hipple and his assistant, Lynn Brown. "He told us the Hawkeyes would score ninety points a game the next year when Hugh was eligible to play," Brown recalled. "All they would have to do was set some screens to get him shots from any place on the floor."

"Leffingwell wasn't a big jumper and he wasn't real fast," Schulz said, "but get him around the basket and you didn't know what he was going to do. He was very nifty. He had a beautiful left hand. He didn't have the athleticism of some of the others, but he could make them look bad." The Fab Five were individually very good players but not superstars, Schulz added. "They knew their positions and what they had to do. They worked so well together, and Hugh did, too. He could have played on any Division I team in the country."

—

Coming off his successful freshman season, Leffingwell continued to work hard on his game. In Marion that summer, Hipple allowed him to use the gym on Sundays. He was joined on at least one such occasion by Darell Failor, who would be a high school sophomore that fall. As a freshman, Failor had been the fastest quarter-miler in the school and had starred on the freshman–sophomore basketball team. "I thought I was pretty damn good," Failor said. The session began with warm-up drills. The two ran up and down the court passing the ball back and forth. Leffingwell ran Failor into the ground. "I couldn't keep up with him," Failor remembered.

"Then we played one-on-one. God, I can't tell you. I was like a third-grader compared to him. I thought I could jump and he couldn't. I think he blocked every shot I took. I don't remember getting one off. You couldn't believe what he could do. I learned humility that day." Leffingwell ended the session by practicing free throws. "He could make 100 or 125 straight in practice," Failor said.

Awestruck though he was, Failor noticed something unusual about Leffingwell: He no longer wore glasses. His vision had corrected itself. Hugh must have considered it a blessing to be rid of his glasses. In fact, his improved eyesight was probably the early sign of a deadly illness.

—

Leffingwell's official Hawkeye varsity photograph—a head-and-shoulders portrait—showed him without glasses. Now nineteen and weighing 190 pounds at six feet three, he no longer looked like the Hughie who played high school ball. The softness in his face was gone. His head seemed to be carved from marble—a young warrior's face.

When the Iowa basketball season opened in December with a game against Washington University of St. Louis, Leffingwell was in the starting lineup along with fellow sophomores Bob George and Roy Johnson. Coach O'Connor made it clear that he had no real starting lineup. He devised a platoon system that allowed him to test all the talent at his disposal. The starters played fifteen minutes and left with the game tied 15–15. The second squad, which included Cain, Logan, Seaberg, and Schoof, took over, and with some other substitutions, including Scheuerman, staggered to a 51–45 victory.

Everyone was "tense and green," wrote Gus Schrader in the *Gazette*. The team's field goal average was a woeful .277. Leffingwell made one field goal and one free throw. He was playing his first game without glasses. "I don't know why I was so tight out there," he told Schrader, "but I guess we were all trying too hard. No, playing without glasses isn't much different. It hasn't seemed to affect my shooting, but I sure missed some shots tonight, didn't I?"

In Iowa's next game, at Nebraska, Hugh started again, scoring only one point as Iowa lost, 81–70. He was demoted to the third string and did not play in the next three games, but remained on the traveling squad. He was one of fourteen players to make the airplane trip over New Years to Los Angeles, where Iowa would play UCLA and Southern California. The trip was a big deal. It included a visit to a movie studio, dinner with actor Don Ameche, who had once gone to school in Marion, and other Hollywood stars, and tickets to the Rose Bowl parade and game, where Michigan was to play UCLA. Forest Evashevski, the football coach, went along to scout Michigan. The athletic director and one of his assistants went too, as did university president Virgil M. Hancher and his wife. Mrs. O'Connor, the coach's wife, was also on the plane.

During this trip, according to several sources, Iowa officials realized that Hugh was not well. Russ Seeks, who was stationed in Japan at the time, said he later learned that when the team's bus stopped at the movie studio, Leffingwell was too exhausted to go on the tour. A related story was that Mrs. O'Connor noticed he was not well and insisted that he see a doctor when the team returned to Iowa. Leffingwell did not play in either California game.

After the return home, on January 9th, Iowa beat Wisconsin, 71–54. Leffingwell was one of thirteen players to see action. He made one field goal. It was probably the last official score of his life.

—

"Leffingwell Out," said the headline on the small, boxed item in the *Gazette* on January 14, 1954. He had entered the university hospital for observation and tests, and would probably miss the next several games. "The illness has not been definitely diagnosed, but it could be some form of anemia," the story said.

The news broke the next day. Leffingwell had leukemia, "a cancerous disease of the blood which causes an increase of white corpuscles and a decrease of red corpuscles," said the *Gazette*. There was no known cure. Leffingwell's parents were at his bedside when the doctors delivered the news. It was, said Bucky O'Connor, "a tremendous blow personally and a shock to the entire basketball team."

The report didn't say so, but Leffingwell probably had been suffering from leukemia for about six months. A radical change in eyesight, it is now understood, is a possible symptom of leukemia. The disease can cause a swelling that changes the shape of the eye, reducing its length in near-sighted individuals and lessening their need for glasses, said Dr. William E. Scott, professor emeritus of ophthalmology at the University of Iowa. "This could have occurred long before he had other signs or symptoms" of the disease, Dr. Scott wrote.

Although his strength had been eroding slowly over the previous six months, Leffingwell never complained of not feeling well. In fact, he probably was suffering from fatigue and headaches. After he was released from the hospital, he stayed on campus and attended spring classes. When asked about his health, he said he felt fine and hoped to play basketball again next year. He had formed a friendship with Ed Failor, a Marion graduate who was studying for his law degree, and the two had lunch together from time to time. "We had long chats about him becoming a coach like Hipple," Failor wrote. "He talked about what systems he would use with various types of teams. He was always positive about his life. He seemed quite mature. I think everyone knew he would not recover."

That summer, back in Marion, Leffingwell hooked up with a friend from his high school days. Don Roby, a year older than Leffingwell, had joined the Marines after graduating and was sent to Korea. He enlisted so he could get a college education on the GI Bill, and now, with his enlistment up, he came back to Iowa to do just that. Sgt. Roby earned three battle stars in Korea for involvement in major combat action, but was safely behind the front lines on July 27, 1953, when the ceasefire was declared. He never forgot how the opposing artillery batteries poured a hailstorm of shells across the 38th parallel, sending up a horrific roar that went on for hours. Then, at midnight, the cannons suddenly stopped and the silence seemed unearthly.

A year later, Roby was granted thirty days' leave. His route home took him to San Francisco, where he boarded a train for the forty-hour ride to Iowa. The train was full of Marines. When it stopped at Green River Valley, Wyoming, some of the Marines spotted a tavern near the tracks. A few of them disembarked, bent on collecting several cases of beer. While they were in the tavern, the train pulled out, and Roby expected never to see them again. But at the next stop, a patrol car pulled up with its lights flashing. The missing Marines piled out, cases of beer in their arms. They thanked the policemen for the ride, and the cops replied, "That's okay. We just didn't want you guys in town overnight."

When Roby got off the train in Cedar Rapids that April, dusty and wrinkled from his ride, the only familiar face he saw was Hugh Leffingwell's. He had learned of Roby's arrival from his friend's mother. Asked why no one else met him, Roby replied, "When you came home from World War II, they held parades. When you came home from Vietnam, they spit on you. When you came home from Korea, they ignored you."

When his leave ended, Roby went to San Diego to muster out of the service, and then returned to Iowa in July. That summer, Roby and Leffingwell hung out together. They went to ball games, ate hamburgers, drank beer, and played pool and Ping Pong. Leffingwell, always the competitor, battled for every point. They rode around in the new white Plymouth Wally had purchased for his son. Hugh had a girl friend during this time, Roby said. "He was very interested in girls."

Leffingwell's spirits were good. "We hoped for a miracle cure," Roby said. Roby decided to attend Coe, where he wanted to play sports. Leffingwell talked about joining him at Coe, and when Roby went there to register, Hugh went along too, ready to offer the ex-Marine any help he might need.

Leffingwell took up golf, playing at the Indian Creek Country Club. He sometimes walked the course alone, working on his game the way he had taught himself basketball moves on his cinder-topped court at home. He celebrated his twentieth birthday on August 3, 1954. When high school football practice began a few weeks later, he went down to the Legion field to watch, remembering to thank assistant coach Lynn Brown for the card he and his freshman–sophomore basketball team sent when they heard of his illness. His attitude was cheerful, Brown noted, thinking Hugh was facing death with great courage.

"He was fine physically that summer," Roby said. "We laughed and joked. I was with him all summer. I'm pretty sure I was with him the night before he died. It was sudden. Suddenly, he was gone."

Hipple was badly shaken by Leffingwell's illness, said his sister, Shirley Shanahan. "The whole town was." Late in the illness, Hipple gathered his wife and daughter for a visit to the Leffingwells, who lived nearby. Hipple's daughter Pat was twelve. She remembered that Hugh did not want to come out of his room to see his former coach and that when he did, he was in tears. "He looked really bad and was so sick. He didn't want my dad to see him in that condition." Her parents talked briefly to the young man, and then he went back to his room.

Hugh Leffingwell died at 11:59 PM, Tuesday, October 4, 1954. Services were held the following Friday at Murdoch Funeral Home. The Iowa basketball team attended. Two ministers officiated: James Gable, Methodist, and C. V. R. DeJong, Presbyterian. The ministers surely struggled to make sense of the death of a young man on the verge of greatness. But Hugh's friend Don Roby, looking back more than fifty years, remembered a fierce spirit.

"Hugh was tough. I knew a lot of tough guys in the Marines, but Hugh could hold his own with any one of them. There's something about Hugh most people didn't realize. He was not a good guy to meet in the alley for a fight. He would kick you in the nuts without thinking twice."

Chapter 22
A Man for All Seasons

In the fall of 1952, after Marion defeated Oelwein in football, a reporter for the *Oelwein Daily Register*, perhaps bitter over the loss, broke the news that Hipple's salary was $5,500 a year, just $200 less than C. B. Vernon's and apparently an extraordinary amount for a coach. The reporter also chided Hipple for his rules and pointed out that outfitting a football squad of ninety-one players was an expensive proposition.

Vernon sprang to Hipple's defense. In a letter to the editor, he disputed the claim that Hipple's salary was $5,500. "In fact, it is $4,800, and that is for nine-and-a-half months of work as a teacher of mathematics, boys' physical education, and head coach of athletics.

"It probably should be $5,500," Vernon went on, "for he has demonstrated during the past seven years that he has done more for the youth of this community than any other single individual. He is truly a builder of men. I might add that on an hourly basis he is the lowest paid man on the faculty."

In fact, Hipple was earning $5,540 a year. Vernon left out Hipple's pay for summer work. Hipple wasn't working nine months a year. He was working twelve months a year, from dawn to dusk and beyond.

After Marion's second run to the state finals in basketball in 1952, Hipple was one of the top coaches in the state. Larger schools were interested in him—overtures came from Iowa City, Davenport, Mason City, Dubuque, and other cities. Vernon, deeply concerned about losing Hipple, signed him in the spring of 1952 to a complex five-year agreement that involved two contracts. The first covered Hipple's work as teacher of physical education and mathematics ($3,410), as head coach of all sports ($1,200), and coach of preseason football for two weeks ($190). This contract totaled $4,800.

The second contract covered four extracurricular jobs, described as "1) Coach of summer baseball; 2) Supervisor of the care of two athletic fields; 3) Repair of the school's athletic equipment; 4) Organizer and supervisor of the Saturday basketball program during the basketball season." This contract paid $740 in 1952 but was scheduled to increase much more rapidly than the standard raises in Hipple's teaching contract, reaching $1,300 for the 1956–1957 school year. It was here it seems that Vernon found the wiggle room to help keep his coach at Marion.

With the unflagging support of Superintendent Vernon, and through his own untiring efforts, Hipple had the entire athletic program under his control, from the brand of thread used to mend jerseys to the length of every blade of grass on the football field.

Here are glimpses of Hipple and his methods as he worked through the seasons.

—

In football practice, Hipple focused on simplicity and repetition to achieve flawless execution. He broke plays and maneuvers into discrete parts so his players could grasp them. His plays were the basic runs by each back to the various holes or around the end. His passing plays were largely variations on the same movements. He installed a split-T offense, using plays that allowed quarterbacks the option of handing the ball off to a running back or keeping the ball and running with it. He chose quarterbacks who were smart, fast, and good ball-handlers and let them call their own plays. Most quarterbacks rarely passed, perhaps four times a game, opting to control the ball and eat up the yards with running plays.

Hipple stressed defense. In the all-time list of Marion teams that allowed opponents the fewest yards gained in a season, Hipple-coached teams occupy the top six places as the stingiest in history.

In practice sessions, Hipple ran plays over and over again, instructing each player on the specifics of his role. "One or two things, [player's name]," he would say, then tell or show him specifically what to do. Bob Malake remembered a Thursday when Lynn Brown took his freshman–sophomore team, "which was full of spit and vinegar," over to the practice field to run plays against the varsity. Malake was only a freshman.

> I was starting right guard on that team. The first play we ran was a *44*. The right halfback was to run between the right tackle and me. On the snap I shot off the line, was fast in the first four feet, hit the man I was supposed to block, got my right shoulder into him, and got absolutely nowhere. I did not move him an inch. I don't think I even straightened him up. He reached over me, grabbed the ball carrier, and he and I, the halfback, and many of his defensive teammates ended up in a pile on the ground with me at the bottom. After the pile was unstacked, I slowly got to my feet thinking, *Let's work on pass plays.*
>
> [But Hipple] grasped me by the shoulder pads and led me over to the man I had just tried to block ... Coach Hipple then proceeded to explain to the defensive player how the offensive player should never be allowed to get his shoulder into his body. He then demonstrated on me how this guy should ward me off with an upward push with his forearm, a forearm shiver. Coach Hipple then turned to Mr. Brown and said these fatal words, "Let's run that play again, Mr. Brown." I thought Coach Hipple was trying to get me killed ... And so we ran the play. The results were very predictable. I remember nothing of the rest of that practice except that I survived.
>
> The next day I seriously wondered why I went out for football. [I] had bruises that had bruises. Then on my way to the lunchroom I stopped and looked at the bulletin board ... where Coach Hipple posted the list of people who got to dress for the game that night. I was stunned. There at the bottom of the list was my name. My aches and pains were forgotten. I was on cloud nine.

Marion always outclassed the other conference teams in appearance. In football, "we were one of the few teams (if not the only one) in the WaMaC that had leg socks," wrote Carl Adkins. "We also had to have two pairs of clean white sweat socks for the games. We had to polish our black shoes and get new laces (or wash the dirty ones) and simonize our helmets. Then we came out on the field at home after the other team was out, and we jogged around the entire field before moving into our circle for calisthenics. My dad always said that MHS was ahead seven points before the game started simply because of our uniforms and our pre-game behavior."

Marion's home squad numbered more than fifty players compared to the visitor's band of twenty or thirty, and the sight of this small army of well-clad Indians circling the field surely intimidated some foes.

Hipple was a natty dresser. On the sidelines during games, he always wore a suit, his good-luck tie, and a wide-brimmed fedora. On cold or rainy days, he wore a tan coat that almost reached his ankles.

—

All during the school year, somehow, Hipple found time to run boys' physical education classes and to teach a class or two in algebra. His PE classes are described in Chapter 18. He was an extremely effective algebra teacher, according to several former students. He had a way of breaking concepts into parts to help students understand the whole.

—

Before each basketball practice, players were required to skip rope three hundred times, do thirty push-ups on their fingertips, and climb the heavy rope to the ceiling twice (once if they could do it without using their feet). Sometimes additional climbs were levied for infractions of training rules, such as driving a car, walking in the hallway with a girlfriend, or being caught not wearing a hat—all players were required to wear hats whenever they went outside as a precaution against catching a cold.

Players climbed the rope often. Irwin Renfer, whose store supplied basketball shoes, was surprised when parents brought them back because they had become badly worn along the sides of the instep. He couldn't understand how basketball shoes could be so severely scuffed in such an unusual place—until someone explained how the boys used their feet to climb the rope and then slide back down.

Hipple ordered the push-ups on the fingertips to build hand and arm strength. At no time in dribbling, passing, or shooting was the ball to touch the palm.

After the warm-up, players practiced shooting, always beginning by standing very close to the basket and concentrating on form, rehearsing the pure motion of bringing the ball up in front of their faces and over their heads before releasing it off their fingertips with a flick of the wrist and a precise follow-through. Gradually, the shooters moved back, still concentrating on form. Next were passing, defensive, and rebounding drills. Hipple stressed the pass instead of the dribble. A frequent drill had three players run the length of the floor passing the ball back and forth without dribbling.

Hipple favored a "tough, hard-nosed, bellybutton-to-bellybutton defense," said Bob Jennings, who coached against him for Immaculate Conception and Regis. "It was man-to-man all the way. Hipple's emphasis on defense was ahead of its time," Jennings said. "In those days, some teams were lax on defense, but I always thought Hipple stressed defense over offense. We liked to set a lot of screens, but Marion's defense stopped us from getting plays off. We had to work our tails off, and couldn't get our patterns going."

In Hipple's checking man-to-man defense, each defender was assigned a man to guard, but would switch to another man when two offensive players crossed paths. The switch, or check, occurred when one Marion player's outstretched hand touched that of his teammate who was guarding the crossing offensive player. When their hands touched, they switched men.

Defensive drills were designed to improve a player's ability to shuffle sideways without crossing his legs. Hipple stood before his players, holding out a basketball, then moved it left or right, forward or back, and the players scuttled along with the ball, arms out, hands up at all times, never allowing them to drop to their sides. It is exhausting for players to keep their arms outstretched all the time, but Hipple insisted on it.

"We liked our players to be ball hawks," wrote Lynn Brown, "since it tires out the other team and causes more turnovers. We did not want our players to get fouls by reaching and grabbing at the ball, but instead keep their hands moving back and forth in front of their eyes so they couldn't see their teammates as well. Move your feet instead of reaching and grabbing with your hands."

Hipple was determined to have the best-conditioned teams. "Marion teams knew they could come from behind in the last part of a game because they were in better shape than the other team," wrote Brown. Marion teams became famous for third-quarter bursts of scoring. After gaining the lead in close games, Hipple often ordered his players to begin a stall with as many as four minutes left to play. "Marion had a four-corner stall and the teams were very good at it," said rival Jennings. "You had no choice but to go out and try to break it up. Marion teams were very good free-throw shooters. I think he was ahead of his time in stressing the importance of free throws, making his kids practice them over and over."

Hipple favored the fast break, and most of his teams excelled at it. Set plays were based on a continuous pattern of passing and cutting. For example, a guard passed to a forward, and then cut around him. The forward might then work the ball to the center, and both the guard and forward would cut around him, one high and one low. In theory, a team could keep cutting and weaving endlessly, but after a few cuts, shots opened up. The closer to the basket they were, the better Hipple liked it.

Opponents often tried to slow a fast-break team with a full-court press, so Hipple drilled his teams on a weaving pattern that almost always broke up the press and often resulted in a fast break as the Indians streaked to the basket ahead of the defenders. The weaving pattern used to counter the press was quite similar to the pattern used for the stall. Hipple wanted his teams to be able to execute flawlessly a few simple but effective patterns.

Hook shots were forbidden. Free throws had to be shot underhanded with both hands. If a player violated these rules in practice, Hipple sent him to the showers. If it happened during warm-ups or a game, he benched the player. Scoop shots were frowned on. Layups should always be made by banking the ball off the backboard, never by trying to dump it over the edge of the rim.

After the drills, the varsity and freshman–sophomore teams took turns scrimmaging. This was followed by free-throw practice, with players often being required to make a certain number without missing. The two-hour practice ended with many of the players running laps to compensate for missed free throws.

—

Hipple demanded that players behave properly at all times during practice and games. There was to be no goofing off. In one basketball practice, George Murdoch felt frisky. As he dribbled the ball up the floor, it came into his head to shoot from the centerline. He got up a run, jumped into the air, and fired. Hipple shouted "Murdoch!" and George just kept going, running through the defending team, out of the gym, and up the stairs to the locker room. He knew without being told that he was through for the day.

In basketball games, the Indians were instructed to chase down balls that went out of bounds and deliver them to the referees. Players always raised their hands when they were called for a foul. Indians were never to argue with the officials or challenge their authority in any way. It rarely happened. Ken Otting remembered a game against Manchester in which he was red hot, leading all scorers. Then he drew a technical foul. His competitive fire had overcome his common sense. Hipple benched him for the rest of the game. "That was the rule," Otting wrote. "I knew the consequences, but it didn't stop me."

Hipple reserved for himself the right to argue with officials, which he did effectively but never boisterously. Hipple, wrote Brown, "could work the officials as well as any coach I have been around, but he respected them and they respected him. I think they liked to officiate Marion games." Bill Quinby, a Cedar Rapids boy who went on to officiate in the National Football League, agreed with Brown. As a young man, Quinby was hired by Hipple for one of his first refereeing jobs, and for about ten years he called football and basketball games at Marion. "He let you know he was watching you," Quinby said. "But after the game, win or lose, he never failed to say, 'I think you worked a good game.' He never chewed you out, never got angry, never blamed the officials for a loss. He was firm, but he was fair."

The four-page programs distributed at Marion basketball games urged spectators to display good sportsmanship. A brief paragraph admonished them not to boo the opposing team and to applaud a good play no matter which team made it. The latter advice was perhaps asking too much of Marion fans, but they were usually polite to the visiting team.

—

Hipple designed the large *M* that graced the side vents of players' basketball trunks. For shoes, he specified PF Flyers, their canvas uppers dyed red, because he believed their traction was superior to Chuck Taylors or Keds.

Although he had a reputation for resisting change, Hipple was fascinated by new developments in equipment and training methods. One year he tested a vibrating device apparently designed to relieve stress or tightness in feet or legs. At halftime during some basketball games, as players sipped their small allotment of water and sucked on a white, chalky dextrose tablet for energy, they also took turns putting their feet on this contraption, which shook rapidly, delivering a sort of massage. Hipple did not keep the machine.

For years, Hipple used an 8mm camera to take black and white movies of players with good shooting form. He then played the films for the edification of youngsters coming along in the game. He introduced weight training in 1956 after learning that it had improved the leaping abilities of players at the university. He rarely missed the football and basketball clinics held each summer, and he came back with notebooks loaded with the latest thinking on both sports.

Don King, a fellow coach, first met Hipple at one of these workshops, and marveled at "the most complete set of clinic notes I have ever seen." Some of Hipple's clinic notebooks have survived, and they show how he filled the page after page with small rectangles representing a half basketball court and meticulously diagrammed each play as it was described by the lecturer, adding captions explaining the moves. The writing is crystal clear. He seemed to have captured everything that was said and shown.

"He was a true student of every sport he coached," said King. "He was determined to be thoroughly knowledgeable with anything that was new and different. It's not so much that he was going to change his game, but that he was not going to be taken by surprise if an opponent initiated a new offense that had started in college. If that happened, he already had it on file and knew what to do."

There is a saying among some coaches that, "I got my best plays on a cocktail napkin" while socializing in the bar with fellow coaches. Hipple never did that. He attended every session, even the optional ones that conflicted with happy hour. As a result, said assistant coach Harold Yeoman, Hipple picked up a special play that his team practiced diligently but used only once—to win a game.

—

Like his parents, Hipple did not take vacations. His only regular summer travel took him to coaching clinics, which were often held in Iowa resort towns such as Spirit Lake and Clear Lake. Sometimes, his wife, Wilma, went along to make a little vacation out of it. There were occasional brief trips to Illinois, Wisconsin, or Indiana to visit relatives, but that was the extent of travel for pleasure. Once, Wilma made detailed plans for the family to visit the Black Hills of South Dakota, which she had always wanted to see. But Hipple refused to go. Wilma had to call off the trip; wives did not readily travel without their husbands.

On evenings he was not coaching a game or repairing equipment, Hipple sat in his living room diagramming plays while his wife sewed and his daughter studied. On game days, he came home for an early supper, put on his good-luck tie, and went back to work. He rarely talked about sports at home.

—

Track, for Hipple, was a form of spring training for football and basketball. He was less interested in winning track titles than he was in keeping his athletes in condition. To do this, he made them all run the 440-yard dash, regardless of their specific strengths or weaknesses as trackmen.

Although Hipple did not covet championships in this sport, the Indians won five titles and finished second four times during his eighteen years as head track coach. Since most boys hated track, a tradition developed in which seniors, their careers in football and basketball at an end, declined to come out for track during their final spring in high school. Had they done so, Marion would have won more track championships. In the years Marion did win, seniors came out in large numbers and contributed greatly.

Hipple's rule of mandatory track unearthed a number of stars who otherwise might not have discovered their gifts at track and field. If baseball had been an option, Jerry Walker, who was the best miler in the state, would have skipped track. The same applied to Norm Rathje, a weight man who went on to be a three-sport star at the University of Dubuque. Was Hipple able to win track championships simply because he turned out such a huge squad? "No," said Jerry Skilling, who succeeded Hipple as track coach at Marion. "You had to be a good coach to win championships." Hipple still had to identify, train, and motivate the athletes, Skilling said.

Walker, who spent decades as a volunteer assistant coach in track and cross country at the University Iowa, said that Hipple's coaching was sound, with one exception. He often held time trials the day before the meet to determine who would compete the next day. Thus he forced some of his athletes to go all out in the trials, increasing the risk they would not fully recover their strength when the meet was held twenty-four hours later.

During the glory years, the track turnouts were huge, sometimes more than one hundred athletes. Hipple tended to work with the runners. Boys good at the field events were largely self-taught, with older students showing the younger ones the rudiments of throwing the shot or high jumping with the Western roll.

Track practice began with a mile jog from the school to the track. Rex Story Jr. lived in the house adjacent to the track. When Story went out for track, it seemed to him the height of good sense that he be allowed to go directly home after track practice, rather than all the way back to the high school, only to have to return to the very place he had just left. "Les Hipple would have none of this," Story wrote. "So my day was off to school in the morning, home for lunch, back to school, down to the track, back to school, and then home for the day." He covered six miles every day, at least two of them running, totally aside from whatever distances he ran during track practice.

—

Although he coached summer baseball during part of the 1940s and 1950s, Hipple probably spent more time in that season caring for the football field, the track, and the school's athletic equipment. He was a familiar sight at the football field, riding his mower and wearing a straw hat or jungle helmet, meticulously grooming the grass so it grew in different directions every ten yards. He also spent hours repairing and weeding the cinder track, sometimes alone, sometimes with student helpers. At home, he used his sewing machines to repair torn jerseys and pants. At the gym, he cleaned and repainted helmets and applied new coats of shellac to pads. Sometimes his wife and daughter helped.

—

Hipple was far ahead of his time in setting up sports programs in the lower grades, extending football into junior high and basketball as low as fourth grade. In high school, he established basketball programs for varsity, junior varsity, freshmen–sophomores, and freshmen. Similar programs were set up in football. No one was cut. Any boy could be a Hippleman.

Hipple's athletic program required an extensive roster of assistant coaches—none of whom he apparently had any say in hiring. While they were all expected to teach Hipple's systems and fundamentals, they were otherwise left to do the coaching as they saw fit. "He was an organizational genius," said George Murdoch, who worked with him as an adult volunteer.

Hipple was an emotionally remote leader who seldom distributed praise. Each of his top assistants during most of his career—successively, Harold Yeoman, Frank McLeod, and Lynn Brown—was intensely loyal. They supported his coaching tactics, his rules, and his strong discipline. It was said of Hipple and Yeoman that they could sit together in the same room contentedly for hours without talking. Brown wrote that he and Hipple often did not need to talk because their views and approaches were so similar.

Hipple insisted that treating all boys the same was essential in team sports. Only this way would his decisions be perceived as fair. If a coach favors any player in any way—whether in meting out punishment or granting playing time—it leads to distrust of the coach and undermines team unity.

Not all coaches agree. Some believe athletes should be handled with more sensitivity to their unique personalities. Bob Justice, a Marion graduate who went on to become a gymnast at the University of Iowa and coached swimming and diving at the College of Marin, said, "I have always tried to work with people as individuals. [When I was in school] I felt no empathy in the personality of Les Hipple. He was a good coach for his time and place, but had he been a little more flexible [in his methods and treatment of players], he could have been a great coach." Justice praised Hipple as a positive influence who set high standards for his players.

—

People in the news media admired Hipple. The *Marion Sentinel* was firmly in his corner. The *Cedar Rapids Gazette* regularly referred to him as "mild-mannered," "quiet," and "gentlemanly." These words never seemed quite accurate to the athletes who labored in his stern regime, but they were correct when applied to his demeanor on the bench, his conduct in interviews, and the behavior he demanded of his players.

"He was one of my all-time favorite coaches," said Bob Brooks, who met hundreds during his more than sixty years in broadcasting. Brooks interviewed Hipple regularly when broadcasting Marion games. "We had the 'Les Hipple Show' before and after each game," Brooks said. "He was absolutely the worst interview. Absolutely colorless as a talker. It was like pulling teeth to get enough out of him to put on a show. He would just say 'yes' or 'no' when answering questions. He thought his teams would never win a game, and he was very slow to praise anyone. But he was a terrific coach, able to get the optimum out of the talent he had."

Hipple was known and feared throughout the WaMaC, and as his basketball teams prospered in the state tournament, his fame spread. His reputation as a disciplinarian grew as well, sometimes taking on mythic proportions. He was known as much for his rules as his victories, his daughter said, and coaches often wrote to him for a copy of his rules.

The coaching community knew him well. When Carl Adkins went to college at Buena Vista, a coach, watching him run laps to stay in shape, often said, "There goes a Hippleman."

When Don Roby walked on for the Coe College football team, he attracted the attention of a coach by making some solid tackles. The coach asked him where he was from. When Roby responded, "Marion," the coach got him a better helmet.

When Bob Malake went to teach at West Des Moines High School in 1976, nearly twenty years after graduating from Marion, the head basketball coach asked him, "Are you a Hippleman?" Malake proudly answered that he was.

When Steve Miller, well into his career as coach at Cornell College, made recruiting trips around the state, parents often asked him, "Did you play for Hipple?" For some of them, it was a thing of wonder, and they wanted to hear what it was like.

Lester's parents, Charles Hipple and Lena Olsson, in photos taken sometime before their marriage in 1907.

Toddler Lester, and as a young basketball star.

Lester when he graduated from the University of Iowa, 1937.

Wilma Winslow in her early 20s.

The young married couple.

Always a natty dresser, the young coach models a coat probably made by his mother. Bosco, the pet rabbit, wants in.

Hipple boards the bus after a football win. This photo appears in his memorial trophy case at Marion High School.
(Photo by Gary Eschman)

Hipple at the track.

Larry Tanner covered Hipple's Marion career from beginning to end, working for the Cedar Rapids Gazette and Marion Sentinel. His Sentinel column, "Larry's Line," often revealed what was on the coach's mind.

Football practice on the Legion field, swimming pool in the background.

The old gym, packed to standing room. (Photo by Gary Eschman)

Hipple treated track as a conditioning program for the other sports, but still turned out five championship teams. (Football and track photos courtesy of Bill Hotle)

—Gazette photo by Johnny McIvor.

AND, AWAY WE GO — Marion Coach Les Hipple got a free ride to the dressing room Thursday night on the shoulders of his happy warriors. Marion came from behind to nip Cedar Rapids Wilson, 55-51, for the class A district championship at Iowa City and a berth in the substate tournament.

A BIG WIN IN THE 1955 STATE TOURNAMENT.
(REPRINTED BY PERMISSION, THE GAZETTE, CEDAR RAPIDS, IOWA)

HIPPLE AND ASSISTANT COACH LYNN BROWN ON THE SIDELINES DURING A FOOTBALL GAME.

BROWN (INSET) SERVED AS HIPPLE'S LIEUTENANT FOR EIGHT YEARS.

HIPPLE OFTEN ATTENDED FOOTBALL AND BASKETBALL CLINICS, TAKING METICULOUS NOTES.

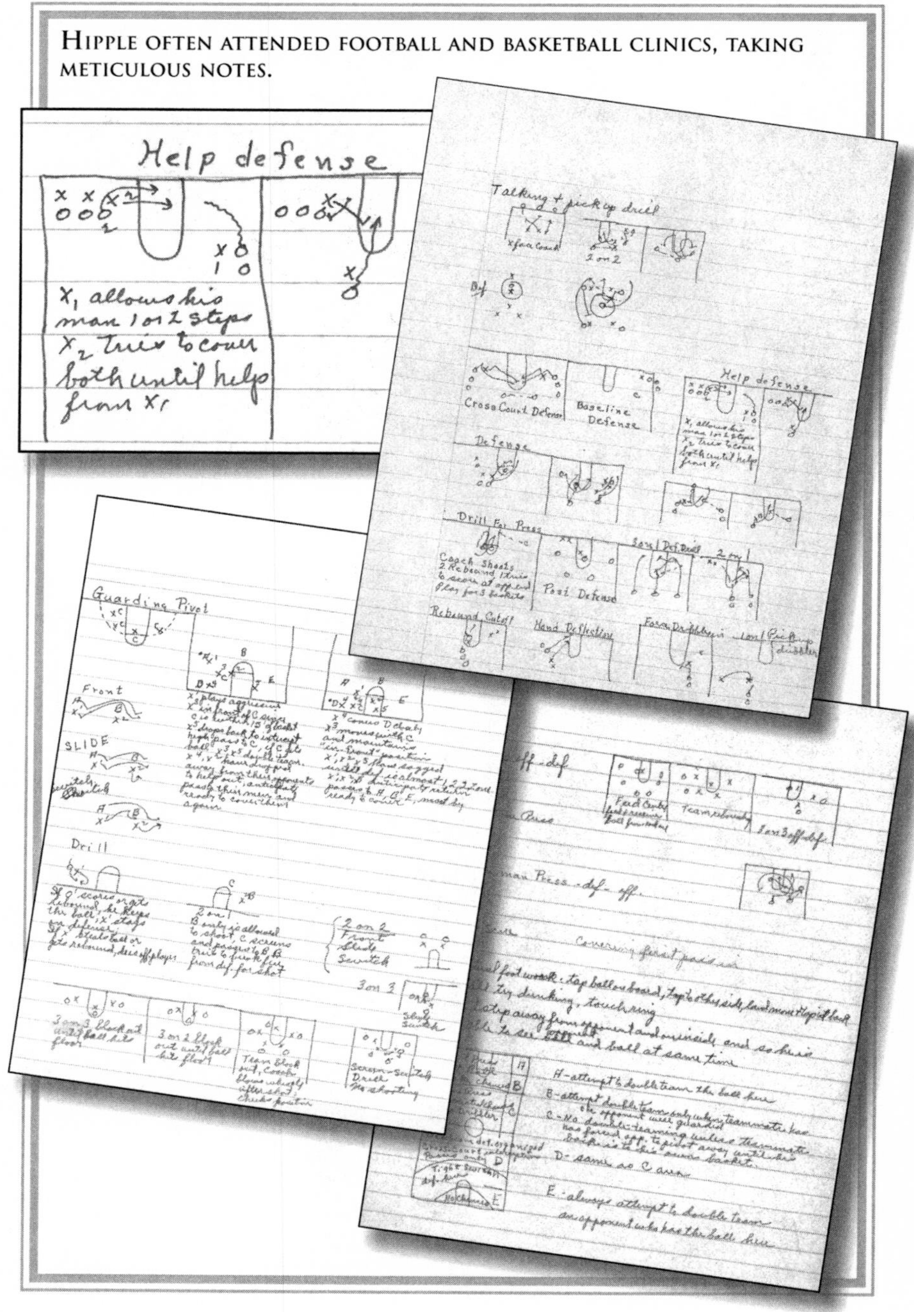

UNTIL THE LATE 1950S, PLAYERS WENT WITHOUT FACE MASKS. MOST STARTERS PLAYED BOTH OFFENSE AND DEFENSE. IN CLOSE GAMES, 15 OR FEWER MEN SAW ACTION. (PHOTO BY OMER D. ESCHMAN)

C.B. VERNON IN THE MID-1940S.

JOHN MESSERLI IN THE LATE 1950S.

Lloyd Olmstead was Marion's first All-State basketball star. At Cornell College (large photo) he set scoring records and was all-conference for three years.

Hugh Leffingwell still holds Marion scoring records and was headed for stardom at Iowa University until he was struck down by leukemia in his sophomore year. He is Marion's only member of the Iowa high school basketball players Hall of Fame.

Perhaps Marion's greatest athlete under Hipple, Ron Altenberg still holds single-season scoring records at Cornell College (large photo). He was named to the small college All-American team, set Cornell track records and later played for the Phillips 66ers.

The Marion pool hall, where some athletes played while others kept watch for Hipple's car. Kenneth "Shine" Domer is behind the counter. (Photo courtesy of Tom Domer)

Les Hipple's cross country teams won eight consecutive state championships. The 1953 version was one of the best, led by Jerry Walker (first row, third from right) and Leo Corporon (first row, center).

At a 1978 ceremony dedicating the athletic fields in his honor, Hipple receives a plaque from Marion's mayor, Bill Grundy.

Chapter 23
The Missed Shot, 1952–1953

"Do you remember the shot Shorty Novotny missed?" Donald Nau and I were sitting on a bench in front of the Marion Public Library on a sunny morning in May 2005 when he asked me that question. Nau had been a young social science teacher and assistant coach at Marion during the 1950s.

I told him I remembered it vividly. I was a reserve basketball player on the Marion bench only a few feet from Novotny when it happened, more than fifty years earlier. Donald Nau never forgot that shot, even though he went on to become principal of George Washington, a large high school in Cedar Rapids, and had witnessed hundreds of basketball games since Shorty's shot.

"You know, he didn't get a letter because he missed it," Nau said.

"Oh," I said, "the story is more complicated than that." Then I told him what I remembered and what I had learned about Shorty's shot and the controversy it helped ignite.

—

After the great Hugh Leffingwell graduated, along with his senior teammates, fans might have expected a dip in basketball fortunes at Marion. But the team that came along next was a powerhouse, too, ranking among the best Hipple ever coached. It lacked the height and the scoring mastery of the former team, but it had terrific speed and athleticism in the starting five and a deep bench with six rugged substitutes who stood six feet or taller. Hipple used those eleven players all season to alternately dazzle and batter Marion's opponents, and when the Indians clinched the WaMaC title in early February with a 68–44 pounding of Vinton, people were already projecting them as a likely member of the Sweet Sixteen in the state tournament.

Reporting on the game that gave Marion its sixth straight WaMaC basketball title, Larry Tanner complained that fans had become complacent. He wrote, "Marion fans are so used to winning basketball titles that they hardly cheered when the buzzer ended the fray. Championships are hard-won affairs in any conference, and the local youngsters deserve more than a few scattered cheers when they finish at the top of the heap in any sport."

Fans had come to take a WaMaC basketball championship for granted. The real action came during the run to the state finals. The Indians had made the Sweet Sixteen in two of the last three years, and many fans thought they would do it again.

But Hipple was worried, despite all the talent on this team. He had been worried for months. These boys, he thought, are so good they don't have to be at their best to win. They have been beating everyone since they were in junior high, but they had not, to his thinking, taken up the habits of sacrifice, discipline, and hard work that are the true hallmarks of champions.

This is how Larry Tanner put it as the football season approached in 1952: "The Indian mentor makes no secret of the fact that he is somewhat disappointed in the attitude of several members of next year's senior class. That attitude is even apparent in some of the underclassmen, too. The attitude is that some of the boys don't feel they have to work hard to achieve success."

Hipple worried that his players had become too much like the fans: They had come to take victory for granted. They weren't working hard enough in the off-season to unleash their exceptional talents.

The results of the football season did nothing to reduce Hipple's fears. When the season opened, he learned that one of his star players had become engaged to his girlfriend—the boy had actually given her a ring. In a world where going steady was against the rules, becoming engaged should have been unthinkable. According to several reports, Hipple made the player take the ring back from the girl and apologize to the assembled football team. He did not throw the player off the team. He could have done so without seriously damaging the team; although this player was a star, there were very capable reserves at his position. But according to Hipple's rules, close relationships with the opposite sex did not merit such drastic action. Hipple believed that being on a team did more good for a boy than being thrown off one.

The football team had a solid core of veterans from the championship team the year before. It was expected to contend for the title, but both Tipton and Anamosa were serious threats in a tough conference. "We aren't sure that Marion can beat both Tipton and Anamosa in one season," Tanner wrote. Marion would play both games on the opponents' fields. As it turned out, Marion lost them both, by the heartbreaking total of two points.

The Anamosa game was a grueling defensive battle, with all the points coming in the final 2:30 of play. Marion scored on a quarterback sneak, but the extra point attempt was wide. Marion's kickoff was fielded by Arnie Ditch, "the great Raider halfback," who ran it back for a touchdown. Anamosa scored the extra point on a running play and the contest ended 7–6. Two games later, against Tipton, Marion held the lead at several points and dominated the statistics, but in the end could not shut down the passing game of the Tigers' star quarterback, Wally Sheets, who completed nine of eighteen passes for 138 yards as Tipton won, 20–19. Tipton won the conference title with a 6–1 record. Vinton and Marion tied for second at 5–2, while Anamosa finished fourth at 3–3–1.

—

As the basketball season opened, Tanner wrote, "Hipple made no secret of the fact that this year's grid squad had more native ability than any team he has coached at Marion." Since the basketball starting lineup was composed of boys who had played key roles on the football team, it's fair to apply the same assessment to that squad as well.

Starting forwards were Jerry Peck, who was about five feet eleven, and Marvin (Shorty) Novotny, about five feet seven. Peck had started as a junior and Novotny had seen a lot of action. They were both very fast. Novotny could reach maximum speed on his second step. They were lethal on defense, preying on opposing guards, trapping them to steal the ball or tie them up. Center was Bob Christensen, six feet three, another starter from the previous year. He was long-limbed and graceful and could run the floor and handle the ball like a forward. At one guard was Harry Oakley, about five feet eleven. "Oakley could guard a guy better than anyone I ever saw," said Frank McLeod, the assistant coach. "He could take a guy's pants off without fouling him."

For most games, junior Bob Fox, who was small, fast, and athletic, filled the other guard spot. Sometimes Hipple started one of his reserves in this position to provide more height. The guards were Larry Morningstar, a six-foot-one senior, and two juniors. I was one of them, about six feet two; the other was Norm Rathje, about six feet. Rathje had moved back to Marion from Coggon. Forwards were juniors Wally DeWoody, six feet one, and Tom Domer, six feet. Reserve center was junior Everett Scott, six feet three. All these reserves saw action in almost every game, and each contributed significantly at various times. "This team's varsity is one of the best-conditioned and fastest units Hipple has put on the floor," wrote Tanner.

Fan interest was high. The gym overflowed for every game. Early in the season, work was finished that enlarged the court slightly and increased the seating capacity from about six hundred to as many as fifteen hundred with standing room. Indian games were broadcast on two Cedar Rapids stations. KCRG sold sponsorships of twelve games to six merchants for a total of $120 a game. Other merchants didn't want to be left out, so KPIG offered to broadcast sixteen games for a total of $1,600, and lined up seventy sponsors.

As his team raced through the regular season, Hipple may have been concerned about the players' discipline and effort, but it's hard to find evidence in the box scores. No starters appear to have been benched, with the possible exception of Christensen, who did not play in the season-opening Springville game, which Marion lost in overtime by two points.

Other than exhibiting a slightly rebellious nature, the most frequent offenses the boys committed involved girls and cars. Peck, Oakley, and Novotny were all dating girls they later married. Peck was frequently caught, both in cars and on foot, with the girl he was soon to wed. "I spent time on the floor boards of Jerry's car," recalled Joanie Justice Peck. "It was bad to be seen driving a car, but even worse with a girl in the car. If we saw Coach, I immediately hit the deck." Christensen was also dating girls, and had difficulty seeing what was wrong about taking them out for a drive once in a while. For all his skill, Christensen was a happy-go-lucky sort who chafed at Hipple's ban on driving and dating. He had been benched for part or all of several football games for this behavior, and his relationship with Hipple was under constant strain.

Thus the Indians entered the state basketball tournament bearing the high hopes of their many fans and the uneasiness of their fretful coach. Their record was 17–2, the losses coming from Springville and a late-season letdown against Tipton, a team the Indians had beaten earlier by thirty-three points. Since their sophomore year, the seniors had played in sixty-three basketball games and had been on the winning side fifty-nine times. Whenever they put on a game uniform, they expected to win.

The Indians cruised through the sectional with easy victories over Mount Vernon and St. Patrick's of Cedar Rapids. Manchester, which had given the Indians trouble before falling in two regular season games, was the foe in the opening round of the district tournament, played at Coe College.

On the Sunday before this game, according to some memories, Bob Christensen took his girlfriend to services at the Methodist church. They sat in the pew directly in front of one occupied that Sunday by Hipple and his wife. The Hipples did not go to church regularly, but there they were, right behind Christensen. During a break in the service, Hipple leaned over the back of the pew and said to Christensen, "You're going to have to come to school early, because you're going to have to run a lot of laps on Monday." Christensen verified the event, but was uncertain of the date. Others said it happened before the Manchester game. Something certainly happened, because when the Indians ran out onto the floor to warm up, Christensen was not among them. He had been banished for a training infraction. But Marion won, 54–39, a larger margin than during the regular season, as Hipple "sent men in and out in an almost constant stream," the *Gazette* reported.

This set up the district final against Belle Plaine. Christensen was back in the starting lineup, and although the taller Plainers opened up a lead in the first quarter, Marion took command in the second period "with a lightning fast break, deadly shooting, and a ball-hawking defense that confused the South Iowa Cedar League club," reported the *Gazette*. It was the Indians' finest game of the season, the paper said, as Hipple used "many of his reserves right from the start, [making it] difficult to tell which spots weren't being manned by regulars." The final score was 75–57. The Indians were peaking for the substate. (There was no district game against Immaculate Conception that year. Vinton had upset I. C. in the sectional.)

Marion's opponent in the first round of the substate was an unheralded team that was also fast improving. St. Mary's of Clinton, with four losses during the regular season, had never gotten out of the sectional tournament in the past. They were a well-conditioned club with good height in the

McAndrews brothers, George and Tom, and Dick Lingle, and speed in the fiery Jim Hyde.

The game was a thriller, played before fourteen thousand spectators at the Iowa University field house. The Indians were ice cold, shooting only .258, but played such tight defense that they entered the fourth quarter with a lead of 35–27, victory in sight. With Peck and Christensen in foul trouble, St. Mary's tied the game at 37–37 with 4:00 remaining. Marion forged ahead to 42–37, and then St. Mary's pulled almost even, to 42–41. Christensen fouled out. Marion squirmed ahead to 46–42. Then Lingle of St. Mary's scored and it was 46–44 with 24 seconds to play.

Now came the key moment, the shot that Shorty Novotny missed. Marion went into its famous stall, needing to hold the ball only a few seconds for the victory. Here is the way the *Gazette* described what happened next: "[Lingle] broke up a Marion stall with less than ten seconds to go. Tying the ball up under the Marion basket, the Clinton sparkplug tipped it away to George McAndrews who wheeled and went in for the bucket with four seconds to go," thus tying the game at 46–46 and sending it into overtime.

This is what I saw from my seat on the Marion bench. Full disclosure requires mentioning that what I witnessed may have happened somewhat earlier or, more likely, somewhat later in the game. I cannot vouch absolutely that it happened in the last few seconds of regulation play, but the essential fact was that Marion was ahead, stalling successfully and in control of the game when Shorty Novotny got the ball on the side of the court nearest the Marion bench. He was wide open, for a second. Hipple's rule was that if a player was wide open in a stall and had an easy basket, he should take it.

Novotny would have to dribble once or twice to score, but his opponent, who must have been Lingle, was on the other side of the basket, seriously out of position. He saw Novotny with the ball, and started toward him. Novotny hesitated for a split second, calculating whether he should go for the basket or continue the stall. Now, Novotny never hesitated. But for that split second, he did. Then he headed for the basket as Lingle closed in on him. As Novotny neared the basket, he was still well ahead of Lingle, but his angle was difficult. He was going to have an uncontested layup, but he might not be able to put it off the backboard, the surest way of scoring. He might have to put it up over the rim. He had the time, the space, and the skill to make the shot either way. It missed. Lingle got the rebound and St. Mary's tied the game with four seconds to play.

Jerry Peck fouled out in the overtime, but his replacement, Tom Domer, made two baskets, and Everett Scott, Christensen's replacement, also scored. As the clock ticked off the seconds, Marion was ahead by four points, then by two, 54–52, with just five seconds to play. But once again, St. Mary's tied the game at 54–54, forcing a double overtime, which was a sudden-death period in which the first team to lead by two points was the winner. Neither team scored until "Lingle took the ball from a wild scramble under the Indian basket and sent it through for the win after 2:01."

Marion, a pretournament favorite, had been ousted by a team nobody had heard of. But before going on to what happened next, it should be noted that other players missed important shots that day.

"Two juniors lost that game," Tom Domer insisted. The two juniors were Tom— and I. Sometime in the second half, Tom came up with a loose ball. I was, uncharacteristically, in the front court. When Tom scooped up the ball I began running toward our basket and found to my amazement that I was ahead of everyone. As we raced down court, I approached the basket from the left side; even a layup would be difficult to make running full tilt. Tom, on the right side, could have driven to the basket, but he did what Hipple always taught: He passed to the open man. I caught the ball, went up and missed the shot—badly, as I recall. I should have tried to work the ball back to Tom or simply dribbled out to set up a play, but to my everlasting chagrin, I didn't. But how could Tom say *two* juniors lost the game? I was the one who blew the shot. Tom's answer was that he could see it was going to be a difficult shot, and he should have positioned himself better to get the rebound.

Bob Christensen remembered with regret that after stealing the ball he blew a key layup because he tried to drop the ball over the front of the rim instead of banking it off the backboard as Hipple had taught.

What about the "wild scramble" from which Lingle emerged with the ball in double overtime? It came about this way. Harry Oakley had been fouled and had two free throws. If he made them both, Marion would win. If he missed the first, however, Hipple directed him to deliberately miss the second, aiming the ball so it would fall off the rim on Everett Scott's side of the lane. Scott could then grab the rebound and put it back for two points. (The rules allowed the shooting team one rebounding spot next to the basket.) Oakley missed the first shot. Following the plan, his second shot fell to Scott's side, but in the scramble that ensued, Lingle got the ball. Oakley has always blamed himself for losing the game. "I wish I could have taken those shots overhand," he said decades later.

Setting aside Scott's failure to get that rebound, there is yet another reason Marion lost that game, and it is one that Hipple used. Wally DeWoody had the mumps. Hipple was going to use DeWoody to patrol the baseline against St. Mary's zone defense. DeWoody was a good rebounder and an accurate shooter, and he would have given Christensen a lot of help with the McAndrews brothers. Before the team left for the game, DeWoody begged Hipple to let him play. "No," Hipple said. "Go home. Go to bed and get well."

The loss to St. Mary's and the players' various roles in it are seared in their memories because of what St. Mary's did in the days that followed. They won their next game for the substate championship against Burlington Central Catholic, 54–47, to make the Sweet Sixteen. Then they beat East Waterloo, 59–49, Sioux Center, 51–39, and Roland, 57–53, to bring them to the championship game, where they would face Ottumwa, which had upset the tournament favorite, Clinton, 53–49, in overtime.

As St. Mary's made its improbable run, Marion players and fans came to believe that those wins should have been Indian victories. Even St. Mary's coach Lou Galactic said that his team had been "more afraid of Marion than any team we've met since."

Ottumwa was widely favored to beat St. Mary's in the championship game, but it turned out to be a romp as St. Mary's won, 61–44. Lynn Brown and his wife went to that game with the Hipples. When it was over, Brown turned to Hipple and was surprised to see that he was crying. "He had tears in his eyes," Brown wrote. "He knew that Marion could have won the state championship, which is the goal of every coach."

Larry Tanner said as much in his column. "All we could think of during the [championship] battle was, 'If our kids hadn't been so generous we might be handing that shellacking to Ottumwa.'"

—

Two months passed before the full repercussions of the loss were revealed. The bombshell fell in May during an all-school awards assembly in the gym.

When it came time to announce the names of boys who won letters, the duty fell to Lynn Brown because Hipple was driving some track stars to the state meet, as he always did.

Christensen and some of his teammates were standing near one of the gym's walls, waiting to be called up to receive their basketball letters. But Brown did *not* read off the names of five players—Bob Christensen, Larry Morningstar, Marvin Novotny, Harry Oakley, and Jerry Peck. They stood in astonished silence as the junior players and one senior were called up. The senior was Jim Lang, a reserve who saw little action but had been on the team for four years. Lang remembered that he was so frustrated and embarrassed to receive a letter when his classmates did not that, in retrospect, "[I] wish I had just walked away."

The boys' parents were shocked and embarrassed. They had been proud of their sons and the records they had achieved, and apparently had no inkling during the season that Hipple had been dissatisfied with the boys' effort. To the parents, the denial of letters was more than a surprise and more than an insult. It was a black mark their sons would carry for life. They didn't understand what the boys had done wrong. They began to protest, and they didn't stop until they had the satisfaction of confronting Hipple in a hearing before the board of education.

The hearing took place in a high school classroom in early July, nearly two months after the boys graduated. The board had the power to overturn the decision and grant the letters. All ten parents and their sons attended the hearing, according to the *Sentinel*. The public was not admitted, but reporters from the *Sentinel* and the *Gazette* covered the first part of the meeting, during which the parents and players questioned Hipple. "The entire meeting was grim," the *Sentinel* report said. There was no byline on the story, but Tanner probably wrote it.

Board president Merrill Smith opened the meeting with a prayer for divine guidance, which had a calming effect. C. B. Vernon explained that rules governing the awarding of letters were made before Hipple was hired and that the awards were not guaranteed by playing time. Vernon explained that Hipple did not make the decision alone—Vernon and Glenn Nicholson, principal of the high school, were members of the letter committee along with Hipple.

Leverne Morningstar, Larry's father, speaking for the parents, said, "We believe the action in not awarding the boys letters will bring discredit on them and their parents in the community. We aren't here to find fault with Mr. Hipple or demand his resignation but to find out why the boys weren't given the letters we feel they deserved."

Then Hipple took the floor and answered questions for nearly two hours. The clearest reason for the letter denial appears in the *Gazette* report. Hipple said that he had repeatedly warned the boys during the season that their attitude and performance were not up to expectations. But in the end, their participation in athletics "had nothing to do with this case," Hipple said. "Most of it was based on the final twelve or fourteen weeks of school" when the boys misbehaved in a variety of ways.

Their defiance, subordinated during the basketball season, flourished when it ended. The most serious charges against them were that four of the boys skipped school the day after the loss to St. Mary's. A few days later, when the coaching staff took the team to Iowa City to watch some state tournament games, three of the boys did not report to the bus for the trip home. "Although it was not brought out directly, Hipple indicated that these two incidents were responsible for the withholding of the athletic awards," the *Gazette* said.

This point was missed by the *Sentinel* reporter, who focused, as the parents apparently did, on their sons' performances as athletes. The parents asked Hipple to describe the shortcomings in effort and attitude of each boy, which he did, and which must have pained him. He was asked whether their refusal to come out for track had anything to do with the decision, and he said it did not, but then muddied the waters by adding, according to the *Gazette*, "But they probably could have redeemed themselves by coming out for track and showing school authorities they were willing to work."

Then came the most complex subject of all: the importance of winning. A parent asked why the boys weren't benched or thrown off the team during the season. Hipple said it was because several would have to be removed and in doing that, "we would have had to change our style of defense." Leverne Morningstar asked whether this meant Hipple didn't want to bench the boys for fear of losing and thus "put winning above the character of these boys?" Hipple did not respond.

Another parent asked the question that must have been on everyone's minds. Would the boys have been given letters if they had beaten St. Mary's and gone on to win the state championship? Wasn't this really what this was all about, losing that game? The question was hypothetical and, as such, unanswerable. If they had beaten St. Mary's, the boys wouldn't have skipped school. If they had been in the state tournament, they would not have taken a school trip to watch the state tournament. If they had won the state tournament, how could Hipple possibly have denied them letters, for their accomplishment would have been exceptional? The *Sentinel* did not report how Hipple answered the question, but it did reveal that he was still angry over the loss. He said that the boys would be remembered as the "give-away" team because they did not play as well as they were able.

As the meeting drew to a close, Vernon said that he had supported Hipple's decision after careful consideration. He said that Hipple was the best coach in the state and that deep in their hearts the boys respected him. He said that when Hipple goes to basketball clinics, he attends every class, never shirking an opportunity to improve. The boys should take a lesson from that kind of behavior. Letters did not mean much, Vernon continued. What mattered was that the boys had been rewarded by being able to play before thousands of spectators.

The *Sentinel* then granted a last word to Shorty Novotny, who was at once accepting and defiant. He said, "If we don't deserve letters, we don't want them."

The board went into executive session without parents or the press, deliberated for two hours, and then voted, four to one, to uphold the coach. The length of the executive session was remarkable because a vote against the coach would also have been a repudiation of Vernon and Nicholson. Apparently the board members needed all that time to unravel the issue and, perhaps, to say what they had to say about it.

For years, many people insisted that Hipple denied the letters because the team lost to St. Mary's. Others, including Christensen, said it was all about attitude.

—

When I finished telling Donald Nau the story, he said, "It was a tremendous mistake not to give those letters. It's an act that will come back to haunt you."

Lynn Brown had a similar view. "I think [it] was the start of [Hipple's] power decline although it was not noticeable at the time." On the other hand, Brown said, Hipple's code allowed him "no other option." Hipple believed that "there had to be consequences for improper behavior. He could not let them get away with it."

The two educators seemed to be saying that in denying the letters, Hipple was true to his principles but had violated his contract with the parents. His act provided ammunition to those who disliked him and his rules. With the approval of Vernon and Nicholson, Hipple had set a flame to a long fuse that might burn for years, but eventually could set off an explosion.

Chapter 24
How Paddles Made a Champion, 1953

In 1953, the town of Monticello buzzed with excitement as the homecoming game for the Black Panthers approached. The team was sitting atop the WaMaC Conference with a 4–0 record. The Panthers had a good shot at an undefeated season. Decorations painted by students on the store windows were "the best in recent years," said the *Monticello Express*. Homecoming was even more exciting because Monticello would play Marion, one of the few teams that had a chance to upset the Panthers.

The town was united in opposition to a reviled foe. On the Thursday night before the game, more than three hundred people snaked-danced through the business district, then gathered at the school for speeches by the coach and other officials. After the cheerleaders aroused the crowd in a series of yells, the pep rally culminated, the *Express* reported, "with the throwing into the bonfire a dummy representing a Marion Indian. With the burning of the dummy are supposed to go the evil spirits." The next afternoon, during a pep assembly at the school, the name of the homecoming queen was to be announced. This was to be followed by a parade through the town, led by the pep band, climaxing "when the group gathers at stoplight corner for a final group of yells."

On paper, Monticello was favored. The Panthers had beaten Independence, the team that had defeated Marion early in the season. In addition, Monticello seemed stronger on both sides of the ball, scoring a total of 103 points while allowing only forty by opponents, while Marion had scored only seventy-three and allowed forty-five in compiling a 3–1 conference record.

The *Express* picked Monticello to win by a touchdown. Monticello coach Harold Shugart was cautious. His coaches had scouted Marion well, he said, but Hipple could be expected to come up with some surprises. "It will be do or die for the Indians and I'm sure they don't want to die."

—

At Marion, Hipple had sifted through an inexperienced squad of eighty-three players to assemble a team that was beginning to surprise its fans. The preseason outlook had been dismal, with only one returning regular among just four lettermen—and they all were backs. They were Norm Rathje, 180-pound fullback, who had been a starter the year before, Wally DeWoody, 170-pound quarterback, and halfbacks Bob Fox, 155, and Bill Hotle, 165. Hipple moved Hotle to right end, installing Lloyd Jordan, a fast and powerful 170-pound farm boy who had recovered from an ankle injury, at halfback.

The rest of the lineup was pieced together from an untested group of juniors and seniors. Hipple had hoped to have two huge underclassmen, each well over 200 pounds, at tackle, but both Merle Folkers and Harold Kuebler had to withdraw because of heart-related problems. The coach had to go with his back-up choices for that position. One of them was Verdean Stade, who weighed 187 pounds. I was the other one, at 172. Hipple probably crossed his fingers when he put me in the lineup. I had played end since junior high, but my appearances in varsity games had been brief and without distinction. Hipple completed the lineup with Jeri Smith, a 160-pound junior, at end, senior Gary Eschman, 150, and junior Bob Murray, 175, at guards, and junior Bill Farmer, 184, at center.

This was a fairly large team. The backs were proven, but the line was woefully green. The linemen had to learn a lot in a short time, and the coaches later said that it was the paddles that made the difference. Almost all Marion football coaches during the glory years carried wooden paddles about three feet long. Hipple supposedly brandished the longest one of all, but it's not likely he carried it around much; he also had to manage a clipboard and a whistle, and a paddle that big would be a hindrance.

Frank McLeod, assistant coach from 1947 to 1952, introduced the paddles as an aid to memory. He explained that Hipple's blocking system was so simple that any lineman who forgot it had to take a swat, usually administered by the person he was supposed to block.

Hipple's playbook contained only five mimeographed legal-sized pages. It illustrated about eleven basic running plays and a similar number of passing plays, plus a few special plays requiring specific blocking assignments. There were also diagrams for such maneuvers as kick-offs and punt returns. Hipple drew all the plays and wrote out the captions by hand. Two of the five pages were devoted to blocking assignments for linemen, and the system, once understood, should have been foolproof. (For a description see the notes for this chapter.)

During practice, Hipple and his assistants drilled the players again and again on the basic plays. Hipple knew the plays so well, it was said, that he could tell from the sidelines when a player blew his assignment. There was really no excuse for forgetting a blocking assignment. Yet it happened, and paddles were swung.

The ferocity with which the paddles were used varies according to who is telling the story. John Nieland recalled a practice in his sophomore year, 1955, when he was playing defensive end against the varsity as it worked on a new play. When a halfback neglected to block him, Hipple instructed Nieland to hit the offender with a paddle, saying that if he didn't do it hard enough, Nieland would be paddled, too. Nieland took the advice to heart and administered a solid whack—the force of which he soon regretted. The varsity ran the play again and again right at him, burying him in blockers each time. "I grew up a lot that day," Nieland said.

Some former players had forgotten about the paddles altogether, and had no memory of being swatted. Others remembered it differently. Norm Rathje, one of the toughest guys ever to pull on an Indian jersey and who later became a coach, said that having one player hit another with a paddle "bordered on brutality. If someone didn't do the job, having someone else hit him is a poor way to teach."

Paddles were fairly commonplace in Iowa schools during the 1940s and 1950s. Willys O. Hulin, who taught industrial arts at Marion, had a paddle. He warned students that if they misbehaved, "I'm going to beat your butt until it shines like a little red apple." However, Hulin was more bluster than action; he may never have used the paddle at all. Instead, boys regularly stole his paddles and drilled holes in them.

Pete Kellams remembered taking up his first teaching assignment in junior high at Newton, Iowa, in the early 1960s. He was shown to his homeroom, which featured a teacher's desk that had been spackled with paint to make it look like an antique for a student play. Inside the top drawer, which was missing some slats, was a paddle. The rules governing its use required that another teacher be present and that the child be granted the option of going to see the principal instead of being paddled. The second choice was not always a wise one, because a guilty verdict usually led to a paddling by the principal.

One day the librarian frantically called Kellams into the library, where he was shocked to see one of his smallest and angriest students throwing chairs out the second-story window. He grabbed the kid and dragged him into the hallway. "You're going to see the principal right now," Kellams said. The boy had no taste for that. He asked, "Can't I just take my whacks right here?" "No way," said Kellams, marching the tiny miscreant down the hall. In the office the boy watched in terror as the principal punctuated his lecture by slapping his paddle against the sole of his own shoe. Suddenly, the boy bolted from the office and fled the building, running toward the center of town, where his father had an auto dealership. The startled principal took off after him, waving his paddle in hot pursuit, only to slow to a walk and then return to school, realizing how fiendish he appeared.

In Marion football, the assistant coaches used the paddles during drills and scrimmages to "swat players who didn't seem to hear the 'hut, hut' at the right time," wrote Ed Reed, adding that these swats often hurt.

Lynn Brown, who replaced McLeod as assistant coach, had a more benign recollection. "We used them in drills to encourage linemen to get across the line of scrimmage quickly. We might tap them on the count to help them remember to get a good start." This reinforcement, he wrote, was a major factor in turning the raw youngsters of 1953 into one of the best lines the Indians ever had.

—

The paddle-trained Indians that year began the season with a surprising 7–6 non-conference win over Oelwein. They were thumped in their WaMaC opener, though, when a reserve back from Independence named Larry Roberts ran wild out of the Mustang's box formation, an especially deceptive version of the single wing. Roberts, who was in the game only because Independence star George Cabalka was injured, rushed for an incredible 240 yards—all but twenty-six of his team's total—on sixteen carries for an average of fifteen yards every time he touched the ball. He was ghostlike dodging tackles. On at least one play, and perhaps others, I had two shots at him before he crossed the line of scrimmage—and of course I missed each time. I can see him still, ducking as tacklers dove at him, squirming out of their grasping arms, and galloping into the night. Independence won, 26–18, and Roberts was permanently installed in the Independence starting lineup and my own personal hall of fame.

Hipple remedied our problem with tackling drills. He had no patience for tackles achieved by grasping jerseys or pads. Jersey tackles tore the fabric, and he was the one who had to mend the rips. He made players run laps for torn-jersey tackles. He wanted shoulders buried in midsections. As their tackling improved, the Indians ground out three straight victories, including a 13–6 win over previously undefeated Maquoketa. The stage was set for the battle with Monticello. The Indians needed a victory to have a shot at the WaMaC title. As Hipple drilled his players week after week on the crisp execution of split-T option running plays, he also began schooling them on a few trick plays.

—

From the start, Marion dominated the line of scrimmage and piled up yardage, but could not break away from Monticello. Marion scored first, but Monticello soon countered to tie the game at 7–7. Before the Panthers kicked off following their touchdown, Hipple drew quarterback DeWoody aside. "Run it up the middle," he told him. Hipple almost never called the plays, but he had seen something.

DeWoody fielded the kickoff on the fifteen-yard line and started up the middle, certain he was going to be smashed by a swarm of tacklers. But Marion's blockers cut down the onrushing Panthers, and DeWoody burst through a gap untouched. He raced to the goal line with an escort of joyous teammates. Marion threatened again, but failed to score, and the first half ended with Marion ahead, 14–7. In the second half, Marion cavorted at will but could not score. "[The kids] were throwing the ball all over the place," wrote Larry Tanner. "Both Jordan and Fox would break through big holes in the Panther line, cut to the outside, then lateral to DeWoody, who was trailing the play."

Penalties shut down several Indian marches, allowing Monticello to stage a comeback. The Panthers combined passes and Indian penalties to move down the field and eventually score, tying the game. Time was running out. The Indians received the kickoff and began a march, but it stalled on the Monticello thirty-three-yard line. It was third down and nine, with less than a minute to play. Unless the Indians could make a first down, the game would end in a tie—condemning Marion to second place in the conference.

Again, Hipple stepped in to call the play. Here's how Tanner described it. "DeWoody faded back to pass. The Panthers swarmed in toward the lanky signal caller. He calmly handed the ball off to Lloyd Jordan, line-smashing right halfback, who came around behind Wally, took the pigskin, and raced to the losers' six-yard line behind a wall of Indian blockers." Hipple had pulled the old Statue of Liberty play, and it had worked beautifully for twenty-seven yards.

Norm Rathje slammed into the eight-man Monticello line. He got three yards. "The pile-driving fullback was given the ball again," Tanner wrote. "He thundered into the line, was hit at the line of scrimmage, bulled his way past two or three tacklers and fell into the end zone beneath a swarm of never-say-die Panthers." There were sixteen seconds left on the clock when Rathje scored, time enough for a kickoff. Marion smothered the return, and won, 20–14.

Marion, said the *Monticello Express* after game, "was the best team [the Panthers have] met this year and they should consider themselves lucky to come out only one touchdown behind." The "terrific Marion line game" and Rathje's smashing runs produced "statistics so lopsided for Marion that we'll not even print them." (Marion made fifteen first downs to Monticello's six, and gained 298 total yards to Monticello's 137.) Marion used fourteen players in the game. Monticello used eleven.

Marion's next game was its own homecoming, against an uncharacteristically weak Tipton team. The Indians romped, 60–18. (Through 2008, the sixty points scored in that game was in a first-place tie for most points ever scored by a Marion team, and the yardage achieved, 648, was more than fifty yards higher than any other team in Marion's history.) Reserves played a great deal of the time and were effective, especially the sophomore passing combination of Darell Failor and Larry Brooks. Failor threw two touchdown passes to Brooks. One of them went ninety-four-yards.

(It is the second longest Marion TD pass of all time, just two yards shorter than the pass thrown by Dutch Coon to Failor's older brother, Ed, in 1944.)

Marion beat Vinton, 19–0, to finish 6–1 in the WaMaC, tied for first with Monticello. In the last game of the season, against nonconference foe Mount Vernon, the Indians were overconfident and sloppy, and left the field at halftime with the game tied at 7–7. There was no locker room at the football field. The team met in the school bus. After all the players were seated, Hipple entered. He was outraged. He did not yell, but he administered a severe tongue-lashing that had players hanging their heads in shame. His major theme was that they had behaved disgracefully. "If you lose this game you will regret it for the rest of your lives," he said. "You will never forget it as long as you live." Each player owed it to himself and his teammates to play to the best of his ability, and each of them should feel nothing but shame. The team was embarrassed and aroused by Hipple's speech and went on to win, 25–7.

When Hipple got on the bus after the game, the squad let out a mighty cheer, and the coach's face broke into the happy smile captured in the photo by Gary Eschman that is displayed in Hipple's memorial trophy case at Marion High School. Seeing that photograph, many people who never met Hipple thought he was a cheerful sort, while those who played for him remembered his steely insistence on always giving one's best.

At Monticello, Coach Shugart said his 1953 team would be long remembered for its outstanding season. At Marion, Larry Tanner pronounced the team "a pleasant surprise" and complimented the line by comparing it to the great front wall of 1949. Years later, at their fiftieth reunion, team members were introduced to the Marion crowd before a high school game. A local man standing nearby recognized Tom Domer as a member of that class.

"Eight and one," he said. "That must have been a good team."

"Oh," said Tom, "about average."

Both men were right.

Chapter 25
Overachievers, 1953–1954

If the football team that year was about average, the basketball team was decidedly below it. After its first three games, Jack Ogden wrote in the *Gazette* that the team had already assured Hipple that it would have the worst record of any he had coached in the previous five years, since none of those teams had lost more than three games, and that's how this one started the season. I played guard on the team.

The first two losses were perhaps to be expected—to Springville, always tough early in the season, and to Grinnell, a power in the west. But Springville crushed Marion by eighteen points, and the Indians were ragged and inefficient against Grinnell, losing by ten points. (The Grinnell game was at a coaches' clinic, to which Marion was invited so Hipple could demonstrate his famous fast break. Of all Hipple's teams, this one had the slowest and clumsiest fast break. After we bumbled through the demonstration, I felt we deserved a tongue-lashing for humiliating our coach, but Hipple said nothing about it.)

The third loss of the season made other WaMaC teams eager to face the Indians. Mount Vernon beat Marion by a single point, 54–53. The Indians seemed to be slogging through mud in Mount Vernon's tiny gym, unable to execute plays they had been running since seventh grade. After the game, a Mount Vernon player said to me, in the friendliest way possible, "Well, we finally beat you guys at something." It felt like a punch in the stomach. The rest of the WaMaC was thinking, if Mount Vernon can beat those guys, so can we.

It's not as if my teammates and I were accustomed to this sort of thing, this losing. We had been undefeated as freshman, playing about five games. We had been undefeated as sophomores, 18–0. As juniors we had played on a team that went 21–3. Our high school career record before the season started was 44–3, and the defeats were by a total of eight points.

The big difference was that we lost our six-foot-three center, Everett Scott, who had been a strong rebounder, scorer, and defender. Scott had broken his arm playing football, and chose as a senior to go out for cross-country to be eligible for basketball. One day, Scott said, he asked Hipple for permission to miss cross-country practice to attend an event related to farming, his chosen career. When Hipple refused, Scott quit, feeling he had to put his future ahead of sports, and the basketball team lost a key man. (Hipple, it should be noted, frequently gave farm boys permission to miss practice for activities related to their careers, such as showing cattle at a fair. It's likely there were other strains between Scott and Hipple.) Scott's replacement was Verdean Stade, a handsome blond as tall as Scott, and nearly as strong, but not as quick or as good a ball handler.

After the Mount Vernon loss, the editor of the *Monticello Express* was convinced his team would trounce the Indians when they traveled to Monticello for the conference opener later in the week. The Panthers were in a mood to stop Marion, he wrote; they were tired of being pushed around. Their center, Carl Egger, should be able to use his height advantage to shut down Marion's Stade and outscore him as well. As the editor prepared his front page for the issue that would come out after the game, he inserted a four-column photo of the team and even wrote a caption describing the victory he anticipated.

Meanwhile, Marion played Wilson of Cedar Rapids in the Coe field house. Normally, Marion fans packed the arena for games against Cedar Rapids schools, but there were many empty seats this time. Few fans wanted to see the Indians lose again. Surprisingly, Marion won easily, 52–28, more through determination than skill. The Indians were "still a far cry from the polished aggregations Hipple has produced in recent years," wrote Jack Ogden.

A few days later, Marion beat Monticello, 64–53, on the strength of a fourth-quarter rally. Stade outscored Egger sixteen to six. The editor of the *Express* had to hurry back to his office and rewrite the caption under the team photo, apologizing in a brief note that it was too late to remove the photo itself.

Thus launched, Marion went through the first half of the WaMaC season undefeated, but not without difficulty. We managed a last-second, one-point victory over Independence when Stade missed a shot but Tom Domer grabbed the rebound and put it in as the buzzer sounded. In the next game, against Maquoketa, Domer missed, and Stade tipped it in for the win. We squeaked by Vinton 64–58. Other games were easier, including a 65–45 payback to Mount Vernon.

Hipple began experimenting with the lineup. The core of the team was Wally DeWoody and Domer at the forward positions, and me at guard. Early in the season, Hipple moved Norm Rathje into the other starting guard spot, replacing Bob Fox. The starters were all six feet or taller, but lacked the speed and grace of earlier Indian teams. Hipple brought Darell Failor up from a sophomore team that was having no problem winning its games by enormous margins. Failor played center, and eventually replaced Stade in the starting lineup. Failor was only about five feet ten, but he was extremely agile. He usually played in front of his taller opponents, using his leaping ability to intercept passes that careless guards thought they could toss over his head. Despite his youth, he played fearlessly and often befuddled bigger defenders with his speed. Juniors Jeri Smith and Dallas Fairley rounded out the rotation.

By this time, the *Gazette* reported, "it's the Marion of old now." But if the Indians were improving, so was the competition, and as the team began its second run through the conference, Monticello beat us at home in a game I can neither remember nor explain. Larry Tanner offered a partial excuse, reporting that Stade missed the game because of an illness. (Or perhaps he was benched for walking in the halls with the girl he later married.) This time, Egger scored eighteen points. At Monticello, the editor of the *Express* was overjoyed. He ran a banner headline across seven columns on the front page that read:

Panthers Beat Marion, 62 to 59

"They said it couldn't happen, but it did," the story began. The fans were ecstatic. It was the first time Monticello had beaten Marion in fifteen games over seven seasons. The coach later said that this victory was the highlight of the year.

The next game was against Franklin of Cedar Rapids, and it, too, resulted in a Marion loss, 52–48. This time, it was DeWoody who was on the sidelines, reportedly because he was recovering from the flu. But the students knew that DeWoody was benched because he had been caught, one too many times, walking down the hallway with his girlfriend, maybe even holding her hand. DeWoody was not allowed to play until very late in the game after Failor fouled out while battling the much taller Franklin players.

Immediately after the loss, Bill James, a senior, charged up to Hipple and snarled, "Well, I hope you're satisfied now." The next school day, the principal, Glen Nicholson, ordered James to write on a blackboard one hundred times, "I'm sorry for what I said." James wrote the sentences out as required and at the end added, "You made me write it but not believe it." James, and many others, thought Hipple's enforcement of his rules had cost Marion a victory. It was not the first time, nor it would be the last, that Hipple put his principles above victory.

Then, with the title at stake, Marion lost to Independence in their tiny gym—a court so small it seemed to be crowded into the school's attic. The score was 45–42. One of Independence's guards (Larry Roberts, perhaps) flagrantly double-dribbled twice but was not called for either violation. It was the first time Independence had beaten Marion in twelve games. The defeat dropped the Indians out of a tie for the conference lead with little chance of getting it back. Hipple neither castigated us at halftime nor consoled us after the game. Not once, all season long, did he remind us of the conference race or warn us that we were facing do-or-die situations. He treated each game as a discrete challenge and behaved no differently after we won than after we lost.

Other teams, long denied a victory over Marion, plotted revenge. "Any time you beat Marion it has automatically been a great season," wrote the *Manchester Press* in chronicling a close but losing game with the Indians.

While fans in other towns gloated over victories over the Indians, or even extolled narrow losses, no fan in Marion looked forward to the state tournament. As pairings were announced, Larry Tanner, who often reflected Hipple's view, cautioned in at least two columns that it was unlikely that Marion would survive the sectional tournament, where opponents would include St. Patrick's of Cedar Rapids, which had lost only a few games, and Springville, which was 22–0 going into the sectional, and had trounced Marion by eighteen points in November.

—

About this time Hipple replaced Rathje at starting guard with Dallas Fairley, a long-limbed junior at six feet one. As Rathje remembered it, the move was preceded by an altercation between the two players during practice ("we were screwing around") that resulted in both being sent to the locker room. "The next game, I didn't start," Rathje said. "I hardly got into the game." When this continued for several games without an explanation from Hipple, Rathje quit. Hipple called the boy out of class and urged him to come back on the team, but Rathje refused. "He said, 'This is the biggest mistake you can make,'" Rathje recalled, "and I said 'I think you are the one making the mistake. I don't like what you do.' I was done, I was out of there."

Rathje was not one for idleness, and his football teammate, Lloyd Jordan, had just the thing to keep him occupied: become a boxer. Jordan was preparing to fight in the Golden Gloves and he thought Rathje should also give it a try. Jordan had been training as a boxer for several winters. Two years earlier, as a sixteen-year-old sophomore, he had stepped into the ring for his first fight without a minute's experience and only a few hours of forethought. It happened this way: One day at school, Richard Bristol, a senior, asked Jordan, a sophomore, if he wanted to go to Cedar Rapids that night and fight in the Golden Gloves. Jordan had a car, and that may have been why Bristol invited him—to get a ride. That sounded interesting to Jordan. He called his father to explain why he would be home late and his father said that would be fine and in fact he would come downtown and watch.

When young men showed up to fight in the Golden Gloves, all they needed was a pair of sneakers. The tournament provided gloves, trunks, and protective cups. The fighters didn't wear headgear or use mouth guards. When Jordan stepped into the ring for the first time, he discovered something he had always suspected: He had a terrific punch—with either hand. The kid was ambidextrous; he could destroy an opponent with his right or his left. He pummeled his adversary and won the fight. Later that night, as Jordan remembers it, he won again. Summaries in the *Gazette* indicate he lost in the quarterfinals in what Jordan remembered was a split decision. Jordan didn't really know how to box, but the whole thing was exciting as hell.

Jordan, a farm boy, was as tough as they come. He had a diamond-shaped face with a broad forehead and high cheekbones that narrowed to his chin. His face was naturally red and he tended to look angry all the time. He didn't talk much. "Jordan was so strong even his face had muscles," said David Martin, an awed underclassman. Jordan continued to train at the YMCA. At some point, Hipple expressed disapproval. Jordan replied that boxing kept him in shape, and the subject never came up again.

Now, two years later, as a senior, Jordan decided to enter the Golden Gloves again, this time as a member of the team sponsored by Eby Sporting Goods, a local retailer. Because he had so few fights he was still classed as a novice. More experienced fighters were placed in the open division. Jordan would fight at 167 pounds, and he wanted Rathje, who weighed 180, to fight on the team as well.

The night the Golden Gloves opened, as Rathje remembered it, he just went along for the ride, keeping company with Lloyd and his older brother, Kenny, who was going to fight as well. An official asked Rathje in a taunting fashion why didn't he fight, too. Rathje didn't back down from challenges. Like Jordan on that night two years earlier, Rathje had never been in a boxing ring. But he'd been in a few street fights, so he had a firm grasp of the principles. He decided to give it a try. Rathje had a square face and a fullback's thick neck. He had a huge grin and was as bombastic as Jordan was stoical.

The boxing tournament was conducted over several days. Each boy had four or five fights. Jordan knocked out one of his opponents, a fighter some had pegged to win the title, in thirty-two seconds of the first round. The crushed fighter lay still for a long time. His tongue curled up in his mouth and his eyes rolled back in his head. A doctor rushed into the ring, and Jordan was afraid for a moment he had broken his opponent's neck. Jordan also whipped Wayne Phillips, a beautifully chiseled halfback for Coe College. Phillips was about four years Lloyd's senior and had trained hard to win the title. The fight wasn't even close. Although Jordan didn't win by a knockout, Phillips never failed to tell him in later years that he had given him the worst beating of his life. Jordan won the crown at 167 pounds.

Rathje, meanwhile, powered his way through his division, beating Lloyd's older brother, Kenny, in the process. He didn't knock anyone out, but overwhelmed his adversaries with a nonstop offense. In one fight, his exhausted opponent refused to answer the bell for the third round. A few days after Rathje won his championship, a man sought him out and offered to be his trainer or manager, assuring him that he had the potential to turn professional. But Rathje, his ears still ringing from the blows he had absorbed, said he wanted no more of a sport that led so predictably to headaches.

That year, as Marion's weakest basketball team prepared for the opening round of the state tournament, schoolmates marveled at the two seniors' championship run in a brutal sport. A *Cedar Rapids Gazette* photo showed them unmarked, clad in robes with towels around their necks, wearing the same scowls they displayed in their football photos.

—

Despite our many loses, I was inexplicably confident as the sectional tournament approached. I bragged to my father that we would beat both St. Pat's and Springville. My father, who went to every game with my mother, rarely commented on my play or the team's. He confined his remarks to a slogan he repeated each time Tom Domer and I left for the game: "Good luck. Go hard. High on the rebounds." But he felt he needed to respond to my rash prediction, either because I was being cocky or because he wanted to prepare me for the inevitable. "You'll beat St. Patrick's," he said, "but you won't beat Springville." Springville was undefeated and had lost only one game over two seasons.

The sectional tournament was again held at Marion. This gave the Indians home court advantage as we beat St. Patrick's, 61–48. The game was easier than expected, possibly because St. Pat's star, Hal Trosky, was playing with a badly bruised ankle.

Now we had to prepare for Springville, which had embarrassed us at home in the season opener. Springville's offense depended on the speed of its guards, who raced the ball down the court and into the hands of the team's scoring ace, Ron Yeisley, or to the center, Dick Biggart. "All year long we had a fast break no one could stop," Biggart recalled years later.

But Hipple devised an antidote. "Hipple came up with a defense that hadn't even been invented yet," Biggart said. "It was a zone press." Marion defenders met the guards deep in their own half-court as they brought the ball down, but did not try to trap them or steal the ball as they would in a full-court press. Instead, the goal was to slow their progress and create frustration. "Our coach told the guards to try to dribble through it, but that didn't work," Biggart said.

Meanwhile, Hipple assigned Fairley to guard Yeisley man-for-man, while the rest of the Indians defended zones. As Springville prepared for the game, Biggart added, the coach, Howard Strong, was so concerned about what Hipple might do that he introduced some new plays. They didn't work well, making things worse for the Orioles.

"Marion's sly fox, Les Hipple, pulled another one out of the bag," wrote the *Gazette*. "Marion, famed for its fire-wagon attack through the years ... slowed down to a mere walk for a 56–49 victory and the Class A sectional championship." Fairley held Yeisley to only twelve points until he fouled out, and the Indians delivered balanced scoring along with deliberate play. With four minutes to play, Marion went into a complete stall, which was interrupted by free throws and a layup. After the game, a victory no one expected, happy fans surged about the team. We carried Hipple into the dressing room, hoping the ride wasn't causing too much pain to his hip.

We had come together as a team, found a style of play that suited us, and were filled with confidence. We must have been focused on the tournament because there were two regular season games to play, and we barely escaped Manchester, and then fell to lowly Anamosa in the last game of the regular season, 57–54. Tom Domer attributed the Anamosa loss to Hipple's overconfidence. He played the reserves for long periods, and when he sent the regulars back in, we couldn't catch the Raiders. Hipple's practice late in the season, and especially during tournaments, was to bring up sophomores to give them varsity experience. Hipple may not have been expecting a long tournament run, so he gave the sophomores more playing time against Anamosa, and the tactic backfired. It was the third conference loss for Marion that season, each coming by three points. The team finished in a tie for second place.

Tournament rules limited squads to twelve players, so to add sophomores Hipple had to drop upperclassmen who had been on the squad all year long. For sophomores, it was a thrill to join the varsity and go to Iowa City, even if all they did was warm up on the big floor and never get into the game. For seniors who were dumped after being loyal scrubs during hundreds of practices, it was an injustice.

Unless a boy grew up in Iowa City, chances are he never saw, nor could have imagined, anything like the University of Iowa field house. It was an enormous building that included a swimming pool with seating for 3,500, a vast dirt-floored armory where athletes practiced football, baseball, track, and other sports, and a huge basketball court with seating for about 15,000 people on two tiers rising high into the sky.

A boy coming out of a small town where he played most of his games in a gym that held a few hundred spectators could be overwhelmed by the cavernous space, the vast playing floor, the glass backboards, and the realization that he was in a shrine where sports legends performed. When games began, the noise from the crowd was deafening. Seating in the tiers was made of steel, and fans stomped their feet to unnerve the opposing team. The stomping was virtually continuous, setting off a tremendous, echoing din. Players dribbling the ball could not hear it bounce. If they listened to the crowd, they couldn't play basketball. Smoking was discouraged, but hundreds of people puffed away, and after a series of day and night games, a bluish-gray fog hung over the court. For a kid from the sticks, it could be nerve-racking.

Now Marion faced Anamosa again. The Raiders were hot. Despite a poor record, they had surprised all of eastern Iowa by beating Monticello, 51–49, to win the sectional tournament, and then they had toppled Marion at home in the last game of the regular season.

The Indians weren't going to let that happen again. But it was the field house, as much as Marion, that defeated the Raiders that day. "We didn't have the jitters," said the Anamosa coach afterward. "We had gone beyond that and were so tense we could hardly move." Facing Marion's relentless defense, the Raiders had difficulty getting the ball past half court. Marion was ahead 41–9 in the third quarter when Hipple sent in the reserves, giving a bunch of sophomores invaluable experience and denying the thrill of a lifetime to some senior reserves watching from the stands. The final score was 70–41.

By this time I was bathed in a completely irrational sense of confidence. I wasn't thinking about going to the state finals. It was impossible to think that far ahead, but I was certain we would win the next game. We could do it, I thought; we had Hipple; we were Marion. The feeling had come over me in the Springville game. I was fouled while taking a jump shot; the defender hit the wrist of my shooting arm, throwing the ball off course. The foul wasn't called, but the wayward ball hit the backboard and bounced through the net. I tried to suppress a grin; I knew then we would win.

I felt like a gambler on a lucky streak. The next game was against Immaculate Conception, which had a terrific team that year, ranked far above the Indians. Surely this was the year I. C. would finally beat Marion. But I. C.'s star center, Dick Cummins, was out with a chipped ankle. The Indians would play a depleted team. In the locker room before the game, as we silently prepared to take the floor, a sudden loud noise came from the next room. It was the I. C. coach, Red Jennings, screaming at his players. We looked at each other and thought, *They must be afraid of us.*

The papers described a battle royal in which the lead changed hands thirteen times and the score was tied on twelve other occasions. I remember it as a game in which we never panicked and slowly took control, then stalled to hold the lead. Final score, 54–49. I believed that had we not stalled, we would have won by a bigger margin. I. C., which supposedly had a deep bench, played only five men, and we wore them out. Make that six straight tournament wins for Marion over I. C.

A few days before the next game, I was walking past the Carnegie Memorial Library on Main Street when a stout man wearing overhauls, a mackinaw jacket, and a billed cap approached from the other direction. He stopped me and asked if I played on the basketball team. When I said yes, he asked who our next opponent was.

"DeWitt," I said.

"Oh," the man said, "You'll beat them."

I thought so, too, but neither of us had any idea what we were talking about. (It was the only time an unfamiliar adult in Marion acknowledged my participation in sports. Every Saturday I sacked and carried out groceries at the Me Too Supermarket and thus saw hundreds of citizens. Not one mentioned sports to me. We may have been stars in Larry Tanner's columns, but people in the real world didn't treat us that way.)

DeWitt had shared the championship of the Iowa Conference with last year's state champion, St. Mary's of Clinton, and had lost about four games all season. They were a rangy outfit, DeWitt's best team in years. But, as was the case with I. C., their star was injured. DeWitt's six-foot-four center and top scorer, Dick Harring, was playing with a badly twisted ankle he had injured the day before. He apparently played well early in the game, because DeWitt burst to an 11–0 lead, the kind of start that could kill an opponent. But Marion remained calm, tightened on defense, and worked its way back into the game, pulling within two points when the first quarter ended. DeWitt spurted to a nine-point lead in the second quarter, but Marion again closed the gap to 25–22 at the half.

At halftime, Haring was in considerable pain, said his teammate John Hinck. With the approval of DeWitt's athletic director, a university trainer took Haring into a separate room and injected him with a painkiller. Haring said years later that he played the second half in a fog-like state.

"Slowing to a more deliberate pace, Marion began its painstaking recovery in the third period," reported the *Clinton Herald*, and the period ended with the Indians ahead by a single point. Now it was Marion's turn to build a lead, which reached 47–42 with less than three minutes to go. Marion began to stall, which DeWitt broke up twice, closing the score to 47–46. Marion continued its stall, pulling ahead by as many as seven points on free throws and quick baskets, and put the game out of reach. The final score was 55–49. As it had against Springville and I. C., Marion won with a tough defense and heady, deliberate play. No doubt Marion benefited greatly from Harring's injury. The DeWitt coach later said he should have removed him from the game. Haring had a twenty-point average, but scored only twelve against Marion. He also had to chase Darell Failor, who scored fourteen, all over the floor.

As the tournament run continued, excitement built in the school. Students wrote slogans on the classroom blackboards urging victories in upcoming games, such as "Ice I. C.," or "Ambush Anamosa." I had an inspiration for the next game and asked a friend to write on the board, "Let's take the grin out of Grinnell," to which I added, "Let's knock the ell out of them, too." I thought we could win, even though they had manhandled us at the start of the season.

Their coach, John Megson, thought the Indians would be no problem. "We had an easy time with Marion," he said, "and we've improved."

Marion's biggest problem would be containing and rebounding against Grinnell's giant center, Dick Reeves, who was six feet five and averaged twenty points a game. Hipple experimented with several defensive combinations and decided to go with a front-back double team by Darell Failor and Wally DeWoody, who gave up respectively seven and four inches to Reeves. We hoped to get him to foul out.

The game, said the *Gazette*, "had 7,000 fans screaming with delirium." Grinnell sped to an 8–0 lead, but Marion caught up at 11–11, and the score was tied seven times after that as the lead repeatedly changed hands. Grinnell was up by four points with 3:14 left in the fourth quarter when Reeves finally fouled out. To Marion's dismay, the player who replaced him was even taller. Marion managed to inch closer, and in the final seconds of regulation, Dallas Fairley sank a thirty-foot shot to tie the game at 56–56. By this time, I had fouled out, and Fairley did the same in the first overtime.

During overtime, Domer had the ball along the baseline near the basket. He faked a drive, and as his opponent started to move backward he lost his balance and stumbled. Domer was wide open. I held my breath because Domer's shot could win it for us and he wouldn't miss from that close. But the defender, as he fell back, reached out and grabbed Domer's left arm. Domer pulled away and shot, but he had lost his rhythm and the ball didn't go in. No foul was called.

The first overtime period ended 60–60 after a strange play in which DeWoody drove in for a shot and scored, putting Marion ahead, 60–59, but was called for a charging foul. The foul could just as well have been called on the defender. DeWoody's basket was declared good, but the charge gave Grinnell a free throw that tied the game, forcing a sudden-death period. Marion had lost its chance to win in overtime on a foul not called and one called against it. The Indians' luck had changed.

In the sudden-death overtime, Grinnell made a free throw to take a one-point lead. One more point for Grinnell and the game was over. Marion had the ball and again DeWoody drove to the basket, again there was contact—and again DeWoody was called for charging, resulting in two free throws for Grinnell. The call could have gone either way; it could just as well have been

DeWoody shooting free throws. But the Grinnell player went to the line and made the first shot to win the game. He made the second shot, too, but it didn't matter; the game was over. The final score was 63–60.

In the locker room after the game, I felt numb. DeWoody was in tears. He sat on a bench, his head in his hands, sobbing. Stade sat beside him, crying, too, more in sympathy than grief. DeWoody had been our leader all through the tournament and had played superbly against Grinnell, drawing fouls from Reeves and making twenty-two points, twelve on free throws. It was not until forty-five years later during a conversation with DeWoody that I understood the depth of his sorrow that day. He blamed himself for losing the game. Although I had thought about the game a thousand times, the idea that DeWoody was responsible for the loss had never entered my mind. I checked with Tom Domer and he had the same reaction. I tried to tell this to DeWoody, then a man in his sixties. He just shook his head and said, "I should have set up a play."

The day after the Grinnell game was a Sunday. I awoke in a state of depression, which my parents tried to lessen by announcing that my photo was in the *Gazette*. They knew how much I liked that. But it was a stupid photo, I thought, showing me jumping helplessly behind a Grinnell player as he drove in for a fast-break layup. I remembered the play and I remembered thinking at the time I jumped, *That was stupid.* I should have pulled up for a chance to rebound.

It was all over. Six years of basketball as a Marion Indian. Well, we had redeemed the season somewhat with a stellar run in the state tournament, finishing among the top ten teams in our class. Independence, which won the WaMaC championship, did go to state, losing in the first round to Paullina, testimony that we lost the conference title to a very good team. But that did not, for me, make up for failing to gain at least a tie for the title, and there is still a bruise left by the loss to Grinnell. (In the state tournament, Grinnell lost in the opening round to East Des Moines, which went on to finish second. Grinnell's center, Dick Reeves, made the All-State third team.)

At the Lions Club dinner for the Indians, the guest speaker was the Grinnell College basketball coach. He said that Marion had played over its head in the loss to Grinnell. He meant it as a compliment, but I took it as an insult. Hipple said that our record was not good (18–8), but that we had worked very hard. Marion had now lost in the substate in double overtimes in two successive years, and that was heartbreaking. "We're still looking for a first-place trophy," he said, adding with a smile that the fourth graders were pretty good. In fact, he would have serious state championship hopes a lot sooner than that.

—

That spring, almost all the senior athletes went out for track, including Rathje and Jordan, and the result was a squad of nearly 120 Hipplemen, well more than half the boys in high school. They constituted what was probably the greatest track team in Marion history.

The team won all of its dual and triangular meets, often by enormous margins, and won the WaMaC championship by scoring 121 points, almost double the sixty-five scored by second-place Monticello. The total was seventeen more points than were run up two years earlier by the great team led by Leffingwell and Seeks. Stars of the meet were Jerry Walker and Rathje. Walker, the best schoolboy miler in the state, won the mile and the half-mile, while Rathje won the shot put and discus and finished second in the football throw. Marion won ten of the eighteen events and finished second in five.

(The WaMaC conference has been lax in its record keeping, and as a result track records are available only through 1981. No team in those years came close to scoring 121 points. Some events were changed to meters from yards in the late 1970s, but the scoring system apparently did not change. In recent years, Marion's track team won WaMaC titles with more points than were scored by the 1954 team, but the scoring system has changed radically with far more total points awarded. The 1954 Marion team won 34 percent of all the points available, an achievement unlikely to be matched in modern times, especially since the WaMaC now has twelve members rather than eight.)

During his high school career, Walker won multiple state championships in cross-country, indoor, and outdoor track, and was the first Marion track athlete to win an event in the Drake Relays, capturing the high school mile run as a junior. Thus, Walker eclipsed his classmate and running partner, Leo Corporon, who was the second-best miler in the conference.

Very often at track meets, Walker finished first and Corporon finished second. Corporon could beat just about every other miler in eastern Iowa, but he couldn't beat Walker. In a meet against Vinton when they were seniors, Walker came around the final turn of the mile run comfortably in first place, Corporon chugging along behind him, well ahead of the rest of the field. Then Walker began to slow down, and as Corporon came abreast of him, Walker reached out his right hand. Instead of passing Walker, Corporon grabbed his hand and they swept across the finish line together in a tie for first place. A teammate, Tom Hutton, writing about it fifty years later, said it was one of the most memorable acts of sportsmanship he'd ever seen.

Chapter 26
Living with the Rules

Discipline, fellow coaches said, was the key to Hipple's success, and the discipline was achieved through his rules.

Hipple "went farther in his rules and enforcing them than any coach I've heard of," said Hall of Fame coach Don King. "As a result, his teams were always in top physical condition and extremely disciplined mentally." Lynn Brown added that all coaches have rules, but not all coaches enforce them. Hipple enforced his rules with an unblinking righteousness that made his players tremble.

As far as most of his players knew, every high school athlete in the country had to follow the same rules. Their parents didn't tell them differently. During the glory years, parents supported the coach. They may have, among themselves, questioned whether some of the rules were absolutely necessary, or whether Hipple was being too demanding, but they almost unanimously believed that once their child had opted into the system, he had to abide by the rules.

Rules were rules, the parents said, and that's all there was to it. They had no patience with complaints about the coach. When Jerry Walker launched into a diatribe about Hipple, his father, who admired the coach greatly, said, "If you keep this up, we're going to have to go down to the basement and fight." Parents almost universally sided with faculty decisions about their children's comportment in school. When Hugh Leffingwell was a sophomore, he acted up in practice one day, and Coach Frank McLeod sent him home early. As practice ended, McLeod saw Hugh's father, Wally, standing in the doorway. McLeod expected an argument, but it turned out that Wally was there to pick up his son. When he learned what had happened, he turned and headed home to further discipline Hugh.

Many people used exactly the same words to describe the parental standard that prevailed at the time: "If you got into trouble at school, you would be in worse trouble when you got home."

Hipple knew how important parental support was. Each fall he wrote a letter to parents, enclosing a copy of the rules and asking their help in seeing that their sons followed them. Sometimes he even asked parents to sign a pledge that they would do so.

"I know you are intensely interested in having your son become a fine man," Hipple wrote in one letter, "and I assure you it is our keenest desire." The letter went on:

> We feel three important phases in every man's life are his physical well being, moral characteristics, and his mental alertness. Physically you have endowed your son with a good sturdy body or he wouldn't be out for football. You will see born in him a new confidence and courage. When you meet and compete each day with your teammates and opponents on a physical basis you soon acquire the confidence and courage for which all men are respected … We do not consider this training a sacrifice on his part because it contributes to his physical well being … We want to win every game if it can be done fairly. We want your son to have the same desire … if we can further his desire at an early age, it should help him to be a winner in his endeavors in later life.

Of course, Hipple's athletes broke the rules. Some of them smoked or drank, and some of them got away with it. But the great majority did not try, fearing they would be thrown off the team. Almost all, at one time or another, used bad language, drove cars, went steady, and stayed up past 10:00 PM. For these infractions they ran laps or climbed the rope. If that didn't work, they might be benched for a game.

Hipple's rules were both written and unwritten, and some were simply inferred by his players.

Rule number one. The most important Hipple rule was not written, but was constantly enforced. "Grades come first," he announced at parents' meetings, "athletics are second." Boys whose grades were borderline C's were required to bring their report cards to him for review. He kept in touch with teachers, and if players were beginning to fall behind, he arranged for them to spend an extra fifteen minutes with their teacher before coming to practice. The dual punishment of extra study and being late for practice seemed to work: The newspapers carried no report of an athlete being declared ineligible because of grades.

When a boy sitting innocently in class opened a note from a teacher that read, *Mr. Hipple wants to see you,* his mind tended to freeze, recalled Tom Domer. "Your butt puckered up and you wanted to throw up in the nearest waste basket."

We are going to be in bed by 10:00 PM on weeknights. Bob Fox, leaving a movie late, sprinted home as if the ghost of Hipple himself was on his heels, startling his mother as he burst into the house and streaked toward his bedroom. Tom Domer loped steadily through the night for more than a mile after leaving a girlfriend's house to make the 10:00 PM deadline. A classmate of Hipple's daughter insisted that the coach had made a nocturnal visit to his house, knocking on the door to inquire whether he was in bed. It was utter nonsense, Pat Turner said, but the boy swore it was true. Bill Rucker, father of two athletes, was a big supporter of Hipple's rules because his sons went to bed promptly without having to be told. John Nieland said that when he was out late at night he was more afraid of encountering Hipple than he was of being caught by the police.

On a January night, Jeri Smith, wearing his red and gold letter jacket, stood shivering in the cold and mist at 19th Street and First Avenue in Cedar Rapids. He had been visiting a girlfriend and was trying to hitch a ride home. Traffic was light, and he was having no luck. He had cut the time too short; it was now slightly past 10:00 PM. Then he saw the headlights of a car pulling up to give him a ride. When Smith saw that the car was a mustard-colored Chevrolet he nearly went into shock. Against all odds, it was Hipple's car, and Hipple was driving it. The coach motioned to him to get in, which Smith did, expecting a tongue-lashing. The two rode in virtual silence into Marion. Smith did not try to explain himself; how could he? At Seventh Avenue and Seventh Street, Hipple stopped the car. As the boy got out, the coach said, "Smith, you are only cheating yourself." Smith bolted for home. Hipple never mentioned the incident again.

During the mid-1950s, as television came into people's homes, WMT-TV broadcast the highlights of Iowa football games on Monday nights at

10:30. There was no TV coverage of the games themselves, so the highlight show was very popular. At football practice one Tuesday, Hipple explained how Iowa had used a button-hook pass to an end who then lateraled the ball to a trailing running back. "That play was on the highlights show last night," Hipple said. "Did any of you see it?" Several players raised their hands. "Okay, men, start running." They had been up after 10:00 PM.

We are going to use proper language at all times. Hipple never cursed, at home or on the field. Not only did he forbid profanity, he didn't like slang. In a speech to parents, he advised them to instruct their offspring to use expressions such as "hello," or "how do you do," rather than "hi."

In football practice, Bill Hotle, a halfback, was tripped up at the beginning of what he thought was going to be a long run. As he hit the ground, he yelled, "Dang!" Hipple took exception to both the shout and the word choice, and set Hotle to running laps.

Dave Carey wrote about an outburst of bad language that Hipple was powerless to punish. It seems that Elbert Waffle, out for cross-country, was plodding around the track to log his daily three miles. Football practice was going on. Charlie Cox, a huge tackle, hoping to provoke Waffle, hollered something derogatory at him. Waffle stopped in his tracks and unloosed a stream of profanity, then resumed his laborious run. "Hipple was nonplussed," Carey wrote. "His usual response to any infraction, including unacceptable language, was to make the offender run laps. But Waffle *already* was running laps. You could almost see the gears turning in Hipple's head as he wrestled with the problem. Finally, he just shook his head in resignation and went on with football practice."

We will drive our car, or our family's car, or motorbike, as little as possible. For most town athletes, driving was limited to a few hours on Sundays. But the rule was frequently broken, usually on Saturdays. While out cruising, the boys scanned the approaching traffic for signs of Hipple's distinctive yellow Chevrolet. When they saw it, the passengers immediately ducked out of sight while the driver crouched as low in his seat as possible. Townspeople joked that an empty but moving car was a common sight for the coach. Many former players insist that Hipple drove around town deliberately looking for violators, but his daughter scoffed at the idea. When she became old enough to drive the family car, which then had a distinctive bug-catching screen on the front, she terrified many players for whom Hipple seemed to be constantly on the prowl.

Few town boys in the 1940s and 1950s owned cars. "There were probably only about five kids in the whole school who had a car and many of us didn't even have a license," wrote Ken Otting, who graduated in 1949. Almost everyone walked to school.

Since there were no school buses, rural students were allowed to drive cars to school, but athletes were admonished by Hipple to return home promptly after practice and to give rides to no other player except when doing so would save someone else from having to drive. One Saturday, Hipple spotted Lloyd Jordan, a farm boy and starting halfback, driving his car in town. Jordan knew he had been sighted, and sure enough, on Monday morning there was Hipple standing in the parking lot when Jordan drove in. The conversation was brief.

"I saw you driving on Saturday."

"Yes."

"Why?"

"My parents sent me to town for medicine."

"Is that the truth?"

"Yes. Call my parents. Ask them. They won't lie for me." *If he doesn't accept that,* Jordan thought, *then I don't want to play for him.*

Hipple turned and walked away. That afternoon, Jordan was told to line up with the first string, and Hipple never mentioned the matter again. Nor did Jordan ever ask his parents if Hipple called them.

On the last day of track practice during his sophomore year, Pete Kellams, barely sixteen, somehow came into possession of his father's Buick convertible, an enormous white car with two-toned green leather upholstery. Since it was the last day of practice, Kellams felt safe in driving it to the track, although he cautiously parked it out of sight near the swimming pool. After practice, he slipped away and drove the car home. The next school day, someone told him to look at Hipple's bulletin board. When he checked it, he found a short list with the names of a few elite athletes—such as Ron Altenberg and Darell Failor—who would be competing in the state track meet and who were to report to the track that day for training. At the bottom of the list was Pete's name. Puzzled but dutiful, Kellams showed up for practice and stood silently in the small group as Hipple outlined the day's program for each of his best athletes. When he finished, the coach turned to Kellams and said, "Pete, start running."

If we date often, go steady, or must see a particular girlfriend between classes or at noon, we will drop athletics. The practice of going steady was invented during World War II and flourished during the 1950s. A survey at the time found that 75 percent of high school students supported the idea and 67 percent of adults opposed it. It was opposed by church leaders and school officials, who felt that going steady was more likely to lead to sexual activity than playing the field, which had been the norm in earlier years.

Some sociologists questioned that conclusion, but the debate was swept aside by actual practice: Going steady was rampant. (Boys and girls commonly went steady with different partners at different times. A survey found that most girls expected to go steady with a number of boys. It was a form of serial monogamy that took some of the stress out of dating.) Hipple, in opposing the practice, threw himself athwart a vast social movement. What's surprising is not that he failed to prevent going steady, but how effectively he modified it.

Couples who went steady observed a variety of rituals. These included exchanging class rings, wearing matching shirts, walking to classes together, eating lunch together, studying together in the evening, and generally being at one another's side as much as possible. Hipple opposed all these observances. He once used the phrase "locker leeches" to describe boys who did those things.

Boys caught practicing these behaviors had to run extra laps or make extra climbs up the rope in the gym. Gordon Rundquist said he was in trouble so often he routinely began every basketball practice by doing extra rope climbs. John Nieland remembered walking down the hallway with his girlfriend, carrying her books. When he saw the coach coming in the other direction, he tried to push the books back into the girl's arms, but she wouldn't take them. At basketball practice that day Nieland ran laps—for two hours. Bob Fox, a four-year letterman, was standing in the hallway talking to Shirley Sills. She wasn't his girlfriend, but when Fox saw Hipple approaching, he was overcome by panic and tried to squeeze into her locker and hide. "And I was just visiting," Fox recalled.

Boys who were in love wanted to be with their girlfriends all the time and these were the ones who got into the most trouble. Being in love was worse for a boy than owning a car, Hipple believed.

Girls had varying feelings about his rule. Some simply accepted it as the way things were. Others were upset that they had to hide their relationships. "We girls were not allowed to talk to our boyfriends during school hours, and therefore we had to pass notes back and forth," recalled Joanie Justice Peck. "This made us feel criminal or guilty of wrongdoing." Some believed Hipple implanted in his boys a destructive message about the opposite sex. Defending his rule, Hipple said he wasn't against dating; he was just trying to discourage highly demanding relationships that distracted boys from their studies and sports.

The answer for many athletes with girlfriends was to go steady (practically a social requirement), but to do it without violating Hipple's rules. They exchanged class rings, for example, but kept them concealed. They scrupulously avoided contact during classes, at lunch, and on weeknights. Boys who practiced this form of going steady seldom had problems. Hipple doubtlessly knew they had girlfriends, but tolerated it because the couple avoided the standard rituals. Russ Seeks and Kay Nietert, who later married, took this route. One year they both were assigned to work lunch hours setting up and taking down tables and chairs in the gym. They felt a guilty pleasure at being coupled this way, but scrupulously avoided behavior that would identify them as going steady. There were no problems from the coach.

You will not go to the pool hall. This rule was neither written nor spoken and may not have been a rule at all. The boys who hung out at the pool hall tended to be those who "rode motorcycles and fixed cars," said Tom Domer, whose father managed the establishment. But every year a few athletes were attracted by the sordid romance of the room and the opportunity to win spending money at the tables. They were convinced, however, that Hipple did not want them in the pool hall and that the consequences would be dire if he found them there. They believed he would come inside looking for them, so they stationed a sentry at the front door. At the sight of Hipple's Chevrolet, the sentry yelped a warning, and the athletes dropped their cues, bolted out the back door, ran into the alley, and dispersed throughout the business district.

In fact, it is almost a certainty that Hipple never entered the pool hall.

Hipple's technique here is in sharp contrast to the way Bob Jennings enforced one of his rules early in his career. Jennings forbade his players and cheerleaders to enter The Butterfly Café in Cedar Rapids. There was no drinking, but it was a pickup place with lots of smoking and a bad reputation. "Our players represented the school, and I didn't want them hanging out there," Jennings said. One day he drove by the café and saw a player's car parked in the lot. He went in and found three of his senior starters and a cheerleader. He threw them all off the team, including the cheerleader.

After a few games and a lot of pressure to restore the players and cheerleader, Jennings put the matter to a team vote, with the result that they rejoined their squads. "I bet Hipple wouldn't have done that," Jennings said. No, Hipple wouldn't have done that; once a player was dismissed, it was all over. On the other hand, Hipple didn't tell his players to stay out of the pool hall, and he didn't go in to check, either. He just let them know he didn't approve of the place. He may have spoken directly to some players who went there, but he never made a specific rule out of it. That was all he had to do to keep most of the boys out of the pool hall.

You will be found out. Coaches know things, said Bob Page, because people tell them things. Parents, teachers, teammates, townspeople, players themselves tell coaches things. Bob Fox found it uncanny that Hipple knew so often when he had driven his car during unauthorized times—then Fox realized he had been spotted each time by a prominent insurance agent in town. During the glory years, many in the community actively supported Hipple's efforts to rein in unruly boys. As they did so, the perception grew among his players that Hipple was omniscient.

Gordon Rundquist recalled what happened after some boys took a homecoming celebration too far by uprooting an outhouse and setting it up in front of the high school. The seniors were convinced that no one, including Hipple, knew who did it. At football practice the Monday after homecoming, Hipple assembled the team and called out, "Boys, those of you who put the outhouse in front of the school—start running." With that, an underclassman, John McKean, broke for the track. The jig was up. When Hipple saw McKean running, "he knew and we knew he knew" who the others were, Rundquist said, "so we all started running. Then another idiot junior [name withheld] asked how many laps we had to do. You never asked the coach how many of anything. We ran the whole practice."

—

Hipple's influence is hard to overstate. He was like a very stern father: Difficult to love and fearsome when crossed. Hipple's power, said his daughter, grew out of his total commitment to his players and their goals. "The kids knew he was following the rules," she said, and this gave him a moral authority most coaches lacked. Don King had a similar view: "The foundation of his success was his discipline. He was going to expect the most from himself and from his players." Although running laps was a mild form of punishment, it was accompanied by a sense of disgrace, a feeling in the athlete that he had somehow let down his team and coach.

Hipple's stare was withering. Ken Otting witnessed this power after a baseball game between Marion and Mount Vernon, which was coached at the time by Hipple's younger brother, Don. As the brothers stood near the Mount Vernon bus talking, the kids on the bus starting yelling at Don Hipple, "Let's go. Come on, Coach, hurry up." Les Hipple didn't like it. "Les stepped out from behind his brother and just stared," Otting wrote. "The whole Mount Vernon bus went quiet."

—

Hipple's rules remained famous long after he stopped coaching. The great Anamosa athlete, Don Norton, who was an All-American end at Iowa and played in the American Football League, was fascinated by the rules. Long retired from football, Norton occasionally spotted Jerry Walker at the University Athletic Club after an Iowa football game. He would bring a companion over to see Walker. "Tell him about Hipple's rules," Norton would say. "We never could beat those guys." After hearing Walker recite them, Norton would exclaim, "Man, I wish I had played under rules like that. I don't know if I would have lasted."

Darrell Shirk, who graduated from Marion High School in 1960, found himself, nearly fifty years later, playing golf with some men about his age who had grown up in Vinton. They asked him about Hipple's rules. When Shirk described them, they said that if there were rules like that at their school, no one would have gone out for sports.

Chapter 27
Piling Up the Wins, 1954–1955

Marion's football and basketball teams were so good in the two years from the fall of 1954 to the spring of 1956 that a debate arose whether Marion should be thrown out of the WaMaC conference. Marion's football teams for those two seasons were undefeated in conference play and the two basketball teams lost only one conference game. The grumbling began as the Indians piled up victories in 1954–1955 and grew louder the following year. Some officials began maneuvers that could lead to dumping Marion.

Neither Hipple nor C. B. Vernon wanted Marion to be cast out. Vernon argued that Marion's success was due to an exceptional group of athletes, and the Indians' dominance would not last indefinitely. While Vernon may have been talking in general terms, what he said applies most accurately to the extraordinarily talented athletes in the class of 1956. As juniors they played key roles on teams that were among the most talented and successful Hipple ever coached. And in the following year, as seniors, they utterly dominated the conference.

—

During preseason football practice in 1954, Hipple tested a variety of lineups and then assembled an artful blend of seniors and juniors. "Coach Les Hipple has in his charge a team with extremely high potential," Larry Tanner wrote as the season began.

Six senior lettermen, three of them starters, were back from the previous year. Hipple moved Bill Farmer and Bob Murray, both now pushing 200 pounds, to tackles. Jeri Smith was back at end. Lettermen Ted Burkhardt and Bill Peck won positions as halfback and guard, respectively. The rest of the line consisted of juniors Terry McEnany, center, Bill Dougherty, guard, and Larry Brooks, end. After extensive experimentation, Hipple switched senior letterman Dallas Fairley to fullback, assigned junior Darell Failor to quarterback, and put junior Ron Altenberg at the other halfback.

Other players also saw considerable action, including seniors Gary Robison (end) and Dick Todd (halfback) and juniors Tom Hutton (end), Jerry Cox (fullback, tackle, and linebacker), Harry Moore (tackle), George Brewer (tackle and fullback), and Doug Ozias (halfback).

Hipple had a powerhouse. The Indians were preseason favorites, but they would face serious challenges from Anamosa and Independence, Tanner wrote. The conference was so tough, he predicted, that no WaMaC team would go through its schedule undefeated.

Marion opened the season with a disappointing non-conference loss to Waverly, 13–6. The Indians displayed a gritty defense, but lost the game because two of their punts were blocked deep in their own territory. Recovering from the loss, Marion ground its way through the conference. The defense played fiercely, allowing a total of only two touchdowns as Marion reeled off victories over Vinton, Independence, Manchester, and Maquoketa. Early in the season, halfback Ron Altenberg was injured. As he recovered, he was used sparingly in special situations, such as punting and pass defense. He rarely ran with the ball. Todd or Ozias took Altenberg's slot on running plays.

Marion's string of four wins set up a clash for the title with archrival Anamosa. The Raiders looked very strong. They were not only unbeaten in conference play but also had not been scored upon. Their backfield—especially junior Don Norton—was reputed to be fearsome. When the teams met, however, Marion completely dominated the line of scrimmage in a thrillingly brutal game. Anamosa could gain a total of only eight yards rushing, as "time and again," Tanner wrote, Marion's line threw Anamosa's runners for losses.

Marion scored in the second and fourth quarters on runs by Failor and Burkhardt to build a 13–0 lead. After Marion's second touchdown, the Raiders' Kenny Taylor took the kickoff and raced eighty-five yards to score. There wasn't much time left when Marion received the kickoff, but the Indians lost the ball on a fumble on their own forty-yard line. Two runs by Norton and one by Taylor made it fourth and one, and Marion fans experienced a heart-throbbing moment as the Raiders lined up to go for the first down. The Indian front wall surged forward to stop Taylor for no gain. Marion took over and ran out the clock to claim a 13–7 victory.

The last chance to reel in Marion came in the next game, homecoming against Monticello, which had one loss. Monticello scored first, on a fake punt, as halfback Carl Morning skirted the onrushing Indians and ran thirty-six yards for the score. "Then lightning struck Monticello for the second time," as Failor fielded the kickoff and ran it back untouched through a gaping hole ninety yards for a touchdown—duplicating and adding five yards to the feat performed by Wally DeWoody against Monticello the year before. Marion's defense tightened in the second half, and the Indians scored twice to win, 19–6. This was followed by a 28–7 victory over Tipton to give the Indians a 7–0 conference record.

It was Hipple's fourth football championship and the first in which his team went both undefeated and untied in the conference (the 1949 team was undefeated but had a tie). Tanner graciously ate his words by asking some of the players what they thought of his preseason prediction that no team would win all its conference games.

"It gave us something to strive for," said Peck graciously.

"I thought you were right at the time," said Fairley, sarcastically.

Tanner said Marion won the title with "comparative ease," and would go down as one of Hipple's great teams. However, he seemed to suggest that while the current team's record was better than that of the 1949 powerhouse, the earlier team had more talent and scoring punch. The 1949 team, he said, had been a victim of overconfidence when it let Monticello gain a tie.

—

The basketball team that year had much in common with the football team. It, too, went through the conference with relative ease. Juniors made a huge contribution. They made up seven of the first nine players and, often, four of the starting five. The seniors were guard Dallas Fairley and forward Jeri Smith. After that it was all underclassmen. Forward Ron Altenberg, center Darell Failor, and guard Jerry Cox started all year long and were sometimes joined by guard/forward Larry Brooks and forward Tom Hutton. Juniors Terry McEnany and Bob Claypool, both about six feet, rounded out the top nine. This was one of Hipple's shortest teams, but it ran a blistering fast break and boasted several players with great leaping ability. The tallest players were guards Cox and Fairley, both about six feet two. Failor was only five feet eleven; although he gave up many inches all year long to his opponents at center, he was extremely agile and tough; few big men could keep up with him. Altenberg, Brooks, and Hutton were less than six feet.

The Indians made up for their lack of height with exceptional athleticism, self-assurance, and speed. They were deadly shooters. The team routinely shot .400 from the field and sometimes made half their field goals. Cox and Altenberg could hit from anywhere. Cox averaged about fifteen points a game, Altenberg more than fourteen, and Failor thirteen. Fairley, Smith, and Brooks had some high-scoring games. If one of them didn't get you, another one would.

The Indians, tight from football, lost to Springville, as usual, in the season opener, then ran off fourteen straight victories, including a 109–57 trouncing of Maquoketa—the only Hipple-coached team to score more than one hundred points. Then came a one-point overtime loss in the first game Independence played in its new gym. As the sectional tournament approached, the Indians were atop the WaMaC with two games to play. They were ranked the eighth best team in northeast Iowa, two places behind Immaculate Conception, which was 22–1 going into the sectional.

The sectional tournament was again held at Marion. The A bracket featured Marion and three Cedar Rapids schools: McKinley, I. C., and St. Patrick's. Cedar Rapids fans howled that the games should be held on a neutral court. In most previous years, I. C.–Marion games had been held at the field houses at Coe (capacity two thousand) or Iowa City (fifteen thousand). I. C. fans said, with some justification, that it wasn't fair to make the team play at Marion. C. B. Vernon held his ground this time, saying that although Marion had applied to host the sectional, it was the state high school association that made the assignment and the pairings. Vernon also said that with standing room and crowding, Marion's expanded gym held fifteen hundred spectators, and could thus accommodate everyone who was a true fan. Vernon didn't want to shift Marion's games to the Coe field house because there would be a large rental fee.

After Marion trounced McKinley and I. C. crushed St. Patrick's, fans began to line up outside the Marion gym in the February gloom at 4:30 PM. The temperature was zero degrees, but the fans endured it to be sure of a seat when the doors opened at 6:00 for the game between the two best Class A teams in the county.

It was another I. C.–Marion classic, "a raging battle," the *Gazette* reported, that was tied nine times and saw the lead change hands seventeen times in the first three periods. It may have been in this game that Jerry Cox attracted wide attention as one of the best players in the state. Altenberg was in foul trouble early, and Cox picked up the burden, making seven field goals on ten attempts in the first half. "His amazing shooting kept Marion in the game," said the *Gazette*.

The first half ended with Marion down by three points, but as happened so often, the Indians burst to a 51–45 lead during the third quarter. I. C. fought back and tied the game at 51–51 in the fourth stanza. The effort may have exhausted the Greyhounds, for Marion broke away to a 61–54 lead, began its famous stall with four minutes to play, and won the game, 64–59. Cox scored twenty-six points. "It wouldn't take much to get Jerry Cox elected mayor of Marion today," the *Gazette* said.

The victory marked the seventh time in as many games that Marion had eliminated a good I. C. team. Fifty years later, I interviewed I. C. coach Bob Jennings. He remembered the game and showed me the story from the *Gazette*. He told me that in a few hours he would attend the fiftieth reunion of the class of 1955. "I think that was the loss to Marion that hurt the most," he said. "Maybe not. Yes, I think so. We played at Marion. If we had played at home I think we would have won." After five decades, the defeats still sting.

The Indians opened the district tournament at Iowa City with a decisive 60–44 victory over Belle Plaine, champions of the South Iowa Cedar Conference. The next game was against Wilson of Cedar Rapids, which Marion had edged by three points early in the season. Wilson had a tremendous height advantage in starter Bob Bradley, six feet five, and reserve Cliff Svoboda, who was even taller. Wilson broke ahead 12–4, and it was a long night for the Indians. They entered the fourth quarter down by six points, but outscored Wilson 13–3 in the final quarter and squeaked by, 55–51. The team hoisted Hipple to their shoulders and carried him off the court. It was a great win for two reasons. One was that Marion would be going to the substate for the seventh year in a row, and the other was that Marion had beaten every Cedar Rapids team it faced: Wilson (twice), Franklin, McKinley, and I. C. Hipple didn't show it, but he loved beating Cedar Rapids teams. All Marion did.

After the district tournament, Marion finished its WaMaC season, sewing up Hipple's seventh title in eight years with a decisive victory over Vinton. This was followed by a three-point squeaker over Tipton, probably the result of a let-down by the Indians, who had mauled the Tigers earlier by forty-seven points. Marion's conference record was 13–1.

That year, officials changed the tournament format. Concern had been growing about the practice of keeping schools in their size bracket until the state finals. This approach, critics said, eliminated many large-school AA teams that were clearly better than most of the A and B teams from midsized and smaller schools that got into the Sweet Sixteen because their competition wasn't as stiff. So officials revised the format to eliminate class distinctions in the substate. The luck of the draw would determine which teams clashed, regardless of school size. If any B or A teams could battle through the AA teams they met in substate play, they deserved to be in the finals. (In a related change, the field for the finals was reduced from sixteen to eight teams. Thus brackets in the substate were expanded from four teams to six.)

Marion's first substate opponent was archrival Anamosa, led by the Norton brothers, Roger and Don. Marion had beaten Anamosa twice, most recently by eighteen points, but the Indians were cold, and the Raiders were determined. Anamosa was ahead by two points at the half, but Marion again surged in the third quarter to take a seven-point lead into the final stanza. Anamosa closed to within four points with two minutes to go, but Marion pulled away to win, 51–45.

That set up a crucial game with St. Ambrose of Davenport. St. Ambrose was an AA school, ranked number one in southeast Iowa and a favorite to win the state championship. This game is well remembered. Decades later, even people with little connection to Marion said the Indians were robbed.

"Marion had the game won," wrote Tanner. "But something happened." It happened in the very last seconds. Marion was ahead all the way, but in the fourth quarter, St. Ambrose briefly took the lead. Marion got it back, and was ahead 48–47 with thirty-seven hectic seconds left. St. Ambrose's Pete Shebler was awarded two free throws. He missed them both, but St. Ambrose controlled the rebound. Marion's Jeri Smith stole the ball. Then St. Ambrose stole it back. With only a few seconds to play, St. Ambrose took another shot. It missed. Marion's Darell Failor grabbed the rebound.

"I jumped so hard to get that rebound that I was off-balance when I came down," Failor said. To avoid traveling, he had no choice but to dribble the ball. Typically, he would have passed it to another player. As Failor dribbled toward the Marion basket to get his balance and preserve a great win, several St. Ambrose players mugged him. Iowa University students who were on the sidelines as ushers said later they could hear the smack of hands on flesh as St. Ambrose players frantically tried to steal the ball. Someone wrenched it out of Failor's hands and threw it desperately to St. Ambrose's Gene Duffy, who was standing under the basket. With two seconds left, Duffy made the basket and St. Ambrose had the victory. Final score, 50–48. (Duffy was St. Ambrose's star and an All-State selection. His game-winning basket was only his third field goal of the game. He was fouled in the act of shooting by Jerry Cox and made a free throw after the game was over. "I knocked him ass over teakettle," Cox remembered.)

For the third year in a row, Marion had lost a substate game by a narrow margin under bitter circumstances. Jerry Cox remembered that as he sat sobbing on a bench after the game, he felt a friendly arm on his shoulder. He looked up to see Iowa coach Bucky O'Connor. "Don't worry, son," O'Connor said. "You can come to Iowa and play and it won't cost you a cent."

Another player sat on a bench that night, and he sat there for the entire game. Larry Brooks, who usually started at forward, got a D in trigonometry. As far as the state of Iowa and the school district of Marion were concerned, he was eligible to play in that game—but not according to the rules of Les Hipple. Brooks was paying the price for subpar academic performance. Hipple used only five men in that game. Would Marion have won if Hipple had allowed Brooks to play? The answer is that studies come before sports. (Among the hundreds of box scores I studied, I saw only one other in which Hipple made no substitutions. His theory of basketball held that a coach needed to use eight players to avoid exhausting the starters.)

St. Ambrose went on to the state finals and finished third. Both the Iowa Daily Press Association and the Des Moines Register named Jerry Cox to the All-State second team. He was lauded for his shot-making, defense, and rebounding. It was a rare honor for a junior, but he was an immensely skilled all-around player with an extraordinary instinct for the game. Ron Altenberg and Darell Failor received honorable mentions from the *Register*.

A few weeks later, Hipple, speaking at an awards dinner, made a shockingly uncharacteristic statement. He said his junior players were so gifted that they could be state champions the following year. To help prepare them, he was going to spend the summer trying to arrange some non-conference games against the best competition he could find.

—

When weather permitted, track season began. The team had "tremendous potential," Larry Tanner wrote. But key seniors followed the tradition of taking the season off, and Manchester and Vinton proved stronger as Marion finished third in the conference meet.

The season marked the emergence of Ron Altenberg as a track star of exceptional talent. At the indoor state meet, which was held immediately after basketball season and provided Altenberg scant opportunity to train, he finished second in the broad jump and fourth in the fifty-yard dash, scoring all of Marion's points. Shortly after that, however, he injured his leg and became ill. He missed most of the season, including the district meet that qualified athletes for the state championships.

He was well enough to compete in the WaMaC meet, however, and there Altenberg emerged as if he were Superman stepping out of a phone booth. He set new records for the 100-yard dash (10.1 seconds) and the broad jump (20 feet 10 inches), won the 120-yard high hurdles, and finished fourth in the 180-yard low hurdles. Teammate Darell Failor won the 440-yard dash and anchored the record-breaking mile relay team. Thus two juniors delivered all of Marion's first-place finishes and almost all the team's sixty-one points.

Altenberg's 10.1 time in the 100-yard dash surprised the judges so much that they wondered if the starting blocks had been set up in the wrong place, shortening the race to ninety-five yards. The previous record was 10.4 seconds. Altenberg had been timed at 10.8 in the qualifying heat, and he ran the final so effortlessly that the judges doubted he could have shaved .3 off the record. He had not run a competitive 100 all season, so there was no history. When the officials went to check the placement of the starting blocks, they found they had been removed. The times for sophomores and freshmen were also unusually fast. It wasn't until February of the following year that the conference officially recognized the new record time.

Despite his heroic showing, Altenberg did not receive a major letter in track. He hadn't participated in enough meets to qualify. Hipple chose not to bend the rules, even for the boy who was becoming the best athlete he ever coached.

That summer, Hipple worked the phones to schedule basketball games against the toughest opposition he could find. Meanwhile, the other WaMaC coaches shook their heads in dismay at what they would face when schools opened in the fall.

Chapter 28

Falling Stars, 1955–1956

Marion's football team of 1955 left no question that it was the greatest to take the field under Hipple. It went undefeated—and practically unchallenged—through all nine games, the first Hipple team to do so. Only two games could be called close—the season-opening 9–0 victory over non-conference foe Waverly and a 13–0 win against Tipton in the next game—but Tanner wrote that the outcomes were never in doubt.

The climactic game was at homecoming in late October against Anamosa. Both teams were undefeated and, while Marion was favored, the game was expected to be close. An overflow crowd of more than three thousand seven hundred spectators turned out to see two of the best running backs in the state: Marion's Ron Altenberg and Anamosa's Don Norton.

It was no contest; Marion won, 45–14. Years later, Norton insisted that Altenberg made three long touchdown runs on three consecutive plays, each play identical to the previous one. The first two, Norton said, were called back because of penalties, so Marion just ran the same play again. Darell Failor, Marion's quarterback, didn't remember that, but he did recall a certain play that almost always went for a touchdown. It involved misdirection as Failor faked a hand-off to the fullback. The halfbacks took a step in the direction of the fake, then reversed field. Failor spun and handed the ball to Altenberg, who followed the other halfback, Doug Ozias, around end.

Failor used the play sparingly, saving it for when the team needed a touchdown. The Raiders were the first team to stop the play: They knew from scouting reports that Failor always set it up by having the fullback plunge into the line on the play before the touchdown sweep. Failor called the play again later without the set-up plunge, and it went for a touchdown. In fact, Altenberg scored three touchdowns against Anamosa, on runs of eighty-six, forty-three, and thirty-one yards. All of them came on "deceptive reverse plays," said the *Gazette*.

After the Anamosa game, Lynn Brown chatted with Jack Fisk, the young Anamosa coach. Brown wrote that Fisk told him that Marion was too good for the WaMaC, and that he was going to try to get it thrown out. Years later Fisk denied any part in trying to evict Marion. He remembered the game. Told that Marion had an awfully good team that year, Fisk replied, "So did we, but Marion's line was better."

Altenberg ran wild behind that line all season. Only about five feet three as a sophomore, he had sprouted to five feet eleven, but weighed only 155 pounds, a skeleton hung with muscle. He was so fast and strong, Hipple said, that once he was past the line of scrimmage, "unless you had two people there to meet him, he was gone. If it was one-on-one, you might as well chalk it up."

Altenberg rushed for 1,105 yards that year, averaging 123 yards per game and 10.7 yards every time he carried the ball. (The first two achievements are reported in Eric Formanek's splendid statistical history, *From the Beginning: Marion Football*, an exhaustive compilation going back to 1922. Altenberg's rushing yardage places him tenth among all-time Marion rushers in a single season and tied for eighth in number of single-season rushing touchdowns with sixteen. Formanek apparently missed the report by Larry Tanner on Altenberg's average yards per rush, for it is not included in his history. Altenberg's 10.7 yards per carry places him second on the all-time list. Altenberg is on other all-time Marion lists: He is ninth in single-season all-purpose yards, 1,176; fourth in extra points kicked in a single season, twenty-eight; and fourth in punting average, 40.05 yards.)

But Altenberg was just the most visible light in a galaxy of stars. The starting backfield of Failor, Ozias, and junior John Jordan was blazingly fast. The line had seniors Larry Brooks (155 pounds) and Tom Hutton (145) at ends, seniors Harry Moore (208) and Jerry Cox (170) at tackles, senior Bill Dougherty (170) and junior Bob Malake (185) at guards, and senior Terry McEnany (175) at center. Many capable reserves saw lots of action. Marion's line was fairly large and very vicious. The team gained 3,208 total yards, more than any other team in the state. Marion outscored its opponents by

299–44, holding five of them scoreless. (On the all-time Marion lists, the team ranks sixth in total points scored, third in total yards rushing, second in rushing touchdowns per game, first in fewest total yards allowed, and fourth in fewest total points allowed.)

After the season, Marion was ranked eleventh in the state. Altenberg was named to the fourth All-State team by the *Des Moines Register* but received only honorable mention from the Iowa Daily Press Association. Terry McEnany, the center and linebacker, received top honors among Marion players. He was listed on the fourth IDPA team. Cox was placed on the *Register's* seventh team and received an honorable mention from IDPA, while Failor received honorable mentions from both the *Register* and IDPA, and the *Register* awarded Brooks honorable mention.

Tanner and many fans were dismayed that the team, Altenberg, and Failor did not receive higher rankings. Apparently reporters thought Marion's competition wasn't tough enough, but Tanner pointed out that WaMaC teams were almost uniformly victorious in their non-conference games, some of them against teams (such as Waverly) that were champions or top contenders in their own loops.

The Indians were never stretched. In the last game of the season, a 47–0 defeat of Mount Vernon, Hipple played his entire squad of 48 men and, in the last two minutes, sent the varsity back in—but told them they had to play an unfamiliar position. Brooks got to be quarterback, so Failor lined up as an end. Brooks threw him a pass for a forty-nine-yard touchdown. Hipple later said that this was the only football team he coached that didn't have to work hard to be good.

Hipple's football teams had now won three consecutive conference titles and twenty consecutive conference games. And every fan knew that the juggernaut would keep rolling through the basketball season.

There was an ominous sign, however. Cox missed two practice sessions before the Mt. Vernon football game and was not allowed to suit up. For punishment, he was denied a major letter, receiving a minor letter instead.

—

As the basketball season opened, Marion's starting lineup consisted of four starters from the previous year: Cox and Brooks at guards, Failor at center, and Altenberg at forward. Senior Tom Hutton was the other forward. This was the same lineup that completely devastated the opposition when they were on the freshman–sophomore team two years earlier. Seniors Terry McEnany and Bob Claypool rounded out the top seven.

The starting five were all natural athletes, fast and smooth, who could play any sport. Brooks had been playing varsity baseball since he was in junior high. Cox tried baseball as a junior and had a late-season batting average of .473; Brooks was hitting .435. Failor would eventually win ten major letters. Altenberg's brilliance in football and track were already legendary. (I once got a vivid picture of Altenberg's hand–eye coordination at a county fair. He was standing on the midway flanked by two girls, each with her arms filled with stuffed animals, fuzzy evidence of his extraordinary skill at carnival games that yokels weren't supposed to win.)

Although they played selflessly, it's not accurate to say the Indians had no stars. They were all stars. They played with a confidence that bordered on arrogance. They were ranked second in northeast Iowa. The *Gazette* ran a story about how the team had been together since sixth grade. The story quoted Hipple as saying that one of the team's weaknesses was lack of depth because there were two juniors, Steve Smith and Bob Wilson, in the top nine. This blatant falsehood illustrated the lengths Hipple would go to avoid praising a team he didn't want to become overconfident. In fact, he never had a team so deep with talented seniors. Lack of depth was the least of his problems.

Hipple might have said that the team's weakness was lack of height. Cox was six feet two and growing, Failor was listed at six feet that year, Altenberg at five feet eleven, Brooks at five feet ten, and Hutton at five feet eight. Claypool and McEnany were each over six feet, and Smith, the junior reserve, was six feet three. But Hipple said that lack of height was not a major problem because the players could jump so high. The year before, after experiments at Iowa University showed that weight training could improve leaping ability, Hipple carved a minuscule weight room out of a storage closet and urged his charges to work on strengthening their legs. He was, in this, decades ahead of his time. He did not insist upon weight work, however, so players tended to be lax about it. Yet when their jumping ability was measured, wrote Lynn Brown, the coaches discovered that Failor had a vertical leap of thirty-six to thirty-eight inches, and Altenberg could soar forty-three inches.

Altenberg's remarkable ability to levitate meant that, with a standing jump, he could bring the top of his head within six inches of the rim. Ron Franklin wrote that Altenberg could spring up and touch the rim with his elbow. Cox could get high enough to "nearly dunk the ball," he said, and McEnany, Claypool, and Smith were respectable jumpers.

Tanner would come to call this squad "the Marion machine." The season was only four wins old when key players began dropping by the wayside. Even with starters out, the Marion machine kept right on grinding up the competition.

The first shock came when Hutton was hospitalized with a mild case of polio. He was out for five games, all resounding Marion victories, and slowly played his way back into the starting lineup. But before he had even returned to sit on the bench, both Brooks and Cox, the stellar guards, were in trouble with the coach.

Problems with Cox came to light after Marion had won eight straight games by an average margin of twenty-nine points. (One of the victims was Belle Plaine, the first of three tough teams Hipple had scheduled to test the Indians.) A few days before New Year's Eve, the Indians prepared to play Clinton, the second of three strong teams new to the schedule. But Cox was not allowed to suit up for the game because he missed school and practice on the last day before the Christmas holidays. Hipple switched Brooks to forward and started Claypool and McEnany at guards. With two of its stars out of the lineup, Marion pounded the River Kings, 50–38. Failor scored twenty-three points and Altenberg scored nineteen.

In the next game, a 78–48 blistering of Vinton, neither Cox nor Brooks played, but Hutton returned to the lineup, playing briefly. Failor scored thirty-two points, Altenberg, seventeen. In the following game, a thirteen-point defeat of a strong Independence team, both Cox and Brooks came off the bench. That was the last game for Brooks. His name does not appear in the lineup for the rest of the season. Neither the *Gazette* nor the *Sentinel* explained why he left the team.

Cox lasted longer. He played well in the only regular-season game the Indians lost, a 50–39 defeat by Franklin of Cedar Rapids, a game in which the Indians were ice cold. Franklin had a good team, but Lynn Brown remembered that Marion played badly without Brooks, and may have been floundering because of turmoil on the team.

Cox missed the next game with a reported case of the flu, and then scored twenty-five points in the lopsided victory over Maquoketa. That was his last game. He was, the *Gazette* reported, "Under suspension … he was suspended by the high school principal."

The loss of Cox and Brooks must have shaken up the team, because the Indians barely defeated Manchester, 45–44, to clinch the conference championship. The loss of Cox, the All-State guard, deflated many fans, forcing them to relinquish hopes for a state championship. The loss of Brooks, Failor said later, was just as harmful—maybe more so. "He was our quarterback," Failor said. Tanner wrote in a column that Hipple was not the only coach in the area who was having problems with players breaking training rules. "It almost makes you cry to see these youngsters … throw college scholarships down the drain because they want to horse around. It doesn't make sense," Tanner said.

Now Failor and Altenberg took on more responsibility. "Those guys were tougher than a nickel steak," Cox said years later. Failor, high-point man all season, maintained his scoring average at around seventeen points a game, while Altenberg upped his production, often scoring in the mid-twenties. Hipple again juggled his lineup, using McEnany at forward and Hutton at guard with Claypool. This lineup easily defeated Cedar Falls, last of new teams on the schedule, 71–55. The Marion cage machine ground on. The Indians won their last two regular season games, bringing their record to 19–1 overall and 14-0 in the conference.

Again, officials changed the state tournament setup. This year, to appease the smaller schools, which were cut out of the state finals the previous year, two champions were to be crowned: one in the A division, which included all schools with more than one hundred students, and one in the B division composed of smaller schools. Marion, in the A division, cruised through the sectional tournament with easy victories over Springville, Olin, and Anamosa—all smaller schools than Marion.

But when district pairings were announced, Marion found itself in what the Gazette called "the toughest district tournament in the state," As luck would have it—bad luck—Marion drew Davenport Central, the largest school in the state and champion of the Mississippi Valley Conference.

"We could have won the game if we had hit our [free throw] average, which was around 65 percent," Hipple said after Marion lost, 65–60, to the heavily favored Blue Devils. Marion made half of its attempts—sixteen of thirty-two—but eight of the misses were in one-and-one situations, where success on the first shot would have allowed a second shot. At several points in the game, Davenport opened large leads, but the Indians kept coming back, to the amazement of their opponents. Davenport had a much taller team and was able to rebound effectively and still keep players back on defense, nullifying Marion's fast break, its best weapon.

But Davenport couldn't shut down Altenberg and Failor. Despite being guarded by Davenport's best defender, Altenberg scored seventeen points. Failor scored twenty-three. "We couldn't do anything with Failor," said Davenport coach Paul Eckert. "If we played behind him, he went over us, and if we played in front he still popped them in." Going into the game, Eckert said, "We were a little bit afraid of them."

Davenport went on to the finals and finished third. Altenberg was named to the *Register's* fourth All-State team and received honorable mention from the IDPA. Failor received honorable mention from both sources. Again, Tanner and many fans thought both players deserved higher honors.

In his wrap-up of the season, Tanner praised the courage of the Indians, who were not intimidated by the largest school in the state. "They were just another team to us," Failor said years later. "But we didn't play as well as we were taught." Tanner insisted that if the state tournament format had been the same as it was two years earlier, with schools staying in their divisions until they reached the Sweet Sixteen, Marion "would have made it to the finals without much strain." But the bigger question still hangs in the air: What would the Indians have done, even with the current tournament setup, if their two superb guards had stayed on the team? "They would have had a good shot at winning state," wrote Lynn Brown.

—

Even though five decades had passed, I felt it was imperative to talk to Cox and Brooks. Other players in other years were either dropped from teams or quit under pressure, but I felt no compunction to single them out. But Cox and Brooks were such good players on such a good team for which hopes were so high that I couldn't gloss over their departure.

Besides, I knew them both; they had been sophomores when I was a senior. I had watched Cox in action and marveled at how smoothly he moved.

Brooks had been a baseball teammate. Playing center field, he kept us in a game against Central City when I was pitching. Some of the Central City batters hit titanic blasts off my fastball. The balls went so far and high that I could turn and watch as they soared almost out of sight. In the distance, this kid, Brooks, moved into position as the balls came rocketing back to earth and—against all odds and my own expectations—he caught them. Those mighty blasts would have torn the glove off most Marion outfielders.

Jerry Cox, when I spoke to him, could not recall clearly why he had been cut from the team. The photo of him that ran in the *Sentinel* shows an inordinately handsome blond boy with a wide, easy grin. He was gregarious, popular, and adventurous. His difficulties with the school system, he said, stemmed in part from his romantic interest in a young schoolteacher—a woman who must have been at least four years his senior. Complications arising from this relationship resulted in him being disciplined by the principal, which led to missed practices and difficulties with Hipple. "I got into some other problems, too," Cox said, "but I can't rightly recall what they were."

Whatever happened, Cox does not hold a grudge against Hipple. "I have nothing but the highest respect for him," Cox said. "He made men out of boys, and he took ordinary players and turned them into good ones. He treated everyone the same. If you didn't follow the rules you were finished, and it didn't matter how good you were."

Larry Brooks also had trouble remembering what happened. He had buried the memory, refusing to talk or think about it for decades. When I contacted him, he suggested we meet for a late breakfast at Huntington's restaurant in Marion. Brooks said he had spent several troubled nights as he dug memories out of the past. "I've tried to block it out of my mind," he said. "I've tried not to be angry about it. I never talked about it with anyone. I didn't want to seem to be attacking Hipple."

As Brooks remembered it, Hipple called him in one day and accused him of being involved in activities that had gotten Cox in trouble. Moreover, Hipple said he had been told that Brooks and Cox had formed a pact, agreeing that if either of them was cut from the team, the other would quit. Brooks adamantly denied this to Hipple (and Cox did the same to me), but Hipple insisted that he had the information on good authority and that Brooks was finished. When Brooks tried to appeal the judgment, Hipple refused to hear it. "I didn't drink and I didn't smoke, but I did drive a car sometimes," Brooks told me. "If the rules were tougher, I would have followed them. That's how much I wanted to play. I was a Hippleman. I still think of myself that way."

Brooks loved sports, but what happened next was even more devastating than leaving the team. Brooks lived with his grandmother and saw his father rarely. His father was an angry man, a hard drinker who could be abusive, but he was extremely proud of his son's athletic accomplishments. If the son continued to excel in sports, the father said, he would send him to college. When the father heard what had happened, he threatened to beat his son and repeatedly tried to break into the house to do it. The police had to be called more than once. Brooks was terrified and, as a result, the boy and his father became permanently estranged. "I was having so much trouble at home that I couldn't think about my problems with Hipple," Brooks said.

—

As the Marion machine mowed down opponents that year, talk increased about the idea of Marion either leaving or being evicted from the conference. Vernon said Marion had no intention of leaving. The WaMaC was more than an athletic conference, he said. There were cooperative programs in music, theater, and other activities, and the locations of the towns meant that trips to other schools did not require an overnight stay.

Speculation about Marion being dumped increased when DeWitt High School applied for membership in the WaMaC. DeWitt was close enough to the other WaMaC towns for the application to make sense. Some people reasoned that if DeWitt was allowed in, Marion would have to get out, but Tanner wrote (no doubt reflecting the official view) that DeWitt was welcome and that scheduling games in a nine-team conference was no problem. Reporters in other conference towns reflected on the situation. Admitting that Marion's teams were very good, they argued that being good was not an appropriate reason for throwing them out. If the other WaMaC schools wanted more championships, they could join other, weaker conferences, or they could get better.

When the annual WaMaC leadership meeting was held that winter at the Terrace Room of the Cedar Rapids airport, officials rejected DeWitt's application and gave little serious consideration to asking Marion to leave. Responding to a friendly query, Vernon asked his colleagues to remember when Marion was at the bottom of the conference (although that was more than a decade earlier). Marion wanted to stay in the conference now that it was winning, Vernon said, just as much as it wanted to stay when it was losing. Marion's dominance wouldn't last forever, he said. There would come a time when Marion would be on the bottom again. Jack Fisk, the Anamosa coach, may not have been so sure. He asked the conference leaders to consider awarding trophies for second place, especially in track.

—

Fisk needn't have bothered. Anamosa won the WaMaC track championship that year, edging Marion by about five points. Only a few Marion seniors were out for track, but one of them was Ron Altenberg, without whom Marion's finish would have been much lower.

At the championship meet that year, Altenberg pulled off a feat described as "amazing" by the *Gazette* and by Tanner as "unquestionably the greatest" ever seen on the Marion track. On a cloudy evening, with rain threatening, he entered four events, won four events and set a new conference record in each one. The most spectacular achievement came in the 100-yard dash, which he won in 9.8 seconds, .3 lower than his previous record, .2 lower than his all-time best, and tying the fastest time turned in by any Iowa high school runner that year. But Altenberg had other business to take care of. He broad-jumped 22 feet ½ inch, shattering his old mark of 21 feet 10 inches. He ran the 220-yard dash in 22.8 seconds and the 180-yard low hurdles in 20.6 seconds, beating the old records by .7 and .9 seconds respectively.

People who saw that performance never forgot it. Ed Failor was a timekeeper, and after clicking the watch to mark Altenberg's time in the 100, he looked at the dial in amazement: The boy had run so smoothly it seemed impossible that he broke ten seconds. Ron Franklin remembered Altenberg's grace and precision in the low hurdles; the way he could glide over them, not really jumping but stepping over each one, his upper body steady as his legs and arms flashed. Bill Huntoon, a junior high student, remembered another scene: Altenberg handing his sweat clothes to a classmate, Tom Keith, to hold as he prepared to enter a race. There was such drama in the moment that it could have been a painting by Thomas Eakins, showing the athlete standing on the floodlit field, outlined against storm clouds in the background. The title: *Altenberg Gets Ready.*

About a week earlier, Altenberg had performed another astonishing feat. He won the same four events at the district track meet in Cedar Rapids, earning the designation as Prep of the Week by the *Des Moines Register*. Now, after his grand slams in both the district and WaMaC meets, he would go to the state meet to see how he could do against the best athletes in Iowa.

Marion was classed AA in track, which meant Altenberg would compete with stars from the largest schools. He had competed against them all year in the Drake, Cornell, Grinnell, and Teachers College meets, sometimes winning, sometimes placing second or third. Among all the talented athletes he would face, none had Altenberg's versatility. The top hurdlers were not competitive in the sprints; the top sprinters did not excel in the hurdles or broad jump; the best broad jumpers did not rank among the top sprinters or hurdlers. Only Altenberg was among the elite competitors in all four events.

He proved it by nipping the defending champion to win the 180-yard low hurdles, won the broad jump with relative ease, finished second in the 220 and third in the 100 (beaten in both races by his nemesis, Denny O'Brien of Des Moines Roosevelt). He accounted for a total of nineteen points, good for a sixth-place finish for Marion. He scored every Marion point.

A few weeks later, Altenberg entered an AAU meet at Iowa City and won each of his four signature events. As a result the Marion team, which may have consisted only of Ron Altenberg, finished second in the meet.

—

With the graduation of the star-filled class of 1956, Hipple's nine glory years at Marion ended. There would be other glorious seasons with exceptional teams, but there would not be the concentration of victories, championships, and basketball tournament runs that occurred between 1947 and 1956. The tide had crested; now it would begin flowing out.

Chapter 29
A House Divided, 1956–1958

In May 1956, C. B. Vernon surprised the school board by announcing his retirement. A month earlier, he had signed a new three-year contract, raising his annual salary by $700 to $8,000. But he'd had second thoughts. "This job is too big for an older man," said Vernon, who had turned sixty-four in January. "It is strictly for a younger man."

Vernon saw serious problems ahead. The school system, already overcrowded, faced a major influx of new students. Wrenching changes would be required. Vernon had been superintendent for thirty years. Local historian Marvin Oxley calculated that Vernon had overseen the education of 60 percent of all the students who had graduated from Marion High School since the first class in 1872. It was time for Vernon to step aside.

After sifting through fifty applications, the board chose John Messerli to succeed him. Messerli, who would turn thirty-three as the school year began, was a Monticello native who had served in the Air Force during World War II, then graduated from Iowa State Teachers College. He had taught commercial subjects and coached at a consolidated school in Ventura, Iowa, then moved in 1951 to Newhall, Iowa, as principal, moving up after one year to superintendent of schools at the age of twenty-nine. Newhall was a village a few miles west of Cedar Rapids. By this time, Messerli had earned a master's degree at the State University of Iowa.

Messerli's salary was $7,000, nearly as much as Vernon's after three decades on the job. The board must have been impressed by Messerli's energy and intelligence, because nothing in his experience had prepared him for the complex political and emotional tangle he would encounter at Marion.

Messerli's challenge was to expand the school system to absorb the tremendous population growth that was taking place in Marion and the surrounding countryside. The district had added two elementary schools under Vernon, but further expansion was required at all levels. The high school was overcrowded. In a few years it would be too small to handle the influx of students from the town, its burgeoning new neighborhoods, and the surrounding farms.

New families were pouring into Marion to work for Cedar Rapids companies, especially Collins Radio (later, Rockwell Collins), which made sophisticated long-range radio equipment for military and industrial use. In 1956, Marion issued a record two hundred permits for new houses, many of them built on farmland, and it was clear the record would be broken in 1957. The town was on a growth path that would take it from a population of five thousand nine hundred in 1950 to nine thousand in 1958—with much more growth on the way.

Messerli responded to the population boom by proposing a merger between the town's school district, where the high school was, and the rural school district, which had a single school building serving students through eighth grade. Since students in the Marion Rural Independent School District had no high school, most rural students attended Marion High School on a tuition basis, with the tuition paid by the rural district. There were almost one hundred rural students in Marion High School—about one fourth the total—when Messerli was hired, but there were many more on the way. Marion High School did not have enough space for them all. This time bomb had been ticking for some time; when Messerli came aboard it was about to explode.

Messerli's efforts to combine the two districts thrust him into the center of the bitterest controversy the Marion community had ever experienced, a controversy so emotional that it destroyed long-term friendships, threatened businesses, and tore families apart. Messerli's eight years as superintendent would be turbulent ones. They spanned a time of wrenching change and disruption in what had seemed to be a peaceful, homogenous community. And they came as many of the basic beliefs and standards of society itself were criticized and challenged by restless and resentful young people and older citizens as well.

—

C. B. Vernon had managed the school system based on values rooted in his upbringing at the turn of the twentieth century. Now Messerli was in charge, and change was imperative. He promptly wielded a symbolic new broom, sweeping out the old, World War II–surplus desks and equipment in the administrative offices, and bringing in new, up-to-date versions. Soon other new ideas were flowing out of his office, including a range of new adult education classes.

As any new superintendent would, Messerli set out to learn everything he could about the school district, and this soon led him to the athletic program. While C. B. Vernon had allowed the program to run at arm's length under Hipple's strong direction, Messerli wanted to be involved. Where C. B. Vernon told parents to take their complaints to the coach, Messerli wanted to hear them. Sometimes he tried to fix the problem.

The 1956–1957 school year had hardly begun when Messerli called a meeting of parents of boys out for football. The purpose was to discuss Hipple's program and rules, according to Lynn Brown, Hipple's assistant coach, who attended the meeting. Messerli had heard complaints and wanted to clear the air. The meeting was intended only for parents of players. But other parents—whose sons were not on the team—showed up as well, perhaps twenty of them, compared to a much larger group of parents whose boys played football.

As Messerli tried in vain to maintain order, the meeting disintegrated into a shouting match between pro- and anti-Hipple parents. One parent, Marvin Edison, owner of one of the town's two drug stores, called Hipple "a little Hitler," Brown remembered. Coming a decade after the end of the war, the insult was shocking. "It was an unbelievable meeting," Brown wrote. "I don't believe Mr. Vernon would have called such a meeting. The conduct of some of the parents was embarrassing."

Hipple's crime in Edison's eyes was that he had prevented Edison's son, John, from rejoining the football team as a senior. Years later, John confirmed that his father had attacked Hipple, but said that he had likened his approach to Russian dictators, not Hitler. John, a physician in California, explained that the summer before the season began, he and some friends were traveling in Mexico, and John realized he would not be back in time for the first days of preseason practice. John sent a postcard on behalf of himself and a friend, notifying Hipple of this fact. When they arrived back in Marion, Hipple allowed John's friend to join the team, but banned John.

As Lynn Brown remembered it, young Edison simply refused to report or, having reported, quit. (It was not Hipple's nature to keep people out of sports; he thought they benefited everyone. The *Sentinel* often reported over the years that boys had missed the first day or two of football practice but joined the team later. In such situations, Hipple often exacted a penalty, such as quarter-mile runs in full gear, and then took the players back.) Looking back, John said he nurtured no animosity toward Hipple and that he had enjoyed his experience that year as a public address announcer at the Indians' home football games.

The stormy meeting, apparently, helped launch a rumor that there existed in Marion a coterie of adults who were conducting a semi-organized, long-term campaign to get Hipple fired. Marvin Edison was often named (or indicated with a nod by those who did not want to say) as a member of this group. But that is unlikely. John said his father wasn't interested in sports. Lynn Brown and others in the school system doubted that Edison was part of such a group.

Still, in the spring following the vituperative parents' meeting, Bill Dougherty, who had graduated from Marion in 1956 after playing football and running track for Hipple, saw his former coach at the Cornell Relays. Dougherty, a freshman at Loras College, was competing. Dougherty's mother, a rabid fan of Marion sports, had told her son of a "purge" attempt against Hipple. Dougherty went to Hipple and told him how sorry he was to hear about the effort to oust him. To his amazement, Dougherty saw tears come to the eyes of his former coach. "It really shook me," wrote Dougherty, "since to an eighteen-year-old he was still an icon whom I didn't associate with having normal feelings."

Although Messerli involved himself from the first in Marion's sports program, and Hipple no doubt chafed at this, athletic reform could not have been high on Messerli's agenda. The program was recognized as one of the most successful in the state. If Messerli saw problems there, they would have to wait until he dealt with the firestorm that grew out of his plan to consolidate two school districts.

—

During the 1956–1957 school year, Marion's Indians failed to win a single WaMaC title for the first time in twelve years. This result supported the assertions made earlier by Vernon that Marion had been blessed in the previous years with extraordinary athletes and did not deserve to be evicted from the WaMaC Conference.

The football team finished in a tie for third with a 5–3 record (4–3 in the conference). The team, an offensive powerhouse, was troubled all year by fumbles, bad luck, and injuries. In one game, the third-string quarterback, junior Buzz Clark, was the starter because both Bob Wilson and Ray Fuller were injured. Clark played ably as Marion won. John Jordan, fullback, wasn't able to dress for the first game because he was nursing a broken rib suffered while competing in a greased-pig contest. He missed the last game with a bone-chip injury, one of three starters on the sidelines as a listless Marion team lost to Anamosa. The Indians, who often gained far more yardage than opponents who defeated them, were basically out of title contention after dropping their first two conference games. Monticello went undefeated to win the championship. Summarizing the season, Larry Tanner pronounced it "not too bad."

A remarkable play occurred during the second quarter of a 51–14 thrashing of Vinton. Marion had the ball near its opponent's goal line when Ray Fuller arched a pass into the end zone. Vinton's Chuck Radcliffe intercepted it and took it 104 yards for a touchdown. When the Marion quarterback came to the sidelines, Hipple called him over and said, "Congratulations, Fuller, you've just set a record for the longest passing touchdown in Marion history." The way Fuller tells the story, Hipple wasn't angry over the interception. He was just sharing a wry joke with his quarterback.

In basketball, Steve Smith, the six-foot-three center, was the only returning letterman. The team sprinted into the season with six straight victories, looking like the Indians of old. Then came four losses. The Indians rallied to win five in a row, but fell out of title contention by losing four straight games (including two one-point defeats). The team finished 12–9 overall and 8–6 in the conference, good for fourth place. Monticello, looking like the new Marion, won the title with a 13–1 conference record. In the state tournament, the Indians beat Olin in the first game of the sectional tournament, but then were crushed by Anamosa, 53–41, losing to a team they had beaten twice during the season. As in football, juniors held many starting positions, and Marion fans looked to renewed success in the year ahead.

During the Christmas break, Larry Tanner reflected in his column on things for which he was thankful. They included young people he knew in the area through his work with Marion Methodist Youth Fellowship. As he wrote about his joy in knowing these youngsters, he added, as a counterpoint, "The pressure under which Marion High School has been competing in basketball during the past few years has sort of dulled my desire to watch the games." Marion's most constant and vocal fan was wearing down.

That spring, the track team scored only twenty-seven points and finished sixth, its worst showing since the conference was founded. Monticello finished first, making a clean sweep of the conference titles. Fans in that town must have been delirious. The school had hired a coach named Dean Nelson and, following the pattern of Hipple at Marion, put him in charge of all three sports.

—

By January 1957, Messerli had been on the job only a few months, and the school consolidation issue was occupying a great deal of his time. What sort of man had the board hired to deal with this contentious matter? The picture that emerges from interviews with former teachers and colleagues—and from Messerli's own writing—is that he was energetic and resolute. He wrote a column on school issues that appeared often in the *Marion Sentinel*, so it's clear he was an activist who was willing to share his opinions. He had to be, to promote the vast change he was charged with implementing. In his columns, he wrote that his guiding principle in all matters was what was best for the students.

Compared to Vernon, Messerli was considered by fellow educators and townspeople to be progressive and liberal, characteristics that were not always seen as praiseworthy.

People who were associated professionally with Messerli said he had a tendency to micromanage. He sometimes ignored traditional hierarchies in dealing with problems. Messerli's experience at smaller schools had perhaps trained him to become more deeply involved in day-to-day matters than would be customary for a superintendent in a larger school system. Some people said he tried too hard to please too many people and that he was inclined to seek compromises in situations that required he take a stand. However, another associate said he had the persistence of "a bulldog" once he settled on an issue. Messerli's son Dave said his father's principal motive was to help people.

Photographs show John Messerli in his thirties with a square face topped by wavy, dark hair. He wears horn-rimmed glasses, and the bridge of his nose is bashed in. Dave Messerli said that his father's nose had been broken, probably when he was a "hard-nosed guard" in high school football.

As the second semester of his first year began, Messerli announced that the number of incoming high school students would exceed the school's capacity of six hundred by the fall of 1958, just eighteen months in the future. New facilities would be needed. But the school board said it would not authorize any new construction when there were 125 tuition-paying students from the rural area. Without them, the board said, the high school was plenty large enough, and the board's first duty was to the students of the town. That meant, unless something changed, the town district probably would be forced to deny enrollment to tuition students by 1958.

Implicit in all this was the knowledge that the rural district was looking into the feasibility of building its own high school. Without knowing what the rural people planned to do, the town district couldn't make its own plans. Would the town, come 1958, have 500 high school students to educate, which the system could handle, or would it have 625, which it could not?

Faced with this quandary, the Marion Board of Education issued what amounted to an ultimatum to the rural district: Merge your district with ours, and your children can go to Marion High School. Don't, and they can't. And decide fast, because we have less than two years to get ready.

The rural people were badly split on this issue, wrote Michael W. Nash in his 1975 college thesis, *The Marion High School Merger Issue of 1958*. Nash wrote the thesis as a history major at Mount Mercy College in Cedar Rapids. He determined that about 30 percent of the rural people wanted to build their own high school, 30 percent favored a merger with Marion, 30 percent wanted a three-way merger with Marion and Cedar Rapids school districts, and 10 percent wanted to merge with the smaller and less threatening school district in the village of Springville, east of Marion. Each of these options was explored and championed by rural contingents—some authorized by the school district and some not—and as the debate raged and the clock ticked, tempers flared.

In time, it became apparent that the rural district had only two choices: build its own high school or merge with the Marion district. Even in early 1957, there were ample signs that most people in the rural district favored building their own high school. A straw vote in February came out 118–54 in favor of building. A pro-building candidate for the rural school board defeated a pro-merger candidate in March. At the same time, the district voted a small increase in its tax rate to finance future expenditures for land and construction.

"Messerli realized that the rural people wanted to build their own high school," wrote Nash. "Messerli and the school board members felt that such a move by the rural people would be a drastic mistake."

For the next year and a half, Messerli was the public voice for merger. His message was simple: A combined school district could provide better educational experiences for the children. Many smaller school districts in the state were consolidating to be able to offer more programs, hire better teachers, and improve their facilities. Messerli championed this cause in his column in the *Marion Sentinel*, which strongly supported a merger, and in speaking appearances before many groups. A merger, he said, would result in reduced tax rates for the town district and increased rates for the rural district, but the rural taxes would be no higher than would result from building a new high school, and the educational programs would be stronger. Both the town and rural people, then, would get more for their money through a merger.

Messerli offered a partnership to the skeptical rural people, wrote Nash. They could become partners in an existing successful school system composed of seven buildings in town. They would be partners in planning and building future facilities, many of which would go up in the rural district. Importantly, Messerli added, they would be partners in a single school district that would help keep the community united.

But the partnership theme didn't resonate with everyone in the rural district. It had two major weaknesses. The most obvious weakness was that the Marion district wanted to retain three seats on the consolidated board of education while offering the rural district only two. The allocation was based on population, but with an unequal voice in a merged system, many rural people felt they would have no control over future spending. Some of them thought Messerli's view of the future was too one-sided, grandiose, and expensive.

The rural people were proud of their school district. Less than a decade earlier, in 1949, they had banded together to build an elementary and junior high school, thus shutting down sixteen one-room and one two-room rural schoolhouses. Lumir Dostal Jr. remembered the joy he felt when he entered that new school as an eighth-grade student: It was the first time he had classmates. The farmers who ran the school were independent and self-sufficient, deeply uncomfortable with the idea of being ruled by town folks.

The other weakness in the partnership theme was that the rural district contained a rich source of future tax dollars—a virtual gold mine that many rural citizens did not want to share with the town. A brief geography lesson is necessary. The rural school district literally surrounded the town district, making the town district an island inside the rural district. The bulk of the rural district lay to the north, east, and south of Marion, mostly in farmland. But a narrow strip of the rural district encircled the town to the west, along a largely undeveloped corridor between Marion and Cedar Rapids. This was the gold mine.

In the late 1950s, the western corridor was beginning to be developed. Collins Radio was located there, growing rapidly. A shopping mall, Lindale Plaza, was in the works. A new motel was going up. These businesses, and those that followed, would be important sources of school tax dollars in the future—and they all lay in the rural district. "Marion had virtually no industrial tax base," Nash wrote. "The only hope of securing any was through a merger with the Marion Rural Independent School District." Why, wondered some in the rural area, should we pledge our future tax dollars for a partnership in which we will have an unequal voice?

There were many in the rural district, however, who shared Messerli's view of the future. Some were families who had moved to new developments just outside of town. Others were long-time rural residents. In fact, when the duly appointed Rural Work Study Group reported its findings after nine months of study in January 1958, it recommended a merger. Messerli and his board must have felt a sense of great relief, if not triumph. But the outcry in the farmland was so great that the rural board of education voted, four to one, to reject the recommendation of its own study group. The lone dissenter on the board, Ralph Hoskins, cast his vote and announced he would not stand for re-election. As a result of his vote some people who were once his friends shunned him.

Citizens' groups on both sides of the issue were formed, and they began to attack one another. Money, children, politics, and pride make an incendiary mix, and acrimony spread throughout the area. In at least one case, brothers ceased speaking to one another. In another, two branches of the same family began to pronounce their last names differently, lest they be confused for each other. Rural district meetings that were supposed to be official and open were held in secret to prevent attendance by those who might disagree.

Merger opponents spread rumors about the high incidence of pregnancies at the town school. A rural woman wrote a letter to the *Sentinel* about how children in town had "to walk in mobs to and from school" and how these hordes would "invade" the business district after school. "What about all the temptations the young people have before them, being so close to the business district where cigarettes, cokes, candy, fountain treats are so readily available and can nickel the parents to death? ... What about the evacuation of 1,000 students in the center of town should we be faced with an atomic war?"

Clearly, emotions were boiling over. Irwin Renfer, a town merchant, remembered that he and his fellow businessmen did not dare mention the subject of consolidation. Doing so raised the risk of offending and losing a customer who was dedicated to one side or the other. At the *Sentinel*, which strongly supported a merger, advertising revenue began to shrink. Eventually, personal attacks against publisher Ralph Young and his wife, together with declining advertising sales and job-printing orders, would contribute to their decision to sell the paper and leave town.

Finally, a time was set to put the issue to a vote. The people in each district would vote at separate polling places on June 9, 1958. For a merger to occur, both districts would have to vote in favor. An anti-merger majority in the rural district would signal approval to build a high school.

Advocates on both sides took their final shots. "For every ad published against the merger, two appeared applauding a merger," wrote Nash. In one ad, angry parents "attacked the rural (school) board for their actions and accused them of avoiding questions concerning their high school students' future."

The most powerful advertisement from the anti-merger faction showed a cartoon of a cat licking spilled cream. The headline read "THE 'HAVE NOTS' WANT WHAT THE HAVES HAVE! ... MARION INDEPENDENT WANTS THE CREAM!" The cream was the present and prospective industrial tax base in the western corridor: "a multimillion dollar shopping center, [the] $2,750,000 new Collins plant, [the] $700,000 motel, plus many other smaller industries and commercials."

The rural district vote was heavy and overwhelmingly against the merger, 548–219. The town vote was light, 551–82 in favor of a merger. The rural district would build its own high school. After the lines were drawn to separate the rural and town districts, some neighbors living side-by-side found they belonged to different school districts. At Lynn Brown's house, the district line ran through one of the bedrooms. The Browns had one school-aged daughter, and she went to Emerson grade school in town.

In 1958, Marion High School found room for the rural students. The new rural high school, christened Linn-Mar in a nod to both the county and the town, was built in part with volunteer labor and equipment from Marion farmers. It opened in the fall of 1959 with 124 students, nineteen of them seniors. Many upperclassmen chose to finish their high school careers at Marion. But the lower classes at Linn-Mar were more heavily populated, and before long all the rural kids were at Linn-Mar and all the town kids were at Marion.

It had been a tough two years for the new superintendent. Messerli had battled tirelessly but futilely. He came into the situation with little knowledge of the history or the personalities with which he had to deal, and it must have seemed at times like fighting a ghost. Even with the matter decided, Messerli refused to leave it at rest. He wrote in the *Sentinel*, "To me [a merger] is still right and I feel time will bear me out. The things we will be able to do for our children as separate districts cannot compare to the many things we could have done if we had united our forces." In the face of movements throughout the state toward consolidation, "Marion was one of the very few [communities] where a step backwards was taken." He went on to hope that the new rural high school would be a good one, providing "all the programs, facilities, and activities that rural boys and girls have a right to expect."

That said, he turned to planning the future of his own school district, which was continuing to grow, though not at the pace of little Linn-Mar next door.

—

Although the merger controversy was the biggest news story of 1957–1958, high school sports remained a topic of interest. Fans had high expectations for the football team, which had a strong core of veteran players. But the Indians were seriously hobbled by injuries and illness, and limped into a three-way tie for third place in the WaMaC with a 3–4 conference record, Hipple's worst since 1945.

A flu epidemic played havoc with practices at Marion and throughout the conference for several weeks. One day, only twenty-nine boys out of a squad of 107 showed up for practice. Things were even worse at Independence, where the flu forced the closing of school and the postponement of its football game at Marion, which was to mark Marion's homecoming.

Although the game was canceled, the homecoming dance was still on. Nevertheless, Hipple called a practice for Friday afternoon. Some of the seniors thought that was a terrible idea. "We felt he was just trying to tire us out before a big date night," wrote John Nieland. A bunch of seniors defied the coach and cut practice. That night they went to the homecoming dance, and some of the players even danced with Mrs. Hipple.

"Coach didn't say anything that night," Nieland remembered, but at practice the next Monday, Hipple said, "All of the seniors who felt they didn't need to come to practice last Friday, go with Mr. Brown over to the track." Their punishment was to run twenty quarter-mile laps in full gear—and to finish each lap in eighty seconds or less. After a few laps, three of the senior starters—Ray Fuller, quarterback, Rich Hendrickson, end, and Buzz Clark, halfback—walked off the track, went back to the locker room, and dumped their equipment in bundles at the door of Hipple's office.

Down at the track, "The rest of us finished our laps," Nieland said. "I'm sure Mr. Brown gave us a break on some of them. I know I wasn't running them in eighty seconds." When the players shuffled back to practice, Brown reported that three had defected. Hipple said nothing, and practice continued.

"The next day it was raining like hell," Nieland wrote, "and Coach decided to have practice in the gym." By this time, two of the players who had turned in their equipment, Fuller and Hendrickson, were remorseful. They asked to be let back on the team. Nieland recalled the scene: "Mr. Hipple turned to Coach Brown and said, 'These two need to finish their laps.' They went down to the track in full equipment and ran their laps in a rainstorm. Mr. Hipple never said anything about this incident again." Years later, Brown confirmed the essence of this story. He had supervised many penalty laps in his time, he wrote, "But I don't recall doing it in a monsoon."

—

If the football season was a disappointment, the basketball season was a glorious surprise. The Indians ran up a string of seventeen straight victories, clinching the conference title with three games left to play. The team had speed, good height, and a strong bench, but its most important characteristic was harmony, according to Larry Tanner. In a midseason column, Tanner noted the balanced scoring on the team, with four starters averaging twelve points or more a game. "There are no point hogs on this club," Tanner wrote. "The boy with the best shooting position usually gets the ball. Teamwork and unselfishness, along with harmony between the junior and senior members of the squad" were the crucial success factors.

The starting lineup for most of the season featured John Nieland, a six-foot senior, and Mike Smith, a six-foot-two junior, at forward; Jim McKean, a six-foot-two junior, at center; and seniors Ray Fuller and Rich Schleuter, both about six feet one, at guard. Key reserves were senior Bob Maly, five feet eleven, and juniors Mike Rucker and Jerry Hempy, both about six feet one.

When, late in the season, Fuller was named Prep of the Week by the *Des Moines Register*, Hipple called him into the office to deliver the news. "Don't let this go to your head," he told Fuller. "You are being honored because you play on a good team." The coach's words echoed those used by Lloyd Olmstead nearly a decade earlier when he was interviewed after being named All-State. In his interview for the *Register*, Hipple called these Indians the best-balanced team he had ever coached.

The rugged, high-scoring outfit averaged just over seventy points a game through its first seventeen contests and won most of them decisively, except for two squeakers against Monticello (50–47 and 73–72). As the Indians approached their final game of the regular season, they had the opportunity to do what only one other Marion team had achieved: go undefeated.

The opponent was second-place Anamosa, the game was at home, Marion had beaten the Raiders by fourteen points earlier in the season, and, although no title was at stake, Marion athletic history hung in the balance. Then a squirrel got into the works. Before the game started, the lights in the gym went out. It took more than three hours to find the problem, which, according to legend, had been caused when a squirrel burrowed into the transformer and gave up its life by gnawing a critical electric part.

Somehow, the delay affected Marion more than it did Anamosa. When the game finally got underway after 10:00 PM, the Indians were listless, losing 64–56. In later years, when they could laugh about it, the players blamed Hipple's training rules. After all, they had to play well past their normal bedtime. Hipple said nothing. "He never got on us one bit for losing that game," Fuller remembered.

That year, Marion was classified as an AA school for the state tournament, making it one of the smallest of the forty or so largest schools. As a result, for the first time in more than a decade, Marion lost its opening game in the state tournament, falling to University High of Iowa City, 72–59.

Tanner praised the team lavishly at the end of the season. "This is one of Marion's best ballclubs," he wrote, doubtlessly echoing Hipple's view.

Tanner made another claim in that column. "Tournaments don't count," he wrote, probably meaning that they didn't count in his assessment of the team. But it also seemed as if, with just three words, he could establish a new way of looking at a basketball season. He was wrong about that. Tournaments do count. Without them, there are no thrilling runs to Iowa City, no do-or-die, nail-biting games broadcast on the radio, no bragging rights for the county, the region, or the whole state, no way to galvanize fans, ignite town-wide interest, and make little boys dream their wildest dreams. The door had slammed shut on all that. And it would remain shut for fifty years.

Worse, Marion fans had become blasé, Tanner thought. Late in the season, when the Indians had wrapped up the WaMaC title and were still undefeated, he wrote, "Winning is still old stuff to many local basketball fans, apparently." The team wasn't drawing large, vocal crowds, either at home or away. "Lack of school spirit shows itself at both home and road games. Most towns are proud of an unbeaten team. But Marion has proven to be different this year. Don't think for a moment the Indians aren't proud of their record. They are. Be nice if the student body was just as proud, and the townspeople, too."

The 1950s were coming to an end. Everything was changing.

Chapter 30
Changing Times

From John Messerli's earliest days as superintendent, parents went to him with complaints about the sports program. Unlike C. B. Vernon, who stood foursquare with Hipple and told concerned parents to work out their problems with the coach, Messerli listened to the complaints and often tried to do something about them.

In his *Sentinel* column in the fall of 1958, after two years on the job, Messerli revealed the extent of his involvement in the program. The column was written as a defense of Hipple and his rules. But near the end of it, Messerli disclosed how much he was interfering with Hipple's program.

Here is most of what Messerli wrote:

> I have watched the Marion athletic program with great interest. Not only because I enjoy athletics but because of the state-wide reputation the program has. Almost every school man I talk with has heard of the program and most often make the statement that he wishes his school could establish such a program. Surely the won and loss record is outstanding, but better yet is the value to the character and discipline it attempts to teach the boy ... Between 150 and 200 boys will take part in some phase of the program this coming year.
>
> Naturally the program is not without its critics. Different parts of the program come under attack by different people. I think all would agree that such things as smoking, drinking, late nights and profane language should be taboo in any athletic program.

> Three types of criticisms reach my ears. 1) Why can't the boys drive cars? Well, the boys can drive cars if they have a reason to, but what Mr. Hipple wants to eliminate is the useless, foolish just driving around that some boys do. I think all of us will again agree that any brake we can apply to such activity the better the community will be.
>
> 2) Why does my boy have to take track if he wants to play football or why football or cross-country if he wants to play basketball? Again let me qualify this by saying that if there is a reason such as work that a boy cannot fill those requirements, just talk to Mr. Hipple about it … It's better that a boy be out for some activity getting good exercise than just sitting around uptown or even at home …. If a boy wants to play bad enough that he will sacrifice … how much better an athlete he will be.
>
> 3) Mr. Hipple is too tough on the boys. Surely he expects each boy to produce near his maximum ability … many times this criticism is due to misunderstanding … I urge every parent to discuss the situation with Mr. Hipple before coming to this conclusion.
>
> I have had the opportunity of reading many letters sent back by former graduates. They attest to the value the program has had for them … I have talked to many people who wish they could have such a program. Many are attempting to copy it. Check with Monticello and look at their performance during the past two years.

Messerli concluded the column by writing, "During the past two years I have personally interceded for many boys by getting them permission to go out or getting another chance after breaking training. Without exception, the boy let me down. One young fellow even showed up at the next home game smoking in the school house."

Hipple rarely threw boys off a team. Drinking or smoking typically resulted in dismissal. Messerli seems to be saying that he went to bat for boys who were thrown off the team for smoking, insisting that Hipple restore them. Twelve years earlier, Hipple had thrown as many as ten boys off the football team for smoking, and Vernon backed him all the way.

Messerli wrote that the boys he supported invariably betrayed him. Did this experience make him more likely to endorse Hipple's enforcement of the rules? The evidence suggests it did not.

Messerli had been on the job for only two years. He did not enjoy the stature Vernon had accumulated over decades. Messerli needed to learn what parents thought and to win their support. But Messerli had a tendency to micromanage situations and intercede in teacher-student relationships, according to several of those who worked with him. He was known to often side with parents rather than teachers. Hipple wasn't alone in experiencing lack of support from his boss.

The relationship between parent and coach and the proper role of school authorities in overseeing that relationship is a difficult and contentious matter. There are no perfect solutions, but there is no question that when a coach's decisions are overruled, his disciplinary power is reduced, and so is his effectiveness.

It's not surprising that parents went to Messerli. While Hipple was always available to parents, his reputation and his manner probably made the meeting difficult for some. He could be distant and reticent. Having heard out the parent and provided his response, he probably considered the meeting over. Parents hoping for a long give-and-take were likely to be dissatisfied, to wonder if Hipple had really heard them.

Messerli would say later that Hipple was too tough. It seems to have been his biggest criticism of the coach. He described Hipple as being like a drill sergeant—that probably meant unfeeling, cold, and even cruel. In Hipple's defense, it should be pointed out that many boys who played for him and later encountered a drill sergeant failed to see a resemblance. Hipple did not scream, curse, threaten, strike, or use demeaning names. He rarely shouted; when he was angry he pressed his lips together, and his face turned red. But, somehow, boys who played for Hipple, on being confronted later in life by a real drill sergeant, were less intimidated than they otherwise would have been.

Messerli—and the parents who complained to him about Hipple—may have been misreading what the players were saying. That's a theory suggested by Bill Huntoon, who graduated from Marion High School, taught and coached there, and later served many years on the board of education. When a boy comes home and says, "You won't believe what he had us do today. It was really tough," the boy is not so much complaining as boasting, Huntoon thought. The boy was proud of the endurance he had shown, and in trying to share that feeling with his parents he instead alarmed them.

Some of Hipple's assistant coaches disapproved of the way he treated his players. The most vocal of these was Bill Page, who had attended Marion High School before Hipple arrived and who came back in the mid-1950s to teach industrial arts and coach freshman football, among other sports. Page later earned a PhD and went on to a career in high school and community college administration.

Page reluctantly agreed to share his views, which were requested because they offer clues to the way Messerli viewed Hipple. The criticisms focus on what Page believed was Hipple's harsh treatment of players and his unbending nature. "If kids didn't do what Hipple said, they became outcasts," Page said. "If they had individual initiatives that violated his principles, they had a terrible time with him. His rules were so rigid that a kid who wanted to be a kid couldn't do it. He tried to control every aspect of their lives. We can't do that as teachers. What we're trying to do is teach them to be good citizens, not control them to be good citizens. I remember kids coming into my room crying because of the way he treated them."

Page and other teachers also resented the emphasis placed on sports and the attention and adulation the coach received. "I'm not a strong supporter of sports," Page said. "It's the tail that wags the dog too often in public education. Coaches are considered good if they win. He was a winning coach. But he didn't personify the kind of educator that should be emulated by people going into the coaching and teaching professions. In my opinion, he was Bobby Knight without the profanity."

Perhaps that was the way Messerli felt, too. But in 1958, it would have been unthinkable for him to try to force Hipple out. Messerli was thirty-five years old and had been at Marion for two years. Hipple was forty-five and had been there thirteen years. Hipple was immensely popular in town and respected throughout the state. Members of the board of education supported Hipple. The most Messerli could do at the time was try to soften some of the rules and urge Hipple to modify his behavior. The only thing Hipple could do, other than quit, which was not a word he recognized, was bend in those areas where his principles allowed it and resist where they would not. The two men became locked in a battle of wills that dragged on for almost ten years.

Richard Sorensen, who joined Marion High School as principal in 1961, said he quickly came to the conclusion that the antipathy between Messerli and Hipple had been "festering a long time." Larry Perkins, who joined the faculty and coaching staff about the same time, echoed this assessment.

—

Resistance to Hipple's rules began to increase in the late 1950s among both parents and students. His rules had been extreme even for the late 1940s and early 1950s, and now change was in the air. New ideas were taking hold. There was a growing feeling that the old ways weren't always best, that some things were wrong in America.

"As we got older, we students were more questioning," wrote Herb Ray, who graduated in 1961. "You have to remember that the late 1950s, despite outward signs of social conformity, were underscored by many rebellions against society. Think of James Dean, Marlon Brando, Montgomery Clift, Marilyn Monroe, and their movies. Think of *Brown v. Board of Education* in 1954, *West Side Story* in 1957, the Montgomery bus boycott in Alabama, the emergence of rock and roll, Sputnik, beatniks, jazz music, and wacky *Mad* magazine. As teenagers, we were profoundly affected by these movements."

In 1957, the nation was riveted as Arkansas governor Orville Faubus called out the state National Guard to prevent nine black children from entering Central High School in Little Rock. "Even as junior high students we knew that the American Legion swimming pool in Marion was racially segregated and we felt that was wrong," Ray wrote.

This unrest among the young expressed itself in the ways they dressed and wore their hair. In the late 1950s it became fashionable for Marion boys to wear their jeans low around their hips with no belt. Messerli ordered them to go home, get a belt, and pull up their pants. "I don't feel a boy is properly dressed for school with any or a combination of the following: ducktail haircuts, engineer boots, tight fitting and low hanging jeans, unbuttoned shirts, and motorcycle jackets," he wrote in a column in 1958. Messerli didn't see kids who wanted to look like Elvis Pressley or Marlon Brando; he saw kids who dressed like hoodlums.

For many years, girls were required to wear dresses or skirts with a sweater or blouse, and by 1961, some of them threatened to step over the fashion line—in skirts that were too short. In Des Moines, school officials sent girls home if their skirts didn't cover their knees, and Messerli warned that Marion would do the same. He also forbade multicolored hairstyles among girls. Dying hair a single color was fine, but mixing several colors would result in expulsion. "We have sent boys home to get a belt or a shirt and suggested hair cuts," he wrote, and there would be no hesitation to doing the same for girls.

Cars were proliferating, and educators were deeply concerned about the consequences. In his *Sentinel* column, Messerli described meetings among fellow superintendents to discuss what could be done to discourage students from driving to school. "Most all agree that students driving cars when not necessary is a scourge to both student and school," he wrote.

In the spring of 1959, Larry Tanner wrote a long column about the evils of driving cars—probably in defense of Hipple's rules. Tanner quoted a column by Florence Hoidahl of the *Mount Vernon Hawkeye* in which she cited a survey taken by a high school that found a direct correlation between driving cars to school and poor grades. The survey found, for example, that no straight-A student had the use of a car and only 15 percent of B students drove a car to school, but that 41 percent of C students and 71 percent of D students did so.

"Coaches in high schools all over the country are also concerned about this problem," Hoidahl wrote. "The degree of ruggedness among high school boys is diminishing." Coaches in Chicago, she continued, said that the desire to own a car was the leading reason for a declining interest in football. Tanner finished the column by describing a visit to the men's room in an opposing team's high school. There he found "big, strong-looking" students standing around "with fags hanging out of their mouths." If their parents had made them go out for sports, he wrote, they might have been better boys, and their team might have been more of a match for Marion.

The phenomenon hit Marion, too. Some of the boys, promising athletes, decided not to go out for sports. They didn't like the rule that going out for track was the price of admission to the football team and going out for football or cross-country was a requirement to play basketball. Herb Ray paid the price, but he resented it. "I considered my time spent running around the track as a form of medieval torture," he wrote, but he did it because he wanted to play so badly. Others were less motivated and turned away from sports. By the 1960s, Hipple's rule requiring track participation may have been hurting his football program as much as it was helping it.

Whether it had to do with cars or track or shifts in social values, fewer Marion boys were eager to play football. Squad photos in the 1957 yearbook show one hundred players out for football, of whom thirty are on the varsity, and seventy are freshmen and sophomores. The following year, the total number of squad members plummeted. The varsity squad remained about the same size, with thirty-seven players, but the number of freshmen and sophomores fell by more than half, to thirty-two. The football team was reduced by thirty-one players in a single year. The *Sentinel* reported that the coaches were particularly disappointed in the small turnout among freshmen. In 1959, with the opening of Linn-Mar High School in the township district, Marion lost 117 students, and the squad size fell to fifty-six.

Hipple stuck to his rules but modified his ban on driving. Parents wanted to be able to send their boys on errands, so he allowed more exceptions to the Sunday-only rule. He allowed players to drive if they had a good reason, had parental permission, and *called him ahead of time* for his approval. Darrell Shirk remembered calling him for permission to drive his family car on Saturday night dates. "He never said no," Shirk recalled. "He just wanted to know what his players were doing."

There is a story, perhaps apocryphal, that a boy called for permission to drive and got Mrs. Hipple on the phone. She said the coach wasn't home but that the boy should go ahead and run his errand. At the next practice, Hipple made the boy run laps because his wife wasn't authorized to grant driving privileges. Whether the story is true or not, it illustrates the tension around the driving rule.

By 1958, wrestling was catching on as a WaMaC sport, and Marion fielded a team. The coach was Bill Linstrom, a young teacher who had wrestled in high school but had never coached the sport. A wrestling room was created in the Lincoln building next door. At first, Linstrom recalled, Hipple opposed the idea, at least in part because he feared it would cut into his basketball program. But after the first year, when he saw how wrestling improved his football players, Hipple supported wrestling. However, Linstrom was not the disciplinarian that Hipple was. "I am sure that [Linstrom's] rules were not as tough as Hipple's," wrote Lynn Brown. As Linstrom recalled it, Hipple's rules were already weakened through Messerli's involvement. Thus wrestlers had different rules than basketball players. A fissure had developed in Hipple's iron control.

—

Meanwhile, Marion was being transformed. Young families were flooding into the area. The town's population grew at a frantic pace. It hit ten thousand in 1960, up from fewer than six thousand in the mid-1950s.

There was an explosion in new housing. Within fewer than twelve months during 1958 and 1959, the *Sentinel* reported three stunning real estate developments. In August 1958, Thomas McGowan announced plans to build about 450 new homes on 110 acres he had purchased from Arthur and Alfred Granger just north of town. The land, with another ten acres McGowan had acquired earlier, included choice lots across the road from the Indian Creek Country Club, which, along with the creek itself, had marked the northern limits of the town. McGowan, who had been a substitute employee at the post office eight years earlier when realtor Earl Brockman offered him a job, was now heading a multimillion-dollar project that was practically a town itself. (Out of gratitude, McGowan named one of the streets in his development after Brockman, but applied his own name to an even grander thoroughfare, McGowan Boulevard.)

In early 1959, news broke of a plan by Cedar Rapids developers to build *another* four hundred homes over a four-year period on ninety acres just south of Marion. This development had a specific market: young families, with children, looking for their first home, earning $4,800 a year, and able to afford the average monthly payment of $74.61 for houses costing from $10,000 to $14,000.

Three months after that, plans were revealed for a "massive" seven hundred-acre development for commercial and industrial enterprises along the highway just east of town. This plan would go forward if Marion agreed to annex the land as part of the town. The city council, eager for the industrial tax base, voted unanimously in favor of annexation just two months later—thus increasing the total area of the town by 25 percent.

The drumbeat had only begun. More developments and annexations followed. Marion was on its way to becoming the fastest-growing town in the state, a claim proudly displayed on the masthead of the *Sentinel* for several years. The value of home permits granted in Marion accelerated steadily during the 1950s and were still climbing in 1959—a year in which the value of new home permits on a national basis *declined* by 19 percent. And Marion had yet to experience the full effects of the recently announced developments.

—

In 1959, Marion High School, for the first time in years, was no longer overcrowded. Linn-Mar opened that year, reducing Marion's enrollment to 468, which Messerli wrote was "just about right" for the building. But new students were flooding into the lower grades.

Twenty-nine new classrooms had been added to the elementary school system by the construction of a new school, Starry, built under Messerli's supervision in 1959, and additions to existing schools. But this did nothing to prepare Marion High School for the crush headed its way. The high school could not accommodate the tide of youngsters already in the system, let alone those yet to move into the district. A new high school was needed, and it would cost much more than an elementary school.

Messerli and the board of education expected resistance from the people of the district, who had to support the school system without much help from taxes on business and industry. All the industrial development was occurring in the Linn-Mar district. As superintendent, Messerli was nearly as frugal as Vernon. In 1958–1959, the average cost of educating a student in the district was $256, compared to a statewide average of $339. Only six districts in the state had lower per-pupil costs than Marion. Yet Marion regularly received high ratings for its educational programs from state agencies. Messerli must have saved money on programming and physical facilities, because teachers' salaries were competitive, or he may have gotten more work out of his teachers than other school districts. The athletic program had been profitable in earlier years, and may have continued to be source of income.

Expecting a tough sell, and having been warned by the editor of the *Sentinel* that there could be a "tax revolt" from the people, Messerli and his board developed an expansion plan. It called for building a new high school to serve grades ten through twelve, using the former high school for grades seven through nine and devoting the Lincoln building to lower grades (it then also housed the junior high).

Messerli used his *Sentinel* column repeatedly to explain the needs and benefits of this plan. As for higher taxes, there was no way around them. "Every new home constructed in the district is a loss of revenue for the district," he wrote. "The amount of taxes paid by the home is not sufficient to pay for the education of the children coming from the home." A quality education cannot be maintained solely through efficiencies, Messerli argued. "The line between an efficient program and a cheap one is very fine."

In 1959, the University of Iowa appraised Marion's facilities and found classrooms overcrowded, the overall land space inadequate, the boys' gym below standard in length, the principal's office grossly inadequate, the superintendent's office barely adequate, and the Lincoln building apparently sound but with hazardous conditions. "I shudder at the thought of the problem we will have by the fall of 1962," Messerli wrote.

In early 1960, as the city council was considering the annexation of one thousand six hundred acres northwest of town, the citizens voted against a bond issue for a new police station and firehouse. This may have spurred Messerli, the board, and their supporters to even greater efforts, for they mounted a full-fledged political campaign to win voter approval for a bond issue for the new school. They surely remembered the failed attempt to create a merged school district a few years earlier, and wanted to take no chances on losing this battle.

Planning and budgeting for the school began in 1960. The public information campaign lasted almost a year. Messerli calculated that he made twenty-five to thirty presentations to community groups, while members of the school board and various advisory groups made many more. Meanwhile, the advisory groups bought advertisements, distributed brochures and flyers, and even made house-to-house visits to get out the vote.

When the matter was put to the people in October 1961, the bond issue was overwhelmingly endorsed by 79 percent of the voters, 1,206 in favor and 300 against. The issue would provide $635,000 of the more than $800,000 the new school would cost.

With this victory, Messerli could now think seriously about how to create a modern high school for the people of Marion. The new school would open in the fall of 1963, and many things would be very different, including the athletic program.

Chapter 31
The Magic Fades, 1958–1960

A stark sign of the changing attitude toward high school sports in Marion—and the changing nature of the town itself—appeared in a headline over a brief item in the *Marion Sentinel* early in 1959.

Marion Stores to Stay
Open on Friday Nights

The Retail Merchants Bureau had polled its customers, and they voted, 332 to 232, to have stores stay open late on Fridays rather than Saturdays. The change would go into effect on Friday, the thirteenth of February. The move would have been unthinkable a decade earlier, when the stores in town closed before 5:00 PM on winter Fridays so everyone could line up for basketball seats.

At the time of the decision, Marion's basketball team was engaged in what Larry Tanner called "the biggest scramble in the loop's history," with at least four teams having a shot at the title as the season entered its final weeks.

That fall, Marion's football team had gone undefeated and untied for the second time under Hipple, bringing home the WaMaC trophy for the sixth time in his thirteen years at Marion. The town did not appreciate the accomplishment, Tanner wrote. "Some of us around Marion take our winning teams for granted. The Indians win a game and fans shrug their shoulders and say it's just another win."

Tanner was correct that many fans in town were accustomed to victory. But the town also was being transformed by a flood of young families; a growing percentage of citizens didn't care whether the Indians won or lost. For many of them, Linn-Mar, not Marion, was the home team. Television was catching on. People didn't need high school sports for entertainment. They had Milton Berle and Arthur Godfrey.

Meanwhile, the rest of the conference was catching up with Marion. In the last four school years of the 1950s, that is from 1956–1957 through 1959–1960, Marion's teams performed well, winning or sharing four conference titles—two in football and two in basketball. But Monticello, where Dean Nelson built a program modeled on Hipple's, won six titles—three in track, two in basketball, and one in football.

—

Although the number of boys out for football in 1958 was dramatically lower than the year before, the loss came among the youngest players and did not immediately hurt Marion's program. The undefeated, untied 1958 team was one of Hipple's greatest. It had a powerful line, one of the heaviest in the conference, anchored at center by 195-pound Gene Dirks and with two big tackles at 190 pounds, Leroy Bufton and Tim Corporan. The backfield was small but fast, spearheaded by senior halfback Mike Smith, the fastest and largest starting back at 175 pounds. The others in the starting backfield were juniors: Terry Conklin, a skinny 130-pound quarterback, Darrell Shirk, about 130 pounds, at halfback, and Don Patschke, 165 pounds, at fullback.

Conklin, who was about five feet seven, was a master at Hipple's belly series. He frisked behind that big line, daring tacklers to grab him as he faked handoffs to fullback Patschke, and then pitched the ball to Smith or Shirk. Patschke and Conklin were so deft at the fake handoff that they often fooled the officials as well as the opposing linemen. Players remember officials whistling plays dead when the fullback went down under a swarm of tacklers, only to apologize later when they saw the ball was in the hands of a halfback. Steve Miller, who played on three Hipple varsity teams and graduated in 1961, insists that several touchdowns were nullified because the quarterback and fullback were so adroit at making the handoff look real.

The 1958 team had only one close game all season, a 14–7 win over Monticello in which all the touchdowns were made in the last quarter.

Monticello scored first, but Marion stormed back with two touchdowns in the last eight minutes. "We were just worn down," said Coach Nelson of Monticello.

The Indians went on to beat two previously undefeated teams back-to-back. They topped Tipton, 21–6, as Smith broke loose for three touchdowns and 191 yards on twelve carries, and Vinton, 28–12. Then they coasted to the championship, scoring a total of 102 points in games against Independence and Manchester. "I can't remember any time I thought we might lose a game," said Conklin years later.

The Indians scored 266 points during the season (ranking twelfth on Marion's all-time list), but were even more effective on defense. They allowed only thirty-eight points in nine games (tying them with Hipple's 1948 squad as the stingiest defensive team in Marion history). Smith, who finished his career with twenty-eight touchdowns (sixth in the Marion record books), was selected for the All-State fourth team, while four of his teammates received honorable mention: Bufton, Dirks, guard Harold Odeen, and end Mike Rucker.

After that perfect season Tanner wrote that, for many fans, victories didn't mean anything anymore.

—

The 1958–1959 basketball season was filled with suspense. Marion was in title contention all the way, but so was almost half the league. With four games to play, there was a four-way tie for first place. It came after Vinton beat Marion for the first time in fourteen years, 65–60. One game later, after Marion had defeated Anamosa, there was a three-way tie, and then, with two games left, a tie between Vinton and Marion.

Then Marion's scheduled game with Tipton, the next-to-last of the regular season, was postponed after an ice storm shut down communications for several days. Vinton and Marion each won the last conference game on their schedules. Thus, Vinton's conference record stood at 11–3, while Marion was 10–3 with one to play. But the state tournament was about to begin, and the WaMaC championship had to wait.

Marion was classed AA, the division with the largest schools. Its first foe was Thomas Jefferson of Cedar Rapids, which had a weak team that year. Marion played poorly, but won, 53–49. The Indians would have to do a lot better than that, the *Gazette* said, to have any chance against their next foe, Regis of Cedar Rapids. Going into the tournament, Regis was ranked as the fourth-best team in northeast Iowa. Marion was barely ranked at all, a distant eighteenth. Regis had been formed a few years earlier by the consolidation of several Catholic high schools, including Immaculate Conception. The Regis coach was Bob "Red" Jennings. This would be the sixth tournament confrontation between Hipple and Jennings, and the eighth between Marion and I. C./Regis.

Regis that year had two scoring aces in forward John Willenborg and guard Larry Wagner. Willenborg was the high scorer, but Wagner, said the *Gazette*, was "one of the most gifted shooters in Iowa high school basketball." All year long, opposing coaches had tried various methods to shut them down and had failed. Marion got balanced scoring from a fairly tall lineup of seniors and juniors. The tallest was senior center Jim McKean, six feet three. Seniors Mike Smith and Mike Rucker played forward, as did junior Bob Berry. Guards were seniors Jerry Hempy and John Cory, backed up by juniors Darrell Shirk and Terry Conklin. When the seniors were in the lineup, everyone was six feet one or taller.

Hipple devised no special defense for Wagner and Willenborg. "You can't take shots away from fellows like that without hurting yourself somewhere else," he said later. "Play 'em tight," he told his team, "man-to-man."

Marion students dressed for the game in crimson and gold and "yelled their heads off," Tanner wrote, as the game turned into another classic. Regis, with Wagner pouring in long shots, took a two-point lead into the final quarter. Marion stuck to its tenacious defense and used its height to dominate the rebounding. With a minute to go, Marion was ahead, 55–54, and was stalling when Conklin was fouled. "With most of the spectators in a state of shock," Tanner wrote, "Conklin rested up and then dropped both free throws into the hoop." The final seconds were thrilling as each team battled for the ball and for shots. Both teams made another free throw; McKean grabbed the final rebound, and Marion won, 58–55.

Regis's Wagner scored thirty points with dazzling long jumpers. Willenborg added seventeen, but Marion's defense held the rest of the Royals to a mere eight points. It was, said Hipple, the Indians' best performance of the year, and it was delivered by defense, rebounding, and superior free throw shooting—traits that Marion had called upon repeatedly over the years in beating Immaculate Conception and, now, Regis. All but one of Marion's victories in those contests were hard-won, but this one came against the greatest odds.

Marion lost to highly ranked Mason City, 68–58, in the district opener, and could then return to the matter of the WaMaC title and Tipton. Marion won, 58–52, in a tough game on the Tigers' home court, earning a tie for the championship.

It was Hipple's tenth WaMaC basketball crown in fourteen years at Marion, a stupendous achievement that went largely uncelebrated by the town. "Victories don't mean anything anymore," Tanner wrote. It's too bad the fans didn't appreciate the teams' accomplishments, because twenty-two years would pass before Marion again won both a WaMaC basketball and football championship in the same school year.

—

The following summer, as the candidates for the football team of 1959 gathered in the gym to be fitted with equipment, a new assistant coach was on hand to help. Ernest Beemblossom, twenty-five, had replaced Charles Kurt, a former Marion player who had been on the staff for several years. Darrell Shirk remembered the scene vividly. After all the players arrived, Hipple called them together to introduce Mr. Beemblossom. As the equipment selection began, Shirk, a senior letterman, addressed the new coach as "Mr. Bloomblossom."

This twist on an unusual name may have brought a smile to Beemblossom's lips, but Hipple overheard it, and pounced. "Start running, Shirk," he ordered. Without a murmur, Shirk did as he was told. "It was a slip of the tongue," Shirk insisted fifty years later, "but he made me keep running around the gym while everybody else got their equipment. I was the last guy to get my gear." For Hipple, it was the perfect teaching moment: The entire team was memorably reminded that they must always show respect for their coaches, no matter what their names were.

Although this team had veterans Shirk, Conklin, and Patschke in the backfield, along with letterman Steve Miller, it was notably smaller and less experienced than the powerful 1958 squad. After losing their non-conference game against Waverly, the Indians recovered and won four conference games to find themselves locked in a tie with Vinton for the lead.

Now, for their homecoming game, the Indians faced Tipton, a team they fully expected to beat. But the Tigers manhandled the Indians. At halftime, Hipple was furious. "In other games where we might be behind, he would just talk to us," Shirk remembered, "but this time he was yelling."

Steve Miller, who also weathered that tirade, said that winning wasn't the point. "It was more about doing things the right way and playing as hard as you could. He would get very upset at players not doing the right thing or not doing the right thing with effort." Hipple's outburst was futile. "We should have won that game," Shirk said, "But there are some days when you think you are playing your hardest and things just don't work." Marion never seriously threatened as the Tigers rolled up three hundred yards to Marion's sixty-nine and won, 14–0.

Now Marion (4–1) would have to beat Vinton (5–0) on its home field to have a shot at the title. Vinton had not beaten Marion since 1951 and was thirsting for revenge. Vinton was rebuilding under a new coach who had been hired to make a run at Marion's dominance. It had rained during almost every game Marion played that year, and the conditions at Vinton were worse—snow, bitter cold, and a strong wind that made passing all but impossible. The game was a brutal defensive battle with neither team scoring until the fourth quarter, when Marion went ahead, 6–0, on a Conklin sneak. Marion seemed in control as the clock ran down. But the Indians had turned the ball over twice in the game and they did it again—this time when the punter mishandled the snap and Vinton recovered on the Marion twenty-eight. Six plays later, with twenty-eight seconds to go, Vinton scored but failed to make the extra point. The game ended in a 6–6 tie, giving Vinton an almost certain lock on the title.

But in the last conference game of the season, as Marion was pounding a weak Independence team, 50–0, Vinton lost to Monticello, 27–13, and Marion was boosted into a tie for the championship. It was Hipple's seventh WaMaC football crown, and his last.

—

That winter, 1959–1960, a small and inexperienced basketball team suffered Marion's first losing season since Hipple's first squad in 1945–1946, finishing in a tie for fifth place with a 6–13 record. Monticello, the emerging power, won the title with a 14–0 conference record. When the season opened, Hipple's tallest starter was six-foot-one Bob Berry, assigned to play center. As the campaign wore on and the losses mounted, the coach constantly experimented with the lineup, even to the point of trying freshman John McKean, who was about six feet three, against an Independence team that had two players measuring six feet five.

It was a weird season. Hipple missed his second game in fifteen years when he and his family suffered food poisoning. Sophomore Jim Luense nearly cut off his big toe with an axe. Hipple apparently had serious disciplinary problems, too, for the box scores show that two of his early-season starters, both capable scorers, were no longer with the team when the season ended. By that time, he had called up as many as four sophomores, who saw considerable action. Only two seniors, both starters, were on the team at the end of the season, Terry Conklin and Darrell Shirk.

—

Hipple's track teams finished sixth and seventh in 1958–1959 and in 1959–1960. There were several reasons for the poor showing. The first was that very few seniors went out for track. The second was that squad size fell precipitously as fewer boys went out for football. Since track was a requirement for football, a smaller football squad meant a smaller track squad. A third possible reason was that it had become fashionable to hate track, and some members of the squad were simply going through the motions with no thought of getting faster or better.

The bright spot in track was the emergence of Steve Miller, who won the WaMaC championship in the mile run in 1959 and went on to repeat the next two years. As a senior in 1961, he set a new conference record for the distance at 4:28.1, beating Jerry Walker's previous record of 4:30.4. Miller's record was not broken for fifteen years.

It had been an extraordinary decade. In the ten years between 1950–1951 and 1959–1960, Marion won or shared seven basketball titles, six football championships, and two track championships. Of the thirty championships available to Hipple-coached teams, Marion won fifteen and finished second five times. In the two team sports that meant the most—football and basketball—Hipple's teams won thirteen out of a possible twenty titles during the 1950s.

—

During the late 1950s, radio broadcasts of Marion basketball games ceased. Perhaps merchants no longer wanted to sponsor them, but a more likely reason is that the broadcasts were cutting into paid attendance. This had been a concern earlier in the decade when football gate receipts dipped after regular broadcasts began. It had not been a problem with basketball because seating was limited. As excitement over the teams diminished, school officials may have stopped the broadcasts to prod more people to come to the games.

There was another sour note in Marion sports as the decade ended. In April 1959, the voice of Marion sports was stilled when Larry Tanner resigned as news editor of the *Sentinel.* For fourteen years, first with Fred Dice, then with Tanner, the *Sentinel* had been an unflagging champion of Marion's sports programs. The two editors always treated Indian games as page-one news, and usually devoted their columns to Marion sports as well. Dice wrote with a fiery passion that reflected the town's growing excitement over Hipple's early teams, and Tanner's tireless reporting on the glory years offered insights into the mind of the inscrutable coach. Tanner left the *Sentinel* to finish work on his degree at Iowa. He resurfaced almost immediately, covering Marion games for the *Cedar Rapids Gazette*, but these brief reports did not permit the range of opinion his readers had enjoyed in the *Sentinel.*

With Tanner's departure, the job of covering the Indians for the *Sentinel* fell to students. For two years, Herb Ray and Steve Miller wrote competent recaps of the games, but readers could learn nothing of what the town or the coach thought of the teams. After Ray and Miller graduated in 1961, there were periods when the *Sentinel* provided no coverage whatsoever of the Indians. The paper had been shrinking in size for several years, and in 1962 the Young family sold it to Willard and David Archie of Shenandoah, who had other publishing interests as well. The new editors devoted little space to the Indians.

Chapter 32
The Beginning of the End, 1960–1962

As new families transformed Marion and new values reshaped society, Les Hipple's professional world changed dramatically. In a few years' time he was surrounded by unfamiliar and, sometimes, disapproving people. It was an unusually lonely time, even for a man perceived to be reclusive.

At the end of the 1959–1960 school year, Hipple's loyal assistant, Lynn Brown, left Marion. He accepted a non-coaching position as a teacher at University High School at Illinois State University in Normal. The move was overdue. Brown had intended to stay in Marion only a few years to get experience under Hipple, but he and his wife enjoyed Marion so much they stayed eight years. Brown had been a completely reliable lieutenant. He supported Hipple in everything he did, understanding and accepting his personality quirks, his silences, and his reluctance to offer praise. Brown said he and Hipple didn't need to talk a lot; they each understood what the other was thinking.

Brown had helped mold some of Hipple's great teams. Brown's junior varsity football team went undefeated for many years and may have lost only one game; the record isn't clear. His freshman–sophomore basketball teams won four conference championships and compiled an overall record that Brown later estimated at 120–40. Now, however, he was burned out from teaching five classes a day and coaching three sports. The offer from Illinois was too good to turn down.

Two young men replaced Brown: Jerry Skilling, 31, who had served in the military and taught at Lansing, Iowa, and Larry Perkins, 22, hired fresh out of the University of Northern Iowa. With the departure the year before of Charles Kurt and his replacement by Ernest Beemblossom, that made three new coaches in two years. Then, at the end of the 1960–1961 year, Ken Otting left as well, marking the departure of another former player and loyalist. Coach Hipple was surrounded by assistants who didn't know him or his systems. Since Hipple had no role in hiring them, they had no reason to be grateful toward him for their jobs. Hipple not only had to train these new men, he also had to win their loyalty.

The year after Brown left, there was another big change in personnel. Glen Nicholson resigned as principal of the high school, announcing that he wanted to concentrate on his graduate studies. Nicholson had been at Marion eight years, entering the system under C. B. Vernon, and he had experienced some of the school's glory years in sports. Nicholson, in his early forties when he left, had worked well with Hipple and, records indicate, thought highly of him as a physical education teacher.

Nicholson's successor was Richard Sorensen, thirty-seven, who had been principal at Nashua (Iowa) High School for eight years following four years of teaching and three years as a Navy pilot. Where the former principal saw in Hipple the embodiment of a superb physical education teacher, the new principal saw a barely adequate one.

For a time during the 1960s, Marion High School used a one-page form to evaluate teachers. Several of these forms were in Hipple's personnel file. The one-page form lists twenty factors that are rated on a five-point scale. A score of five was superior, four was good, three was average, two was fair, and one was poor. Among the factors rated were *cooperation with other teachers; general appearance; acceptance of criticism, all-around good influence on students;* and *discipline and control.* None of Hipple's evaluation forms were signed, but one was dated 1960–1961. That was Nicholson's last year as principal. On this form, Hipple received an average rating of 4.65. He was rated superior on twelve factors and good on eight.

Two other forms have handwriting that matches writing on other documents in Hipple's files that can be attributed to Sorenson. On these forms Hipple's overall ratings are 2.6 and 2.65—below average. Where Nicholson rated Hipple as superior in influence on students and superior in discipline and control, Sorenson rated him as fair—that is, below average—giving him a two on both factors. How could anyone rate Hipple a two on discipline and control? He was famous for discipline and control; they were his bedrock qualities. A partial explanation is contained in a note at the bottom of the form: "When I rate him poorly on influence, etc., I again refer to his negative approach to problem-solving."

The note must refer to Hipple's manner and technique—the *way* he went about solving problems, not the results he got. Hipple had a very direct way of solving problems with students: He told them what to do and they did it. Problem solved. So it seems reasonable to infer that Sorenson did not approve of Hipple's *style* of leadership and discipline, his stern, brook-no-nonsense posture, his apparent lack of flexibility, and the distance he maintained between himself and his students. It seems that Nicholson and Hipple were "old school," while Sorenson was "new school." (Nicholson died before research on this book began. Sorensen said he had no memory of events involving Hipple.)

With Nicholson gone, Hipple lost a protective buffer between himself and the superintendent. Nicholson's support, spoken and unspoken, must have modified what Messerli said and did about Hipple. Now, with Sorenson aboard, it seems that the superintendent and the principal were of like minds—strongly critical of Hipple's methods. A third member of the school administration, John Fowler, was principal of the junior high. He was also the junior high coach, and had his own problems with Hipple. Although Fowler had no authority over Hipple, he was described by many sources as an adverse influence.

In 1960, the board of education was expanded from five to seven members. Over the next several years, all the members who had known Hipple during his glory years and who had worked with C. B. Vernon were replaced.

Thus, by 1961, Hipple was operating in isolation. He must have been shocked by his suddenly low ratings as a teacher. He probably never had received such bad reviews in his life. His key assistant coaches were unproven in their skills and loyalty. His supervisors disapproved of his teaching methods. The board of education had new members with new ideas. Hipple tended to keep matters to himself. He did not go out of his way to make friends or converts. He didn't play politics or curry favor. He was in trouble, and things were going to get worse.

—

In the early 1960s, with Hipple still at the helm, Marion's basketball teams continued to show flashes of glory. In 1960–1961, a promising team with only three seniors won two of its first three games. Then the entire season was threatened when five junior players, including two starters, seriously breached the training rules. A classmate, who was not out for sports, had a fake ID that was honored by a tavern in Newhall. The boys drove there, and the classmate went into the tavern and bought some beer. The boys drove out on a country road, and some of the players, although not all of them, drank some beer.

Hipple found out about it. He called the team together in a classroom. "It has come to my attention that some of you were drinking beer," he said. He knew who they were. He did not throw them off the team. Instead, he benched all five of them, told them to continue to report for practice and ordered them to climb the rope ten times and skip rope a thousand times each day. He said they wouldn't play again until Marion won a game. He called up some sophomores to bolster the team.

Jim Luense, a starter, had been with the group but had not consumed any beer. He made no attempt to use this fact to reduce his penalty. He was not good at climbing the rope. As he climbed it and slid back down, he held the rope between his thighs instead of his feet, with the result that he got rope burns on his legs. "Before long, I was limping home with raw legs every night," he said. "I was scared to death to tell my parents I was off the team for a time." When he finally confessed, his parents said they hoped he had learned his lesson. "My folks never bad-mouthed Coach Hipple," Luense wrote.

The reserves performed well. The Indians lost the next game, to Independence, by only one point, 44–43. They lost the next one, to Tipton, 73–58. Then Hipple restored the five juniors to the lineup, even though Marion hadn't won. "It was the only time I remember him not keeping his word," Luense said.

Hipple's change of heart was almost certainly the result of a directive from Messerli. In fact, the scope of punishment was mild by Hipple's earlier standards. Fifteen years before, he had unhesitatingly thrown a group of players off the football team for smoking. Left to his own remedies, he might well have done the same thing in this instance. He certainly would not have gone back on his promise to keep them on the bench until Marion won.

Luense went on to a career as a high school guidance counselor. Looking back on the event, he thought the punishment was appropriate. "It's better to have students stay on the team and practice than throw them out into the streets where they could end up with the wrong crowd," he wrote.

With the Indians at full strength, they won eleven of their next twelve conference games (losing to Tipton again). They took over the conference lead by winning a barn burner at Maquoketa, 98–84, in which both teams shot over 50 percent. Maquoketa's tiny basketball court was built on a stage—an architectural approach that harked back to the 1920s. "The ten-second lines were the same as the free throw lines," remembered Steve Miller, "and both teams had shots going up every twenty or thirty seconds." Marion clinched the title in the last conference game of the season, nipping Anamosa, 52–47. Its regular season record was 13–5 and 11–3 in conference play.

The team had fair height, balanced scoring and synchronized play. The starting lineup for most of the season had seniors Steve Miller and Dave Fernow, both well under six feet, at guard, Luense, six feet, and sophomore Bob Hoglund, six feet one, at forward, and junior Ron Hartgrave, six feet three, at center.

In state tournament play, the Indians squeezed by Prairie of Cedar Rapids and crushed Vinton to become sectional champions. In the district opener, they faced Washington of Cedar Rapids, which had overwhelmed Marion by twenty-seven points earlier in the season. Before the game, Hipple gathered his team in a huddle. Suddenly, an uncharacteristic grin spread across his face. "Just go out there and have fun," he told his team.

"That image of him has stuck in my mind ever since," Miller said. The Indians played their best game of the season and were ahead 50–45 late in the game. But Washington came back to win, 62–59. After the game, Washington coach Don Shupe went into the Marion locker room to personally congratulate the Marion players, telling them that they were the better team that day, but that the better team doesn't always win.

The following year, Marion posted a 14–4 record and earned a tie for the WaMaC title. The tie came in a thrilling, late-season victory over Tipton, which had beaten the Indians by fifteen points earlier. Tipton had a prodigious scorer and rebounder, Al Koch, a six-foot-three forward who averaged twenty-eight points a game. As Luense remembered it, he was assigned to guard Koch. The Tipton star made thirty-two points, but it wasn't enough, as Marion won 49–45, with Luense scoring the winning four points on free throws. Marion's defense couldn't stop Koch, but it threw a blanket over the rest of the Tigers and repeatedly intercepted passes intended for Tipton's scoring star. Once again, a gritty, team-oriented defense brought a victory to Marion. Starters on the team included seniors Luense and Gordon Rundquist at guards, senior Ron Hartgrave at center, and juniors John McKean and Bob Hoglund at forwards.

Hipple had now guided Marion to twelve basketball championships in sixteen years, an awesome coaching feat.

In 1962–1963, the Indians floundered through a 7–11 season, finishing in fifth place as Tipton took the crown.

The football teams, hurt by the loss of players to Linn-Mar and by the reduced turnout of eager players, had only one winning season in the first three years of the 1960s. The 1960 team, which had few experienced players, was hobbled by injuries all year. Miller, the quarterback and star, hurt both ankles in the first game and limped through the entire season. The team played some close games but had difficulty scoring and went 2–5–2, finishing in a tie for sixth place. The Indians bounced back the following year, tying for second with a 6–3 record. But in 1962, the Indians finished fifth, going 3–5–1 for the season. For a school with a history of victories, the football record for the first three years of the 1960s was dismal: 11–13–3.

—

The poor football record was not responsible for what came next. In December 1962, Messerli announced that the board of education had approved a reorganization of the athletic department. There would now be a different head coach for each of six sports. Hipple, forty-nine, would no longer coach football and track, jobs he had held for eighteen seasons. He would serve as athletic director, basketball coach, and head of physical education. Ernest Beemblossom, twenty-eight, would take over as head football coach. Jerry

Skilling, thirty-three, would head track. Bill Linstrom would continue to coach wrestling, a program he had established four years earlier. Jan Flickinger, twenty-seven, would handle cross-country. Vince Woodson, twenty-nine, would be responsible for starting a spring and summer baseball program. While other WaMaC schools were strengthening their athletic programs with seasoned coaches, Marion had instituted a youth movement. It appears that among this group, only Hipple and Skilling had head-coaching experience before coming to Marion.

The change probably came as a shock to Hipple and his supporters. It was dramatic enough to rate a three-column headline and an "end-of-an-era" story on the first sports page of the *Cedar Rapids Gazette*. The change was "subject to acceptance by the six coaches named," reported the paper. It seems strange that Messerli did not obtain agreement from all parties before making the announcement. Perhaps Hipple wasn't consulted; perhaps the board thought he would resign. The *Gazette* ran a photo of Hipple, Beemblossom, and Skilling, standing in a row and staring blankly at the camera. No one looks happy. Hipple looks positively ill.

The *Gazette* story also said that the board approved a new "set of training rules for athletes, a program that has been under fire at times in past years."

With the new high school scheduled to open for the 1963–1964 school year, Messerli wanted to modernize the athletic program. By this time, it was rare for an athletic director to be head coach of more than one sport. "One man can no longer do it all," Messerli said. "The new program is designed to include all the desirable facets of the present one and yet spread responsibility among several people."

The upshot was that Hipple's control of the program and its athletes was immeasurably weakened. The school board, in adopting Messerli's plan, had endorsed a program that Hipple doubtlessly didn't like and had dumped it in his lap. The change also reduced Hipple's pay somewhat. In 1962 his compensation was $8,550. The following year, under the reorganization, it fell to $8,477. So he lost $73 on the deal, plus whatever automatic increase he would have received in his teacher's salary.

Some people believed that Hipple might have welcomed the opportunity to stop coaching football. His former assistant, Frank McLeod, thought so. The cold weather late in the season caused a lot of pain in the coach's hip. McLeod remembered how Hipple stood under the shower after practice, turning his left hip into the steaming water and holding it there as his flank turned bright red. McLeod never heard Hipple complain about the pain, but felt that the coach had endured enough cold and rainy days of football.

Larry Perkins, an assistant coach at the time of the change, didn't agree. He thought Hipple wanted to keep coaching football and track. "He would have crawled out there if he had to," Perkins said. "I'm sure he felt he had given for so long and that he had been stabbed in the back."

Hipple wasn't impressed with the athletic director title. It was a job he had held for many years, whether it carried the title or not. He would later say that being athletic director was basically a glorified secretary's job, involving tasks such as scheduling games, preparing reports, filling out forms, and writing plans required by Messerli as part of his move to modernize the department.

—

The *Gazette* story on the change pointed out that Hipple's record was stellar. Through 1962, he had delivered at least one WaMaC championship to Marion in fifteen of the seventeen years he coached—twenty-four titles in all. His basketball teams had won or shared twelve basketball championships in his seventeen years at Marion. He had only three losing seasons in compiling an overall record of 298–98, for a winning percentage of .753. It's true that his current basketball team was stumbling, but over at Cornell College, Paul Maaske, the basketball coach, praised Hipple's ability to teach the game, and said he would gladly take any player Marion would send him, whether he was from a winning team or not.

The man was a basketball genius, but some people were blind to Hipple's accomplishments. At the same time, parents increasingly questioned the validity of his rules. "Parents weren't backing Hipple the way they did earlier," remembered Irwin Renfer. "They were letting their kids do their own thing. The parents weren't necessarily undercutting him, but they weren't backing him with their own kids." Discipline was breaking down all along the line. Lots of mothers didn't want their boys to go out for three sports, Doris Renfer added.

By this time, a small group of people had mounted a campaign to get Hipple fired.

Chapter 33
A Thousand Cuts, 1963–1964

The minutes for the board of education meeting of April 4, 1963, contain the following: "It was moved by [Harold] Klink and seconded by [Lowell] Sebern that the Board of Directors go into a closed, executive session during the interview with Athletic Director Les Hipple. Votes all aye. The athletic policies, programs, procedures and experiences were discussed extensively by the members of the Board and Athletic Director Hipple."

Minutes are not taken at executive sessions. This allows individuals to talk freely about difficult topics without concern about what will be published later. There are no written directives from the board to the coach in Hipple's personnel file, but later notes by Superintendent Messerli indicate that Hipple was being told that if he did not do a good job of implementing Messerli's plan for the athletic department, he would be fired.

Messerli was not at this crucial meeting. He had been away for nearly three months, studying in Europe on a Fulbright Scholarship. He was due back soon, but the board had to decide what to do about Hipple's contract and went ahead without him. It might have been better for Hipple if Messerli had been on hand. Messerli's nature was to seek compromise, and he might have indicated a willingness to work with Hipple and thus take a share of responsibility for making the program work. As it turned out, when Hipple told the board he would do what was required, he was on his own, with his fate in the hands of the board.

Board members were tired of hearing complaints about Hipple, which came from two sources. One was Messerli himself, who disapproved of Hipple's approach to discipline and had come to believe that Hipple was refusing to put his best effort into the new program. Complaints also reached the board from parents who didn't like Hipple's rules and thought he was too tough on the boys. Among them were a group of parents who had joined forces with the goal of getting Hipple fired.

There's no way to tell when this group formed, but it became increasingly visible and vocal during the 1960s. Perhaps its complaints were directed at first to Messerli. With Messerli away on his scholarship for three months, it seems likely that members of the group focused on the board of education, discrediting the coach whenever they could. Many individuals interviewed for this book mentioned the group, describing it as small, but dedicated and intense. (No strong effort was made to discover the members of this group. Most had probably died or were quite old. They were doubtlessly acting out of what they believed to be the best interests of their children. That the group existed and made a great deal of trouble for Hipple is enough for this story.)

It's not as if Hipple—or any coach or teacher—expected to please every parent or to live without controversy. Hipple took it in stride when boys drove by his house screaming obscenities. He just shook his head and cleaned up the mess when they threw eggs on his car. Hipple took meticulous care of his Chevrolet, which made it a target for mischief. One day, four boys threw paint on his car when it was parked outside his house. The parents of one of the boys turned them in when they overheard the boys talking about it. The boys had to come up with $50 to have the paint removed. At least one of them later played under Hipple.

The coach was probably livid, but unable to do anything, after someone threw something that broke the window of his daughter's bedroom, raining shattered glass on the pillow where she had been sleeping seconds earlier. The shouts that preceded the barrage woke her up, and she got out of bed just before the glass broke.

Parental complaints are the stock-in-trade of coaching. Dick Sloan, a lifelong coach, said that basketball parents are the worst, probably because fans and players are so close during games. "In any given year, at least two sets of parents are upset because their child doesn't get enough playing time," said Sloan, who was head basketball coach at Marion for a decade. "So after ten years you have forty people who don't like you."

Hipple had coached at Marion for eighteen years—long enough to generate a small group of people who wanted his head. Unless Hipple had protective cover from Messerli and the board, they would have it one day.

"Thinking back, there was an undercurrent of dissatisfaction that was going on," said Larry Perkins, who came to Marion in 1960. "There was turmoil and it was known that people were after him. There was lots of talk about 'He's not doing a good job; he's behind the times; we've got to get rid of him.'"

It's true that Hipple had a lot of backing in town, Perkins said, "But people started chipping away. A little cut in the back here, a little poke there. It adds up."

The Chinese call it *lingchi*, an ancient form of execution known as "death by a thousand cuts."

—

In addition to complaining about his rules and his methods, Hipple's enemies said he had grown too old and the game had passed him by. He still banned hook shots and forbade freelance play, which had become commonplace. If a boy tried to take the game into his own hands, if he started trying to play basketball like the professionals, Hipple pulled him out of the game. When he saw a boy shooting hook shots during a pre-game warm-up, he ordered him to the locker room and didn't let him play.

Most damning was his insistence on the underhand free throw. It was sometimes called "the granny shot," but not around Hipple. Players were taught to dip the ball between their bent knees, then bring the arms up, not stiff, but relaxed, letting the ball slide off the fingers with only a slight wrist motion and as little spin as possible. The dead ball was more likely than a spinning one to get a favorable bounce off the rim or backboard.

Hipple stuck with the underhand free throw long after it had gone out of style. It was probably a source of mockery by players on other teams. The last practitioner of the form in the National Basketball Association was Rick Barry, a Hall of Fame player who retired in 1980. For many years, Barry held the NBA record for highest career free-throw percentage, .900. Barry coached a professional team in Cedar Rapids after retiring. He explained to Tony Pantini of Marion why he used the underhand method. In essence, he said, the arm motion was simpler, involving principally the shoulders, while a one-handed shot required the coordination of multiple movements from the shoulder, elbow, wrist, and fingers—movements that can easily be compromised by nervousness or exhaustion during a game. Time and again Hipple's teams won games because of their accuracy from the foul line.

Almost invariably, however, Hipple's players switched to the one-handed shot after graduating. It seemed more comfortable and natural because the shooting motion was the same as for field goals.

Eventually, Hipple yielded to pressure from Messerli to allow his players the choice of shooting either the underhanded way or overhanded. "But they won't make as many," Hipple groused, according to Messerli.

—

In its executive session that day, the board of education wanted Hipple's commitment to implement Messerli's athletic program. It also wanted an end to the clashes that had gone on for years between Messerli and Hipple. And it wanted the parental complaints to stop. Hipple could work on the first two, but there was nothing he could do to stop the campaign against him.

When the executive session met, Hipple had been in his new role as athletic director about three months, hardly time enough to overhaul the program. But according to notes by Messerli in Hipple's file, his resistance to making changes had been going on longer than that. Messerli typed up the notes in early 1965, nearly two years after the events now being discussed. The notes appear to be written hurriedly to build a case should Hipple appeal his being fired or start a lawsuit. It is unlikely that Hipple ever saw these documents. They cover problems and dealings with Hipple dating back to the fall of 1962. They are roughly typed with some spelling corrections and hand-written notations. There are also some related documents intended as attachments to the memo in progress. This material will be referred to in the next chapter as "Messerli's background notes." There is little in the file that presents Hipple's side of the controversy.

According to the notes, in the fall of 1962, with the move to the new high school a year away, Messerli informed the coaching staff that the board of education wanted to expand the athletic program, and it wanted the rules to be modified. The board expressed the view that it opposed the requirement that boys go out for three sports and it wanted parents to have a greater say in deciding when their sons should be able to drive cars. Messerli instructed the coaching staff to draw up an athletic program based on the board's directive. When, after a period of time, no proposal was submitted to him, Messerli wrote the program himself and presented it to the board, which gave its approval. This led to the announcement in December 1962 that the athletic department would be restructured.

In addition to the restructured department, Messerli's program called for the institution of spring baseball, which was to occur in 1964 on a playing field at the new high school. Another key section described the duties of the athletic director. He was to handle all the managerial, administrative, and scheduling duties required to run a district-wide sports program encompassing five major sports (football, basketball, wrestling, track, baseball), one minor sport (cross-country), and involving all grades from junior high on up, with separate squads and schedules for freshmen and sophomores (freshmen were no longer to play on sophomore teams). There is a suggestion in the program that two minor sports, golf and tennis, should be added.

On top of that, Hipple, as director of boys' physical education, was assigned to "direct and develop" a sweeping new physical education program for elementary, junior high, and senior high students "that will serve as a guide to the people working in this area." Among its components was to be a health program ("care of the body, sex education, etc.") to be developed with the school nurse. On top of that, he was to "work toward an intramural program that will include all students."

It was a massive workload for a single person who was also head basketball coach. Some educators, hearing about this workload, suggested it was a setup—designed purposely so Hipple would fail. Hipple tended to try to do everything himself; he was not much of a delegator, but there was no one to whom he could delegate. All his coaches had teaching duties. There is no indication that he had even a part-time assistant in either of his roles as AD or director of physical education. According to Messerli's notes, Hipple told him the program couldn't be done with the current staff, which Messerli took as Hipple's negativism, a signal that he wasn't going to try. Perhaps it could have been done, in time, with close cooperation between an AD and a superintendent who trusted and liked one another and shared common views. The program would have to be built in increments, with a clear understanding between both parties about goals and techniques. They would have to help each other through it. In other words, given the relationship between the two men, it was impossible.

The new rules in Messerli's program must have made Hipple blanch. They said "it is desirable and should be encouraged" that a boy should go out for three sports, but not doing so was insufficient grounds for prohibiting him from playing on a team. Instead of being banned outright, "smoking, drinking, strong language, and steady dating that may lead to late hours, low moral standard, etc., are undesirable attitudes and should or may lead to dismissal … or other disciplinary action as the coach may see fit." Driving cars "just for fun" was forbidden; driving to school "should be" forbidden; driving for errands as instructed by parents was not forbidden. The new rules were so nebulous that Hipple would have been justified in claiming that some of his old rules were reasonable interpretations of the new ones.

But when Hipple walked out of that executive session in April 1963, three days after his fiftieth birthday, the board had his pledge to implement a program he considered impossible to pull off. Other coaches, seeing the inevitability of failure, would have found work elsewhere. But Hipple did not believe in quitting. He believed in facing into trouble and doing his best. Quitting was a sign of weakness. Quitters never win and winners never quit. Hipple was trapped in the vise of his own principles.

—

With the new Marion High School set to open in the fall of 1963, a young former Marine and recent Iowa State University graduate named Larry Twachtmann was hired to teach industrial arts and coach the ninth-grade teams. As usual, Hipple had no role in the hiring process, but he was one of the first persons Twatchtmann heard from when he moved to town in July. "[My wife and I] had been in town only two days when Les Hipple called me," Twachtmann wrote. "After some discussion on the phone he invited me to attend a three-day football workshop with him at Clear Lake." Twachtmann had other ideas about how to spend those three days, but he could hardly say no. "Little did I know what I was in for."

From the minute the twenty-six-year-old Twachtmann met the fifty-year-old athletic director, it was all business. "On our auto ride to Clear Lake I learned the football offense in three hours (I took notes). At Clear Lake I seldom left the motel complex, much less got to the pool or a bar. We arose talking football and coaching, we ate football and coaching, we studied football and coaching philosophy, and went to sleep late talking coaching and football. I was rubbing elbows with a legend and didn't know it. Those three days are permanently embedded in my soul. He gave me an introduction to teaching, coaching, enthusiasm, dedication, discipline, and focus. I was lucky. It was probably the most intense three days I've ever spent in my life," wrote the man who had served in the Marines.

With his job hanging in the balance, and with building a freshman sports program on his long list of assignments, Hipple was, as usual, giving it everything he had. That he took charge of Twachtmann's indoctrination, rather than assigning it to the head football coach, was probably due to his natural inclination to take matters into is own hands, but it may also have indicated lack of confidence in his football coach.

That fall, under Beemblossom, the varsity football team had a miserable year, going 2–6–1 overall and finishing sixth in the WaMaC. The Indians were held scoreless in six of their nine games and managed only thirty-four points all season.

In basketball, Marion had only three returning lettermen from a team that had finished fifth the season before. Lacking both experience and height, the Indians relied a great deal on junior players as they struggled to a seventh place finish in the WaMaC. The Indians' record of 5–13 was the worst since 1945–1946, when Hipple's first Marion team had an identical record.

George Duvall, who went on to lead many successful teams at Ames High School and was elected to the Hall of Fame, coached basketball at Independence at the time. His team tied for the WaMaC championship with Monticello in 1964. Marion was not considered a power, he said. "Monticello was tough. Tipton and Maquoketa were more feared than Marion. I think Hipple was tired."

"He was probably tired of the hassle," wrote Lynn Brown. By this time it seems certain that rumors were circulating about Hipple's precarious position. But if Hipple was getting any official written assessment of his progress as athletic director, copies never reached his personnel file. Whatever feedback he was getting was oral.

That spring, Marion fielded its first baseball team to compete in the WaMaC Conference. Athletic Director Hipple had come through on at least two of the tasks assigned him in Messerli's policy: an energized and focused freshman sports program under Twachtmann and a varsity baseball team.

But he was found deeply wanting on other matters, according to Messerli's background notes. In them, Messerli wrote that during 1963–1964—the first year after the athletic program was restructured and the first year in the new high school—"Mr. Hipple failed to follow the program and assignments" and was called before the board several times. It also describes a critical meeting in which Messerli, with board member Harold Klink present, spelled out his and the board's position. Hipple's file includes a script of what Messerli said—or intended to say—at the meeting. The meeting took place early in 1964 as the board considered renewing Hipple's contract for the next year. It's not possible to determine whether the script was written before or after the meeting, and some of its pages are missing.

In the script, Messerli said he told Hipple, "The need for these particular conferences at this time of the year every year is always due to pressure brought upon me and the board of education by parents and citizens to relieve you of your coaching duties or dismiss you altogether. I have always recommended your reappointment with the promise that I would talk with you about the problems and see if I could get the desired changes."

The areas where Hipple fell short, Messerli said in the script, involved "such things a[s] better relations with parents, a more relaxed relationship with students and faculty members, a less unbending attitude in dealing with specific problems, and [failure] to develop an imagination that will meet the various situations we come on due to changes in the school, the people, and the community."

Elsewhere in the background notes, Messerli wrote that at a meeting such as this Hipple was asked to resign, but refused to do so. Finally, the background notes say, "After a promise that he would do the following four things, [Hipple] was granted a contract for the 1964–1965 school year. 1) Organize and develop a physical education program that would include more than just conditioning; 2) Organize and develop an extracurricular [athletic] program coming up with agreements from the coaching staff on such things as training rules, awarding of letters, participating in two sports at the same time, etc.; 3) Develop a public relations program with the parents so that they would feel free to talk with him, etc.; 4) Develop a more positive relationship with all boys."

There is no indication how Hipple responded to these charges and assignments. On his behalf, it should be pointed out that parents were going to Messerli and the school board because they were in effect being invited to do so instead of being sent to Hipple to work out the problems first. Hipple would later say things such as, "They aren't coming to see me." He might have pointed out that the complaints, for the most part, were coming from a small group of enemies who were determined to get him fired and that they were unlikely to stop until he got support from the superintendent and the board. He might have said that he was only one person, that he had been assigned an overwhelming number of tasks in his new positions, and he could use more help. He could have argued that he was making progress, citing the accomplishments of his first year. He might have told them to take the job and shove it, but he didn't use that kind of language, and he didn't quit.

It's impossible to know what was said by any of the parties at this crucial meeting, since the only record is a script that Messerli typed before or after the meeting—almost certainly to establish, in the event of a lawsuit, that Hipple had been properly instructed about his shortcomings and what was expected from him.

It may have been true, as Messerli states, that Hipple was slow to change the rules, particularly through some sort of democratic discussion with his staff of young coaches. He may have been sticking with his old rules as long as he could, even though his head coaches were doubtlessly enforcing them inconsistently. It was even more likely that he hadn't changed in his behavior as a coach.

Messerli and the board believed that Hipple was unable or unwilling to change his behavior. This was a key point made by an individual who was a close observer of the events at the time. He spoke under the condition of anonymity, which was granted because of the unique perspective he offered. His point was this: Hipple could have kept his job if he had been willing to change. People are able to change, and Hipple simply refused to do it. His insistence on the underhand free throw was not an example of him being out of touch with the game, but another proof of his obstinacy. Hipple, this source went on, misjudged the board of directors. He thought he could defy them and get away with it, and in this he was completely wrong, the source said.

Hipple may have refused to make certain changes as a matter of principle. More than one contemporary saw it that way. They said that his sense of integrity would not allow him to change his behavior. Hipple repeatedly insisted that he wasn't doing anything wrong.

However, there were indications that Hipple was making changes—or trying to. He paid several visits to the home of board member Arthur Bezdek to better understand what the board wanted from him. He administered comparatively light punishments when he discovered, in 1960, that some of his basketball players had been drinking. He permitted overhand free throws. Bill Huntoon, who had returned to Marion as an assistant wrestling coach, remembered at least one meeting of all coaches in which Hipple established ground rules. Vince Woodson, the baseball coach, had similar recollections. Asked whether the athletic program was in disarray at this time, Bill Linstrom replied, "Not from the point of view of the coaches."

It's also clear that Hipple relaxed the rules about driving a car and going steady. Steve Rucker, who graduated in 1966, remembered that the coach no longer required players to ask his permission before using the family car to run an errand; there was still a ban on aimless riding around in groups, however.

Several players confirmed that Hipple dropped the rule against going steady. Rucker remembered that at some point Hipple took him aside for a quiet talk about his spending too much time with his steady girlfriend. "He actually was pleased with my choice of girlfriend, but told me he thought it might be impacting my dedication to the game," Rucker wrote. "Actually he was right and I adjusted my behavior. It worked out anyway, because the girl ultimately dumped me for an upperclassman with a sports car." In an earlier time, Rucker's behavior would have drawn penalty laps and, if he persisted in it, benching.

—

By the spring of 1964 rumors about Hipple's troubles "were rampant" all over the school, wrote Genny Yarne, an elementary school teacher. During this time, Shirley and Tony Pantini, who lived in New Jersey and were in town to visit Shirley's family, stopped by to see the new high school. When they visited Hipple, he told them that a group of parents were campaigning to get him fired. While Hipple knew Shirley as a former student and fellow teacher, he had never met Tony. It was rare for him to speak so openly about his problems to anyone, and even more unusual to do so with a stranger present. The loneliness and the pressure must have been getting to him.

There is a clue to the degree to which it was known around the school that Hipple was under fire. It came in the form of praise from one of the groups with which he supposedly had poor relationships, and it appeared in the 1964 high school yearbook, *The Quill.* The student editors dedicated the yearbook to Hipple, devoting a page to his photograph and a tribute that said:

> Athletics at Marion High School has long been recognized as a force contributing to the development of true sportsmanship, a force which has diffused itself through the school, adding a measure of health, vitality, and enthusiasm to student life ... Head Coach Lester C. Hipple is a fitting leader of an outstanding athletic department. This distinguished mentor of the gridiron and the basketball court has in his eighteen years lifted the name of Marion to the top not only in conference standings but in public acclaim. To this scholarly strategist who has faithfully and tirelessly served our school, we humbly dedicate the 1964 Quill.

Thus the student editors uniquely honored the man who had no friends in the administration or the school board, and who was supposedly at odds with parents. It was not common practice to dedicate the yearbook to anyone, let alone a teacher. There were only three dedications in the previous thirteen years: 1962, foreign exchange students; 1955, parents as a group; and 1952, Anna Jean Marchant, a student who had died of polio in 1950.

Chapter 34
Hipple Is Fired, 1964–1965

That summer, rumors about Hipple's future swirled around town. Businessmen who gathered for coffee at Leon and Jerry's debated the matter. Many were disturbed about what was happening to Hipple, but felt there was nothing they could do.

One man decided he would do something. When Doug Hutchins was a senior on Hipple's first Marion football team in 1945, the coach sent him to the locker room for talking too much. Since then, Hutchins' admiration for Hipple had grown. When Hutchins came back to Marion in 1952, he volunteered to help the sports program. He piled football uniforms and equipment into his pickup truck when Marion played out of town and drove them to the competitors' schools so players could suit up in the locker room. He ran the line markers at home football games and the scoreboard at home basketball games. In summers, he umpired baseball games.

Now, he decided, he would run for the school board and try to help Les Hipple in another way. If he was elected, he thought, he could support Hipple and perhaps convert other members to his side. To do it, he would have to beat one of two incumbents, Harold Klink, who had served since 1960, or Norman Stoockey, a Marion dentist. Hutchins, who worked for the Rural Electric Cooperative and had managed community baseball and basketball programs, was a "late entry," reported the *Sentinel.* In what the paper called a "larger than usual" turnout, Hutchins garnered 244 votes, forty-six more than Stoockey and just ten fewer than Klink. Some voters knew where Hutchins stood on Hipple, and this surely helped him win the seat.

But when he attended his first board meeting, Hutchins realized he was too late. The board members had made up their minds to release Hipple. A few members, Hutchins said, actively wanted him gone, while the others were tired of the conflict between the athletic director and the superintendent and wanted to get it over with. These directors saw the situation as a management problem that could be resolved by removing the coach. Hutchins agreed that a problem existed, but "I thought the solution should be applied to the superintendent."

That idea went nowhere. On a trip to Denver to survey schools using the open classroom design, Hutchins and another director began discussing Hipple during dinner. Their argument became so loud and angry that the two men had to be calmed down by their colleagues. After that, the other board members didn't talk about Hipple when Hutchins was around.

I interviewed Doug Hutchins three times in 2003 and 2004, once on the telephone and twice in his home. In one of the personal interviews, I asked him to identify the main reason for board dissatisfaction with Hipple, offering him three choices: 1) Failure to perform his duties; 2) Conflicts with Messerli; 3) Complaints by parents. He left no doubt that conflict with the superintendent was by far the dominant reason. He could not remember any discussion of operating shortcomings by Hipple, and parental complaints played a role only insofar as they provided fuel for those who wanted Hipple removed.

Hutchins was adamant that there was no flood of complaints from parents. "There was not an overwhelming number of parents complaining. There was not a moderate number of parents complaining. There were only a few parents complaining. But these parents were considered influential; they were people who had the ear of Messerli and the board."

When research for this book began, only two other school officials with inside knowledge of these events were still alive. Former board member Harold Klink said that his memory had been impaired by a bad fall. "Over my lifetime, I have put aside unhappy events, unpleasant confrontations, if you will, and this was certainly an unhappy event." He said that as far as he could recall parental complaints had played no role in the matter and that the board's action came about because Hipple was unwilling to make changes. "It had a good deal to do with the strictness of his rules," Klink said.

The third insider, Richard Sorensen, Marion High School principal at the time, said he had no memory whatsoever of those events, although he did recall that difficulties between Messerli and Hipple had been "festering" even before he arrived in 1961.

—

Hutchins discovered that Hipple's fate had been decided before the 1964–1965 school year began. This was confirmed by another event: As soon as school opened, Marion began to recruit a new basketball coach. Jim Morrow, who eventually replaced Hipple, was approached about the job in September of that year. The man who contacted him was Ernest Beemblossom, the head football coach. Instead of assigning the recruiting task to Richard Sorensen, who was the principal and thus Hipple's superior, Messerli or the board, or both, gave the job to one of Hipple's chief lieutenants, who had little choice but to play an active role in the demise of his own boss.

Since Morrow did not accept the position for many months, it's almost certain that Beemblossom approached other potential replacements as the year wore on. And that means that rumors were spreading throughout the high school coaching community of eastern Iowa. Although Hipple tended not to fraternize with other coaches, the rumors must have reached his ears—and he must have known that his own football coach was doing the recruiting. He spent the whole school year with a sword hanging over his head.

"He knew it was coming," said Larry Perkins, his assistant basketball coach that year.

—

Marion's 1964 football team under Beemblossom improved its ability to score but still won only two games, finishing 2–6–1 and in sixth place for the second year in a row.

Before the basketball season began, Hipple attended a clinic for coaches at Coe College organized by Don King, Coe's basketball coach. Despite his problems, Hipple was as focused as ever, taking his usual meticulous notes. He got an A for the course and was praised by King for his extraordinary ability to absorb and understand the material.

So began Hipple's bitterest season. He was the center of constant rumors, the easy target of a small group of parents out to discredit him, mistrusted and undermined by his superiors, and viewed with pity, bewilderment, or distrust by some assistant coaches and players. How could he coach under those circumstances? That he would even try raises the question whether he was thinking clearly, whether he was somehow out of touch with what was happening. But his contemporaries said he wasn't in denial. Instead, they said, he blocked out the negatives as best he could and addressed the job at hand. When Doug Hutchins was asked what Hipple's strategy was during this period, he responded that Hipple's only strategy was to do his best and hope that things worked out.

Hipple's last team had skilled, experienced players who had seen a lot of action on a weak team the year before. There were six returning lettermen, led by Ken Backsen, six feet three, a strong rebounder and prodigious scorer who was installed at center. Backsen, who had been quarterback on the football team, was smart, wiry, and deceptively quick. He could drive equally well to his left or right and had an almost flawless jump shot. The others in the starting lineup were all seniors: Tim Ledvina and Everett Weaver, both six feet, at forward, and John Fowler, five feet nine, and Larry Stick, five feet ten, at guard. Hipple also had a strong bench, with senior Porter Reed and juniors Steve Rucker, Bill Long, Bill Null, and Ivan Rundall.

It was a typical Hipple team, athletic and well-drilled, but without a really big center. The team was capable of putting up a lot of points, but was often lax on defense. This was rare for Marion, but it takes a lot of discipline to play defense, and this team was operating under a serious burden: Their coach was an outcast.

"No one thought he would be fired during the season," wrote Steve Rucker, the junior sixth man, "but the turmoil had a significant impact on team discipline and cohesion." Some of the players did their best to ignore the rumors and play hard. Others were inconsistent; surely they had trouble following orders from a man their parents wanted fired.

During this period, Hipple increased his emphasis on weight training. He was well ahead of his time in this. He first made strength equipment available to his players in 1956, but now, as Steve Rucker remembered it, he fashioned homemade weights from coffee cans filled with concrete that he attached to long and short bars. The weights were light and were used to build endurance rather than muscle mass. "Pretty advanced for the time," Rucker wrote. Hipple also experimented with a new offense and a new approach to a pressing defense. "The charge that the game had moved beyond Coach Hipple was nonsense," Rucker insisted.

On January 6, 1965, with the team holding a 3–1 conference record, Messerli put Hipple on notice. He wrote in his background notes, "Informed Mr. Hipple that I was still dissatisfied with his manner of handling young men. Told him I believed the drill sergeant approach was all he knew and perhaps he couldn't make changes … Referred to such things as degrading talk, blisters from pull-ups, rope burning from rope climbing … Told him I would report my opinion to the board of education [the next day]."

The notes continue, for January 7: "Made my report to the board of education. I did not recommend Mr. Hipple be dismissed but informed the board that he could not change in the areas discussed and that it would continue as is if he remained as basketball coach. Also that I might be wrong in my appraisal and that they should decide for themselves and take such action as they feel necessary."

The following night, Marion lost a key home game to Maquoketa, 69–62. Messerli's entry for that day reads, "Mr. Sorenson arranged for cookies and pop for the team after the game. Mr. Sorenson did all the arranging."

The Indians split the following two games, moving their conference record to 4–3, not great, but good enough to remain in contention if they put together a string of victories. The next game would be at Tipton, which Marion had barely beaten at home earlier in the season.

The afternoon of the Tipton game, as usual, the players loaded their uniforms on the school bus and went home for an early supper. After eating, Tim Ledvina and Ken Backsen, neighbors and friends, began to walk back to school to get on the bus. They lived out east of town. It was more than a mile. "I don't remember us being in a hurry," said Backsen. "We often screwed around on the way to school."

"Ken and I were walking and talking, and I thought we were on a good pace," Ledvina said. "It was snowing hard, so maybe that slowed us down."

As the two boys approached the school, the bus started to move. When the boys reached the driveway, the bus pulled even with the sidewalk. The boys smiled and waved, waiting for the bus to stop. But it didn't stop. Instead, the door popped opened to reveal Hipple looking down on them. "You guys are late," he said. "You need to find another way to get to the game." The door closed and the bus rolled out into the street and headed through the falling snow toward Tipton.

When they recovered from their shock, the boys hurried home. Ledvina's mother drove them to the game. Hipple allowed them to dress, but didn't let them into the game until the second half. Marion lost, 90–57.

Messerli was stunned when he heard the news. He wrote in his notes, "This action is against school procedure and decidedly improper from any standard of decency or conduct. The two most modest terms that might describe this action [are] stupid and childish … Discussed this matter with Mr. Hipple. I tried as emphatically as I could to impress Mr. Hipple that this could not go on and that I could not defend him in such actions."

In his own defense, Hipple might have told Messerli that promptness in all things is a bedrock requirement of athletics, and that once the door shuts and the motor starts, a player is either on the bus or off it.

Ledvina supports Hipple. "Can you understand the courage Hipple had to do that to two starters, and one of them his leading scorer? How many coaches would have the guts to do that? He had enough guts to teach us a life lesson. I've always been grateful for it; I'm never late for anything." When Ledvina tells the story to others, they always blame the coach for losing the game. "But you know who I blame? Us. We were late. Rules are rules."

It's impossible to know what motivated Hipple to act this way despite all the warnings he had received. Was he being principled, defiant, or foolhardy? Whatever his motive, it was not the act of a man who was afraid of being fired.

Two days after the Tipton game, Hipple gathered his team at practice to talk to them. Ledvina and Backsen were talking to each other while Hipple was speaking. "You know how Hipple hated to have anyone talk when he was trying to teach something," Ledvina recalled. "He said, 'Ledvina, shut up,' so I stopped talking. Then Backsen said something else to me and I replied and Hipple said, 'Ledvina, I told you to shut up. Come up here.' And he got some tape from the equipment manager and put it on my mouth. 'Now maybe you'll be quiet,' he said. Some of the guys were laughing a little, but Hipple was serious. I was surprised he singled me out and didn't put tape on Backsen's mouth, too."

When practice resumed, Hipple had the squad run "killers"—they had to sprint up the floor to a point, then turn quickly and run back. "I kept pointing to the tape on my mouth, but Hipple wouldn't let me take it off," Ledvina said. "You can imagine how tough that was."

When Ledvina got home that night, his parents were waiting for him.

"What happened at practice today?" they asked him.

"Oh, I got into a little trouble and he singled me out," Ledvina replied. Then he told them the story.

When he finished, his father said, "Well, that'll teach you, won't it? Did you learn anything from that?" Ledvina's dad was strictly old school.

A few years later, Ledvina learned the whole truth. Before he got home that night, someone had called his parents, told them what happened, and urged them to complain to the board of education. Clearly a teammate had reached his own home first and told his parents about the incident. Then the anti-Hipple network sprang into action and the phone calls started. After hearing his son's version, Ledvina's father called the tattletale back and said that his family would not complain to the board and that it wanted no part of any movement to oust Hipple.

Messerli was aghast. "I GIVE UP," he typed. "Either Mr. Hipple does not understand what we are saying … or he is deliberately defying us. Perhaps Mr. Hipple needs psychiatric help."

The act of placing tape on a boy's mouth was not typical of Hipple. He did not do physical things to players. Ledvina was five inches taller than the coach; the boy must have had to lean over to accept the tape. That Hipple did it this time was perhaps a measure of the pressure he was under. "Yes, it was unusual," Ledvina said, "but he wasn't wrong and I don't resent it. I deserved it."

The day after the taping incident, Ledvina was in the starting lineup against Monticello and made eight points as Marion lost, 69–59. Backsen, then reigning as top scorer in the Cedar Rapids metropolitan area, made twenty-two points. In the following game, a non-conference contest against Prairie of Cedar Rapids, Hipple started junior Bill Long in Ledvina's place. He did not explain his move to Ledvina. The boy sat on the bench in confusion and anger. "I burned and burned," Ledvina said. At some point, Ledvina got up from the bench and walked away from the game. When Hipple called Ledvina's name to send him in, he wasn't there. Marion won, 80–61, as Long scored sixteen points, Backsen made fourteen, and guard Ivan Rundall made twenty-two. The next day, Hipple told Ledvina he was off the team.

The day after that, the board of education personnel committee met to discuss Hipple's future. The committee directed Richard Sorensen to see Hipple and suggest he resign. Sorensen did so the next day, January 29, and Hipple refused, saying that those who were complaining did not come to see him. That night, Marion beat Vinton, 78–65, climbing to 5–5 in the conference as Everett Weaver scored eighteen points and played defense so brilliantly that, wrote Larry Tanner in the *Gazette*, he "reminded longtime Marion fans of a decade ago when small players made the Indians an eastern Iowa cage power."

The following day, the board of education personnel committee, Harold Klink and Arthur Bezdek, met with Hipple. They came away with the sense that Hipple didn't understand some of the things they were telling him.

The statement that Hipple "didn't understand some of the things they were telling him," is puzzling. Perhaps it was a bit of gamesmanship by Hipple, not unlike his mysterious behavior twenty years earlier when Superintendent Vernon and the Rev. Gable recruited him for Marion. Hipple was far too intelligent and cool-headed not to understand what was being said. His basic stance throughout the ordeal was that he had done nothing wrong. Acting as if he didn't understand may have been a way of saying that the board members had not convinced him that his actions were improper. Many former Hipple players, for example, would find it difficult to understand what Messerli meant when he said that Hipple used "degrading talk." Nor would they understand serious objections to blisters or rope burns, which were the inconsequential byproducts of being in shape.

Two days later, on February 2, Hipple contacted a local attorney, Morris Allen, who in turn scheduled a meeting with Messerli and Gordon Harstad, president of the school board. The specter of legal action almost certainly prompted Messerli to begin typing up his notes. However, the meeting was never held because Hipple decided not to involve the lawyer. Allen said through his associate, John Vernon, that he neither started a file on the matter nor sent Hipple a bill.

That Thursday, February 4, when board members convened for their regular monthly meeting, they were greeted by an audience of at least twenty-five citizens who were there to support Hipple. Leader of the group was Bill Rucker, father of two Hipple athletes: Mike, who graduated in 1959, and Steve, a junior. When Rucker asked the board what it was planning to do about Hipple's contract, board president Harstad urged the group to meet with the board in a closed, executive session "so that the individual to be discussed would be protected from unnecessary publicity." But Rucker replied that he had Hipple's permission to bring the matter to public attention and that Hipple wanted the press to hear what was said.

Rucker identified himself as president of the Marion Alumni Association and submitted a series of questions. Had the board reached a decision on Hipple's contract, and if, not, when would it do so? Had the board received formal charges against Hipple? If so, had Hipple been given the opportunity to respond? Finally, had Hipple been asked to resign?

Harold Klink, chair of the personnel committee, did not directly answer that last question. Instead, he said his committee had not yet made a full report to the board on the Hipple matter. He added that asking for a teacher's resignation is a standard procedure that allows the teacher to leave the school without negative material being included in his or her personnel file.

With that, the board went into executive session to talk the situation over. When the members emerged, Klink told the gathering that yes, Sorensen had asked for Hipple's resignation, but "as far as we know, [Hipple] has not given any indication what he plans to do," according to Larry Tanner's story in the *Gazette*. "Rucker countered that Hipple said he would not resign," Tanner wrote. "Klink said he had no information of this nature."

Harstad refused to answer the questions from Rucker about formal complaints against Hipple, but said that that Hipple as athletic director had failed to develop the policies and programs required by a school district of Marion's size. Parental complaints, he said, were not a factor in the board's deliberations.

That's not what the alumni group believed. "It is our opinion that the school board is receiving outside pressure from a person or persons in the school system," Rucker's statement said. "How does the school board expect to render a fair and honest decision when they are receiving over a period of years information from individuals who are of the minority rather than a majority?" Finally, the statement said, the alumni association would request an inquiry by the Iowa State Education Association and, if Hipple was not offered a contract, would appeal the matter through official channels to the county superintendent of schools.

Harstad said that the board always tried to protect the school system, students, and teachers, and that this gathering had not allowed it to protect Hipple from public stigma. The matter had yet to be decided, he said.

At least one member of the audience disagreed with the alumni group. He was William Reed, the former World War II pilot and war hero who was known as "Dick" at the time. (He was the nephew of Bill Reed, the Flying Tiger who died in China.) Reed defended the board, saying he had faith in its ability to handle the matter and that the pro-Hipple group was doing serious damage to Hipple's ability to get a job in the future. Reed's statement precisely echoed the board's point of view. Reed was the father of Porter Reed, a basketball teammate of Bill Rucker's son, Steve. Thus, two fathers of current players were in opposite corners on the Hipple matter.

Contrary to what Reed said, the appearance of the pro-Hipple group and its threat to ask for a formal appeal actually helped Hipple. Until this point, the board was on course to dismiss him from the school system. But after this board meeting, Messerli wrote in his notes, "Supt. Messerli recommended that an alternate position be offered Mr. Hipple … Majority of board agreed to follow this plan." Messerli, seeking compromise, would keep Hipple at Marion.

The board adopted a plan to allow Hipple to request reassignment to another position in the school system. The plan did not specify a position, but the board had only one job in mind—that of math teacher. The schedule gave Hipple until March 1 to make his request for reassignment, after which the "contract for the new position should be issued whether he requests it or not." Hipple would then have until March 8 to sign the contract. If he didn't sign it by then, a month-long termination process would begin.

The next night was Friday. Marion traveled to Maquoketa to play the conference-leading Cardinals. Marion fell behind early, staged a furious third-quarter rally but finally lost, 61–56. Hipple received no help from the referees. The Cardinals got forty-one free throws and made twenty-nine; Marion got five and made two.

The next day, board members Klink and Hutchins met with Hipple to tell him he could request reassignment to another position in the system. Hutchins was the only pro-Hipple member of the board. His participation may have been an attempt to improve communications. There is no record of what the two men told Hipple, and subsequent events raise the question of whether they made it clear that in requesting reassignment he had only one choice.

Hipple seized the opportunity to ask the board to consider a variety of alternatives. In an undated handwritten letter on lined paper, he wrote:

> To whom it may concern:
>
> Although I do not fully realize what the conditions are or were to prompt the actions the Board of Education is considering at this time, I am very much interested in all youth and especially those of our school and community. It is with this in mind that I present some plans as follows:
>
> 1) Continue in the school system in my present position.
> 2) Continue in the school system at my present position without athletic director.
> 3) Be transferred to the Math department and coach basketball.
> 4) Be transferred to the Math department and no coaching.
>
> I sincerely desire that each plan will be properly considered.

A period of temporary quiet followed. The board of education met in an undisturbed special session on February 8 to ratify a new three-year contract for Messerli (starting at $14,000 with subsequent annual increases of $800 and $700) and one-year contracts for principals Sorenson and Fowler. Discussions on Hipple's contract were put forward to the next regular meeting, March 4, pending the resolution of his request for reassignment.

Although Hipple undoubtedly had kept his wife up to date, it wasn't until the story broke in the press that his sisters and brother learned he was under fire. He probably didn't talk about it much to them. Said his sister Shirley, "I used to send my kids off to school and then call Wilma to find out what was happening." Hipple's daughter was living in Colorado and was out of the loop.

Meanwhile, Hipple received support from a variety of sources. Mike Rucker drove to Des Moines to see if he could involve the state education association. Ray Fuller and doubtlessly others asked Hipple what they could do on his behalf. Hipple thanked them but gave them no instructions. Members of the news media offered off-the-record support. Tait Cummins, the voice of sports at WMT radio and television, was among those who called Hipple and urged him not to quit.

Frances Rucker, Bill's wife and mother of Mike and Steve, went to Messerli to plead Hipple's case. She recounted the conversation: "He said, 'Well, he's outlived his usefulness.' I said, 'You are talking about a man, not a horse.' I told John Messerli that Hipple will be remembered and honored. It was the only time I ever protested anything."

With board action on hold for several weeks, Hipple tried to concentrate on basketball. Surely he hoped to lead his team to a strong finish. It didn't happen. The Indians threw a scare into Jefferson of Cedar Rapids, but faded to lose by nine points. They lost to Anamosa on two free throws in the final second. They fell to Independence in overtime. They beat Manchester.

Then, on February 22, in the opening game of the sectional tournament, they mounted a second-half rally against Jefferson that gave them a one-point lead with five minutes left, only to be nipped in the final seconds and lose, 58–57. The season was over. Marion finished 7–11 overall, losing five of its last six games, and went 6–8 in the WaMaC for a sixth-place tie. The Indians had good players but fell far short of their potential as a team. Ken Backsen was named to the all-metropolitan area first team; he was the second-leading scorer in the area with an average of 18.1 points per game.

—

Meanwhile, Hipple's supporters were restless. The *Marion Sentinel*, which had published nothing on the controversy, ran an editorial under the headline "Never Say Die," praising the basketball team and Coach Hipple, but remained silent on the matter of his future.

The next day, February 26, several Hipple supporters attended a special meeting of the board of education to ask what was being done about the coach's contract. One of the supporters was Joe Green, who warned the board, "The people are being aroused." He argued that if Hipple was not retained as athletic director he should be kept on as basketball coach.

Messerli, according to the *Gazette*, responded by saying the board did not want to divide the community, to which Green and others responded that it was too late; the community was divided. The board said the coach's contract would probably come up for discussion at the next regular meeting, the following Thursday. After discussion of other matters, just before the meeting ended, the board went into an executive session. When it came out, a motion was passed to offer Hipple a job teaching math. The board said it had accepted the last of the alternatives Hipple listed in his letter. This it was decided there would be no sports in Hipple's future at Marion. The *Gazette* reporter must have left the building, for there was nothing in the paper to indicate Hipple was through as a coach.

When Hipple was offered the math contract, he refused to sign it. This meant he also refused to relinquish the athletic positions. As the March 4 meeting approached, the matter was still unresolved. On the day of the board meeting, the *Sentinel* ran another editorial, this time an angry one, castigating the board for not coming forth with the facts concerning "internal personnel problems" and for allowing the situation to become so controversial.

That afternoon, knowing it would face a large, hostile crowd of Hipple supporters, the board made a last-ditch effort to defuse the situation. Personnel committee members Harold Klink and Arthur Bezdek went to see Hipple, hoping to persuade him to sign the math contract. Sorensen, the principal, went along as an observer. If the three men could persuade the coach to sign the contract, it would take the steam out of the meeting later that night. If Hipple signed, they could tell the crowd that he had accepted the contract and the matter was closed. If he didn't, they would face a firestorm of questions and then have to vote against him in front of his most loyal supporters.

The meeting began at 4:00 PM with Sorensen taking notes for the first ten minutes or so. The visitors apparently tried to get Hipple to focus on the contract, but instead he said, "No visits here and all at once it hit." He may have been complaining that he had little warning of what was to come.

Klink said that in the February 6th meeting, he and Hutchins had made it clear that the only alternative was the math job. Klink threatened that the math contract might be rescinded. "We're trying to give you every consideration. [At] 7:30 this evening … I'm going to make a decision: [either] a signed contract for mathematics or [I'll] make a motion [you] refused reasonable reassignment." It didn't work. Hipple responded, "You've been here seven years."

Klink continued, telling Hipple, "This is not about something [that happened] this week, this month, this year. The major basis of my decision is that you have not given your support to our plan."

Hipple responded, "[People] complaining about everything and no one has been down here this year. When was he [Messerli] down here and visited a class? He has been keeping it alive."

Bezdek then took over the conversation, saying he called four teachers to inquire about Hipple and, based on that, decided he would vote to release him. "I have had parents call, complaints, not mean, just disapproving of the way [you are] handling it. [It's] not about one deficiency … I don't want to face this next year, do you? … It's time to hang the whistle up … We are not enjoying it either." Bezdek's decision to vote against him may have startled Hipple. He had visited the board member in his home several times, seeking his help in understanding the board's position.

Klink then asked Hipple what he wanted the board to do. "I'd like to retain [my] present position. [You] took the fourth one without considering the first three."

About here Sorensen wrote, "Did not continue with notes." And yet the discussion lasted two hours more. The men continued talking, arguing, urging Hipple to sign the contract, until 6:15, according to a notation by Sorensen.

When it was over, the three men were vanquished. Hipple had not budged an inch. He would not quit. If the board members were going to dismiss him, they would have to do it before an angry crowd.

There were more than one hundred people sitting on the north bleachers of the old gym in the C. B. Vernon school building when the board meeting convened. Larry Tanner was there for the *Gazette* and Gene Raffensperger was covering for the *Des Moines Register and Tribune*. This was going to be statewide news. The board sat at long tables on the gym floor where Hipple's teams had thrilled so many fans. A legal-sized pad was passed around; the board asked everyone to sign it, enter his or her address, and indicate why they were attending the meeting. Bill Huntoon, the young wrestling coach, saw the sign-up sheet as an act of intimidation. "If they can fire Hipple, they can sure fire me," he thought. He signed it anyway. So did about seventy other people. Most of the people in the gym were Hipple supporters, the newspapers said.

The tense, two-hour meeting was in some ways a replay of the prior two board meetings. Hipple supporters tried to get the board to disclose the reasons for their actions. Board President Harstad reminded them that the board was prohibited by law from disclosing the reasons, unless a public meeting was held at Hipple's request.

Bill Rucker, head of the alumni association, apparently wanted to make the point that Hipple was overburdened with work. He asked board members if they were aware of Hipple's daily schedule. They were not. Sorensen provided it. Rucker reminded the board that Hipple repaired equipment, wrote contracts, tended bruises, and went to the gym on Saturdays to encourage young athletes. Rucker said he wanted neither a public hearing nor a court battle, but that Hipple would get a lot of support if either came to pass. What his group wanted to know, he said, was "What was the big problem?"

Allan McKean, father of former athletes, said that many of the charges against Hipple were secondhand. He urged further study. Another parent, Merle Hanson, said, "For a while I hated Les Hipple's guts. Today I have more respect for him than any other man I know. I think we need to back this kind of guy."

Joe Green, self-appointed gadfly, began to question board members individually whether Hipple's disciplinary methods were a factor in his being released. Some board members refused to comment, but Hal Klink was quoted as saying, "Absolutely not. When we select a new athletic director and coach, he will have to be more strict than Hipple."

This exaggeration may be a clue to the pressure the board was feeling, as well as to its sensitivity on the subject of discipline. The reporters, and probably many in the audience, knew about the two recent incidents involving the bus departure and the tape on the boy's mouth. Hipple's opponents had probably tipped off the reporters, and Hipple had confirmed the events in interviews earlier that day. Both reporters mentioned the incidents in their stories.

At this point, Messerli took the floor, saying that discipline "was one small factor." He said, according to the minutes, that he had many conferences with Hipple on this subject and that "he had never suggested that Mr. Hipple lessen the severity of the discipline but that he did however question some of the methods Mr. Hipple used in administering discipline." (Messerli's claim that he never lessened the severity of discipline is directly contrary to what he wrote in 1958: "During the past two years I have personally interceded for many boys … getting them another chance after breaking training.")

William Reed again stood up for the board. He was careful not to attack Hipple. Reed called the whole matter "a great disaster." He defended the board and criticized Green for directing "a lot of tripe" at the board and for implying that its members had a vendetta against Hipple. "You're going to make it impossible for the school board to give him a decent break," Reed said.

Green said he didn't feel the board had a vendetta against Hipple, but he wondered why Hipple was being forced to resign after so many years of faithful service. He wouldn't be doing this, Green said, if he thought it would bring harm to the coach.

Bezdek then took the floor and provided a masterly summary. To quote the minutes: "Mr. Bezdek expressed his respect for Mr. Hipple's intent and his coaching techniques. He pointed out that the administrative problems have been over a period of years and that no one factor involved in this situation created the problem as it now exists, rather it was an accumulation of a number of problems, no one of which was sufficiently serious in itself to alone create the present situation."

The meeting went on, but no one got any closer to the truth than that. No wonder Hipple was confused about what he was doing wrong. He wasn't doing things that were seriously wrong; he had just been doing them too often over too long a period in the wrong place.

Finally, Klink introduced a motion that termination procedures be initiated "at the earliest possible time." Hipple's rights were described. He could still take the math job if he wanted it. If he did take it, he had a letter granting him release from the contract should he find a coaching job elsewhere. He could demand a public hearing, but that would have been futile since the board of education itself would determine the outcome of the hearing and it was highly unlikely to overrule its previous decision.

Then came the vote: "Upon the question being put on the adoption of this motion the following directors voted aye: Klink, Hutchins, Bezdek, [Herbert] Kohl, Harstad, [Lowell] Sebern, and [John] Andrea. Nay: None. Motion carried."

"We sincerely believe before God we are doing what is right for Marion and for the children," Bezdek said.

—

A week later, after a meeting with Harstad, Hipple signed the math contract. It paid him $7,301 (equal to about $47,500 in 2007), about $1,100 ($7,200) less than he had received as athletic director, physical education director, and coach. Announcing the deal, Harstad said, "The board of education regards Mr. Hipple as being of high moral character and is confident that he will continue to exert his good influence upon the young people of the community."

There is nothing in Hipple's file describing the negotiations that led to his signing the contract. Perhaps this was because Messerli was in Germany on a study mission sponsored by the American Association of School Administrators. When the *Gazette* contacted Hipple, he declined to explain why he accepted the contract. He said he would issue a statement later. It appears that he never did.

Chapter 35
Aftermath, 1965

The story of Hipple being fired simmered in the sports pages of the *Gazette* for a few days. Charles Kurt, former Marion player and assistant coach, wrote a letter praising Hipple, which sports editor Gus Schrader printed, adding a few words about his own high regard for the coach.

Verdean Stade, a 1954 graduate living in Albuquerque, wrote to the *Gazette*, too, saying, "You can't blame a coach for having a poor record when you can't discipline the boys … The championship teams of the past would still belong to Hipple if he didn't have to pat the players on the head and cope with obnoxious parents."

William Reed, continuing to defend the board, promptly responded. His letter to the *Gazette* essentially said that Stade didn't know what he was talking about. "Mr. Stade's contention by inference that boys today are a sorry lot by comparison with the boys of his day is perhaps the sorriest of all his generalizations … I'm sure little will be accomplished by further bickering, so if you are inclined not to print this … please do just that." Schrader printed the letter, but agreed that "there doesn't seem to be much good in continuing this discussion," and that was the end of it.

In early April, Ernest Beemblossom, then thirty-one and with two years of head-coaching experience at Marion, was named director of athletics. Messerli had recommended him, saying it would be best if the new AD came from the existing staff. Beemblossom was described by a number of individuals as a fairly easygoing man with a good sense of humor who was popular with the students. He was no pushover, they said, but not strung as tightly as Hipple, either. "You could talk with Ernie," said Ken Backsen, who played quarterback for him. "Hipple you just obeyed."

Before the week was out, Beemblossom announced that James Morrow, twenty-nine, had accepted the job as basketball coach. Morrow had compiled an outstanding record at Lincoln High School, which served the nearby towns of Mechanicsville and Stanwood.

Shocking news came a month later. John Messerli, who had just signed a new three-year contract, tendered his resignation. He had accepted a position with a new cooperative educational agency in Wisconsin that provided goods and services to public schools in the area. The position was definitely a career advancement, according to Richard Sorensen. He added that it was unlikely Messerli could have landed it in the month since he returned from Germany. Applications and interviews would have required more time than that. Messerli would later say he left Marion because he was blamed for firing Hipple. There were rumors that he had received phone calls threatening physical harm from men who were furious about what had happened. When I asked Messerli's son Dave about his father's motive for leaving, he said, "Let's just say the opportunity to go someplace else came along at the right time." Later, he wrote, "As far as I was told or knew, we left Marion because a better opportunity presented itself."

Announcing his departure, John Messerli said it was a difficult decision, "but the opportunity was such that it couldn't be passed up." After thanking the community and the board of education, he added, "My sole interest was in the welfare of the young people, and all of the decisions and recommendations I've made have been with that in mind." Sorensen succeeded Messerli as superintendent.

As for Hipple, "He was devastated, just devastated, just completely devastated," said Bill Huntoon, who became a close friend of the Hipple family. Fired, discredited, treated as a pariah by some members of the faculty and administration, giggled at by some of the students, Hipple said nothing.

"He was devastated," agreed his daughter, Pat Turner. She was living in Colorado when her father was fired, but learned about his reaction in discussions over the years with her mother. Only Wilma knew how Hipple really felt, and he probably didn't talk much about it to her, either. "He was devastated that the vote against him was unanimous and that even a good friend voted against him," Turner said.

She was referring to Doug Hutchins, who had won election to the board of education to protect Hipple, but in the end joined the others in voting to terminate him. Hutchins was surely under great pressure to make the vote unanimous. "I don't really know why I voted with the board," Hutchins told me. "I didn't know what I was going to do when I went to the meeting. I knew my vote wouldn't make a difference. I did it partly for things down the road. The board needed to be together for future decisions. I didn't want the fight to continue."

Shortly after the vote, Hutchins sought out Hipple, tried to explain his action, and asked Hipple's forgiveness. Hipple granted it, and the two men resumed their friendship. "I think he understood there was nothing I could do to stop it," Hutchins said. Hipple seemed to have accepted his fate, Hutchins thought. "I never saw any difference in his behavior on the surface."

Few men who were hurt so much complained so little. When friends or family members brought up the subject, Hipple refused to participate. He squirmed in his chair and tried to steer the conversation away from Messerli and the board. Some friends thought the subject was too painful for him to discuss. Or perhaps he was trying to put it behind him, treating the tragedy the same way he handled a lost game or a poor season—moving on without getting caught up in pointless discussions about things he couldn't change.

When Wilma's temper flared and she used a mild curse word or two, Hipple tried to shush her. He didn't approve of swearing. "Lester," she responded, "There are times when 'golly' just doesn't fit the occasion."

No one I talked to ever heard him say a single word against Messerli or the board members or anyone else, either right after he was fired or any other time as long as he lived. Instead, said Genny Yarne, a family friend, he made himself the butt of the joke.

"I'm not good enough to coach," he might say, "but I can teach math. What kind of math department do we have that they let me be part of it?" That was as angry as he allowed himself to sound. Whatever else he felt, he kept to himself. (Genny Yarne had come to know Hipple when she was a fourth-grade teacher and was married to Larry Tanner, the reporter who loved the Indians. Later, Tanner and Genny divorced. She remarried and introduced her new husband, Andrew Yarne, to the Hipples.)

The summer after being removed from his job, Hipple faced a yawning gulf of time with no duties for the athletic department. No fields to mow, no equipment to mend, no clinics to attend, no plans to make. Nothing. For the first time after twenty-eight years of coaching, nothing. For a man whose every minute had been filled with work, nothing.

He bought a paint-by-numbers kit. He chose a large painting, about two feet by three feet, with very intricate patterns. Finishing it could take weeks or even months. He completed two paintings that size, then stopped. There was no pleasure in it.

He tried to sell his extensive collection of coaching magazines and books, writing letters by hand to coaches and organizations listing the titles and dates of the publications. He made few, if any, sales.

He had a box full of newspaper clippings—stories about Marion teams and games—that his mother had cut out of the *Gazette* year after year and sent to him. The articles had never been sorted. Instead they had been collected randomly in a thin white cardboard box, the kind that might be used to hold the gift of a shirt or blouse. The articles were clipped meticulously, but there were no dates on them. Hipple began to sort them by school year into manila file folders, perhaps intending to make a scrapbook. But he stopped well before completing the project.

There were two or three sewing machines in the basement that Hipple had used over the years to repair sports equipment and uniforms. He began going down there to make things. Working with vinyl and canvas, he started with bags and totes of various kinds. Somehow this developed into a small business. Perhaps some coaches remembered his skill at repairing equipment and brought him some odd jobs. Maybe they wanted to show him how they felt about him. Maybe they told him he got a raw deal. He didn't want to talk about it. He began spending more time at his machines. The work required concentration. It helped take his mind off what had happened.

—

Why didn't Hipple seek a job elsewhere that included coaching, and leave Marion? Other school systems would have been interested in him. In fact, at the very moment Hipple was being publicly fired, the superintendent of schools at Tama wrote a letter to Messerli saying his school needed a basketball coach who could "exercise effective control over the varsity squad" and could teach mathematics or biology. The job sounds tailor-made for Hipple. Tama's superintendent was well aware of what was happening in Marion but was interested in Hipple anyway. He asked for Messerli's "frank and candid opinion" of Hipple's strengths and weaknesses. There is a handwritten note at the bottom of the letter: "Answered by personal conversation 3/8/65 by R. M. Sorensen at Washington High approx. 9:00 PM." Given Sorensen's low opinion of Hipple's methods, it's unlikely he offered a favorable recommendation.

Hipple may not have been the hot property he was ten years earlier, but there were surely others in the region who believed that Marion's educational leaders had made a mistake and who would have been open to a conversation with the coach. But he apparently made no attempt to look elsewhere.

Why? He was fifty-two, not the ideal age to look for a new job. Further, starting someplace else might have required giving up some salary or retirement benefits. He also had his wife to consider. She was ill, suffering from severe depression. Hipple was her primary caregiver. A move might be too upsetting for Wilma. Besides, "He really liked Marion," said his daughter. "He was happy here."

When I asked the question of Doug Hutchins, he put a different twist on his answer. Hipple couldn't leave Marion, he said, "Because we all loved him so much."

There may have been another reason. Perhaps he thought he would have the opportunity to coach again.

Chapter 36
Just Teaching, 1965–1978

In the fall of 1965, Hipple began the first school year of his professional life without coaching. He taught two math courses, both for slower students. One course was called consumer math—dubbed "dummy math" by the students. It was for seniors who had not mastered such skills as calculating interest, balancing checkbooks, understanding the costs of installment buying, and filing tax returns. Hipple was shocked to learn that some didn't know how to make change. He brought cash from home to teach them, and some of the money disappeared into his students' pockets.

He also taught a course called pre-algebra, intended for ninth graders who weren't ready for the real thing. The course was designed to give "a good review of the basic operations of whole numbers, common and decimal fractions," Hipple wrote in one of his evaluation forms.

Some fellow teachers said administrators assigned him these courses in the hope that he would become bored with them—or insulted by them—and quit. Instead, he bent himself to instructing students who had little aptitude for what he had to teach and less interest in learning it.

He remained a strict disciplinarian. Some students lacked respect because he had been fired, but he tolerated no backtalk or horseplay. He made students sit up straight, keep both feet on the floor, and pay attention. He was quick to call down students whose concentration wandered. He drilled them, over and over, on the basics. "I learned a lot of math from him," one student said years later. "I was afraid not to."

He kept his room spotlessly clean, carrying out duties normally left to janitors, such as washing down the blackboard, cleaning desktops, and picking up scraps of paper. Janitors said he had one of the neatest rooms in the school.

In his evaluations, Lowell Morgan, high school principal from 1965 to 1976, evaluated Hipple as "good" to "very good" on a long list of factors. "He is well qualified in math, and does a good job of controlling the type of student he has in most of his classes," Morgan wrote in 1967. "He is withdrawn and doesn't mingle with the other teachers. He is difficult to talk with, but he will do anything you want him to do." In a later evaluation, Morgan commented that Hipple did not seem happy in his job, but added, "You cannot always tell how he feels about a problem or a situation."

Shirley Post Pantini, who taught at Marion High School, remembered a classroom tour organized by the principal. All the teachers went from room to room to hear presentations from their colleagues. She was impressed by the clarity with which Hipple explained his courses.

When I described Hipple's firing to Pantini as a tragedy, she responded, "It may have been a tragedy for him, but it was a blessing for any student who was having trouble with math and wanted help." Hipple met any willing student before or after school or during free periods to tutor them. He turned no one away.

Mike Nash was one of those special students. Nash had won an appointment to West Point. He knew his math wasn't good enough for the military academy, so he asked Hipple to help him with geometry and college preparatory math. "I was scared to death" by Hipple's reputation before going into the classroom with him, Nash said, but found him to be kind and giving. Hipple explained math problems in a way Nash could understand. Although Nash didn't go to West Point, he scored high enough on his entrance tests to be admitted. "He was the greatest math teacher I ever had," Nash said.

As they worked together, Hipple told Nash stories about some of the great Marion teams and players of the past. Nash and some of his buddies started going to see Hipple during breaks to hear more stories. Some were funny and some were sad, Nash said, but they all had an educational point. Some of their friends chided the boys about their visits. "What are you going to see that old goat for?" they asked. But Nash and his buddies liked the stories and liked the old guy a lot. Hipple turned fifty-seven in 1970, the year Nash graduated.

—

When the 1965–1966 school year began, Hipple made a new friend, a surprising one, many thought. He was Jim Morrow, the young man who replaced him as basketball coach. Morrow came to Marion with sterling credentials. Only twenty-nine, he had been coaching basketball at Lincoln High School since graduating from the University of Iowa in December 1959. Over six seasons, his teams compiled a record of 89–13, advancing to the substate round in 1965.

Although the job was a career advancement, Morrow wasn't interested at first. "I thought it was absolutely ridiculous," Morrow recalled. "Hipple was a legend. I didn't want to go to a school that treated him that way. The community of coaches in Iowa was shocked. There was no sympathy among coaches for the people of Marion and what they were doing. I didn't want to follow that."

But Marion officials persisted. Morrow met several times with Ernest Beemblossom, the football coach who eventually replaced Hipple as athletic director. He also met with Richard Sorensen, who checked out his teaching credentials and looked into his relationships with parents. Morrow came through with flying colors. Morrow had at least one dinner with John Messerli, who offered him the job.

Morrow was an ideal replacement for Hipple. He was young, which meant he should relate well with players. He stressed conditioning, mastery of the fundamentals, a pressing, man-to-man defense, and a fast-breaking offense, just as Hipple had. He built winning teams. He was a disciplinarian with strict training rules, but not as strict as Hipple's. He got along with parents. In Morrow, Messerli and Sorensen must have believed they had found a younger, more personable, more flexible version of Hipple.

The deciding factor for Morrow was not what Marion officials said, but what he was told by a fellow coach. Gay Dahn coached at Thomas Jefferson in Cedar Rapids, a frequent Marion opponent. He encouraged Morrow to take the job. "You are following a legend, probably the best coach the state of Iowa ever had," Dahn said. "But Les Hipple himself will never cause you any problems."

Hipple more than lived up to Dahn's promise. He became a friend and mentor to his successor. "I went to him privately for a lot of advice," Morrow said. "He was a private supporter over the years." The advice Hipple gave wasn't about coaching strategies, but about principles and politics. "I would go to his classroom to talk about problems and issues that might result from a strong decision on my part," Morrow said. "The decisions were mine; what I wanted from Hipple was his assessment of what might happen next. He knew all the families. I wanted his advice on how to deal with parents. He understood the school system and the town. I don't think I would have lasted five years without him."

Morrow's friendship did not go unnoticed. Some people thought it was unseemly for the new coach to be spending time with the former one. When they remarked to Morrow about it, he just said, "Yep, he kept me after school today."

Eventually the superintendent himself had a word with Morrow. "Sorensen approached me and said that people were talking about my meetings with Les. He said, 'You know, Les Hipple is not held in the highest esteem around here.' I said that if anyone had a problem with it they should come and see me. That's what Les would have done. If I saw Les at the Hy-Vee and we started chatting, I'd say 'Do you think anyone's watching us?' He got a chuckle out of that."

Morrow welcomed complaints and questions from parents because he saw it as a way of keeping tabs on the mood of the town. Most parental concerns, Morrow said, have at their heart the desire to get more playing time for their children. He heard his visitors out, and then explained that they couldn't tell him how to coach or whom to play.

It wasn't long before parents started going around Morrow to higher authorities, just as they had done with Hipple, and the authorities listened, just as they had when Hipple was coach. One night, unannounced, a member of the board of education showed up at Morrow's home. "He didn't call first, just dropped by," Morrow remembered. "He said he was disappointed because he was getting complaints about me from parents. He was upset because I didn't have more flexibility. And here I was the one who was supposed to understand young people."

This happened even though Morrow loosened Hipple's rules considerably. He lifted all bans on driving and made no objections to going steady. He did not require his players to go out for football or track, although he encouraged them to do so. He gave players more leeway in missing practice if they had a legitimate reason. Morrow had been stricter in his previous position, but saw that his rules had become impractical.

"Les coached at the end of an era when discipline was respected," Morrow said. "Parents and kids simply weren't going to follow rules as strict as his. In small towns, the coach was like a minor god, and parents didn't argue with him. But that was all changing."

After coming to Marion, Morrow discovered that some people resented him because he had replaced a beloved coach. But in all their time together, Hipple never showed the slightest animosity toward him, nor did he show a tinge of resentment about being fired. "He was a complete gentleman," Morrow said. "It's the only way I know how to put it. I admired him so much for the way he handled adversity. Les was a mentor to me. He came into my life and filled the role of my father." (Morrow had been twelve years old when his father died.)

When the basketball season began, Morrow sensed that some of his players might be showing disrespect for their former coach. He called a meeting and warned his players that if any of them spoke or acted against Hipple he would be thrown off the team. Their former coach deserved their greatest respect, he told them. "Marion is Les Hipple and Les Hipple is Marion."

That first difficult year under Morrow the Indians posted a record of 8–9, finishing in a tie for third in the conference. Morrow coached the team to three winning seasons and two district championships in the following four seasons, compiling a five-year record of 54–40. Then, asked to become a student counselor, Morrow withdrew from coaching because he felt the two jobs conflicted.

Looking back on his role in replacing a legend, Morrow said, "I was completely supportive of everything Coach Hipple believed and did. I wasn't a lot different from Coach Hipple. I just wasn't as good."

—

From the very first, Hipple could not stay away from the games. He went to as many as he could and watched from the stands, choosing an inconspicuous seat. "He never sat in a place that was prominent," said Larry Perkins, a Marion coach. "I used to talk with him about what was happening. He never second-guessed the coaches even though our teams weren't very good. He never said we should be doing this or that."

John Vernon noted similar behavior at football games. Hipple said nothing, although "It must have galled him that the safety was making most of the tackles." Marion did not have a winning football team until Les Dollinger arrived in 1969. In four years under Ernest Beemblossom and two under his successor, Tom England, the Indians went 13–37–4.

—

In 1974, Bob Thurness took over as football coach at Marion. At an early practice he noticed a man standing off at a distance, half-hidden in some pine trees at the edge of the field. Thurness walked over and introduced himself. The man said his name was Les Hipple.

"Coach Hipple, I know your name," Thurness said. "You're a legend around here. As long as I'm coach, you're welcome here. You don't have to stand over here. You can come and stand on the sidelines. You can listen in on the huddle. You can come down and stand on the sidelines at games if you want." Hipple remained at a discreet distance.

On the night of the first home game, Thurness rode the bus to the playing field with the team. As the bus passed through the gates, Thurness saw Hipple working as a ticket-taker. *What's going on?* thought Thurness. When he saw Hipple next, he asked him why he was taking tickets. Hipple explained that if he worked enough events, he would get a free pass to all the games.

That didn't sound fair to Thurness. He went to see the new athletic director, Les Dollinger, who had been football coach. "For all Hipple has done around here, he should be given a free pass," Thurness said. Dollinger immediately agreed, and so it was done.

Thurness often took equipment to Hipple to repair. Hipple showed him photos and talked about teams of the past.

"I think he was frustrated as hell that he wasn't coaching," Thurness said.

—

As basketball season approached in 1974, Hipple was finally offered a coaching job. Dick Sloan, previously an assistant, was named head basketball coach. When the freshman basketball coach resigned, Sloan asked Hipple to take the spot. "I had heard great things about him," Sloan said, "and we got along well." Hipple was sixty years old. He hadn't coached in eight years. Practice started at 6:00 or 6:30 in the morning. Pay was $750. He had won more than three hundred games as a varsity coach and had never been an assistant. Hipple immediately said yes.

Mike Ryan was a team member that year. Even though the freshmen were entering high school nearly a decade after Hipple had been fired, practically a lifetime for these youngsters, they were keenly aware of Hipple's reputation. "When we heard Hipple was coming out of retirement to coach us, we rolled our eyes and said, 'Oh-oh, we're in for it now,'" Mike said.

On the first day of practice, Hipple was ready for them. He marched them into a classroom and for an hour and a half made them watch old 8mm movies he had made of players in the 1950s to show them how to shoot properly, keeping the ball on their fingertips, and how to pass the ball. "I remember that Wally DeWoody was in the movie," Mike said. DeWoody graduated in 1954, two decades before Mike was a freshman.

Hipple made them do push-ups on their fingertips. They had to jump rope before practice. He found or made them uniforms that were just like those worn by players in the 1950s. Their shorts had the signature *M* on the side vent, the design that Hipple had created years earlier. He made them practice the two-handed pass until they thought they would die of boredom.

When a player got out of line or stopped paying attention, Hipple raised his arm, "slowly and deliberately," said Mike Ryan, acting it out, bringing up his arm with the pointed finger, his eyes narrowing, sighting along the finger, showing how Hipple brought fogbound freshmen to attention with his piercing gaze. Then Mike showed how Hipple lowered his arm slowly to his side, the finger still pointed, like a cocked gun, ready to be raised again to drill anyone who thought this was not serious business.

"We had had a semi-successful eighth-grade team," Mike said. "What Hipple did was bring us together, make us a more cohesive team, more disciplined." The team had a poor won-lost record, but Mike said the freshman experience was crucial to the way they performed later.

Sometimes Sloan went to practice to see the old coach at work. He watched as Hipple drilled the kids over and over again on the proper shooting form. "He had a bunch of cocky kids with short attention spans, but as they saw themselves begin to improve they paid more attention to what he said."

Sloan was surprised that Hipple insisted on push-ups; strength building was not associated with basketball at the time. He watched as Hipple ran the same offense he had used in the 1940s and 1950s, teaching the boys to pass and cut. "I had never seen it before," Sloan said. "It was interesting."

As Sloan remembered it, Hipple taught the underhand free throw but did not insist that the players use it. Brad Albaugh, who played for Hipple, remembered it differently. "Oh, he made us use it," Albaugh said. The kids hated it because opponents razzed them unmercifully, even though they made about 80 percent of their shots, Albaugh said. Once, Hipple missed a game because of a scheduling conflict. So the players got together and decided to shoot free throws overhand. "We made about 50 percent," Albaugh said. When Hipple found out about it, he made them run sprints until their tongues hung out. "I'm glad I didn't have him as a varsity coach when he was younger," said Albaugh. "He was tough."

Sloan remembered a meeting of the coaching staff to discuss training rules. The idea under consideration was to have three stages of punishment for infractions. The first infraction would draw a warning, the second a moderate penalty, and the third the maximum penalty, such as being benched or even dismissed from the team. Hipple hated the idea. "You're just encouraging them to break the rules," he said. Where others saw a system of deterrence, Hipple saw an invitation to cheat.

Dick Sloan noticed that after a game, he couldn't tell by Hipple's behavior whether his team had won or lost. "We didn't talk a lot," Sloan said. "You know how he was. You could take five minutes to frame a question and all he would say would be 'yes.'"

After his second year as freshman coach, the players had a plaque made for him that read:

To Coach Hipple

We wish to express our appreciation for your time and effort put into improving our team.

Freshman Class of 75–76

Record 12–3

And then it was over. Hipple didn't coach the following year. Sloan couldn't remember why. Lowell Morgan, the principal, said he couldn't recall the details but that the reason wasn't related to any dissatisfaction with his performance. Perhaps, said Hipple's daughter, he had proven what he wanted to prove—that he could still coach.

Many years later, Marion High School held its first all-school reunion. Mike Ryan, a member of Hipple's first freshman team, made a point of going. "The guy I wanted to see most was Les Hipple. I was able to tell Mr. Hipple that we really loved him as a group."

—

Coming off his successful stint as a freshman basketball coach and nearing the mandatory retirement age of 65, Hipple began a quiet campaign to find a spot coaching basketball at Marion. Thurness remembered Hipple seeking his support. Hipple also made unofficial inquiries among members of the Marion board of education, but was discouraged from having any hopes of coaching because he was too old and too strict. He also contacted Lumir Dostal Jr., who was on the board of education at Linn-Mar. When Dostal brought the idea to his fellow board members, the response was the same. Hipple was too old; he would not relate well with the kids.

As the 1997–1978 school session ended, Hipple turned sixty-five and had no choice but to retire. Formality required a letter to the school board. Hipple's was written by hand. "I shall comply with the policy," it said in part. "It has certainly been a short enjoyable 33 years."

Then he added a final sentence:

"I do feel that I am in a position to add a great deal to the basketball program, regardless of age."

There were lots of kids out there who needed to learn the fundamentals. Les Hipple never got the chance to teach them.

Chapter 37
Redemption

"I never cared what a boy thought of me when I was coaching him, but I cared a lot what he would think of me later," Hipple said.

As his retirement approached, Hipple discovered how successful he had been. The first honor came when former players Chuck Kent and Ray Fuller mounted a campaign to nominate Hipple for the Iowa Basketball Coaches Hall of Fame. Some years earlier, he had been elected to the Football Coaches Hall of Fame, which is maintained by an association of football coaches. The Iowa High School Athletic Association maintains the Basketball Hall of Fame. As part of their campaign, Hipple's supporters presented him a plaque at a basketball game in January 1978 and called upon his colleagues and former players to write to the IHSAA on his behalf.

"If Les Hipple … doesn't belong in the Basketball Hall of Fame, no one does," wrote Bob Hersom in the *Gazette*, citing Hipple's won-lost record, his string of championships, and the names of some of the stars he turned out. Hersom wrote that Marion's basketball teams dominated the Cedar Rapids metropolitan area for years, going 26–6 against Cedar Rapids schools before they consolidated in 1957 to form bigger schools.

The letters from former players didn't mention victories and statistics. They described Hipple's values, the lessons he taught them about discipline and hard work.

"Aside from my parents and wife, Coach Hipple has done more for my life than anyone, and I honestly believe this feeling is shared by the hundreds of other graduates who were under his guidance," wrote Russ Seeks, director of personnel at American Red Ball Transit.

"Les Hipple is a hard-working, honest, giant of a man. A man I respected and admired in my youth and whose ideals and confidence I carry with me in my later years," wrote Dallas Fairly, superintendent of utilities at Altamont, Illinois.

"Coming from a home with divorced parents and not having any male figure to identify with, Coach Hipple gave me the guidance and discipline to shape my life," wrote Gordon Rundquist from Maquoketa, where he was about ten years into a high school basketball coaching career that would produce more than 550 victories.

After Hipple was inducted into the Hall of Fame that March he received letters of congratulations. Jim Luense, a guidance counselor in St. Ansgar, Iowa, wrote that he didn't always agree with Hipple's rules, but "I really feel I am a better person today because of my association with you and athletics."

Len Bruce, a teacher in Waukon, Iowa, wrote that although "at the time, running laps, doing push-ups, and climbing the rope seemed terribly cruel, I look back on those days and your discipline with a great deal of gratitude."

Jerry Peck, sales manager for E. S. Dysart Co. in Cedar Rapids, wrote a seven-paragraph letter recalling his playing days and thanking the coach for his many sacrifices. Peck assured Hipple that he always had everyone's respect, "even during the most difficult times." Peck may have been referring to a controversy that occurred fifteen years earlier, when Hipple denied letters to five senior basketball players. Peck was one of them.

Meanwhile, plans were underway for an honor that Hipple surely treasured more than his induction into the Hall of Fame—the naming of the athletic fields at Marion High School in his honor. Bill Huntoon proposed the idea to the board of education, of which he was then president. "One or two of the board members might have opposed it," Huntoon said. "I was shocked when someone said, 'Maybe we should wait until after he is dead.' I got some petitions typed up and run off and got them to different athletic contests and got input from people. Almost everyone was positive. I took the petitions to the board to convince them that it was a good idea to do this radical thing of creating a memorial for a living person and a controversial person. The mayor, Bill Grundy, was just delighted."

On June 29, 1979, Mayor Grundy issued a proclamation declaring "Les Hipple Day" and saluting the old coach for his "devoted and unparalleled services to our community." In ceremonies at the school, a monumental stone marker was unveiled reading, "Les Hipple Athletic Complex." Town leaders and former athletes spoke at the ceremony. A photo of the event shows Hipple nattily dressed in a tan sports coat and white slip-on shoes with a woven pattern. He is rocking back in his metal chair and has a huge grin on his face, convulsed, apparently, by a wisecrack from the speaker.

The engraved stone that marks the Les Hipple Athletic Complex is about five feet high and twelve feet wide. It's the first sign a visitor sees as he approaches the high school from the north, well before the eye catches the large *Marion* on the school building higher on the hill. Behind the stone marker are a lighted baseball field, a lighted softball field, five lighted tennis courts, a soccer field, and practice fields for football and baseball.

In his speech that day, Hipple was true to his nature: grateful, gracious—and demanding. The honor, he said, was "unbelievable. For the last few weeks, I've been pinching myself to see if I'm awake or dreaming."

He thanked those responsible, and especially his "most important backer, my wife. She has been through many victories and some defeats." He said that whenever he drove by the marker, he would think of Marion athletes, past, present, and future, including "maybe a small boy or girl here tonight who in a few years will become a great athlete." He asked his audience to think of the marker in the same way, as a tribute to all Marion athletes.

Typically, he urged his audience to achieve even more: "I would like to compare this development to about a fourth grade athlete, one interested in all sports and having great potential but needing a lot of coaching to develop [that potential]. Some future needs could be a track, basketball courts, volleyball courts, a football field with lights." (A sport he didn't list, soccer, surged in popularity, and today the complex includes one of the finest soccer fields in the conference.)

—

With classes no longer occupying his time, Hipple turned to his sewing in earnest, building a small business that he worked at daily. He eventually owned five specialized machines. He repaired equipment, mended uniforms, and made bags for a growing list of coaches in the area. He also made items in canvas and vinyl for friends and their children—school bags, purses, backpacks, attaché bags, soft luggage, bags of all shapes and sizes. They often bore a sports motif—usually the Marion Indians or the Iowa Hawkeyes.

Perhaps for no other purpose than to increase the challenge, he began to design and make some apparel as well, such as jackets, warm-ups, foul weather clothing, pullovers, and mittens, even bibs for babies. He may have given some of these items away, but he made no serious attempt to sell them.

Several contemporaries described taking work to him and spending a few minutes talking about sports. Unlike some former coaches, Hipple had no photographs or newspaper articles framed on his walls as reminders of past glory. The basement walls were bare except for shelving he built to hold his materials. Once in a while he pulled a photo or an article out of a drawer to illustrate a point for a visitor. In another room, he displayed some plaques he had received over the years.

For all the work he did in that basement, Hipple's financial rewards were small. His daughter, who handled his tax reports, said that his annual gross income was typically about $2,000. He was essentially giving the stuff away. Wilma used to say, "Lester, I don't know why you spend so much time down there for so little money." To keep busy, to fill the hours, to be *working*, he might have replied, but probably didn't have to.

—

Hipple's daughter, Pat, and her husband, Jim, had six children, four boys and two girls, born between 1968 and 1982. In 1973, the Turners moved to Marion from Bloomfield, Iowa. When the children visited their grandparents, "they had his complete time and attention," Pat Turner recalled. "When it was time for them to learn to tie their shoelaces, I just took them over to Grandpa's house. When I came back to get them, they knew how to do it. Every time I walked into the house, I found one of them sitting on his lap."

From the time they were very young, his grandchildren went to his sewing room to watch him make things, sometimes sitting on his lap as he worked. "Every good sewer sews over his finger at least once," he told them. As they grew older, he listened carefully to their problems and concerns, often responding by telling them the story of Marion athletes and how they had met adversity through hard work and discipline.

He made popcorn that was so good his grandchildren thought he had a secret formula. He baked frozen pizza for them, putting bologna on top. He fed them ice cream and candy. When it was time for them to go home, he made up a little package of cookies for the journey. As they grew older and went off to college, he insisted they stop at his house on the way to pick up a sack of sandwiches.

—

Throughout his career, Hipple received letters from former athletes who had joined the military. The young men thanked him for the mental and physical training he put them through, which had prepared them to deal with the shock of basic training. While some of the other recruits were frightened or uncertain of their ability to survive the ordeal, the former Hipplemen had no such qualms. An obstacle course that involved climbing a rope looked familiar. A forced march with rifles at port arms was tough, but they knew it wasn't going to kill them. Hipple took great pride in these letters and often showed them to others.

In his later years, when he was teaching algebra and after he retired, some of these soldiers showed up on his doorstep to thank him in person. One was Gary Eschman, a former football player who attended the University of Iowa and, after graduating in 1959, entered the Army, survived the Infantry Officer Leadership Course, and then went to Airborne School at Fort Benning, Georgia. Years later, and "with no prior warning," Eschman went to see Les Hipple.

"I was treated very warmly," Eschman wrote. He had interrupted Hipple and his wife at work. "They'd been sewing and repairing football shoulder pads. Les explained that this gave them a little extra money to meet their living expenses. I realized that this was the living room of relatively poor people." Everything was extremely clean, Eschman remembered, but the furniture was sparse and the carpet was worn. The Hipples sensed his thoughts and described an opportunity that Hipple had turned down some years earlier to go into real estate in Marion. Had he done that instead of coaching and teaching, they would have been more prosperous.

This wasn't a social call. Eschman had never been on friendly terms with the man. He had come to tell him about Airborne School, and especially about "The Run." There were about one hundred men in Eschman's airborne class, including twenty Marines. It was July, a time of blistering heat and boiling humidity in southern Georgia. Each morning began with two hours of calisthenics followed by The Run—two miles at first, but quickly escalated to five miles. The Run was used to weed out the weak. "If you dropped out of any scheduled run, you washed out of Airborne School. No second chances. No appeal. Our class quickly dwindled to sixty-five students."

In the fog of harsh training, deprived of sleep, harassed by the cadre, confronted by a host of challenges such as being "free-dropped" repeatedly from 350-foot towers, Eschman began to realize "that somewhere along the way I'd acquired something that was missing in some of the other men. Occasional thoughts of Hipple and Marion High School football training floated through my mind."

All this Eschman told the Hipples—and more. He told them about the ecstasy of completing his first real jump, about the jumps that followed and the parties that followed the jumps and the thrill of having his jump wings pinned on the top left pocket of his dress uniform out on the regimental parade ground.

"By the time I finished my story, Hipple and his wife were beaming," Eschman wrote. He told them again that if it hadn't been for Hipple he might not have made it through airborne training.

"They asked me a few questions and that was pretty much it. We'd run out of things to say to each other. I thanked Coach once more. We shook hands very formally and then said our goodbyes. I walked out their door and never saw either one of them again."

—

When former athletes who had moved away came back for a visit, they often went to see Hipple. Some visited just once, to say something that needed to be said. Others called regularly. Gordon Rundquist, himself a basketball coach of note, liked to stop by and swap plays. "My concept is that there is really nothing new in basketball," Rundquist said. "I would ask him what he would do in certain situations—out-of-bounds plays, for example—and he would diagram it for me. I keep files on all these things. All coaches have these kinds of files." Rundquist never brought up the subject of being fired.

—

Every year, when the alumni from his coaching years assembled for their class reunions, Hipple was invited to the dinners and often asked to speak. He attended as many as he could. To prepare, he pulled out that class's yearbook (he had one from every year he taught at Marion) to remind himself of the players and games. He told the aging students about their years of glory and effort and sometimes showed movies he had made of some of the players and games. His former players were delighted to see him, but "you made sure you didn't have a beer in your hand when you talked to him," wrote Bill Lundquist.

One year, the class of 1955 made "A Les Hipple Roast" the theme of its dinner. "You always said that you were preparing us for success in later life," one of the speakers told him. "Well, I've had four different jobs and not one of them made me run laps." The audience roared, and Hipple bent double with laughter.

At another reunion, John DeJong, who had been trouble-prone in high school, described his religious conversion as an adult. DeJong was the son of the Presbyterian minister in Marion. Although he was interested in sports, DeJong rebelled. "By my sophomore year, my life was not going all that well," he said. Hipple tried repeatedly to get DeJong to come out for sports. "I knew he was right, but I simply would not listen." Hipple never gave up on DeJong, but he didn't beg the boy. "He was constantly telling me how I was screwing up my life."

Then, in his mid-thirties, DeJong told his reunion classmates, he began going to church from time to time with a friend of his father. He usually avoided these people, dismissing them as "Bible thumpers." One day in church, the minister said that he sensed there was someone in the congregation who sought a spiritual awakening. He asked that the congregation pray along with him. "I did what he asked in the silence of my own mind," DeJong said, "and a feeling came over me as if I had been dipped in a rain barrel, a feeling of being clean and new."

After DeJong gave his testimony at the reunion, Hipple approached him with a wide smile. "He told me how glad he was that I'd turned my life around and how proud he was of me," DeJong said. "I was just stunned because he was so friendly and nice. The man never said anything kind to me in high school. He was highly uncomplimentary of my lifestyle."

—

Jay Kacena tells the story of a party at Bill's Tap in Marion arranged for Butch Stade by a group of friends who wanted to show their affection for him. Stade and others in his family suffered from an incurable brain disease known as hereditary olivopontocerebellar atrophy. Stade, who was about fifty, was beginning to weaken and would soon have to enter a nursing home.

At the party, Stade reminded his friends of his most memorable prank in high school: He stole Hipple's football paddle from his office, took it to the industrial arts shop, sawed it in half, and then returned the two pieces to the office. No one else in history had the guts to do that.

Naturally, the hosts thought it would be fun to have Hipple come to the party, so Kacena and his brother Charles went to Hipple's home to invite him. "You could see he really wanted to come," Kacena remembered, "but Wilma didn't want him to go out so late." He told the men he was sorry he couldn't come, but invited them to have Butch call him from the bar.

The Kacena brothers hurried back to the bar and placed a call to Hipple, telling Stade someone wanted to talk with him. "They talked for a while," Kacena said, "and then we heard Butch shout, 'Yeah, I ran it through the buzz saw!' He was laughing, so obviously they both enjoyed the story. Then Butch talked quietly on the phone for a long time. We couldn't hear the conversation. When Butch finally hung up, tears were streaming down his face."

Chapter 38
Later Years, 1978–1998

As the Hipples grew older, Wilma's depression worsened. She often stayed in bed for long periods. "Her mental problems consumed her," Pat Turner said. "Her legs were strong." Lester took care of her and the house. He cleaned, shopped, cooked, handled the finances, managed his wife's medical care, and served as a constant comfort and presence.

His health was strong, but his damaged hip kept getting worse. Although he never complained about it, friends saw that it bothered him constantly. Even when sitting in a chair he had to shift position often to reduce the discomfort. He was told he needed a hip replacement, but was unwilling to undergo the surgery until a friend, Andrew Yarne, Genny's husband, began talking to him about it. Andrew had been a medic in the Navy, and through persistent questioning was able to understand that Hipple was enduring a great deal of pain.

Andrew showed him medical books and described a successful operation his father had experienced. The clincher, however, came when Andrew showed Hipple a copy of *Machine Design* magazine that described new materials used in hip replacements. Finally, in his mid-seventies, Hipple had the operation, exercised faithfully, and recovered fully. He was able to walk normally without pain for the first time in fifty years. He told Yarne he felt young again.

As Wilma's illness progressed, there were times she could not be left alone. Sometimes their daughter or friends stayed with Wilma, allowing Hipple time to run errands. His need to care for his wife limited his freedom to pursue his own interests, but he never complained about it.

Since he ran all the errands, people saw him around town a lot. He was extremely friendly when meeting someone he knew, and people were often amazed that he was able to remember the names of their parents, siblings, or children. He enjoyed chatting with former players, but prolonged conversation with a minor deity made some of them nervous. They could not reconcile this chatty gentleman with the demanding coach who had haunted their youth. Even George Murdoch, who had gone to Dartmouth, served in the Marines, led many community groups, and built a multibranch funeral service, tended to squirm mentally as Hipple made small talk on Main Street. "He was always the left hand of God to me," Murdoch said.

Hipple, who had once insisted on formality among his players, now tried to persuade them, as grown men, to call him by his first name. "You can call me Les," he told them. They couldn't bring themselves to do it. The name stuck in their throats. Since "Mr. Hipple" was too ceremonial, they went on calling him Coach.

One day Hipple saw a former player walking toward him on Main Street. The man, well into middle age, was smoking a cigarette. When he spotted Hipple, he was so stricken with panic that he stuffed the lighted cigarette in his pants pocket and held it there as the two men passed. "Hello, Coach," the man said, as the cigarette, presumably, burned a hole in his trousers.

Hipple probably enjoyed going to the supermarket. He had spent many years working in A&P stores as a youth, and it is likely that he marveled at the variety and abundance of food in the large new stores. People who lived through the Great Depression often tend to occupy one of two extremes in food shopping: They either shop only for immediate needs or they hoard against going hungry in the future. (My mother, for example, was one of the former. She did not like the idea of spending on any day any more than was absolutely required, fearing that anything extra would go to waste. In her later years, when she asked my brother to bring her a banana, she meant *one* banana; she refused to reimburse him for any overage.)

Hipple bought for the future. His kitchen shelves were loaded with carefully arranged canned goods, assurance that the family could survive being snowbound for weeks. He was not an adventurous eater. He knew what he liked. In those days he had oatmeal for breakfast almost every day. At noon, for dinner, the largest meal of the day, he often had soup and a bologna sandwich. Perhaps from feeding his grandchildren, he developed a fondness for Spaghetti-Os and canned ravioli, and one of those dishes might be supper. He ate moderately, stayed active, and remained trim all his life.

Hipple maintained a tenuous connection with Marion sports, such as helping to officiate at track meets when his commitments allowed. As he traveled about town he often stopped to watch a pickup basketball game in a neighbor's driveway. He once told an interviewer, "[By themselves, players] will start out practicing their skills, but as soon as another player comes along, they'll be playing one-on-one or two-on-two. They want to be like players they see on TV. They develop bad habits. I don't like to see all the styles they are playing right now. Players might have one good game out of four. I expected our players to have four good games out of five."

As his grandchildren grew older and attended Marion High School, some of them went out for sports. He couldn't always see their games because he had to care for Wilma, but sometimes when the grandchildren played baseball or softball, he took his wife in their car to a spot from which they could watch the games. Afterward, as likely as not, he asked Wilma, "Why don't they teach fundamentals anymore?"

Chapter 39
Messerli's Memories

Two years after he resigned as superintendent and left Marion for Wisconsin, John Messerli and his family returned to eastern Iowa. Messerli came back to serve as second-in-charge of what became the Grant Wood Area Educational Agency in Cedar Rapids, which, like the agency he joined in Wisconsin, served as a central provider of goods and services to area schools. However, he found this work unfulfilling and sought to return to education.

Messerli became superintendent at Monticello, his hometown, and then moved on to a similar position in Faribault, Minnesota. Then Messerli and his wife Lorna fulfilled a long-held ambition by buying a twenty-unit motel in Anoka, Minnesota. "Mom loved it, but Dad missed getting out in the community and being on boards and committees," wrote their son Dave, so the couple returned to Marion, where Messerli planned to become a realtor. However, the Lisbon school district asked him to serve as interim superintendent, and this turned into a job lasting several years.

At some point after leaving Wisconsin, Messerli inquired about a position with the Marion school system, according to Bill Huntoon, who was on the board of education at the time. The board turned him down.

After his retirement from education, Messerli and his wife moved back to Marion, where John became a real estate agent. He became active in community affairs. He was a member of the Masonic Lodge and served on the board of the library and the Marion school foundation. He was an elder at the Presbyterian church.

His son Dave graduated from the University of Iowa and applied for a job in the Marion school system because he wanted to stay in the area. He was hired as a teacher and coach at Vernon Middle School in 1972 and later transferred to the high school. When he was hired, Richard Sorensen, the superintendent, commented that Dave was "carrying a lot of baggage," a reference to his father's role in Hipple's being fired. But Dave never felt that way. In his thirty-seven years with the school, very few people have mentioned it to him. Dave had outstanding years as freshman football coach under Les Dollinger and Bob Thurness. He replaced Thurness as head coach in 1981, and held the position for eighteen years, compiling a record of 98–69. His teams won seven WaMaC championships before the state switched to a district football format, which had the effect of dissolving the conference for football.

Dave had been a sports nut as a kid at Marion when Hipple was coaching and was in ninth grade when Hipple was fired. He was in the gym all the time and went down to the football field often to watch the varsity practice. He greatly admired Hipple; he'd even taken up the clarinet as a boy because that was the instrument Hipple's daughter played. When I told Dave that he shared the Marion record for most WaMaC titles with Hipple, he shook his head, looked up at the ceiling, and said, "There's no one like Hipple."

As a football coach, he said, "I was tough. I never swore. I tried to help the players have fun. I took a lot of pride in being a football coach with compassion for the kids." He said he thought a lot about getting reserves into the game. "Did he get to play enough? That was on my mind a lot. Maybe it shouldn't have been." Coming off a 3–6 season in 1999 and with his son a candidate for starting quarterback the following year, Messerli decided it was time to quit. "That whole season I was uptight," he said, "I wasn't enjoying myself."

Dave and I met for interviews twice, once in a classroom and once at Mr. Bean's, a casual restaurant near the school. His main concern was to protect his father's memory and to alleviate any pain this book might cause his children and his mother, "who thought the world of my father." Perhaps he feared that I would trash his father. He wanted me to understand that, whatever role his father played, he did not act out of vindictiveness but according to what he thought was best for the students. He also said that his father should not be held solely responsible for Hipple being fired because an action such as that requires the participation of many people.

I told him that I believed what he said and that I hoped the book would reflect that. I said my view was that both men were at fault to some degree, because they were unable to find a way to work together. I told him that Hipple's personnel file contained a lot of material explaining the reasons he was fired. Hipple would not escape criticism in the book, but neither would John Messerli.

I also said that I believed that his father felt pain over this event all his life, just as Hipple had, and I somehow had to make that clear. I thought Dave and his mother understood this very well, because while Hipple never talked about the subject, John Messerli talked about it a lot. Dave said that maybe his father was provoked into talking about it, but that was not the case.

"To John Messerli's dying day he said that [Hipple's firing] wasn't his doing," said Bill Huntoon, who had worked with Messerli at the Grant Wood agency and was on cordial terms with him. "He told me that many times over the years. He said it was the board's decision and that he was forced to carry out their dictates."

It may have been the board's decision, but Messerli made it very clear that he did not approve of Hipple's methods. He held the board responsible, but indicated that he believed it had done the right thing.

In mid-2000, the Marion Independent School Foundation, a fund-raising arm of the school, received a gift of $1,600 from the Les Hipple Memorial Fund, which was established at his death. The foundation board decided to spend some of the money to create a display case in Hipple's honor that would be placed in the school's cafeteria. The purpose of the display was to tell the students something about the man after whom the athletic fields were named.

The case was mounted on the wall with a photograph of Hipple, some trophies, his old red and gold necktie, a whistle, and other artifacts. Messerli was on the foundation's board of directors at the time. During board meetings, he raised no objection to the trophy case. But shortly after the decision was made, he approached Laura Vint, executive director of the foundation, while she waited in line at the concession stand during a football game.

"He started talking to me about how he couldn't understand why we would give this honor to Hipple," Vint recalled. "He railed at me about it." Messerli told her that Hipple mistreated his players, that people disliked him, that he had been removed from his job. "He carried on in a negative way about how Hipple wasn't worthy of the honor," Vint said. Feeling cornered, Vint protested her innocence, responding that she hadn't known any of that. "I was amazed," she said, "because all I had heard about Hipple was that he was awesome."

About a year later, Tony Pantini and Ken McMurray, who were working on an oral history of veterans of World War II, interviewed Messerli, who had served in the Air Force in Italy during the war. The two men made an audiotape of the interview. After they covered Messerli's wartime career and the interview seemed to be coming to an end, Messerli talked briefly about his academic career, then, with no prompting from the interviewers, brought up the Hipple matter. "I should have stayed longer [at Marion]," he said. "I had a three-year contract in my pocket, but that last year was the hassle we had with Hipple. And I got the blame for it."

Messerli was suffering from cancer at the time of the interview; he would die six months later, on January 5, 2002. He knew he was being taped. It is reasonable to conclude that he wanted to go on record.

McMurray said he didn't know much about the controversy. The interview continued:

> MESSERLI: Well, he was an old drill sergeant. He had a lot of wins, but he had no way of dealing with kids, and I put up with him for nine years. I tried to make it easier. But the board finally said, "John, we've got to do something." So they called him in … They said, "You will have to do this." And he said, "Yeah, yeah, I can do that." The next year—that was the last year I was here—they said, "John, did he do it?" They knew better of course, but I said, "No, he's no different. He's still doing the same things." Art [Bezdek] says, "I move we fire him." He'd been there nineteen years.
>
> MCMURRAY: Lots of backers?
>
> MESSERLI: Oh, yeah, they came out of the woodwork from all over, backing him. "He's done such great things

> for our football team and our basketball team," and all that. We had two open meetings in the old gym just packed with people. Of course, I wanted to explain all the things, dumb things, he did to kids ... He just, he abused kids is what he did, and, of course, they put up with that. And if you were ready to put up with that, you were ready to sacrifice the boys on the field or on the court.
>
> But anyway, they had done everything proper. They had counseled him. There was a math job open. He was qualified to teach math. I said, "Fellas, he's been here nineteen years and if we were going to do this we should have done it a long time ago. I recommend offering this man a job. Get him out of coaching, offer him this job."
>
> That was the same year I was offered a trip to go study education in Germany. While I was gone ... [board president Gordon Harstad] called; "He's accepted the math job." And, well, I was to blame. It was because he couldn't get along with the superintendent. That's why I said I didn't want to put up with this. That's why I left.

Messerli had guided the Marion school district through a period of tremendous growth and had overseen the construction of a new elementary school and a new high school. "A lot of people thought John Messerli was jealous of Hipple," said Bill Huntoon. "Messerli was extremely disappointed that we didn't name a field or building after him.

"Everyone wanted to be a Hippleman," Huntoon said. "No one wanted to be a Messerliman."

Chapter 40
Farewell, 1998–1999

Early in 1998, as he was approaching his eighty-fifth birthday, Hipple was diagnosed with colon cancer. An operation removed the cancer. The doctors did not prescribe chemotherapy or radiation.

During his time in the hospital and part of his recovery, Wilma was also hospitalized for an illness. In fact, over the preceding decade or so, she often had to go to the hospital for monitoring and testing that resulted in changes in her medication. She also spent some time in a nursing home. Now, with Hipple recuperating from his operation, there were two sick people in the house. Nevertheless, Hipple continued to care for his wife. "The devotion and patience he showed over the years was beyond belief," said their daughter.

The two struggled together with the assistance of friends, helpers, and their daughter for about a year. Then Hipple was told the cancer had returned and was in his liver. It was untreatable. He did not have long to live. He did not accept that judgment, and sought a second opinion. It was no more favorable than the first. "He was not ready to die," his daughter said.

He weakened. Wilma had to be taken to a nursing home. She did not want to go, and fought the orderlies and nurses. Soon, Hipple asked his daughter, who was teaching at Kirkwood Community College, "How much longer are you in school?" He knew he would need her in the house. "He was trying to hold out until I was finished with school," Pat Turner said. He did, and she began to spend the days at her parents' house, while nurses came at night.

There was time to say goodbye to the family. His sisters came from Cedar Rapids and Florida to see him; his brother visited from Illinois. His granddaughter Lue flew in from Utah. Hipple joined them in the kitchen in his bedclothes, very tired and, as usual, not saying much. He laughed quietly at the family banter. He never acted as if he was in pain. "We prayed he wouldn't suffer," Turner said. "I don't think he did."

People in town knew he was dying. He was under hospice care in his home. George Murdoch decided something had to be done for Les Hipple. He would write a letter and read it to him. He asked Turner to let him know when she thought her father was dying. Then he began writing. "It took me about a week," Murdoch said. "Then I called Patty Jo and told her I had a letter that I would like to read to him on behalf of myself and all the boys he coached."

Murdoch went to Hipple's bedside, took his hand, and began reading the letter on behalf of all the student athletes and himself. Murdoch was so near tears he could hardly finish the letter. It took about five minutes.

"You set your standards high … you taught us to play by the rules … you stressed mental and physical fitness … you demonstrated leadership by example … it was always reassuring to look to the sidelines or courtside and see you in control …

"And so today … we say thank you for having been there at such an important time in our lives. You prepared us well."

Murdoch finished the letter. There was a pause. Then Hipple said,

"Thank you, George. And thank all the boys for me."

Les Hipple died the next day, June 3, 1999.

Acknowledgments

Many people helped write this book. The names of most of them appear in the section called "Sources and Notes."

I am especially grateful to the following. Pat Hipple Turner, Les's daughter, was monumentally patient and always helpful, answering all my questions and opening her father's papers to my inspection. Lynn Brown, Hipple's former assistant coach, responded to my many questions with long, thoughtful e-mails. Shirley and Tony Pantini and John and Stevie Ballard opened their homes to me on my visits to Marion. Shirley also opened doors to many important sources and carefully read a draft of the manuscript. Staff members at Marion High School, including Shane Ehresman, Laura Vint, LaNisha Cassell, and others were consistently helpful and supportive. I am very grateful to the football and basketball departments for their meticulously assembled record books charting the history of their sports at MHS. Joyce Hutchins, Nancy Thornton, Jerry Walker, and Nate Wiley provided invaluable research assistance, unearthing facts and resources I never would have discovered on my own. Michael Toomey's design ideas and expertise were invaluable. Ed Reed was a constant source of encouragement and ideas.

I spent many pleasant hours in the Marion Public Library, in its real and Internet guises, poring over its priceless bound volumes of the *Marion Sentinel* and clicking through its online copies of the *Cedar Rapids Gazette*.

My wife, Elaine, was unwavering in her support of my work on this project over many years. She also edited the first draft mercilessly, for which I am deeply grateful.

Appendixes

Hipple's Record at Marion

Unless otherwise indicated, all statistics are based on material published by Marion High School. Total numbers of wins and losses may vary slightly from reports published in newspapers.

Football

Coached eighteen years (1945–1962)
Career record: 105–42–10 for a winning percentage of .714
Conference record: 84–34–8 for a winning percentage of .698
Seven WaMaC championships, four runners-up
Member of the Iowa Football Coaches Hall of Fame

Through 2009, Hipple led all Marion football coaches with most victories. Dave Messerli (who also coached eighteen years and also won seven WaMaC championships) was second with ninety-eight victories. Current coach Tony Perkins (who had coached ten years through 2009) was third with eighty.

Through 2009, Hipple's winning percentage of .714 was fifth among all coaches, behind Bob Thurness (who coached seven years) .814; Les Dollinger (five years) .761; Don Wolfe (eight years) .758; and Tony Perkins (ten years) .755.

Hipple also coached football for three years at West Branch, compiling a record of 21–5–1 (.796), for an overall career record of 126–47–11 and a winning percentage of .715.

Hipple's Marion record by decade
1945 to 1949: 28–12–4, .682
1950 to 1959: 66–17–3, .785
1960 to 1962: 11-13-3, .463

Most successful teams
Conference champions, with points vs. opponents

1955: 9–0, 299–44
1958: 9–0, 276–38

1954: 8–1 (undefeated in conf.), 127–32
1949: 8–0–1 (tied in conf.), 235–47
1953: 8–1–0 (conf. loss), 197–84
1951: 6–1–1 (conf. loss and tie), 174–70
1959: 5–2–1 (conf. loss and tie), 170–91

Two runners-up of note
1948: 8–1–0 (lost title game to Tipton, 13–7), 244–38
1952: 7–2–0 (lost two one-point conf. games), 160–47

Basketball

Coached twenty years, 1945–1965
Career record: 310–120, for a winning percentage of .721
Conference record: 201–71, for a winning percentage of .739
Twelve WaMaC championships; one runner-up
Two substate championships
Seven district championships
Eleven sectional championships
Member of the Iowa Basketball Coaches Hall of Fame

Hipple leads all Marion basketball coaches in victories, winning percentage, and conference championships. Dick Sloan, who coached from 1975–1985, compiled a record of 116–83 (.583) while winning three WaMaC and one district titles. Corby Laube, who coached from 2000–2008, compiled a record of 111–68 (.620) and won three WaMaC and two district titles.

Hipple also coached basketball at West Branch, Walker, and Callender. The won-lost records are unclear. His teams at West Branch won three sectional and county championships, averaging about sixteen wins per season. His teams at Walker and Callender lost most of their games.

Hipple's Marion record by decade
1945–1946 to 1949–1950: 82–26, .759
1950–1951 to 1959–1960: 180–51, .779
1960–1961 to 1964–1965: 48–43, .527

During the nine "glory years" (1947–1948 to 1955–1956), Hipple's teams went 196–27 (.879), won eight WaMaC championships, seven district championships, and two substate championships.

Most successful teams
1948–1949: 23–1, undefeated in regular season, advanced to substate final.
1949–1950: 25–2, one regular season loss, advanced to quarterfinals of the state tournament.
1951–1952: 24–2, one regular season loss, advanced to quarterfinals of the state tournament.
1950–1951: 23–2, one regular season loss, advanced to substate final.
1955–1956: 22–2, one regular season loss, lost in district.
1954–1955: 22–3, two regular season losses, advanced to semifinal of substate.
1952–1953: 21–3, two regular season losses, advanced to first round of substate.
1957–1958: 17–2, one regular season loss, lost in first round of sectional tournament.

Other teams to win conference championships (season records): 1947–1948, 18–4; 1961–1962, 14–4; 1960–1961, 15–6, 1958–1959; 15–7.

Track

Coached eighteen years, 1945–1962
Five WaMaC championships, four runners-up

Most successful squads
Conference champions: points scored out of a total 358 awarded

1954: 121, the most on record in the WaMaC through 1981. (The format has since changed.)

1953: 104 1/10
1949: 93
1947: 81 ½
1948: 54 ½

Three other teams nearly won. In 1946, Vinton edged out the Indians by three points. In 1953, a junior-dominated team finished second to Tipton by three points. In 1956, four record-smashing efforts by Ron Altenberg helped the team score sixty-five points, five behind Anamosa.

Hipple coached more WaMaC champions than any other Marion coach, although Chad Zrudsky, who was still coaching in 2009, has brought home two champions in his brief career at Marion.

Cross-Country

Hipple fielded state championship teams at eight consecutive meets: 1945, 1946, 1948, 1949, 1950, 1951, 1952, and 1953. (No meet was held in 1947 due to heavy rain.) Marion also won a state championship in 1959 with John Schippers as coach. Through 2005, no other coach in Iowa won as many cross-country championships as Hipple.

Hipple vs. The WaMaC

Number of championships during years Hipple coached, including ties

Basketball	Football	Track
Marion 12	Marion 7	Marion 5
Monticello 6	Monticello 5	Manchester 3
Independence 3	Tipton 3	Monticello 3
Anamosa 1	Anamosa 2	Tipton 3
Maquoketa 1	Independence 2	Maquoketa 2
Vinton 1	Maquoketa 2	Anamosa 1
Manchester 0	Vinton 2	Vinton 1
Tipton 0	Manchester 0	Independence 0

Source: WaMaC records

Outstanding Athletes

In 1980, the *Cedar Rapids Gazette* asked its readers to vote for the greatest all-time high school athletes in the metropolitan area. On what must have been a heavy turnout of Marion voters, Hugh Leffingwell was voted the top basketball player, receiving eighty-eight votes compared to the runner-up, Jim Cummins of Regis, who received fifty-three. Ron Altenberg was voted into fifth place as best overall athlete, and Jerry Walker was voted into fourth place as outstanding track athlete.

As part of the article, the *Gazette* asked Hipple to name the most outstanding athletes who played for him. He said, "Three that come to mind right away would be Hugh Leffingwell ['52], Ron Altenberg ['56], and Lloyd Olmstead ['49]." Adding that he "wouldn't dare" pick out just a few, he also mentioned Steve Miller ('61), Darell Failor ('56), Don Roby ('51), and Norm ('54) and Dave ('49) Rathje. Miller, Roby, and Norm Rathje had outstanding college athletic careers. Failor was injured in college and had to give up sports. Dave Rathje joined the Navy after high school.

The Rules

(Note: This version of the rules was dated, by hand, *Sept. 1, 1953.* The rules were typically mailed to parents of boys coming out for football and remained in force throughout the school year. The boys didn't need to see a copy of the rules; they already knew what they were. Hipple believed totally in his rules. "The success of our athletic program depends on how sincerely your son follows them," he wrote in one letter. Note the complexity of the rule on driving a car; this was one that parents objected to from the beginning. It was often modified from year to year and, in later years, was changed to simply discourage the practice rather than ban it under most circumstances. Those who were required to drive to school were almost invariably farm boys; there was no school bus service for rural students. He also had many unwritten rules, such as the requirement that all basketball players wear caps during the winter. Note rule No. 9, dealing with the proper site for putting on and removing shoes. Hipple wrote this requirement into all versions of his rules, going back to his time at West Branch. Why it rises to the importance of being included as a major training rule is a mystery.)

The Marion High School INDIANS Training Rules

Through the years Marion High School has developed a tradition for championship teams which it proudly and jealously treasures. Students, parents, and townspeople alike have made many sacrifices for this community enterprise of winning athletic teams.

Let us repeat again, it has taken a terrific amount of sacrifice, especially by the players themselves. They were willing to pay the price for playing on a good ball club. They were willing to live up to the training rules which in themselves have become traditional in this wonderful community. For many years they have accepted the rules as set down by their coach and have lived up to them faithfully. Some have made a name for themselves in college athletics, and more will continue. The point is, they were willing to go "all out" for 48 minutes every game. They were able to do so because of superb condition. They are the ones who have proved that training rules are a necessity. Are you capable of stepping into their shoes? No matter how big you are, or how fast you are, nothing will give you the feeling of confidence of filling their places as that thrill of knowing that you are physically able to go "all out."

Here are the rules which all Indian players have had to follow:

1. We are staying away from smoking and drinking entirely as they have no part of our athletic program.
2. We are going to be in bed by 10:00 PM every night except Friday and Saturday—and on these nights we may stay out until 12:00 PM although this will not be done often.
3. We will keep our dates at a minimum (school parties after home games, Saturday night or Sunday afternoon) and not let them interfere with our football. If we date often, go steady, or must see a particular girl friend between classes or at noon, we will drop athletics.
4. We are going to attend every practice. If this is impossible, we are going to be excused before practice that day.
5. We may drive our car, the family car, or motor bike under the following conditions:
   a. Anyone having to drive to school is to see Coach.
   b. We may drive when accompanied by our parents.
   c. Anyone with a valid drivers license may drive Sundays from 12:00 noon to 6:00 PM, providing he is not just driving around.
   d. We may drive to school functions after home games on Friday nights.
   e. Only those driving to school are to drive to school functions during the week; we will go directly to school and return home immediately afterwards; no one is to ride with us unless we can save some other boy from driving in.
   f. These provisions are not intended to encourage driving; therefore, anyone taking advantage of the driving privilege will be placed on probation and if continued will be dismissed from the squad.
   g. Any necessary exceptions will be talked over with the Coach beforehand.
6. We are going to use only the proper language on or off the field, on trips, and around the building at all times.
7. We are going to take the best possible care of our equipment, as it is for our own protection to have our equipment in the best condition.

8. We are going to keep our dressing rooms at home and on trips as clean as possible by throwing all waste materials in the waste basket, by keeping all our football equipment in our lockers or on top when drying.
9. Our football shoes are to be <u>put on</u> and taken off outside when muddy; in the lower exit when not muddy.
10. These training rules have been discussed with the squads and each boy has agreed to follow them in every detail.

George Murdoch's Letter

June 2, 1999

A Letter to Our Coach

As a tribute to you, Les, on behalf of the many student-athletes who had an opportunity to have you as a teacher and coach, and from me personally, I want to express to you and your family how much we have valued those experiences through the years.

I know some of us have told you personally how much we appreciated what you did for us, and I think this letter is an appropriate and timely way to let your family know also.

You set your standards high, Les, and in so doing inspired us to set our standards high—high standards for sportsmanship and high standards for work ethic and preparedness. You taught us on the field to play by the rules, to be magnanimous in victory, and to be gracious in defeat. Off the field you expected us to have the respect of our fellow students and to represent well our school and community. The modern adage, "It isn't how you play the game, but whether we won or lost" wasn't in your playbook. We learned that it wasn't just whether we won or lost—it really was how we played the game. You stressed the importance of being fundamentally sound—that we should practice fundamentals until we were proficient. You stressed mental and physical fitness so we could cope with critical situations and have the endurance to be strong at the start, during, and at the end of the game.

Les, you also demonstrated leadership by example. You were soft-spoken. I can't remember you yelling—but I do remember you communicated pretty good with body language. A stern look, a grimace, and the shaking of a head and we knew your displeasure. Yet, with a twinkle in your eye, a wry grin, and appreciative nods, we knew you were enjoying the situation.

Physically, you were not a big man, but you stood tall among your coaching peers, and even the refs respected you highly, because you were not a complainer on the sidelines or courtside. To your athletes you were determined, methodical, calm, and cool, with an air of being in control. It was always assuring to look to the sidelines or courtside and know you had the situation in control. We learned that practice had to be tough, grinding, and well organized. By being so well grounded and fundamentally strong we had confidence and we were able to enjoy the game. We didn't realize it at the time, but you were preparing us well to face the rigors, the challenges, the risks, and the competition of the real world after high school.

In 1945, I was an eighth grader when you came to Marion. At that time there weren't organized sports in the lower grades. I remember before we were to enter high school that you gathered the eighth grade boys in the gym to give us a pep talk about high school sports. You worked up our enthusiasm to a point where you challenged us—by asking, "Do you want to be a champion?" Of course we said, "Yeah! Yeah!"

Then you held up papers to give us and told us, "These are the things you won't be able to do and these are the things you will need to do to be a champion." What it all meant was some sacrifice, hard work, and dedication.

Well, we did become champions, as did several classes before us and many classes following us.

And so today, with the spirit of the student-athletes within us, but now as older and wiser men, to our teacher and coach we say thank you for having been there at such an important time of our lives. You prepared us well.

Written from the heart by George Murdoch on behalf of Les's boys.

Sources and Notes

Three documents provided by Marion High School were used as references for game scores and statistics related to Marion teams. They were Marion Basketball, *a statistical history of the sport since 1946–1947;* From the Beginning, Marion Football, *a statistical compilation by Eric Formanek that goes back to 1922; and records of WaMaC Conference track meets from 1943–1981. They are mentioned here to avoid repeating them in each chapter.*

Chapter 1: Author memories. Interviews and/or correspondence with Tom Domer and Darell Failor.

Chapter 2: Robert Dana, "A Short History of the Middle West," from his book, *Starting Out for the Difficult World*, Harper & Row, 1987, used with permission from the poet. Dorothy Schwieder, *Iowa, the Middle Land*, Iowa State Press, 1996.

Chapters 3 and 4: *Des Moines Register, Cedar Rapids Gazette, Iowa Heritage* magazine; "History of Tipton Public Schools," 1935; "A City Called Tipton," *Annals of Iowa*, Summer 1981; articles from an unidentified Tipton newspaper; Hipple family genealogy. Interviews with Bess Hipple Zvacek, Florence Hipple Hamacher, Shirley Hipple Shanahan, and Pat Hipple Turner. Correspondence from Herb Ray. Hipple personnel file at MHS.

As the number of workhorses dwindled on farms during the first half of the century, so did the number of blacksmiths. A few stayed open by doing metal work and machinery repair. Lester's father kept his business going through the Depression and World War II. His was the last blacksmith shop in Tipton and perhaps all of Cedar County. In 1964, Charles suffered a heart attack while working in the shop at the age of seventy-nine. He died a few weeks later. Lena died four years later at the age of eighty-two.

A brief report of the student's drowning, apparently taken from a newspaper article, appears in a historical record on Tipton. It reads, "Tragedy struck Tipton Junior College on October 12, 1933, when Roger Morton, a college sophomore, drowned at the Cedar Valley quarry. Roger, the son of J. Earl and Laverna Morton, was attending a Tipton Junior College picnic party at the quarry. He accidentally stepped off the rock bluff and into the water. Two of his classmates, Lester Hipple and Richard White, attempted to rescue him, but in the darkness could not locate their classmate. He was deeply mourned by the college and the community."

Chapter 5: Callender scrapbook. Interviews and/or correspondence with Don King, former coach and Iowa basketball authority; Bud Legg, information director, Iowa State High School Athletic Association; Shirley Hipple Shanahan. Hipple's MHS personnel file.

Chapter 6: *Walker News*. Interviews with Bess Hipple Zvacek, Florence Hipple Hamacher, Shirley Hipple Shanahan, and Pat Hipple Turner. Hipple's MHS personnel file.

Chapter 7: *West Branch Times*; other unidentified newspaper articles. Interview with Warren Rummells by Jerry Walker. Letter from Winton Gable. Interviews with

Bess Hipple Zvacek, Shirley Hipple Shanahan, Pat Hipple Turner. Hipple's personal papers.

Chapter 8: *Cedar Rapids Gazette, Marion Sentinel.* MHS yearbooks. *The History of Marion, Iowa,* compiled by MHS students and published by the school district in 1999. Interviews and/or correspondence with John Ballard, Ed Failor Sr., Tom Fisher, Winton Gable, Jane Blessing Gibson, Joyce Kolda Hutchins, Chuck Kent, Bill Lundquist, Joyce Fosdick Parks, Mary Lou Pazour, Joanie Justice Peck, Don Roby, Jon Smith, Jeri Smith, John Vernon. Internet research.

Chapter 9: *Marion Sentinel*; *The History of Marion, Iowa.* Interviews and/or correspondence with Bob Brooks, Ed Failor, Winton Gable, John Vernon. Hipple's MHS personnel file.

C. B. Vernon was recruited as superintendent of schools at Marion in 1926 after his predecessor was forced out for committing a mistake that became a scandal. One day he entered the girls' locker room to investigate noises long after the room was supposed to be vacant. There, he saw two girls who were not completely dressed. This indiscretion supposedly underlay the school board's decision to dismiss him on more public grounds (such as an undisciplined approach to holding teachers' meetings). There was no charge that the superintendent had molested anyone. He fought the dismissal right up to the state board of education, but eventually lost his appeal and apparently lived out his life in shame before dying at a relatively young age.

Chapter 10: *Marion Sentinel.* Interviews and/or correspondence with Winton Gable, Pat Hipple Turner, John Vernon. Hipple's MHS personnel file.

Pat Turner, Hipple's daughter, remembered a less complex scenario leading to her father's going to Marion. In this version, Hipple agreed to stay on at West Branch, but then asked to be released when Iowa City recruited him. West Branch first said no, and then angrily withdrew its contract, leaving Hipple stranded until the Marion opportunity came along. Whatever the truth, Hipple's leaving West Branch did not cause bad blood with Superintendent Maley. The two families remained close friends and correspondents all their lives.

Chapter 11: *Cedar Rapids Gazette, Marion Sentinel.* Buck Turnbull, *Iowa Hawkeyes Men's Basketball,* Morris Book Publishing, Inc. 2007. Interviews and/or correspondence with Doug Hutchins, Don King, Winton Gable, Bob Page, Don Roby, Shirley Hipple Shanahan, Bob Shulz, John Vernon, Jerry Walker, Ken Winkler. Hipple's MHS personnel file.

Ken Winkler, executive secretary of the Iowa Football Coaches Association, said that he could think of only two men other than Hipple who were in both the Football Hall of Fame and the Basketball Hall of Fame.

Chapter 12: Judith Yarger Hull, *Around the Park: Marion Merchants Then and Now,* Marion Historic Preservation Commission, 2008. *Marion Sentinel.* Maps and photos from the Marion Historical Society. Author memories. Interviews and/or correspondence with Mel Campbell, Tom Domer, Jane Blessing Gibson, Jay Kacena, Ed Reed, Irwin and Doris Renfer, Jeri Smith, Joyce Fosdick Parks.

By the late 1980s, some of the buildings in the block stretching from the Club Royale to the depot had fallen into disrepair. Some had been torn down. Stores were empty. The Milwaukee Railroad had entered bankruptcy and abandoned the depot. To the east and west of Main Street, little strip malls and chain restaurants had replaced many houses, stretching out the business district. In an attempt to revitalize the original uptown, the entire block was demolished, even the depot. Historian Judith Yarger Hull has dubbed the area "The Ghost Block." After demolishing the buildings, the developers, in a monumental failure of vision, replaced them with a strip mall, repeating and expanding the same undistinguished architecture that was already crowding in on both sides of the business district. Today, the heart of Marion is occupied by a mall that is little different in character from others that sit at the edge of the old downtown and stretch away for miles in both directions. If it weren't for the town park, where a pavilion was built using materials from the roof and walls of the depot, there would be almost nothing on the south side of Main Street to distinguish downtown Marion from the surrounding commercial roadside.

Chapter 13: *Cedar Rapids Gazette, Marion Sentinel.* Interviews and/or correspondence with Floyd Domer, Winton Gable, Bob Page, Bob Peck, Ken Otting, John Vernon.

As Winton Gable remembered it, Hipple put the matter of the dismissal to a vote of the team, telling them, "If you vote them off the team, you probably won't win the conference; but I promise you that you will have begun a new era for Marion High School. You will set an example for future players and make possible a winning tradition for years to come." The team then voted the other players off, Gable wrote. Teammate John Vernon could not remember such a speech and said that if indeed the matter was put to a vote, Hipple did it with full confidence in the outcome. It is highly unlikely Hipple left a matter such as this to the team. It's more likely that he spoke separately with Gable about it, since he was the team captain.

Chapter 14: *Marion Sentinel.* Lyle Touro eulogies by Rev. Howard B. Chapman and Linda Cory Touro. Interviews and/or correspondence with Bill Huntoon, Doug Hutchins, Steve Miller, Harry Oakley, Mike Rucker, Gordon Rundquist, Ken Touro. Lyle Touro papers.

As the years passed, Lyle Touro continued to pursue his dream of a softball league. He bought bats, balls, and gloves and even paid for the lights to put on some night games. He took his players to the A&W root beer stand after some games and bought them all a round. Lyle was a great fan of the minor league baseball team in Cedar Rapids, and often took two or three kids to the games. They caught a bus in Marion that went to Armstrong's Department Store in downtown Cedar Rapids, where they transferred to another bus to the stadium. After the game, they sometimes had to dash for the last bus leaving Armstrong's for Marion. Most Marion parents had no hesitation about turning their sons over to Lyle.

By the mid-1950s he had formed at least one full-time team and by 1957 had created a three-team league that played many of its games at the Emerson schoolyard. The Se*ntinel* occasionally reported game results. Touro's Tomcats vied with teams coached by two boys, Gordon Rundquist and Larry Smith. Rundquist remembered the games as very informal affairs, and only vaguely recalled his role as a coach.

That summer, however, the *Sentinel* reported that three Little League baseball teams had been formed for boys aged eight to eleven and that plans were proceeding for a fourth. The effort, begun a few years earlier by Doug Hutchins, a long-time sports booster, and John Fowler, junior high school principal, was spreading through the town. Lyle's days as softball manager were coming to an end.

About forty at the time, Lyle refused to retire from coaching. Instead, he formed a boys' bowling league, with his own Touro's Tomcats as one of the teams. Lyle had been an ardent bowler for years. Harry Oakley, who worked as a pinsetter at Marion's bowling alley in the 1940s, remembered that when Lyle threw a bowling ball, it remained airborne for about half the distance to the pins.

For decades Lyle organized winter bowling leagues and tournaments for Marion boys. He solicited town merchants as sponsors, arranging for door prizes and trophies that Lyle, wearing a jacket and tie, presented at an annual supper at the Presbyterian church. The supper was potluck, the food contributed by the boys' parents.

Lyle kept autograph books with padded covers that he asked his bowlers to sign. There is no particular order to the signatures. A group of autographs from the early '60s, for example, is followed by messages from five years later. Touro's Tomcats filled page after page with messages of gratitude ("We had a great team"; "You are my best friend"; "You are the best coach").

Lyle was a fixture at high school sporting events. He was made an honorary member of the booster club. He went to the industrial league basketball games featuring former Marion stars. He sat in the first row and always put money in the hat. He sometimes delivered the children's sermon at the Presbyterian church. He showed up at school playgrounds on Saturdays with bats, balls, and other equipment for kids who gathered there. He went around town looking for opportunities to help youngsters.

Lyle was the family celebrity, said his brother, Reginald. Whenever Reginald met someone new and introduced himself as a Touro, the other person would say, "Are you any relation to Lyle?"

After his parents had to leave the farm because of their age, Lyle boarded with a local family in town, helping support himself by doing odd jobs. Somehow he became a crossing guard at Starry Elementary School, drawn there no doubt by his love of children. In his sixties, he continued to promote an annual bowling tournament for Starry kids.

As he grew older, school officials became worried about his ability to do the job and about liability issues that might arise should there be an accident. When he reached sixty-eight, the board of education decided that Lyle would have to retire.

When Lyle Tuoro was forced into retirement, it was done with a celebration that included a certificate of appreciation from the Marion Education Association, a proclamation from the mayor declaring "Lyle Touro Day," and the presentation of a plaque from the citizens of Marion and Cedar Rapids that read "Lyle Touro—Benefactor of Youth."

Lyle's boarding arrangement ended when he was about seventy. He moved into an apartment on his own under the watchful eye of his nephew Ken and Ken's wife, Linda, who visited Lyle often and taught him new skills in communications, hygiene, and diet. He lost 94 pounds and learned to take better care of his money.

He lived this way for several years, then, after an extended stay in a nursing home, died in November 1995 at the age of seventy-eight. More than 150 people attended his funeral.

Speaking at the funeral, his sister-in-law, Linda Cory Touro, said, "Lyle was labeled mentally retarded, handicapped, limited, and sometimes given much crueler labels. But Lyle never thought of himself as less than you or I. He accepted himself as just exactly what God intended him to be.

"I never heard him say a negative remark about any person, place, or thing. He never uttered a racial or sexist slur. He accepted and was serene.

"He believed in God without question or reservation. He perceived no person as his enemy. He treated all people as equals and with respect. He served his community. He gave unconditional love to family and friends and asked nothing in return."

Chapter 15: *Cedar Rapids Gazette, Marion Sentinel, Independence Conservative.* Author memories. Interviews and/or correspondence with Chuck Carney, Ray Fuller, Chuck Kent, Ed Reed, Russ Seeks, Ken Otting, Bob Page.

Chuck Carney, who graduated in 1962 and was mechanically gifted, went to elaborate lengths to obtain water during football practice. He wrote, "I made a water container that fit inside my Riddell helmet suspension [straps] above my head with a piece of plastic tubing … running down around my left ear, supported by the cheek pads with the end folded over, held by a paper clip. So when convenient, I could unfold the tube and suck water out of the plastic bag over my head."

Chapter 16: *Cedar Rapids Gazette, Marion Sentinel.* ISHAA website. Cornell College athletic records. Author memories. Interviews and/or correspondence with Bob Brooks and George Murdoch.

Although there were fine teams in other years, the glory years for Marion sports under Les Hipple were from 1947 through 1956. During that time, the Indians won or shared seventeen of the twenty-seven WaMaC championships that were contested in football, basketball, and track, and finished second seven other times. Marion won eight of nine basketball championships, finishing in a tie for second in the year it didn't win. It won or shared five football championships, finishing second three times. In track, it won three WaMaC titles, finishing second three times. During the glory years, Hipple's football teams went 64–10–5 for a winning percentage of .842. In basketball, the overall record was 196–27, or .879. In conference basketball play, the Indians were 115–9, or .927, as three Inidan teams went undefeated in the WaMaC. Marion's overall record in state tournament play during this period was 44–9, or .830.

In the 1949 state tournament, Montezuma lost its first game to Waverly, 47–42, and Waverly lost its next game to the eventual fourth-place finisher, Winfield, 50–45.

More than 50 years after the Montezuma game, Olmstead was inducted into the Marion Athletic Hall of Fame along with Jerry Walker, an outstanding distance runner a few years younger than Olmstead. As they talked about the game, Olmstead told Walker that Marion would have won had he not been injured. He was playing with a badly injured thumb and it seriously affected his play. He made eleven points in the game.

Olmstead went to Cornell College, where he was a first-team All-Conference selection for three years and set several scoring records, including total career points (1,230), points per season (468), and most points in a single game (42). All his records have been broken, but he still ranks eighth in career points, even though freshmen were not allowed to play varsity ball. Olmstead was twice captain of the team, as a sophomore and as a senior, and led his team to a share of the Midwest Conference title in 1953, his senior year. In a curious repetition of his high school experience, Olmstead went out for football during his senior year at Cornell—after not playing the sport for three years in college. He earned a letter and, presumably, toughened himself for his senior year of basketball. Olmstead is a member of Cornell's Athletic Hall of Fame. He was drafted by the Minneapolis Lakers and approached by a professional team in New Mexico, but elected to become a high school coach, working at Garnavillo and Osage, Iowa, for more than twenty years. He left the field in 1976 to become an insurance agent. Olmstead declined to be interviewed for this book.

Chapter 17: *Cedar Rapids Gazette*, *Marion Sentinel.* Interviews and/or correspondence with Pat Hipple Turner, Genny Yarne.

Chapter 18: *Marion Sentinel.* Author memories. Interviews and/or correspondence with Lynn Brown, Tom Domer, Kay Kearns Francis, Sharron Ozburn Grundy, Joyce Kolda Hutchins, Lillie Fuller James, Harry Oakley, Elaine McGee O'Malley, Bill Page, Shirley Post Pantini, Ed Reed, Marjorie Reynolds, Janet Gordon Vikdal, Genny Yarne. Hipple's MHS personnel file.

The Marion High School of that era is now the C. B. Vernon Middle School. Additions were made to the building. The gym was covered over by classrooms and a computer lab. Players of the Hipple era who visit the school try to find their way to the old gym and their instincts take them as close as possible, bringing them to walls and dead ends just short of where the bulletin board hung. The gym floor, they are told, is still there. It was never pulled up. It's down there; the old gym is down there, under an overlay of lumber and plaster and computer cable. They can't see it, those old Indians, but they can feel its pull. In 2009, it was announced that the building would be torn down and replaced.

Miss Haffa's "step-together-step" foxtrot involved mastery of the following steps for the male: "step" (left foot ahead) "together" (right foot up even to left) "step" (left foot ahead); "step" (right foot ahead) "together" (left foot even with right) "step" (right foot ahead). Repeat.

Bailey's Milk Bar became Cira's Snack Bar in 1950, but for some reason many people continued to call it Bailey's.

Chapters 19, 20, and 21: *Cedar Rapids Gazette*, *Marion Sentinel*, *Daily Iowan*. Buck Turnbull, *Iowa Hawkeye Men's Basketball*; George Wine, *Black and Gold Memories*. SUI sports department archives. ISHAA records. MHS yearbook, *The Quill.* Interviews and or correspondence with Lynn Brown, Bob Christensen, Darell Failor, Ed Failor, Ron Franklin, Ray Fuller, Joyce Kolda Hutchins, Pete Kassler, Chuck Kent, Bud Legg of the Iowa State High School Athletic Association, Frank McLeod, Ken Otting, Shirley Post Pantini, Ed Reed, Norm Rathje, Don Roby, Steve

Rucker, Dr. William E. Scott, Sharm Scheuerman, Bob Schulz, Russ Seeks, Shirley Hipple Shanahan, Pat Hipple Turner.

After Hugh Leffingwell's death, Hipple had a memorial plaque created and placed on a wall in the gym.

Long-time Marion residents recalled that several years after their son's death, Wally and Pat Leffingwell were divorced. Wally moved away and died at a relatively young age. Pat stayed in the Marion area and died in a nursing home in 2002 at the age of ninety-two.

As this book was being published, more than fifty years after he played, Leffingwell still held Marion records for most career points (1,309), most points per season, and highest average points per game—in fact, he held both first and second place in the latter two categories. As a junior (1950–1951), he scored 609 points for an average of 24.4 points per game then topped both marks as a senior, scoring 673 points for an average of 25.9 per game. Among Leffingwell's other Marion records are most free throws made in a single season, first and fifth places, with 143 in 1951–1952 and 109 in 1950–1951; most field goals in a single season, both first and second place, 265 in 1951–1952 and 250 in 1950–1951; most free throws made in a career, second place, 254.

Leffingwell's basketball teams went 23–2 in his junior year and 24–2 the next season, for a winning percentage of .922. He was named to the All-State second team as a junior and to the first team as a senior, one of only a handful of Marion players so honored and the only one to be named twice.

Several sources identified Barbara Paul, a high school classmate of Leffingwell, as his girlfriend during his final months. I wrote to her, inviting her comment. She returned my letter, writing at the bottom, "I have in my hand an award, 'The Iowa High School Basketball Hall of Fame Presents This Honor Award to Hugh Leffingwell for his Outstanding Contribution to Iowa High School Basketball.' Hugh's mother gave me this award. I loved him sincerely and have had this plaque for all these years."

Despite weighing only 150 pounds, Don Roby was starting center on Coe's football team for two years. He was also a key reserve on the basketball squad. He graduated to spend a lifetime in education, beginning as a high school coach and later as president of Northeast Iowa Community Colleges. His coaching experience included six years as linebacker coach for Marv Levy's teams at William and Mary. Well into his seventies, Roby was a volunteer assistant football coach for Luther College.

Russ Seeks returned to Coe after his tour of duty in the medical corps and obtained his degree, but did not play sports. He spent forty years as an executive in the household moving industry. He and his wife live in Florida.

Bob Schulz, an All-State forward from Davenport, was a four-year letterman at Iowa. He coached basketball at University High in Iowa City before becoming freshman coach at Iowa. He was later basketball coach at Coe College. He left the field for a career as a lobbyist for the oil industry.

Bucky O'Connor, the Iowa coach, was killed in an automobile accident two years after the Fab Five went to the NCAA finals.

In 1980, the *Cedar Rapids Gazette* reported the results of a poll in which it asked its readers to name the top all-time high school athletes in the area in various sports. Riding what must have been a tide of votes from Marion readers, Hugh Leffingwell was named the top basketball player—twenty-eight years after he graduated.

Chapter 22: *Cedar Rapids Gazette, Marion Sentinel, Oelwein Daily Register*. Author memories. Interviews and/or correspondence with Carl Adkins, Bob Brooks, Lynn Brown, Tom Bullis, David Carey, Tom Domer, Bob Fox, Bob Jennings, Bob Justice, Chuck Kent, Don King, Bob Malake, Frank McLeod, Steve Miller, George Murdoch, Ken Otting, Bill Quinby, Norm Rathje, Irwin Renfer, Don Roby, Russ Seeks, Jerry Skilling, Rex Story Jr., Pat Hipple Turner, Jerry Walker. Harold Yeoman remarks at Hipple's funeral. Hipple's MHS personnel file.

Chapter 23: *Cedar Rapids Gazette, Marion Sentinel.* ISHAA records. Board of education minutes. Author memories. Interviews and/or correspondence with Bob Christensen, Lynn Brown, Wally DeWoody, Tom Domer, Jim Lang, Frank McLeod, Chuck Morningstar, Donald Nau, Harry Oakley, Bob Peck, Joanie Justice Peck.

I have been troubled all my life by the denial of letters to the senior members of the varsity team I played on. I have never been able to justify the action and it was not until 2009, when I discovered the report of the 1953 hearing in the *Cedar Rapids Gazette*, that I fully understood the reason. It was a disciplinary action by the school aimed at punishing some basketball players for transgressions that were not directly related to their performance in practice and games. Some of the boys skipped school the day after the loss to St. Mary's. Some did not report for the bus ride home after a trip to Iowa City to see some games. The boys were apparently misbehaving or defiant in other ways that spring, the way seniors often are. All these things happened after the basketball season ended. Vernon, Nicholson, and Hipple must have believed the transgressions were serious. They did not want to see them repeated by future seniors, so they hit the boys where it hurt the most. The punishment, in my view, did not fit the crime. The players earned the letters during the season. They should not have lost them for actions after the season. They should have been punished as students, not basketball players.

Christensen, Novotny, and Peck received All-State honorable mentions from the Iowa Daily Press Association.

Although fans thought the Indians could have won the state championship had they beaten St. Mary's, Marion would not have been matched against the same teams. Tournament teams were seeded according to an alphabetical system based on the name of their city. So the Indians would have had to face tournament favorite Clinton in the second round, had they gotten that far.

Harry Oakley attended Iowa State University. After graduation, he was commissioned in the Air Force and flew B-52s until 1966. He then joined TWA as a pilot and flew with them thirty-one years. He was co-pilot on a plane that was hijacked by Palestinian terrorists in 1969. They redirected a flight bound from Rome to Athens, forcing a landing in Syria, where the terrorists damaged the plane and were treated as heroes. Oakley has no memory of the events surrounding the denial of letters, and never discussed the matter with anyone until he was interviewed for this book. He became friends with Hipple, exchanging letters and gifts. He lives in Holstein, Iowa, where he played full-court playground basketball well into his sixties.

Bob Christensen played basketball in Cedar Rapids industrial and AAU leagues, principally on a strong team sponsored by Sanitary Dairy, until he was thirty. Hipple attended one of the games, a special exhibition, and walked over to Christensen to say hello, but Christensen ignored him. "I walked right by him," he said. Christensen built a trucking business hauling milk from farms to bottlers. He is retired and lives in Florida.

Jerry Peck rose from a supermarket produce manager to a parts inspector for Collins Radio to becoming part owner of a company that distributed hydraulic seals for tractor manufacturers. It is known today as Fusion, Inc. Peck received several patents for inventions related to this company. As an adult he was a top amateur golfer and bowler. Peck died in 1997. His widow said he always respected Hipple for the lessons he taught about discipline and hard work.

Larry Morningstar went to the University of Dubuque, where he played football and basketball and ran track, graduating with degrees in mathematics and physics. He then joined the Navy, serving on aircraft carriers and submarines, reaching the rank of lieutenant. After his discharge, he worked at the Naval Undersea Center in California, where he was one of the lead designers for sonar test systems used on the research submarine USS Dolphin. He and his family later moved to Dallas where he worked as an underwater acoustics engineer, wrote several technical manuals, and received patents for three inventions. He died in 1994.

Marvin Novotny did not respond to requests for an interview.

Chapter 24: *Cedar Rapids Gazette*, *Marion Sentinel*, *Monticello Express*, *Independence Bulletin-Journal*. IHSAA records. Author memories. Interviews and/or correspondence with Lynn Brown, Wally DeWoody, Tom Domer, Darell Failor, Bob Fox, Pete Kellams, Chuck Kent, Bill Hotle, George Murdoch, John Nieland, Norm Rathje, Ed Reed.

Two of the five pages in Marion's 1954 football playbook are devoted to blocking assignments. Hipple used what he called "rule blocking." Linemen were taught a system by which they learned to recognize the defensive formation (such as a 5-3-2-1 or a 7-1-3) and then assign numbers to the defenders. Once the numbers were assigned, the linemen knew which defender to block. "The defensive players near the line are now given numbers instead of guard, tackle, end, and linebacker," Hipple's explanation reads. "Each man is given a number from the center out to both sides, with the exception of the first man who plays on the offensive center and is therefore in position for the center to block; this man is not given a number."

The explanation may sound confusing, but in practice it was simplicity itself. Once a lineman understood the counting system, his blocking target was obvious. For the left tackle, for example, if the play came to his side of the line, his blocking assignment was to take the number 2 man, and if the play went to the other side of line, he was to cut off the number 2 man and run downfield to block a defensive back. The left tackle was especially concerned with plays with odd numbers. The space between him and the left guard was hole number 5. A running play with the number 35 called for the fullback (the number 3 back) to run through the number 5 hole. Block accordingly and be quick about it, for Rathje is on the way.

Here is how Hipple wrote it out his rule-blocking scheme: "L. T. on all even no. plays (weak side) against even or odd defenses, except 16H and 36H, drive inside the no. 2 man & block downfield ahead of ball carrier. On all odd no. plays (strong side) against even or odd defenses, block no. 2 in or out as the play indicates." The same rule applied to the right tackle, who was concerned with the number 2 man on his side of the line. The ends were instructed to block the number 3 man and the guards were to take out the number 1 man. The center took the man with no number. If a player could recognize a defense and count to three, he always knew whom to block.

My recollection is that the use of paddles was essentially benign. I had forgotten about them until I began research for the book. Although most coaches carried paddles, I believe they were largely symbolic, like riding crops carried by British military officers. To the extent we were paddled, we were protected by hip pads that had a flap covering the tailbone. As Lynn Brown remembered it, the use of paddles ceased in the late 1950s.

There was another football ritual that might seem brutal or at least crude by today's standards. During games, when Marion was on defense, the linebackers routinely kicked the butts of the linemen. This was not to punish them, but to deliver a charge of energy for the next play. The linebackers kicked us with the sides of their feet. Norm Rathje was the linebacker who kicked me. He had a powerful leg and was our kickoff man. I remember raising my butt to him often, and he hammered it each time for grit and good luck.

In the Tipton game, sophomore Brooks caught a total of three passes for a total of 137 yards, good for tenth place for receiving yards per game in the Marion record books.

Chapter 25: *Cedar Rapids Gazette*, *Marion Sentinel*, *Clinton Herald*, *Independence Bulletin-Journal*, *Manchester Press*, *Monticello Express*. Buck Turnbull, *Iowa Hawkeyes Men's Basketball*. Author memories. Interviews and/or correspondence with Dick Biggart, Lynn Brown, Wally DeWoody, Tom Domer, Darell Failor, Bob Fox, Bill James, Lloyd Jordan, Chuck Kent, John Hinck, David Martin, Norm Rathje, Everett Scott.

Rathje was not the only player who described Hipple's practice of demoting them from the starting basketball lineup without an explanation. Hipple may have thought an explanation was unnecessary. He was always very clear about what he wanted a player to do and may have presumed the player knew why he was being demoted. I had a similar experience. For no other than a teenager's reason, I played listlessly for a few days. One day in a practice scrimmage, Hipple put Gene Brown on the first team in my place. I was on the second team. I stole the ball on the tip-off and did everything I could to give the first team fits. The next day I was back on the first team. Hipple never said a word about it and none was necessary. I knew I had been goofing off and I knew what I had to do to reclaim my spot.

The summer after their Golden Gloves championships, Rathje and Jordan went around to county fairs, offering to fight the visiting strongman. Jordan said he would box him; Rathje said he would wrestle. Jordan said that no one wanted to box him, and it's unlikely any visiting strongman took on Rathje. These contests were largely put-up jobs involving volunteers who agreed ahead of time to lose.

Norm Rathje attended the University of Dubuque and starred in football and track for four years and in wrestling for three years. As a senior, he was undefeated in wrestling and is in the university's Athletic Hall of Fame. He played semi-professional football for many years, coached college and high school, then retired from coaching in 1980 to teach. He now lives in Illinois.

Lloyd Jordan continued to box for a few years and won several fights, but did not again enter the Golden Gloves. He stopped boxing when he got married in 1956. He and his wife, Shirley Sills Jordan, and their sons farm several homesteads just east of Marion.

Jerry Walker attended Southern Methodist University then transferred to the University of Iowa. He gave up running competitively, obtained a degree in dentistry, and eventually taught pediatric dentistry for many years at SUI while helping to coach the cross-country and track teams and serving as dentist for the wrestling and hockey teams.

Chapter 26: Matthew J. Bruccoli and Richard Layman, editorial directors, *American Decades 1950–1959*, Gale Research International, 1994. Internet research. Author memories. Interviews and/or correspondence with Lynn Brown, David Carey, Wally DeWoody, Tom Domer, Bob Fox, Lloyd Jordan, Pete Kellams, Chuck Kent, Don King, Bill James, Bob Jennings, Jim Morrow, John Nieland, Elaine McGee-O'Malley, Ken Otting, Bob Page, Joanie Justice Peck, Ed Reed, Gordon Rundquist, Russ Seeks, Darrell Shirk, Jeri Smith, Pat Hipple Turner, Jerry Walker.

Chapter 27: *Cedar Rapids Gazette*, *Marion Sentinel*. ISHAA records. Interviews and/or correspondence with Larry Brooks, Lynn Brown, Jerry Cox, Darell Failor, Don King, Ed Reed, Jeri Smith.

Chapter 28: *Cedar Rapids Gazette*, *Marion Sentinel*, *The Cornellian*. Cornell College historical sources, Midwest Conference website. Author memories. Interviews and/or correspondence with Larry Brooks, Lynn Brown, Jerry Cox, Tom Domer, Darell Failor, Ed Failor, Frances Parton Altenberg Farrow, Jack Fisk, Ron Franklin, Bill Huntoon, Ed Reed, Audrey Altenberg Thompson.

Altenberg's 9.8 time in the 100-yard dash was still the WaMaC record when the conference switched to metric distances in the late 1970s. It is still listed in the Marion record books. Using a standard conversion method, his time in the 100-yard dash equals 10.7 seconds for 100 meters. The current Marion record is 10.66, set by Grayline Ross in 2006. Altenberg's WaMaC 220-yard dash record stood for eleven years and his 180-yard low hurdles record stood for twelve years. His broad jump of 22 feet ½ inch stood for many years. The Marion record is now 22 feet 5 inches, set by Ben Humiston in 1998. Current WaMaC records for the 100-meter dash and the long jump were not available.

In the WaMaC meet that year, Don Norton of Anamosa was involved in setting three new records: He ran on two relay teams and tied for first in the high jump.

After graduation, Jerry Cox ignored expressions of interest from Marquette, Duquesne, and other schools, and become a lineman for Iowa Electric Light and

Power. He played industrial league basketball. One year his team beat the Coe College freshmen, and the Coe coach offered him a scholarship on the spot—tuition would cost only $500. He couldn't even consider the offer. "I was 26 and had four children," Cox said. "I didn't have a nickel. I went back to climbing those poles." He became an expert in high voltage lines. For many years he toured the country teaching his skills to other linemen. "I was very good," he said, "I could bare-hand 500,000-volt lines." He is retired and he and his wife live in Mississippi.

Larry Brooks turned away from sports and any hopes of going to college. He went to work for Rockwell Collins and spent his career there, rising to become a supervisor in the maintenance department. He and his wife live in Anamosa, where he plays golf in fair weather and foul. He spends winters in Alabama to keep on golfing.

Ron Altenberg and Darell Failor were recruited to the University of New Mexico by Dick Clausen, who had been football coach at Coe College and was moving up to Division I. Neither boy was happy there, and both moved back to Iowa. Failor enrolled at the University of Dubuque. In an early football scrimmage, he suffered a career-ending knee injury. He spent most of his work career in various supervisory positions with the Milwaukee Railroad. He lives in Robins, Iowa.

Altenberg, consulting with Hipple, chose Cornell College. He was still maturing when he left high school, and he became one of Cornell's greatest basketball and track stars. Because of the transfer, he was ineligible to play for Cornell until the second semester of his sophomore year, in 1958. So he played AAU ball in Cedar Rapids and, in February 1957, led his team to the championship of the twenty-eight-team state tournament, averaging twenty-four points a game, and was named to the first all-star team. Several other Marion players were honored for their performances in that tournament: Bob Christensen (second all-star team), Jerry Cox and Tom Domer (third team), and Don Christensen (honorable mention).

In two-and-a-half basketball seasons at Cornell, Altenberg made 1,274 points, breaking Lloyd Olmstead's record. His total would have been much higher if three-point shots were allowed and he had played three full seasons. According to Cornell's sports information office, in his final year, 1959–1960, Altenberg set three season records that still stand: most points (604), scoring average (26.2 points), and most field goals (234). During the regular season he averaged 28.1 points per game. That year, Cornell put on a late-season run (with Altenberg consistently scoring thirty points or more) to tie for the Midwest Conference championship. Cornell was selected to compete in the NCAA Small College basketball tournament. Lacking height, Cornell used a full-court press to advance to the final four in the tournament, beating the favorite, Prairie View (Texas) A&M, along the way. Many Marion fans enjoyed going to the Cornell games to watch Altenberg. He had a terrific jump shot that was accurate from great distances. He could jump so high that he seemed to hang in midair as he launched his shot. If guarded closely, he slipped around his defender and drove for the basket; he could take off from the free-throw line and lay the ball over the rim.

Altenberg was named to the small college All-American team (Little All-America) and was one of the top small-college scorers, playing guard at Cornell. His fellow guard was an awkward-looking player named Rich Merz, who specialized in twisting, driving shots that seemed impossible to make but were, instead, impossible to stop. He scored more than 1,000 career points. Both men were named to the Midwest Conference All-Star team.

Altenberg played one season of football at Cornell, but did not go out as a senior, apparently to avoid injuries. He still weighed only about 155 pounds.

In track, Altenberg won nine individual conference championship events. In 1959, his junior year, he won every event he entered, setting new conference records in two of them, the 100-yard dash (9.5 seconds) and the 220-yard low hurdles (23.2 seconds). His winning time in the 220-yard dash was .2 off the record time and his distance in the broad jump was ¾ inch off the record. The previous year, as a sophomore, he had won the same sprint and hurdle events but apparently did not enter the broad jump.

Cornell had won the conference championship in each of Altenberg's first two years, and might have won again in his senior year except for a change in the event schedule. Altenberg won the 100-yard dash in 9.7 seconds on a muddy, rain-soaked track. Then he won the 220-yard dash in 21.2 seconds to tie the conference record. Immediately after the 220, he had to run in the 220-yard low hurdles and finished a "winded fifth," the *Gazette* reported. Originally, the two-mile relay was scheduled between Altenberg's two races, but the schedule was changed by a vote of the coaches. Had Altenberg been able to recover and then win the hurdles, Cornell might have won the meet. At some point during the meet, he pulled a hamstring and was held out of the broad jump.

One of Altenberg's track teammates at Cornell was Dennis O'Brien, the Des Moines sprinter who had beaten him in the state high school meet. By this time, Altenberg was consistently posting faster times than his old nemesis. He ran the 100 in 9.5 seconds several times. This was only a few tenths of a second off the world record, and there was talk of him trying to make the 1960 Olympic Team. Altenberg had competed against some of the top sprinters in the country at one or more Drake Relays or other top meets, and had finished in the lead pack each time (various newspapers say he placed third, fourth, and fifth in these races). Thus he held his own against the nation's fastest sprinters, none of whom, it is safe to assume, had spent the winter playing intercollegiate basketball. However, his injury that spring in the Midwest Conference meet probably ended his Olympic hopes. According to a standard conversion method, Altenberg, at his fastest, would have run 100 meters in 10.4 seconds, faster than the current records at Cornell (10.73) and the Midwest Conference (10.61).

Altenberg was named Outstanding Amateur Athlete in Iowa in 1960. He was elected to the Cornell College Athletic Hall of Fame in 1971, its inaugural year.

He was drafted in the twelfth round by the Cincinnati Royals of the National Basketball Association, and indicated in a newspaper interview that he was going to give it a try. But in December of 1960, when he was finishing work on his degree from Cornell but was no longer eligible for intercollegiate sports, he played on a team assembled by Sanitary Dairy of Cedar Rapids that traveled to Fort Dodge to play an exhibition game against the Phillips 66ers, perhaps the most famous of the

National Industrial League teams that prospered in those times. Although the 66ers won the game easily, Altenberg stole the show, scoring twenty-eight points in three quarters of play and bedeviling the much taller 66ers on defense.

This led to his being offered a position on the 66ers, which many top players of that era saw as a better deal than anything the NBA could offer. NBA salaries were modest because television revenues had not yet enriched the league. Earning a position with the 66ers guaranteed a full-time job with Phillips Petroleum when the playing days were over. Gary Thompson, the former Iowa high school star and Iowa State All-American, was a member of the team. So was Bobby Plump, Butler All-American, whose famous last-second shot in the 1954 Indiana state tournament propelled tiny Milan High School to the championship against Muncie Central. (That game inspired the movie *Hoosiers*.)

There were about twelve players on the 66ers squad, and Altenberg was a reserve. He averaged about six points a game in his first season. The following season he scored eighteen or more points in several games, but did not get as much playing time as he would have liked. Playing for the 66ers was almost a full-time activity. The team traveled internationally to play exhibition games and then played almost fifty regular season and tournament games that often involved extended road trips. With training and exhibitions, the season could last nine months. Altenberg played for two years (1961–1962 and 1962–1963), during which the team was twice national AAU champion, posting an overall record of 85–11.

Altenberg worked in sales for Phillips for more than a decade. In 1974, he and his wife, Frances Parton, a Marion girl he married in 1959, settled in Temple, Texas, where he opened a Phillips jobbership, wholesaling gasoline and auto supplies to service stations. In 1982, he became a national sales manager for Circle K Stores. He and Francis had four children (Brad, David, Julie, and Kristin). Ron remained active in sports, coaching youth teams, playing basketball in a men's league, playing racquetball, jogging, and skiing. One day he injured his shoulder playing basketball. When a doctor examined him, he discovered that Altenberg had lung cancer. Less than three weeks later, in December 1988, at the age of fifty, Altenberg died.

Hipple remembered him as probably the best athlete he coached at Marion. "Whatever he wanted to do, he could do," Hipple said, "and he could do it so easily." Hipple was also impressed, as were many others, by Altenberg's modesty. "If you saw him around school, you'd think he was just one of the kids," Hipple said.

In the spring of 1989, after receiving a petition signed by nearly three hundred citizens, the Marion board of education voted to name the high school track after Ron Altenberg.

Chapter 29: *Marion Sentinel.* Michael Nash, "The Marion School Merger Issue of 1958," a college thesis. *Celebrating 50 Years, 1949–1999*, a history of Linn-Mar and the rural school district. Board of education minutes. Interviews and/or correspondence with Lynn Brown, Lumir Dostal, Bill Dougherty, John Edison, John Fowler, Ray Fuller, Greg Hapgood, Don Hoskins, Bill Huntoon, Joyce Kolda Hutchins, Dave Messerli, Michael Nash, George Murdoch, John Nieland, Ann Young Oakley, Bill Page, Shirley Post Pantini, Tony Pantini.

By 2008, Linn-Mar was one of the largest school districts in the state, encompassing sixty-four square miles, 6,200 students, and nine school buildings—and still growing rapidly. The Marion Independent School District, completely surrounded by Linn-Mar, covered 3.6 square miles and had 2,000 students in five schools.

John Nieland, the youngest of several siblings, was the first in his family to graduate from high school. His father had demanded that the other children get jobs and fend for themselves at an early age. His mother insisted on John's right to an education, and prevailed. For a graduation present, John's father gave him a suitcase with these words, "I don't know where you are going to spend tomorrow night, but it won't be here." John enlisted in the Army, became a paratrooper, obtained a college degree, and retired with the rank of major. He returned to Marion where he served six years on the city council and four years as mayor.

In 2009, the Indians made it to the state basketball tournament for the first time since 1952, losing in the first round by a single point.

Chapters 30 and 31: *Cedar Rapids Gazette*, *Marion Sentinel.* Interviews and/or correspondence with Lynn Brown, Terry Conklin, Pat Hipple Turner, Frank McLeod, Steve Miller, Ken Otting, Irwin and Doris Renfer, Herb Ray, Darrell Shirk, Jean Tanner, Genny Yarne. Hipple's MHS personnel file. MHS yearbooks.

Marion's official basketball history shows seven Hipple-coached victories over I. C.: 1948 (27–24); 1949 (31–25); 1950 (39–36); 1951 (43–41); 1952 (62–37); 1954 (54–49); 1955 (64–59). Five of the I. C. teams were coached by Bob Jennings. The victory over Regis and Jennings (58–55) came in 1959.

Bob Jennings was born in 1927, grew up to play basketball for I. C., graduated from the University of Iowa in 1950, and returned to his alma mater as coach. When I. C. merged with other Catholic schools in the 1960s to form Regis, he became the school's basketball coach and guided it to the state championship in 1962. He compiled a lifetime record of 330–77, for a winning percentage of .810. He retired from coaching in 1966 at the age of forty, after which he became athletic director and associate principal at Prairie High School in Cedar Rapids. He is a member of the Iowa Basketball Coaches Hall of Fame.

Chapter 32: *Cedar Rapids Gazette*, *Marion Sentinel*, Interviews and/or correspondence with Lynn Brown, Pat Turner Hipple, Bill Huntoon, Bill Linstrom, Frank McLeod, Steve Miller, Larry Perkins, Herb Ray, Jerry Skilling, Dennis Stickney, Richard Sorenson, Vince Woodson. Hipple's MHS personnel file. MHS yearbooks.

It appears that Beemblossom (who is deceased) had no coaching experience before joining the faculty at Marion. Skilling had coached several sports at Lansing, Iowa. Woodson had no previous coaching experience, but had received coaching certification at Northwest Missouri State. Linstrom had no prior experience as a wrestling coach before starting the program in 1958. I was unable to contact Jan Flickinger.

After teaching at University High School in Illinois for five years, Lynn Brown took a sabbatical to study for a PhD from the University of Iowa then returned to Normal to join the mathematics department at Illinois State University, from which he retired in 1992. As part of his PhD dissertation, he developed a special program for teaching algebra that allowed students to write their own definitions and theorems. He retired in 1992. Although he never coached after leaving Marion, he remained an ardent sports fan and golfer.

Steve Miller attended Cornell College, where he starred in football, basketball, and baseball, winning nine varsity letters. He was twice named to the All-Conference football team, as a defensive back as a junior and as quarterback and tri-captain as a senior, when Cornell tied for the Midwest Conference championship with St. Olaf and Ripon. After teaching and coaching briefly in a high school, he returned to Cornell where he coached six different sports over the years, winning conference championships in swimming, golf, and football. He left Cornell in the 1970s to coach at Carroll College and Morningside College, and then returned to his alma mater as football coach, compiling a record of 87–55 and winning two conference championships. He was also athletic director for many years and served the college as a development officer. He is in the Cornell Athletic Hall of Fame.

Chapter 33: *Cedar Rapids Gazette*, *Marion Sentinel*. Board of education minutes. Interviews and/or correspondence with Tom Bullis, Ken Backsen, George Duvall, Ray Fuller, Doug Hutchins, Bill Huntoon, Jim Morrow, George Murdoch, Shirley Post Pantini, Larry Perkins, Steve Rucker, Larry Twachtmann, Vince Woodson, Genny Yarne, one anonymous source. Hipple MHS personnel file. MHS yearbooks.

Larry Twachtmann served Marion schools for thirty-three years, retiring as principal of the high school in 1996.

Chapter 34: *Cedar Rapids Gazette*, *Des Moines Register*, *Marion Sentinel*. Board of education minutes. Hipple personnel file. Interviews and/or correspondence with Ken Backsen, Ray Fuller, Doug Hutchins, Bill Huntoon, Don King, Harold Klink, Tim Ledvina, Jim Morrow, Elaine McGee-O'Malley, Shirley Pantini, Larry Perkins, Irwin and Doris Renfer, Frances Rucker, Mike Rucker, Steve Rucker, Shirley Hipple Shanahan, Richard Sorensen, Pat Turner, John Vernon, Genny Yarne.

Tim Ledvina attended Lea College in Albert Lea, Minnesota, where he was a four-year letterman in football and golf. He later coached in high school for about ten years then spent many years as a golf-teaching professional. He works for the Gainesville, Florida Chamber of Commerce. On several occasions when he returned to Iowa to see his family, he visited Hipple in his home. He is never late for meetings.

Ken Backsen attended Iowa State University, where he made the basketball squads as a freshman and sophomore before quitting the sport. He obtained a degree in geology and spent his entire career in exploration and research. He is retired and lives in New Orleans. He is often late for meetings.

It was shocking to learn that Joe Green had emerged as one of Hipple's supporters. Green, a feisty, curly-haired blond, had been a year ahead of me in school. He went out for sports and was a good athlete, but was too small to get much playing time. He was constantly at war with Hipple. While I couldn't remember the specifics, visions of him railing against Hipple and everything he stood for came back clearly. Green died before I could contact him. His ex-wife, Elaine McGee-O'Malley, said that Joe had been in a serious car accident in 1963. Although his foot and leg were badly injured, he had managed to crawl fifty feet up an embankment to wave down a passing car. After his hospitalization, he endured months of rehabilitation and physical therapy. He always credited Hipple for instilling the stamina and fortitude it took to escape from the vehicle and go through rehabilitation.

Larry Tanner covered Hipple's coaching career at Marion from his first game to the day he was fired. Tanner was born near Central City, Iowa, on September 30, 1923. After graduating from Franklin High School in Cedar Rapids, he studied journalism at the University of Iowa for a while and began covering sports for the *Cedar Rapids Gazette* before moving to the *Marion Sentinel* as news editor from 1949 to 1959. He went back to the University of Iowa and earned a bachelor's degree in history in 1961 while working part-time as a sports reporter for the *Gazette*. He then returned to his beat as Marion reporter for the *Gazette* and remained there until 1978. In 1981, he earned a master's degree in journalism from the University of Iowa and taught journalism at Western Illinois University in Macomb, Illinois for several years, again returning to the *Gazette*. He later taught journalism at Cornell College. He died May 23, 1988.

Chapter 35: *Cedar Rapids Gazette*. Interviews and/or correspondence with Ken Backsen, Bill Huntoon, Doug Hutchins, Dave Messerli, Richard Sorensen, Pat Turner, Genny Yarne. Hipple's MHS personnel file.

Chapter 35: Interviews and/or correspondence with Lumir Dostal Jr., Doug Hutchins, Bill Huntoon, Lowell Morgan, Jim Morrow, Mike Nash, Mike Ryan, Dick Sloan, Dick Snyder, Shirley Post Pantini, Larry Perkins, Bob Thurness, Pat Hipple Turner, Genny Yarne, John Vernon. Hipple's MHS personnel file. Hipple personal papers.

In the mid-1970s, Jim Morrow transitioned from teaching into the insurance business. Today he and his wife, Shirley, have their own personal financial advisory firm in Cedar Rapids.

Bob Thurness's Marion teams were all very successful, and in 1980 the Indians won the state championship. The following spring, the school administration wanted Thurness to take over girls' junior high physical education, which would require that he spend much of his time at another location. Thurness told his supervisors that it wouldn't work; a coach needs to be around the school during the day to communicate with his players, monitor injuries, and solve problems. He threatened to quit if they insisted he take the assignment. State championship notwithstanding, they told him to do it. So he quit. Thurness went to Coe as an assistant coach and the following year became head coach and athletic director. He later coached at Cornell and the University of Northern Iowa while maintaining a home in Marion. In 2008, he was honored, along with five other successful Coe football coaches, with his name and photo on a bronze plaque on the stadium wall. Thurness's coaching career spanned thirty-six years, including stints at five high schools and the University of Dubuque before he came to Marion.

Dick Sloan coached basketball at Marion for ten years and taught there from 1970 until he retired in 2002. While teaching at Marion he was an assistant coach in football and basketball at Coe College. He is now an assistant football coach at Marion.

Larry Perkins spent his entire career teaching and coaching at Marion. He continues to serve the football program as a volunteer assistant to his son, Tony, who became head football coach in 1999. Larry was also an assistant football coach at Coe College.

Chapter 37: *Cedar Rapids Gazette*. Interviews and/or correspondence with John DeJong, Gary Eschman, Bill Huntoon, Jay Kacena, Chuck Kent, Bill Lundquist, Gordon Rundquist, Nancy Thornton, Bob Thurness, Pat Hipple Turner, Alice Wallace. Eulogies and letters by Hipple's grandchildren. Hipple's personal papers.

Chapter 38: Interviews and/or correspondence with Pat Turner, George Murdoch, Andrew and Genny Yarne.

Chapter 39: Interviews and/or correspondence with Bill Huntoon, Dave Messerli, Laura Vint. John Messerli taped interview provided by Tony Pantini.

Chapter 42: Interviews with George Murdoch and Pat Turner.

Les Hipple's funeral service lasted two hours. There were tributes from eighteen individuals, including grandchildren, whose letters were read. Seven former athletes spoke, spanning the years from 1945 to 1965. Marion "was blessed" to have had Hipple, said John Vernon. George Murdoch read his letter. John Nieland, who grew up in a tiny house along the railroad tracks, said Hipple "didn't care whether you had $100 in your billfold or holes in your shoes; if you worked hard, you got to play." Bill Huntoon and Gordon Rundquist said he was a father figure they loved. Steve Miller said Hipple's influence extended beyond athletes, affecting everyone in the school. Steve Rucker said that Hipple's training helped save the lives of athletes who had fought in Vietnam.

Wilma Hipple was in a nursing home when her husband died. She came to a visitation the day before the funeral, but was unable to attend the service itself. When her daughter asked her what she wanted said on her behalf, Wilma responded, "He was just very, very kind to me." Wilma died in a Cedar Rapids nursing home nine months later, on March 14, 2000.

George Murdoch died in 2004.

In the late 1990s, the administration at Marion High School decided that the school possessed more sports trophies than it wished to house or display. Many of these trophies were from the Hipple years. The school conducted a public auction, and some of the trophies were purchased and preserved by individuals. Many others were dumped in the trash.

About the Author:
Dan Kellams

Author Photo: © 2009 Michael Toomey

Dan Kellams, who was born and raised in Iowa, is a free-lance writer in New York City. He has often written about sports during a 50-year career writing for business organizations. He is a 1954 graduate of Marion High School, where he played four sports under Les Hipple.

This book is the fulfillment of his long-held ambition to explore the Les Hipple legend and the coach's impact on so many lives. Kellams attended Cornell College, where he was active in journalism, drama and sports. He was awarded a fellowship to Columbia University and earned a master's degree from its Graduate School of Journalism. He and his wife, Elaine, live in New York City and Litchfield County, Connecticut.

Breinigsville, PA USA
19 November 2010

249641BV00001B/8/P